# THE EUROPEAN UNION SERIES

**General Editors: Neill Nugent, William E. Paterson**

The European Union series provides an authoritative library on the European Union, ranging from general introductory texts to definitive assessments of key institutions and actors, issues, policies and policy processes, and the role of member states.

Books in the series are written by leading scholars in their fields and reflect the most up-to-date research and debate. Particular attention is paid to accessibility and clear presentation for a wide audience of students, practitioners and interested general readers.

The series editors are **Neill Nugent**, Visiting Professor, College of Europe, Bruges, and Honorary Professor, University of Salford, UK; and **William E. Paterson**, Honorary Professor in German and European Studies, University of Aston. Their co-editor until his death in July 1999, **Vincent Wright**, was a Fellow of Nuffield College, Oxford University.

Feedback on the series and book proposals are always welcome and should be sent to Steven Kennedy, Palgrave Macmillan, Houndmills, Basingstoke, Hampshire, RG21 6XS, UK, or by e-mail to s.kennedy@palgrave.com.

---

## General textbooks

### Published

Laurie Buonanno and Neill Nugent **Policies and Policy Processes of the European Union**

Desmond Dinan **Encyclopedia of the European Union** [Rights: Europe only]

Desmond Dinan **Europe Recast: A History of the European Union (2nd edn)** [Rights: Europe only]

Desmond Dinan **Ever Closer Union: An Introduction to European Integration (4th edn)** [Rights: Europe only]

Mette Eilstrup Sangiovanni (ed.) **Debates on European Integration: A Reader**

Simon Hix and Bjørn Høyland **The Political System of the European Union (3rd edn)**

Dirk Leuffen, Berthold Rittberger and Frank Schimmelfennig **Differentiated Integration**

Paul Magnette **What is the European Union? Nature and Prospects**

John McCormick **Understanding the European Union: A Concise Introduction (6th edn)**

Brent F. Nelsen and Alexander Stubb **The European Union: Readings on the Theory and Practice of European Integration (4th edn)** [Rights: Europe only]

Neill Nugent (ed.) **European Union Enlargement**

Neill Nugent **The Government and Politics of the European Union (7th edn)**

John Peterson and Elizabeth Bomberg **Decision-Making in the European Union**

Ben Rosamond **Theories of European Integration**

Sabine Saurugger **Theoretical Approaches to European Integration**

Ingeborg Tömmel **The European Union: What it is and how it works**

Esther Versluis, Mendeltje van Keulen and Paul Stephenson **Analyzing the European Union Policy Process**

Hubert Zimmermann and Andreas Dür (eds) **Key Controversies in European Integration**

### Forthcoming

Magnus Ryner and Alan Cafruny **A Critical Introduction to the European Union**

### Also planned

**The European Union and Global Politics**

**The Political Economy of European Integration**

---

**Series Standing Order** (outside North America only)
ISBN 978–0–333–71695–3 hardback
ISBN 978–0–333–69352–0 paperback
Full details from www.palgrave.com

Visit Palgrave Macmillan's
EU Resource area at
www.palgrave.com/politics/eu/

## The major institutions and actors

*Published*

Renaud Dehousse  **The European Court of Justice**
Justin Greenwood  **Interest Representation in the European Union (3rd edn)**
Fiona Hayes-Renshaw and Helen Wallace  **The Council of Ministers (2nd edn)**
Simon Hix and Christopher Lord  **Political Parties in the European Union**
David Judge and David Earnshaw  **The European Parliament (2nd edn)**
Neill Nugent  **The European Commission**
Anne Stevens with Handley Stevens  **Brussels Bureaucrats? The Administration of the European Union**

*Forthcoming*

Ariadna Ripoll Servent  **The European Parliament**
Sabine Saurugger and Fabien Terpan  **The European Court of Justice and the Politics of Law**
Wolfgang Wessels  **The European Council**

---

## The main areas of policy

*Published*

Michele Chang  **Monetary Integration in the European Union**
Michelle Cini and Lee McGowan  **Competition Policy in the European Union (2nd edn)**
Wyn Grant  **The Common Agricultural Policy**
Martin Holland and Mathew Doidge  **Development Policy of the European Union**
Jolyon Howorth  **Security and Defence Policy in the European Union (2nd edn)**
Johanna Kantola  **Gender and the European Union**
Stephan Keukeleire and Tom Delreux  **The Foreign Policy of the European Union (2nd edn)**
Brigid Laffan  **The Finances of the European Union**
Malcolm Levitt and Christopher Lord  **The Political Economy of Monetary Union**
Janne Haaland Matláry  **Energy Policy in the European Union**
John McCormick  **Environmental Policy in the European Union**
John Peterson and Margaret Sharp  **Technology Policy in the European Union**
Handley Stevens  **Transport Policy in the European Union**

*Forthcoming*

Karen Anderson  **Social Policy in the European Union**
Michael Baun and Dan Marek  **Cohesion Policy in the European Union**
Hans Bruyninckx and Tom Delreux  **Environmental Policy and Politics in the European Union**

Sieglinde Gstöhl and Dirk de Bievre  **The Trade Policy of the European Union**
Christian Kaunert and Sarah Leonard  **Justice and Home Affairs in the European Union**
Maren Kreutler, Johannes Pollak and Samuel Schubert  **Energy Policy in the European Union**
Paul Stephenson, Esther Versluis and Mendeltje van Keulen  **Implementing and Evaluating Policy in the European Union**

*Also planned*

**Political Union**

---

## The member states and the Union

*Published*

Carlos Closa and Paul Heywood  **Spain and the European Union**
Andrew Geddes  **Britain and the European Union**
Alain Guyomarch, Howard Machin and Ella Ritchie  **France in the European Union**
Brigid Laffan and Jane O'Mahoney  **Ireland and the European Union**

*Forthcoming*

Simon Bulmer and William E. Paterson  **Germany and the European Union**
Brigid Laffan  **The European Union and its Member States**

---

## Issues

*Published*

Derek Beach  **The Dynamics of European Integration: Why and When EU Institutions Matter**
Christina Boswell and Andrew Geddes  **Migration and Mobility in the European Union**
Thomas Christiansen and Christine Reh  **Constitutionalizing the European Union**
Robert Ladrech  **Europeanization and National Politics**
Cécile Leconte  **Understanding Euroscepticism**
Steven McGuire and Michael Smith  **The European Union and the United States**
Wyn Rees  **The US–EU Security Relationship: The Tensions between a European and a Global Agenda**

*Forthcoming*

Senem Aydin-Düzgit and Nathalie Tocci  **Turkey and the European Union**
Graham Avery  **Enlarging the European Union**
Thomas Christiansen, Emil Kirchner and Uwe Wissenbach  **The European Union and China**
Tuomas Forsberg and Hiski Haukkala  **The European Union and Russia**

# The European Union

## What it is and how it works

Ingeborg Tömmel

palgrave
macmillan

First published 2014 by
PALGRAVE MACMILLAN

Palgrave Macmillan in the UK is an imprint of Macmillan Publishers Limited, registered in England, company number 785998, of Houndmills, Basingstoke, Hampshire RG21 6XS.

Palgrave Macmillan in the US is a division of St Martin's Press LLC, 175 Fifth Avenue, New York, NY 10010.

Palgrave Macmillan is the global academic imprint of the above companies and has companies and representatives throughout the world.

Palgrave® and Macmillan® are registered trademarks in the United States, the United Kingdom, Europe and other countries.

ISBN 978–1–137–42753–3      hardback
ISBN 978–1–137–42752–6      paperback

This book is printed on paper suitable for recycling and made from fully managed and sustained forest sources. Logging, pulping and manufacturing processes are expected to conform to the environmental regulations of the country of origin.

A catalogue record for this book is available from the British Library.

A catalog record for this book is available from the Library of Congress.

Typeset by Aardvark Editorial Limited, Metfield, Suffolk, England, UK.

Printed in China.

# Contents

# List of Illustrations

## Tables

## Figures

# Preface

This book is the result of long-standing experience in research and teaching on the European Union (EU). In earlier years, there were hardly any books that described or explained what European integration was all about, but now, the market is overcrowded with textbooks on the EU. These books highlight in detail the Union's institutional structure, its working methods, its policies, and its weaknesses. So, in face of this abundance, why would one write yet another book?

Despite a wide variety of valuable books on the subject, I felt that something was still missing. I was looking for a book that could give a lean description of the EU as an emerging political order beyond the nation state. I wanted a book that highlights the basic features of the EU's institutional structure and the 'why' of this apparently unusual structure. I needed a book that describes the Union's institutions not just one by one, but also in their complex interactions. I also required a book that places European integration in a consistent theoretical framework, without reverting to the grand theories of international relations, or to those capturing the nation state. The present book is a response to what I felt was missing. Of course, it does not satisfy all my aspirations. Nevertheless, I hope readers will view this book as a missing link in the crowd of textbooks on the EU.

A book is never the work of its author alone. Instead, many contribute in some form to its successful completion. I can mention only a few of them here. First, I wish to thank the practitioners of European integration whom I had the opportunity to meet in the framework of various research projects. They provided me with deep insights into their activities, the underlying motives, and the interwoven paths of European decision-making. In particular, I wish to thank Gert-Jan Pöttering, Member of the European Parliament (EP) and former President of the EP (2007–2009), for his continuing support of my work. Furthermore, I am most grateful to Wolfgang Gaede, head of department at the General Secretariat of the Council, for a wide range of support. I also owe considerable gratitude to generations of students, who, with their enthusiasm for the European cause and their commitment to understanding what the Union is, kept my motivation alive and gave my studies new impulses. In finalizing the manuscript, Steven Kennedy, the publisher at Palgrave Macmillan, was particularly supportive and encouraging. Moreover, the two series editors, Neill Nugent and Willie Paterson, were of great support with advice and helpful comments. Neill Nugent, himself an outstanding and experienced author of many textbooks on the EU, carefully read the whole manuscript and made numerous valuable suggestions for improvements. I am most grateful to them all. Many thanks also go to two anonymous referees for their comments on the draft manuscript. Finally, I am most grateful to Heather MacRae, who, as a native speaker, helped to bring my English writing style into a pleasant, readable form. In addition, as a colleague in political science and expert in European integration studies, she gave numerous insightful suggestions on how to improve the book in substantive terms.

Finally, with deep gratitude, I dedicate this book to my parents, Josef Tömmel and Henriette Tömmel-Dohmen.

INGEBORG TÖMMEL

# List of Abbreviations

| | |
|---|---|
| ACP-States | African, Caribbean, and Pacific States |
| AFSJ | Area of Freedom, Security and Justice |
| ALDE | Alliance of the Liberals and Democrats for Europe (party group in the EP) |
| BEPA | Bureau of European Policy Advisers |
| CAP | Common Agricultural Policy |
| CEEC | Central and Eastern European Countries |
| CEEP | Centre Européen de l'Entreprise Publique (European Centre of Enterprises with Public Participation and of Enterprises of General Public Interest) |
| CEFIC | European Chemical Industry Council |
| CEN | Comité Européen de Normalisation (European Committee for Standardization) |
| CENELEC | Comité Européen de Normalisation Electrotechnique (European Committee for Electrotechnical Standardization) |
| CFSP | Common Foreign and Security Policy |
| COGECA | General Committee for Agricultural Cooperation in the European Union |
| COPA | Committee of Professional Agricultural Organisations |
| CoR | Committee of the Regions |
| COREPER | Comité des Représentants Permanents (Committee of Permanent Representatives) |
| COSAC | Conférence des Organes spécialisés en Affaires Communautaires (Conference of the Community and European Affairs Committees) |
| DCT | Draft Constitutional Treaty |
| DG | Directorate-General |
| EBA | European Banking Authority |
| EC | European Community or Communities |
| EAEC | European Atomic Energy Community |
| ECA | European Court of Auditors |
| ECB | European Central Bank |
| ECJ | European Court of Justice |
| ECOFIN | Economic and Financial Affairs Council |
| ECR | European Conservatives and Reformists (party group in the EP) |
| ECSC | European Coal and Steel Community |
| EDA | European Defence Agency |

| | |
|---|---|
| EDC | European Defence Community |
| EEA | European Economic Area |
| EEA | European Environmental Agency |
| EEAS | European External Action Service |
| EEB | European Environmental Bureau |
| EEC | European Economic Community |
| EES | European Employment Strategy |
| EESC | European Economic and Social Committee |
| EFC | Economic and Financial Committee |
| EFC | European Fiscal Compact |
| EFD | Europe of Freedom and Democracy (party group in the EP) |
| EFSA | European Food Safety Authority |
| EFSF | European Financial Stability Facility |
| EFTA | European Free Trade Association |
| EIB | European Investment Bank |
| EIOPA | European Insurance and Occupational Pensions Authority |
| EMA | European Medicines Agency |
| EMU | European Monetary Union |
| EMS | European Monetary System |
| EP | European Parliament |
| EPC | European Political Cooperation |
| EPP | European People's Party (party group in the EP) |
| EPP-ED | European People's Party-European Democrats (former party group in the EP) |
| ERT | European Round Table of Industrialists |
| ESCB | European System of Central Banks |
| ESDI | European Security and Defence Identity |
| ESDP | European Security and Defence Policy |
| ESM | European Stability Mechanism |
| ESMA | European Securities and Markets Authority |
| ETUC | European Trade Union Confederation |
| EU | European Union |
| EUMC | European Union Military Committee |
| EURATOM | European Atomic Energy Community |
| EUROPOL | European Police Office |
| EWL | European Women's Lobby |
| FRG | Federal Republic of Germany |
| FRONTEX | European Agency for the Management of Operational Cooperation at the External Borders of the Member States of the European Union |
| GDP | Gross Domestic Product |
| GDR | German Democratic Republic |
| GREENS-EFA | Greens – European Free Alliance (party group in the EP) |

| | |
|---|---|
| GUE-NGL | European United Left-Nordic Green Left (party group in the EP) |
| HR | High Representative for the Common Foreign and Security Policy, or High Representative of the Union for Foreign Affairs and Security Policy |
| IGC | Intergovernmental Conference |
| IMF | International Monetary Fund |
| IND/DEM | Independence/Democracy Group (party group in the EP) |
| INTERREG | Community initiative of the European Fund for Regional Development (EFRE) |
| ITS | Identity, Tradition, Sovereignty (party group in the EP) |
| JHA | Justice and Home Affairs |
| MEP | Member of the European Parliament |
| NAP | National Action Plan |
| NATO | North Atlantic Treaty Organization |
| NI | non-inscrit (MEP not belonging to a party group) |
| NRP | National Reform Programs |
| OECD | Organisation for Economic Co-operation and Development |
| OEEC | Organization for European Economic Cooperation |
| OJ | Official Journal |
| OLAF | Office Européen de Lutte Antifraude (European Anti-Fraud Office) |
| OMC | Open Method of Coordination |
| PES | Party of European Socialists |
| PHARE | Poland and Hungary Action for Reconstructing of the Economy |
| PR | Permanent Representation |
| PSC | Political and Security Committee |
| RRF | Rapid Reaction Forces |
| S&D | Alliance of Socialists and Democrats (party group in the EP) |
| SEA | Single European Act |
| SG | Secretariat General |
| SGP | Stability and Growth Pact |
| SME | Small and medium sized enterprises |
| SWIFT | Society for Worldwide Interbank Financial Telecommunication |
| TACIS | Technical Assistance to the Commonwealth of Independent States |
| TEC | Treaty on establishing the European Community |
| TEC-A | Treaty on establishing the European Community (consolidated version after the Treaty of Amsterdam) |
| TEC-M | Treaty on establishing the European Community (consolidated version after the Treaty of Maastricht) |

| | |
|---|---|
| TEC-N | Treaty on establishing the European Community (consolidated version after the Treaty of Nice) |
| TEU | Treaty on the European Union |
| TEU-A | Treaty on the European Union (consolidated version after the Treaty of Amsterdam) |
| TEU-L | Treaty on the European Union (consolidated version after the Treaty of Lisbon) |
| TEU-M | Treaty on the European Union (consolidated version after the Treaty of Maastricht) |
| TEU-N | Treaty on the European Union (consolidated version after the Treaty of Nice) |
| TFEU | Treaty on the Functioning of the European Union (consolidated version after the Treaty of Lisbon) |
| TSCG | Treaty on Stability, Coordination and Governance |
| UEAMPE | European Association of Craft, Small and Medium-Sized Enterprises |
| UEN | Union for Europe of the Nations (party group in the EP) |
| UEN-EA | Union for Europe of the Nations – European Alliance (national conservative political group in the CoR) |
| UK | United Kingdom |
| UNICE | Union des Industries de la Communauté Européenne (Union of Industrial and Employers' Confederations of Europe) |
| US | United States |
| VAT | Value added taxes |
| WEU | Western European Union |

# Introduction:
# The Political System of the EU

The European Union (EU) constitutes a political system that shares powers with the member states, a fact that makes it difficult to comprehend its true nature. On the one hand, the Union appears to be superordinate to the member states and, as such, significantly constrains national sovereignty. On the other hand, the Union seems to depend on the member states, since it is national governments that decide on any transfer of powers to the European level. For their part, most European citizens perceive the Union as being too powerful, as its decisions clearly impact on domestic politics and policies in fundamental ways. For example, citizens attribute the dismantling of welfare state measures at national level to decisions and policies that originate in the EU. At the same time, however, they wonder why the EU is often unable to make forceful decisions and take common actions in the face of pressing political problems – as, for example, with the economic and financial crisis or foreign policy issues. Overall, the European Union appears to be a political system full of contradictions, with widely varying perceptions and assessments of its nature.

In this introductory chapter, I will explore some of these contradictions, in order to offer some preliminary insights into the true nature of the EU. I will additionally present an overview of the issues and themes that I address in this book.

## Paradoxes of the EU

One of the most striking aspects of the EU is the large discrepancy between a comparatively 'weak' or poorly codified institutional structure, and the far-reaching impacts of its political decisions and actions. This institutional structure – insofar as it is perceived as such – appears to lack transparency and is difficult to comprehend using knowledge of existing forms of political order. The EU is neither a clearly defined federal or supranational state, nor a genuine international organization. It is, furthermore, difficult to pinpoint clearly the centre of the political

1

system where political power is concentrated and exercised. Neither the Commission (the Brussels-based administration, charged with promoting integration) nor the Council and the European Council (as the representatives of the member states in decision-making) seem to have decisive authority. The European Parliament (EP) (as the representative of the citizens of Europe) appears to be an even weaker player.

This complex constellation – where individual actors and institutions have substantial power, yet a clearly defined central authority is absent – often results in stalemates in decision-making. Commission proposals regularly fail to be adopted by the Council; the Council often fails to take decisions because of dissent among the member states. The Parliament can hardly stand up to the Commission, let alone to the Council. If the European Council is to take decisions, then heads of state or government seem to be compelled to make far-reaching concessions and accept compromises. More often, however, they fail to reach consensus, so that intergovernmental conferences and summit meetings end in non-decision or weak compromises. These situations appear to highlight a collective powerlessness of the EU.

And yet, in spite of these hurdles, European integration seems to proceed at a steady pace. When major integration projects appear on the agenda, individual politicians often boastfully announce their intentions to stop, or at least to slow down, the European 'train'. Yet, when they see that train pulling out of the station, they rush to jump on board out of fear of being left behind. In contrast, when the reform of the institutional structure of the EU is on the agenda, the train moves much more slowly. Although European leaders debate far-reaching proposals at every stage of integration – in particular, with regard to improving democratic accountability – at best, they achieve piecemeal and watered down compromises. More comprehensive steps towards reform are regularly put on the back-burner.

As a result of these contradictory developments and in the face of pressing transnational problems, the Union evolves in a specific way. Its institutional structure as defined by the Treaties is complemented by a series of informal or under-formalized arrangements and regulations, only to have these arrangements often transformed into Treaty-based institutions at some later date. In short, the EU has evolved into a complex and inventive patchwork that has, to a certain extent, altered its original institutional design. On the one hand, this enables policy-makers to overcome the structural weaknesses of the European polity and thus maintain, or even improve, its operability in the short term. On the other hand, this very approach exacerbates the complexity of the system and its lack of transparency. This, in turn, undermines the ability to hold the system democratically accountable. Consequently, public support for European integration has dramatically decreased.

In summary, the political system of the EU is marked by a series of contradictions that are manifested in striking discrepancies:

- The discrepancy between an apparently 'weak' institutional structure and the far-reaching impact of European decisions and actions.
- The discrepancy between a highly fragmented process of decision-making and the centralizing impacts of decisions.
- The discrepancy between powerful individual actors and institutions and a collective weakness in exercising power.
- The discrepancy between 'grand designs' for focused reform and the Union's piecemeal institutional evolution without a clear vision of its final shape, the so-called 'finalité'.

These discrepancies give rise to a series of questions. Should the discrepancies be regarded as merely coincidental or as unintended outcomes of the process of integration? Or, are they inherent to an emergent political order beyond the nation state? Are these discrepancies undesirable developments or, rather, core characteristics of the European polity?

As a preliminary answer to these questions, I posit here that these discrepancies are not coincidental but are core characteristics of the European polity. The central question underlying the following analysis of the European polity is why this is the case. The puzzle will be solved through a step-by-step process of unravelling the evolution of the Union as a political system, looking in particular at the unfolding of its institutional structure and its ways of operation. This includes, first, analyzing the concepts and premises underlying the creation of the European Communities and later the Union, as well as the dominant patterns that have structured its subsequent evolution. Furthermore, it implies an analysis of the EU's institutional structure, as well as its reorganization and expansion in response to increased external pressures and evolving internal dynamics. Finally, it involves addressing the procedures of decision-making and consensus-building in the process of policy formulation and implementation. Taken together, it is my objective to elaborate the specific features that characterize the EU as a political system and to clarify the dynamics that not only shape the evolution of the Union but also, at the same time, supplement, transform, and transcend the political systems of the member states.

## Overview of the book

Against the background of the questions and theses raised in the previous section, I conclude this introduction with a brief overview of the issues and themes that I intend to address in this book.

The analysis starts with a chapter that looks into the academic debate on the EU as a newly-emerging political order beyond the nation state. It examines a rich variety of theoretical approaches aimed at conceptualizing and explaining both the impressive dynamics of European integration and the political system that has emerged from this process. Starting with neo-functionalism and intergovernmentalism as the cornerstones of integration theory, the chapter proceeds to present modern variations of these approaches, as well as some completely new avenues towards understanding the EU. Furthermore, the chapter delineates the most recent turn to theorizing the EU as an emerging political system that transcends the nation state. The chapter concludes by summarizing these insights and elaborating a basic conceptual framework of the EU as a bicephalous (two-headed) system.

The Chapters 2 and 3 analyze the historical origins and the evolution of European integration and system-building. Chapter 2 presents the first three phases of this process, which established the basic features of the European polity. The first and the third phase are primarily characterized by forceful steps towards creating a supranational polity, whereas the second phase is marked by equally forceful steps aimed at expanding and diversifying its intergovernmental dimension. The chapter shows that these contradictory developments are induced, on the one hand, by the need to create an institutional framework for common action at European level and, on the other hand, the will to safeguard national control over these actions. Furthermore, the chapter explains why phases of accelerated integration alternated with phases of stagnation. In conclusion, the chapter highlights the core characteristics of the European polity, as it evolved through supranational dynamics and intergovernmental configurations.

Chapter 3 presents the fourth phase in the historical evolution of European integration, where the European polity is well-developed, but undergoes further transformations. After the third phase, characterized by supranational dynamics, this fourth phase is, again, dominated by intergovernmental forces; however, this dominance does not result in stagnation (as was generally the case during the second phase) but, rather, in improving the capacity of the intergovernmental institutions to act. Consequently, this phase is characterized by concurrent processes of widening the EU's membership and deepening integration through fundamental Treaty reform. However, in spite of these accomplishments, the Union soon faced new challenges of formerly unknown dimensions: the international financial and sovereign debt crisis, which resulted in a crisis of the Euro. The chapter shows that these challenges triggered further institutional and procedural innovations in the European polity without, however, altering its basic structure. The chapter concludes by summarizing the whole process of system-building from its inception by specifying the factors that caused the unbalanced course of integration, its unexpected or unintended consequences, and also the dualistic structure of the political system that thus emerged.

Chapter 4 provides a thorough overview of the Union's institutional structure and the characteristics of the Union's core institutions: the Commission, the Council, the European Council, the Parliament, and the Court of Justice. Four of these five institutions were already established with the creation of the Communities; a fifth institution, the European Council, consisting of the heads of state or government, was later added. It began as an informal body, then figured as a specific Council formation and, finally, constituted a separate institution formally based in the Treaty. The chapter describes the functions, competences, and internal organization of the five institutions; it also highlights the rationale of their existence, the interests they represent, and the contradictions that characterize them. The chapter concludes that the Union's most outstanding characteristic is its dualistic, bicephalous structure, combining intergovernmental and supranational institutions into a unique political system. This institutional configuration serves to mediate between the supranational aspirations of European leaders and the concerns of national governments to contain integration to a minimum.

The Chapters 5 and 6 analyze the procedures and practices of decision-making and consensus-building in the European polity as they evolved among and within its institutions. Chapter 5 examines the interaction among the core institutions of the EU in the legislative process, in fundamental decisions, and at the executive stage. It first describes the complex procedures of adopting legislative acts and the different roles that the Commission, the Council, and the Parliament play in this process. It then highlights the institutional constellation and practices with regard to fundamental decisions on European integration, such as Treaty amendments or enlargements, which are clearly dominated by the European Council. Finally, the chapter outlines decision-making at the executive stage, where interaction between the Commission and the Council plays the pivotal role. The chapter pays attention to both the formal distribution of powers among the institutions, and the practices of the individual institutions systematically to use, expand, and transgress these powers. It shows how the individual institutions engage in power struggles yet, at the same time, aim at mutual cooperation and consensus-building. Overall, the chapter highlights the exercise of political power in the EU and the ability of each institution to shape European policies and politics, as well as the overall course of integration.

Chapter 6, in contrast, analyzes each institution's internal mechanisms of decision-making and consensus-building. This analysis highlights how every institution searches to maximize its actual power and influence in the European concert by making optimal use of its institutional resources and improving its performance. The chapter explores the internal organization of these institutions, the divergences or even cleavages that result from their heterogeneous composition, and the opportunities and constraints that determine their activities. Furthermore, it takes a look at the various strategies, tactical skills, and increasingly sophisticated procedural mechanisms, as well as additional institutional arrangements that the European institutions developed for coping with the omnipresent constraints. In this, their overall aim is to achieve consensus internally in order to maximize their influence vis-à-vis their counterparts. We thus learn how the institutions build and improve the consensual spirit in their own ranks, which also characterizes their external relationships. In summary, the chapter argues that the Union's core institutions seek to improve their capacities of decision-making and their overall influence on integration by establishing elaborate internal procedures and institutional arrangements, which combine to facilitate consensus-building.

Chapter 7 elaborates on the EU's institutional expansion and diversification in both vertical and horizontal directions. The chapter starts with the insight that the original design of the EU's institutional structure soon proved to be insufficient to promote rapid integration while, at the same time, coping with the diversity among the member states. Therefore, European leaders created additional institutional structures and arrangements for specific purposes: distinctive intergovernmental institutions for dealing with foreign policy and justice and home affairs (the so-called 'second and third pillars'); independent agencies (such as the European Central Bank (ECB)); and forms of differentiated integration (e.g. monetary union). The chapter highlights the rationale underlying these institutional choices and also their unintended consequences: the dilution of power among a wide variety of actors and a lack of transparency in the systemic structure. Finally, the chapter shows that the institutional expansion and diversification of the EU is, for a large part, a path-dependent process shaped by prior institutional choices; it thus tends to reproduce the dualistic structure of the EU.

Chapter 8 explores EU policy-making and governance in its various dimensions, ranging from the evolution and expansion of the policy portfolio, via the emergence and differentiation of corresponding policy processes and governance modes, to the development and successive reforms of selected policy areas. The chapter shows how the policy portfolio evolved in four phases, alternating between building and expanding European policies and developing and sophisticating the governance modes. Furthermore, the chapter presents the basic patterns of European policy processes and the corresponding modes of governance, particularly in their process dimension. It highlights that variations in the policy process depend on the distribution of competences between the EU and the lower government levels and, consequently, the varying involvement of institutional actors in the governance process. Similarly, variations in the distribution of competences result in variations in European governance and the extent to which these are binding on the addressees. Finally, the chapter presents three selected policy areas that are representative of specific modes of governance: competition policy, cohesion policy, and the European Employment Strategy (EES). Overall, the chapter shows that European policy-making and governance evolve according to the opportunities and constraints inherent to the institutional structure of the EU; at the same time, however, policy-making also shapes institution-building and fosters integration.

Building on these insights, Chapters 9 and 10 examine how the European polity expands beyond the realm of its core institutions by incorporating national political systems as well as non-state actors into the dynamics of integration and system-building. Chapter 9 looks at the involvement of the member states – or, more precisely, public actors, institutions and organizations – in the decision-making, legislation, and policy implementation of the EU. This includes an analysis of the manifold interactions between the European and the national levels in the process of policy-formulation and implementation. These interactions create both a direct and an indirect nexus between these levels. Furthermore, the chapter highlights the increasing interactions between the European and the regional government levels. Initially, these interactions were triggered by the Commission. Over time, however, the regions themselves have claimed a direct voice in the European arena. Overall, the chapter shows that the incorporation of the national and regional government levels into European decision- and policy-making transformed the EU into a multi-level system.

Chapter 10 analyzes how non-state actors are incorporated into the European polity. It begins by outlining the performance of non-state actors as representatives of specific interests and as lobbyists at the European level. In this context, the chapter points to specific organizational forms of EU interest representation, as well as the strategies of interest organizations and lobbyists to achieve their objectives. At the same time, it considers the strategies of the European institutions to make optimal use of interest representation while concurrently containing negative spin-offs. In addition, the chapter analyzes the role of non-state actors in various phases of policy-making. This includes their involvement in legislation at European level; their role as relatively independent rule-setting agents within a regulatory framework set by the Union; and their activities in policy implementation, where they are even charged with administering the allocation of public funds. Overall, this chapter shows how the European polity tends to expand in both horizontal and vertical directions, and how it evolves not only as a multi-level, but also as a complex, multi-actor system that delegates far-reaching responsibilities to non-state actors.

Chapter 11 focuses on a critical assessment of the EU by calling into question its efficiency and effectiveness. Although these qualities are hard to measure accurately, the chapter highlights some of the EU's achievements and deficiencies in this regard, and discusses the conditions that aggravate or alleviate them. The chapter evaluates the efficiency of the EU's institutional structure, questioning whether it is functional and adequately staffed, given its tasks and objectives. Furthermore, the chapter examines the efficiency of decision-making in the Union in both quantitative and qualitative terms. Overall, it concludes that the Union has achieved a considerable degree of efficiency, in spite of manifold inefficiencies in detail. The effectiveness of the EU is then evaluated by analyzing the governance of European policies. The analysis of various policies from across the EU's regulatory, distributive and cooperative spectrums leads to the conclusion that the effectiveness of European governance may widely vary, depending on such variables as the competences of the European level, the length of the chain in political steering, and the degree of autonomy of the institutions and actors involved in the governance process.

Chapter 12 focuses on the EU's democratic legitimacy and accountability. First, the chapter delineates the 'democratic deficit' of the EU as it is widely discussed in the literature. It identifies this deficit in a number of specific features of the European polity that clearly deviate from democratic constitutions and practices of nation states. The chapter then evaluates various proposals to remedy the democratic deficit of the EU, ranging from cautious, incremental steps to alternative models for establishing post-national forms of democratic representation and participation. Finally, the chapter considers nascent forms of democratic practice in the EU that might form a realistic starting point for further improving the system's democratic legitimacy and accountability. Such practices are identified in the existence of certain checks and balances within the EU; in a specific, post-national democratic performance of the EP; and in institutionalized forms of interest representation at European level. The analysis leads to the overall conclusion that the democratic deficits of the European polity form the starting point for the emergence of alternative forms of democratic representation, participation, and legitimacy.

Finally, Chapter 13 provides an overall conclusion. It returns to the basic questions that were raised at the beginning and that underlie the analysis of all chapters. Specifically, it reconsiders how to characterize the Union as a whole and how to explain the dynamics of integration. Based now on a rich account of the EU's institutional structure and decision-making practices, the chapter answers the first question by characterizing the EU as a multifaceted political system. The facets of this system are identified as a negotiated order, an intertwined system, and also as a multi-level system. Taken together, these facets constitute the Union as a dualistic, bicephalous system, based on a unique combination of intergovernmental and supranational institutions. With regard to the second question, the chapter concludes that the dualistic or bicephalous structure of the EU, once established, causes the dynamics of the integration process, as well as the evolution and diversification of the EU's institutional structure. It thus reproduces the EU in its dualistic form. Chapter 13 closes by providing an outlook on the future of the EU. In doing so, it critically assesses how the Union might cope with the manifold external challenges that confront it and the persisting internal frictions that hamper forceful decision-making and unified action at European level.

# Chapter 1

# Theorizing European Integration and the Union as a Political System

The features of the European polity outlined in the introductory chapter have stimulated academic analyses and debates in a variety of ways. In political science, in particular, there is a long tradition of theorizing the creation and evolution of the European institutions, beginning first with the EC (European Community) and, later, the EU and the political system that subsequently emerged. Two core questions underlie these theoretical approaches: first, what explains the dynamics of integration? Second, what are the characteristics of the polity that emerges from this process? Depending on the perspective and objectives of the analysis, scholars conceptualize the EU either as a state-like political order, or as an international organization or regime (for summaries, see Rosamond 2000; Wiener and Dietz 2004; Neyer and Wiener 2011). Whereas the first perspective was primarily launched in comparative politics, the latter was developed in international relations. While the international relations perspective initially dominated the academic debate, the comparative perspective has recently become more influential. Yet, both perspectives are increasingly combined to pose new research questions and to elaborate alternative explanatory approaches.

## Traditional explanatory approaches: neo-functionalism, intergovernmentalism, and federalism

Within the framework of international relations, two theoretical traditions were crucial in shaping the analysis of European integration: neo-functionalism, a special variant of functionalist approaches; and intergovernmentalism, grounded in the theoretical tradition of (neo-) realism. These theoretical strands constitute the 'two great monoliths at the gate of the study of European integration' (Hix 2005a: 15), and they continue to inspire scholars today. Neo-functionalism was specifically developed to study the EC/EU. Its purpose is to highlight the internal dynamics that propel integration (Haas 1958; Lindberg and Scheingold 1970). In contrast, intergovernmentalism addresses international organizations in general; and poses questions of why, to which extent and under what conditions cooperation or collective action evolves among self-interested states (Axelrod 1984; Keohane 1984).

*Neo-functionalism* presents an explanatory approach to the internal logic and dynamics of the process of European integration (Haas 1958; see also Lindberg and Scheingold 1970; Schmitter 1971). The approach builds on functionalist normative models of international cooperation (Mitrany 1966). Haas defines political integration as *'the process whereby political actors in several distinct national settings are persuaded to shift their loyalties, expectations and political activities toward a new centre, whose institutions possess or demand jurisdiction over the pre-existing national states'* (Haas 1958: 16, emphasis in the original).

The core explanatory concept of neo-functionalist integration is the mechanism of spill-over. This asserts that integration in an initial, limited policy area triggers additional steps towards integration in adjacent policy areas as a result of functional needs. This leads to a series of transfers of political tasks and functions to the European level until the latter eventually becomes the main level for governance and policy-making. Haas even assumed that '[t]he end-result of a process of political integration is a new political community, super-imposed over the pre-existing ones' (Haas 1958: 16).

However, according to neo-functionalism, the transfer of policy areas and functions to the European level is not an automatic or pre-determined process. Instead, neo-functionalists assume that integration-minded actors, primarily national governments and political elites, recognize the advantages of successively integrating related policy areas and thus will consciously advance the process of integration. As progressively more tasks and functions are transferred to the European level, other actors – including political parties, interest groups, and transnational associations – will increasingly shift their activities and loyalty to this level. For Haas, 'integration is the result of specific decisions made by governments acting in conjunction with politically relevant, organised groups' (Haas 1958: 285).

Unsurprisingly, neo-functionalist theory was elaborated during the early years of European integration, when major steps towards building the Communities were taken. The theory is particularly well-suited to explaining the incremental nature of European integration and specific steps in this process. Thus, it might give an account for the founding of the three Communities, the transition from the creation of a common market to a common agricultural policy (CAP), and the transition from the completion of the single market to monetary union. However, it does not provide explanations for stagnation in the process of integration, or the fact that certain steps towards integration were never realized despite functional pressures and concrete proposals for implementation (Sandholtz and Zysman 1989). For explaining such events or constellations, intergovernmentalism appeared much better suited.

*Intergovernmentalism* basically aims to explain international co-operation among utility-maximizing, self-interested, and rational states. In international organizations or regimes, cooperation among states occurs when actors expect benefits that would not materialize without cooperation (Keohane 1984). Further motivations for cooperation might be the possibility of concluding advantageous package deals, or simply a fear of disadvantages if excluded from cooperation (Moravcsik 1991). According to intergovernmentalist approaches, the emergence and evolution of European integration can be explained as a series of bargains among national governments that may result in partial trans-fers of powers to the European level, and the creation of institutions for decision-making and collective action. Integration moves forward when actors' interests and preferences converge, or when diverse interests are reconciled by convening package deals or additional compensatory arrangements such as side-payments (Hoffmann 1966, 1982; Taylor 1983; Keohane and Hoffmann 1991). However, intergovernmentalists are sceptical about the possibilities of achieving lasting cooperation within the framework of a regional entity such as the EC/EU. Thus, Hoffmann (1966) argues that the nation state remains the most impor-tant entity in the international system. Furthermore, since 'the first truly *global* international system' has emerged, states participating in a regional entity 'are differently subjected and attracted to the outside world'; hence, the diversity among them 'seems to sharpen rather than shrink' Hoffmann (1966: 865). More broadly, Hoffmann (1966: 867) assumes that the move towards regional integration 'can fail ... when there are differences in assessments of the national interest'. To underpin this claim with empirical findings, he gives a comprehensive account of the manifold differences among the original six founding members of the European Communities.

Intergovernmentalist approaches appeared particularly meaningful after the first major crisis, initiated when de Gaulle, the French president at that time, stalled the integration process. The intergovernmentalist approach is particularly well-suited to explain why predicted steps towards integration do not materialize and why the process of integra-tion frequently stalls or stagnates (Taylor 1983). Furthermore, the approach successfully explains the asymmetries of European integration – for example, between economic and political integration, between market integration and public regulation, and between economic and social policy domains. While all member states perceive economic integration as beneficial, issues of social policy or political integration are much more contested among them and, as a result, progress in these domains is harder to achieve. However, intergovernmentalism barely addresses the significance of the supranational actors and political forces and, specifically, the role of the Commission for promoting integration.

The two theoretical approaches outlined above refer primarily to the dynamics of European integration; that is, the processes of decision-making and the actors that advocate or promote integration. However, these approaches do not explicitly address the nature of the political system that evolves from this process. While intergovernmentalism primarily perceives the EU as a specific form of an international organization or regime (Hoffmann 1982), neo-functionalism assumes that, in the long term, a 'new political community' will emerge (Haas 1958: 16) which, however, is hardly defined in concrete terms.

*Federalism* has provided a concept that attempts to define the EC as a political system. Thus, in contrast to the international relations approaches described above, various scholars of comparative politics have developed an understanding of the EC as an emerging federal system, modelled after the United States. Particularly in the early years of integration, scholars and politicians alike hoped to build the 'United States of Europe'. Accordingly, in these early years, federalism served more as a normative objective for European integration than an analytical tool for specifying the nature of the European polity (Rosamond 2000: 23; Burgess 2004: 31–4). Nevertheless, some scholars attempted to view the early Communities as the building blocks of an emerging federation. The two-level nature of the EC and the far-reaching powers of the supranational institutions, as well as joint decision-making in the Council, appeared to confirm this interpretation. The federalist perspective on the EC also highlighted the deficiencies of the emerging polity: the imperfect separation of powers among the European institutions, the unclear allocation of competences, and the democratic deficit of the system. In sum, the federalist perspective on the EC served to highlight the preliminary state of European integration and the hybrid nature of the emerging polity. However, federalism hardly offered insights into the origins and dynamics of European integration, let alone the recurring phases of stagnation.

The three theoretical strands outlined above – intergovernmentalism, neo-functionalism and federalism – were developed and gained importance during the early years of integration. They essentially refer to the origins and evolution of European integration, as well as to the basic structure of the EC as a political system. Furthermore, these theoretical strands refer to different aspects of the European polity; hence, the explanatory power of each is limited. However, a synthesis of these theories would pose problems. If used consistently, the theories are mutually exclusive and can thus hardly be combined to form an over-arching explanation in the sense of a 'grand theory'. Therefore, the theoretical approaches discussed above should be viewed as providing a framework that allows us to comprehend the EU *with reference* to an intergovernmental, a supranational or a federal system. Yet, we should not directly equate the Union with any one of these systems.

## Traditional approaches revisited

Rapid institutional and procedural changes in the European polity that began in the mid-1980s changed the scholarly perspective on the dynamics of integration and the nature of the EC/EU. The academic debate generally continued to rely on the theoretical strands outlined: intergovernmentalism, neo-functionalism, and federalism. However, departing from these theories, a few scholars presented more elaborated explanatory approaches that reflected the actual state of European integration and the EC/EU as a political system. Furthermore, these approaches served explicitly to explain specific aspects of integration: major turning points in building the Community or Union, the role of individual actors and institutions in this process, or the interplay between the European and the national level within the EC/EU.

Theoretical approaches inspired by either neo-functionalism or intergovernmentalism particularly sought to identify the forces, institutions, and actors relevant for building the European polity. Accordingly, a heated debate emerged on the question as to whether national governments or supranational actors were the driving forces in European integration.

Early contributors to this debate were Wayne Sandholtz and John Zysman (1989). They explained the re-launch of European integration and the building of the single market after 1985 as the work of supra-national and non-governmental actors. On the one hand, the European Commission 'exercised effective policy leadership' and, on the other hand, a transnational industry coalition, 'supported the Commission's efforts' (Sandholtz and Zysman 1989: 96). However, the authors also acknowledged other factors as important for 'recasting the European bargain' (the title of their article). In their view, shifts in the situational context – structural changes in the international economy and the trend towards neo-liberal solutions to economic problems – caused national governments to reconsider their policies and to embark on elite bargains on the proposals of the Commission. Particularly important in this context was French President Mitterrand's turn to European solutions for economic problems instead of national solo efforts. Even though the authors understood their explanatory approach as a new concept, it was later identified with neo-functionalism. Particularly, the authors' strong emphasis on the importance of the Commission and non-governmental actors for the re-launch of European integration underpinned this interpretation.

Andrew Moravcsik (1991, 1993, 1998), drawing largely on inter-governmentalism, reacted to this explanatory approach by explicitly taking the opposite position. At first, he presented an empirically-based understanding of the member states as holding the dominant role in the creation of the single market (Moravcsik 1991). Later, he elaborated this approach into a concise theory that he labelled 'liberal intergovern-mentalism' (Moravcsik 1993, 1998). This theory conceptualizes major integration steps, culminating in treaty reforms, as the relevant stages in building the EC/EU. Accordingly, Moravcsik assumes that it is the preferences of the member states and the bargains among them, together with the ensuing institutional choices, that decisively shape integration. In his view, the bargaining position of every single state is first determined through a process of preference formation at national level. This preference formulation is largely determined by economic and – to a lesser extent – geopolitical interests. The member states then engage in intergovernmental bargains; the outcomes of which are shaped by the intensity of national preferences and the asymmetrical interdependence among the member states (Moravcsik 1998: 60). Member states with strong interests in further integration will act as policy entrepreneurs. The institutional choices finally agreed on are mainly induced by the member states' wishes to establish credible commitments. Altogether, progress in integration – mainly laid down in Treaty reforms – comes about when the governments' preferences tend to converge. But progress is also possible when preferences do not converge, as states with much to gain will be willing to make concessions or provide side-payments to those opposing reforms. States may even agree to undesired reforms because they are concerned that they may otherwise be excluded from the benefits of integration. This has been the case for the United Kingdom (UK) during the negotiations around the SEA (Moravcsik 1991). Consistent with this view on the central role of the member states, Moravcsik explicitly rejects any major influence of the Commission on the process of integration; in his view, the Commission acts merely as a secretariat that implements the decisions of the Council.

Moravcsik's theory has the merit to provide an intergovernmentalist explanation for progress in European integration, even when the preferences and positions of the member states do *not* converge. Furthermore, his theory has been widely noted because of the rigour of his reasoning and the many variables that he included in the approach. Nevertheless, his concept has provoked a plethora of criticism (e.g. Sandholtz and Stone Sweet 1998; Wallace *et al.* 1999). Scholars particularly criticized

Moravcsik's strict rejection of any role of the supranational institutions – above all the Commission – in the process of integration, and his view of national governments as the exclusive promoters of this process. Furthermore, critiques consider the empirical basis of liberal intergovernmentalism to be comparatively thin. In spite of Moravcsik's extensive description of the bargaining processes among the member states, he analyzed only the preferences and positions of three states in depth: France, Germany, and the UK.

However, the merit of Moravcsik's position has been that it has induced a flood of studies that all sought to refute his theoretical propositions. Initially, this led to the formulation of alternative concepts drawing primarily on neo-functionalist arguments. I now briefly present a few examples of these concepts. In the long term, however, scholars rejected Moravcsik's theory by elaborating new explanatory approaches grounded in alternative theoretical concepts. Thus, as I will show in the following section, they slowly transcended the dichotomy between intergovernmentalism and neo-functionalism.

Some scholars attempted to revive neo-functionalism by applying it to actors other than those mentioned by Haas, or by re-defining the concept of spill-over. Thus, in 1993, Burley and Mattli presented 'A Political Theory of Legal Integration' (the subtitle of their article) as an explanation for the rapid evolution of the EC/EU. In their view, the European Court of Justice, 'an unsung hero', is the main actor promoting integration, since 'the thirteen judges ... managed to transform the Treaty of Rome ... into a constitution' (Burley and Mattli 1993: 41–2). According to the authors, this process is best explained with 'the original neo-functionalist model developed by Ernst Haas' (Burley and Mattli 1993: 43). In particular, the authors emphasized the logic of spill-over as a forceful mechanism for pushing forward integration. Thus, through a chain of judgements, the Court established, among other matters, the precedence of European law above national law and its direct effect on the citizens (for details, see Chapter 4). In their telling, legal spill-over also occurred from initially pure economic regulation to a number of other domains. Furthermore, the authors claim that neo-functionalist theory adequately captures the independent variable of legal integration, since 'the drivers of this process are supranational and sub-national actors pursuing their own self interests' (Burley and Mattli 1993: 43). Even though the authors deal primarily with legal integration, they also emphasize the Commission's role as a supranational actor capable of overcoming 'national barriers' (Burley and Mattli 1993: 54). They thus claimed to revive neo-functionalism as a means of explaining European integration.

Similarly, in 1995, Cowles proposed an approach that emphasized the role of non-state actors in creating the single market. In her view, it was the European Round Table of Industrialists (ERT) that acted as the main promoter of this project. According to Cowles, the business group managed not only to set the agenda for the single market programme, but also to influence its implementation. Cowles explicitly rejects inter-governmentalist theory, as it 'cannot explain the activities of the key non-state actors in the 1992 process' (Cowles 1995: 521). However, she also questions neo-functionalism, and concludes her article with the remark 'that new conceptualizations of European integration are neces-sary' (Cowles 1995: 523). Nevertheless, her reasoning is clearly rooted in neo-functionalist assumptions.

By contrast, in 1995, Corbey – determined to explain both stagnation and progress in European integration – presented a completely new and original version of neo-functionalism that she termed 'dialectical func-tionalism'. The concept of dialectical functionalism: 'provides a concep-tion of the internal dynamic that drives the cycle' (Corbey 1995: 253). Central to this approach is the interaction between the EU and the member states. The 'cycle' starts with steps toward integration in one sector. Member states then react to these steps by protecting their sov-ereignty in adjacent areas. They tend to 'safeguard functionally linked areas against integration' (Corbey 1995: 263). In addition, they respond by increasingly intervening in adjacent areas, 'either to compensate for the loss of autonomy, or to improve national competitiveness in relation to other countries, or both' (Corbey 1995: 263). The result is stagnation in the process of European integration. As an example, the author points to the proliferation of non-tariff trade barriers at the national level after the creation of the customs union. However, when policy rivalry increases and becomes counterproductive, 'policy preferences converge and further integration is demanded ... or supplied by the European Commission' (Corbey 1995: 265). Interest groups also have a place in dialectical functionalism. They often exercise pressure on national governments to safeguard adjacent areas or to intervene in them. There-fore, when national governments turn to new integration steps, they also aim at freeing themselves from interest group pressures.

The theoretical approaches presented above are important for their efforts either to revive (Burley and Mattli) or even to renew neo-function-alism (Corbey) and for focusing on institutions and actors as well as dynamics (Burley and Mattli; Cowles; Corbey) which are largely excluded by Moravcsik. As such, they formed an important step towards over-coming the one-sidedness of liberal intergovernmentalism. Yet, these approaches themselves only considered certain aspects, phases, or dynamics of European integration, while other dimensions remained out of sight. Furthermore, these approaches remained grounded in international rela-tions theory, whereas the EU had already transformed into a political system in its own right. Not surprisingly, theoretical approaches inspired by comparative politics therefore gained ground. Even though the debate continued to focus on Moravcsik's shortcomings, or even mistakes, his critics no longer rejected his theory by turning to neo-functionalism but, rather, by opening up completely new theoretical avenues.

## New theoretical avenues

### Institutionalism

While, during the 1990s, some scholars revived neo-functionalism, others discovered *institutionalism* as a tool for more accurately theorizing why the process of integration did not exclusively depend on the choices and decisions of the member states. As early as the 1980s, March and Olsen (1984, 1989) opened up this theoretical avenue by presenting a new understanding of the role of institutions in political life. Their approach, termed 'new institutionalism', caused an enormous resonance among political scientists and received much attention from scholars of European integration. The authors' main thesis was that institutions do not simply mirror societal forces; instead, they are 'collections of standard operating procedures and structures that define and defend interests. They are political actors in their own right' (March and Olsen 1984: 738). Furthermore, the authors stressed that collective choices are not simply induced by the logic of consequentialism but, rather, reflect a logic of appropriateness. This means that collective choices are rarely 'based on calculated self-interest' (March and Olsen 1984: 735). Instead, the authors assume 'that political actors associate certain actions with certain situations by rules of appropriateness' (March and Olsen 1984: 741). The new perspective on institutions as actors in political life was quickly adopted by many scholars. However, it soon fell apart into a number of different strands. In 1996, Hall and Taylor presented a concise overview of three variants of new institutionalism: historical, rational choice, and sociological institutionalism.

According to Hall and Taylor, *historical institutionalists* conceptualize institutions as formal organizations and analyze the power relations among them. They largely explain institutional behaviour through path dependency; that is, previous decisions, choices and institutional arrangements will, to a significant extent, mould ensuing decisions and developments. Furthermore, historical institutionalists assume that unintended consequences play a major role in political life. *Rational choice institutionalists*, by contrast, conceptualize institutions as organizational forms – formal organizations, rules, or norms – that structure the behaviour of actors. They assume that actors have a fixed set of preferences and behave entirely instrumentally. Thus, strategic interactions among them, structured and constrained by institutions, determine political outcomes. *Sociological institutionalists* for their part use a much broader concept of institutions. They include in their definition 'not just formal rules, procedures or norms, but the symbol systems, cognitive scripts, and moral templates that provide "the frames of meaning" guiding human action' (Hall and Taylor 1996: 947). Accordingly, scholars adhering to this strand assume that the driving motive of actors is not rational or strategic considerations but, rather, culturally-specific practices.

The concept of new institutionalism induced a fundamental change in theorizing European integration and the EU. While initially used to refute liberal intergovernmentalism, new institutionalism soon became the dominant theoretical lens for analyzing the EU (Pollack 2004). This meant a shift from explaining the causes and dynamics of integration to the analysis of institutional behaviour and interaction. It also implied a shift from international relations theories to those developed in comparative politics. In turn, these shifts opened up the path towards applying a host of other theoretical approaches – mainly derived from the analysis of national political systems – to the study of the EU. Yet, initially, it was historical and rational choice institutionalism that played the most prominent role in transcending traditional theoretical thinking.

Paul Pierson (1996) was one of the first to present a historical institutionalist account of 'The Path to European Integration' (the title of his article) (see also Bulmer 1993, 1998; Olsen 2010). Arguing against the shortcomings of Moravcsik's liberal intergovernmentalism, he claimed that member states, for various reasons, lose control over the process of integration. This may result from autonomous action of the supranational institutions, from member states' preoccupation with short-term concerns, from unintended consequences of their decisions, or instability of national policy preferences. Furthermore, 'once gaps in control emerge, change-resistant decisions and sunk costs make it difficult for member states to reassert their authority' (Pierson 1996: 123). In other words, Pierson argues that not only supranational actors, but also the path of the historical process, the unforeseeable consequences of decisions and institutional choices, and the hurdles to adapt institutions to changed needs, make it difficult for national governments to exercise full control over European integration. With this explanation, Pierson clearly transcended not only liberal intergovernmentalism, but also neo-functionalism.

Similarly, in the same year, Pollack made a strong case for rational choice institutionalism as the appropriate theory to study European integration, as it allows researchers to overcome the 'impasse' between intergovernmentalism and neo-functionalism (Pollack 1996: 430). In his view, both historical and rational choice institutionalism depart from the same assumptions. Both believe that '[o]nce created, institutions 'take on a life of their own,' acting as independent or intervening variables between the preferences and the power of the member governments on the one hand, and the ultimate policy outputs of EC governance on the other' (Pollack 1996: 431). Initially, institutional choices are the result of intergovernmental bargains shaped by national preferences; yet, with these choices, national governments delegate certain functions to supranational agents, which 'enjoy considerable discretion from the collective preferences of the member states' (Pollack 1996: 433). Pollack's main claim is that the relationship between the member states and the EU's supranational institutions is best understood as a principal–agent relationship, where the member states act as collective principals, and the supranational institutions perform as their agents (see also Pollack 2003). Against this background, he first defines the mechanisms of institutional choice and the conditions that constrain institutional change, for example the unanimity rule in the Council, or resistance 'from below'. He then goes on to determine the conditions that enable supranational institutions to 'exert independent causal influence on EC policy outcomes' (Pollack 1996: 444). This might occur, for example, when they have informational advantages over the member states, or when the principals fail to exercise effective control over their agents. Finally, Pollack sheds light on the Commission's agenda-setting powers in both formal and informal terms. Drawing on rational choice institutionalism, Pollack defines a whole range of circumstances that provide supranational institutions a high degree of discretion in their activities and, thus, a certain degree of independence from their principals. However, he concedes that 'the primary emphasis in institutional analysis is indeed on institutions as intervening rather than independent variables, and the ultimate causes of European integration do typically remain exogenous to the theory' (Pollack 1996: 454; see also Pollack 2004: 154). With this conclusion, Pollack clearly points to the limits of the new theoretical approaches: they explain what may happen in the framework of the EU's institutional structure, but they do not theorize the origins and dynamics of integration.

New institutionalism not only shed light on the discretion of supranational agents, or the constraints that member states face when attempting to hold control on them, it was also successfully applied to other dimensions of the EU. Simon Bulmer (1993, 1998), for example, used historical institutionalism to analyze European governance, particularly the adoption of the single market programme. Fritz Scharpf (1988, 2006) developed a theoretical approach to decision-making in the EU. According to his theory, member states may end up in a 'joint decision trap' – that is, non-decision – particularly in those situations where the unanimity rule applies. Geoffrey Garrett and George Tsebelis, using a rigorous rational choice approach, analyzed the relationships among the core institutions of the EU in decision-making, and defined the conditions that allow supranational agents discretion, or provide national governments full control (see, e.g., Tsebelis 1994, Garrett 1995; Garrett and Tsebelis 1996; Tsebelis and Yataganas 2002).

## Multi-level governance

In 1996, Gary Marx, Liesbet Hooghe, and Kermit Blank presented another approach rooted in new institutionalism, which later evolved to an independent theoretical strand: *multi-level governance*. In the title of their article, the authors juxtaposed state-centric versus multi-level governance. The authors explicitly rejected the 'state-centric model', as it poses national governments 'as ultimate decision-makers, devolving little authority to supranational institutions' (Marks *et al*. 1996: 343–5). As an alternative, they presented the multi-level governance model, where 'decision-making competencies are shared by actors at different levels' and 'supranational institutions ... have independent influence in policy-making' (Marks *et al*. 1996: 346; see also Hooghe and Marks 2001). Furthermore, they argued that 'collective decision-making among states involves a significant loss of control for individual national executives' (Marks *et al*. 1996: 346). Marks, Hooghe and Blank also claimed that states can no longer monopolize the relationships with sub-national actors, since the latter act in both national and supranational arenas. The reasons given for member states' willingness to delegate power to the supranational level are mainly those known from other theories. National governments may expect benefits that exceed the loss of control, or they hope to achieve desired policy outcomes that they otherwise could not achieve. Finally, Marks, Hooghe and Blank highlighted the practice of multi-level governance. Distinguishing four phases in the policy-making process – policy initiation, decision-making, implementation, and adjudication – they attributed to every phase a particular set of actors, institutions, and government levels. Thus, they once again proved that national governments or executives are by no means in full control of European integration and the 'polity creating process' (Marks *et al*. 1996: 342).

The multi-level governance approach, once formulated, soon evolved into an independent conceptual tool (see, e.g., Kohler-Koch and Eising 1999; Jachtenfuchs 2001; Scharpf 2001; Benz 2007; Treib *et al*. 2007; Tömmel and Verdun 2009; Börzel 2010; Sabel and Zeitlin 2010). As such, it served to capture the specific features of European policy-making rather than those of the integration process, or the Union's political system. As a heuristic concept, it inspired scholars to define more precisely the characteristics of European governance, and sometimes even the manner in which the EU functions. Thus, scholars coined terms such as 'network' governance, 'experimentalist' governance, or 'innovative' governance (Kohler-Koch and Eising 1999; Tömmel and Verdun 2009; Sabel and Zeitlin 2010). All these analyses have in common the conceptualization of the EU as a multi-level polity with a multitude of actors involved in decision-making. Hence, influence on policy-making, policy outcomes, and polity-building is largely diluted among them.

## Social constructivism

By the turn of the century, another theoretical avenue gained ground among scholars of European integration: *social constructivism*. Social constructivism may be seen as an offspring of sociological institutionalism, as it strongly emphasizes the role of cultural norms and identities on human action (Leuffen *et al.* 2012: 85–7). Yet, constructivism as a meta-theoretical approach also has independent roots based in social sciences more generally. In EU research, social constructivism is used to explain the motives of agents, the interactions among them, or changes in rules, norms, and behavioural practices. Applied in this sense, social constructivism constitutes a meso-level theory rather than an all-encompassing approach for explaining European integration, or the nature of the European polity. Jeffrey Checkel (1999) was the first to define the baselines of social constructivism in EU research. Criticizing historical and rational choice institutionalism for their narrow view on institutions as constraints on actors' behaviour, he argued that these institutionalisms 'need to be complemented by a more sociological understanding of institutions that stresses their interest- and identity-forming role' (Checkel 1999: 545). Such an understanding is provided, first, by sociological institutionalism, which assumes that 'institutions constitute actors and their interests'. Thus, institutions 'can provide agents with understanding of their interests and identities' (Checkel 1999: 546). Checkel, however, goes even further by proposing social constructivism as the appropriate tool 'to explain theoretically both the content of actors' identities/preferences and the modes of social interaction' (Checkel 1999: 548). He exemplifies this approach in two issue areas suited for a constructivist analysis: 'learning and socialization processes at the European level; and the soft or normative side of Europeanization at the national level' (Checkel 1999: 548). The first issue area, social learning and socialization, involves 'a process whereby actors, through interaction with broader institutional contexts (norms or discursive structures), acquire new interests and preferences – in the absence of obvious material incentives' (Checkel 1999: 548). Checkel underpins this statement by formulating some hypotheses about the conditions that might facilitate social learning and socialization processes. Similarly, as the second issue area, the author defines the construction of norms at European level and their diffusion to the national level, as well as the conditions that favour such developments.

Social constructivism aims at analyzing complex relationships between institutions and actors, which are rarely the subject of other theoretical approaches. Accordingly, Checkel (1999) emphasized that constructivism complements, rather than substitutes, existing theories and explanations. In spite of these limitations, the approach soon gained currency among scholars of the EU. It served to explain certain choices of European leaders or other relevant actors; it provided an under-standing of the role of norms and ideas in decision-making and integra-tion steps; and it helped to understand identity-building in the context of the European polity. A few examples will illustrate this. In sharp contrast to liberal intergovernmentalism, Craig Parsons (2003) explained the preferences of French presidents during the initial and subsequent steps towards increased integration that are usually laid down in treaty reforms as a 'particular set of ideas' (Parsons 2003: 1). Similarly, Jachtenfuchs *et al.* applied a constructivist approach to the analysis of the European Union, arguing that 'the development of a polity depends not only on interests but also on normative ideas about a legitimate political order (polity-ideas)' (Jachtenfuchs *et al.* 1998: 409). Schim-melfennig (2003) found that EU member states' choices on Eastern enlargement were not motivated by strategic considerations of utility-maximizing actors, but were the outcome of lock-in-effects that resulted from normative claims underlying European integration. Rittberger (2005) claimed that member states' choices to create and subsequently empower the EP were induced by concerns about procedural legitimacy and, ultimately, shaped by the polity-ideas of the most influential govern-ments. Finally, Risse concluded that emerging forms of European iden-tity can best be explained with constructivist arguments, since 'European identity ... is a specific construct in time and space' and the EU 'consti-tutes 'Europe' as a political and social space in people's beliefs and collective understandings' (Risse 2004: 171).

In summary, we can conclude that the theoretical approaches presented in this section significantly widened the realm and scope of EU research. New institutionalism shifted the focus of analysis from the integration process to the EU's institutional structure and, particularly, its 'thick' institutional fabric. Scholars now theorized the logic of insti-tutional choice, the structuring or constraining impact of institutions on actors' behaviour, and the role of cultural norms and practices in shaping actors' identities as well as institutional change. Furthermore, with terms such as 'multi-level' or 'network' governance, they captured the EU's institutional architecture more precisely. Finally, they successfully applied social constructivism in order to deal with issues that otherwise escape scientific reasoning. Thus, at present, scholars of European inte-gration have a much wider range of analytical tools, mainly derived from comparative politics, at their disposal. However, these approaches tend to cover specific dimensions of the European polity. They rarely provide answers to the basic questions of EU research: the ultimate causes of European integration, and the nature of the polity that emerges from this process. Against this background, it comes as no surprise that scholars recently reintroduced at least one of the big questions; that is, how to capture and explain the nature of the EU.

## Theorizing the EU as a political system

Even though the approaches outlined above continue to dominate the analysis of certain dimensions of European integration and the EU, scholars have recently turned again to the question of how to conceptualize the EU as a whole. This turn was induced by the perception that not only international relations theory and, particularly, liberal inter-governmentalism, but also comparative politics did not provide satisfying explanations or concepts to capture the emerging European polity in its entirety.

### The EU: a system sui generis

Acknowledging the limits of comparing the Union to other existing forms of political order, a consensus quickly gained ground that the EU might be a system '*sui generis*'. Even though many political scientists shared this idea, it remained largely unclear what '*sui generis*' exactly implies and how to define the actual nature of the EU in such terms (Jachtenfuchs 1997). Some scholars rejected the *sui generis* concept, arguing that it would exclude any comparison. However, this argument is hardly valid since it is only by comparisons that the specific features of a system *sui generis* can be defined.

Unsurprisingly, comparisons – not only with certain dimensions of a political system, but also with entire systems – remained high on the agenda. In this context it was, again, federalism that first provided the template for theoretical reflections on the EU. In general, scholars of federalism agreed that the Union should not be considered a federal *state*. Rather, they conceptualized the Union as a specific form of 'federal balance' (Sbragia 1993) that displays characteristics of both federations and confederations (Burgess 2000, 2006; Howse and Nicolaïdis 2003; Laursen 2011). Accordingly, scholars coined new terms to define the EU as a federation that clearly deviates from existing forms; for example, 'unachieved federation' (Harbo 2005: 141), 'confederal union' (Burgess 2000), 'new type of federal union' (Burgess 2004: 27), 'transnational type of federalism' (Nicolaïdis 2006: 60), or 'hybrid type of federalism' (Hueglin and Fenna 2006: 240). All of these terms emphasize, in some form, the mixed nature of the EU. Furthermore, they point to the fact that the EU somehow constitutes a new type of federation. Michael Burgess, the most prominent analyst of the EU as a federation, clearly expressed this when he argued, '[t]here is no historical precedent for the creation of a multinational, multicultural and multilingual federation composed of 15 to 20 established national states ... with mature social, economic, political and legal systems' (Burgess 2006: 39). Accordingly, he concludes, '[t]he EU seems to point the way forward to a much more imaginative, flexible accommodation of organized local, regional, national, supranational and international interests than the United States of America' (Burgess 2006: 43). In this way, attempts to compare the EU with federations generally lead to the conclusion that the Union, if at all, constitutes a completely new type of a federal political order, a federation '*sui generis*' (Tömmel 2011a).

Other scholars have attempted to analyze the EU as a whole by using the analogy of state, but without actually equating the Union with a (nation) state. For example, Simon Hix (2005a: 2–5; see also Hix and Høyland 2010: 12–15) in his comprehensive textbook conceptualizes the EU as a political system, but not a state. In his view, the EU displays the core characteristics of a political system: a set of stable institutions for collective decision-making; demands on the system by citizens and social groups; decisions that impact on the allocation of resources and values; and, finally, feedbacks between the system and its constituencies. Furthermore, as with national political systems, he distinguishes between executive, legislative, and judicial politics of the EU. The distinction between these three dimensions allows him to analyze each dimension with reference to the respective theories of comparative politics and to identify differences between the Union and national political systems. Yet, since such a distinction suggests a clear separation of powers in the EU, which obviously is not a given, it blurs some characteristics of the European polity such as the specific separation of powers between European institutions; the eminent role of the Commission in legislation; the emergence of alternative forms of democratic representation; and, finally, the role of less formalized institutions and procedures of the EU (for details, see Chapters 12 and 13).

### The EU – political order beyond the nation state

Finally, a few scholars succeeded in breaking new ground by elaborating conceptual or explanatory frameworks that compare the Union to historical forms of political order, or define it as an emerging new form, but within a longer-term historical context. A few examples are now outlined, all of which refer to the EU as a more or less developed political system constituting an emerging post-national type of political order.

Giandomenico Majone (1996, 2005, 2009) conceptualizes the EU as a political system of 'mixed government'. He sees the EU as a combination of intergovernmental and supranational institutions that are representative of different interests; namely, those of the nation states and those of the Union as a whole (Majone 2005: 59). More specifically, he compares the EU to pre-modern, medieval systems of mixed government. Such a 'polity is composed, not of individual citizens, but of corporate bodies balanced against each other and governed by mutual agreement rather than by a political sovereign' (Majone 2005: 46). Majone characterizes the EU with reference to three 'estates: national governments, represented by the Council; supranational institutions (the Commission and the Court); and the peoples of the states, represented by the EP' (Majone 2005: 47). Such an institutional structure excludes majoritarian forms of rule and democracy. Instead, the system is governed by the 'principle of institutional balance' (Majone 2005: 48). Accordingly, 'sovereignty is shared among the constituents of the polity', and decisions are taken 'by a political exchange among the three law-making institutions' (Majone 2005: 49). Furthermore, Majone ascertains an imbalance in the EU's exercise of state functions. In his view, the EU is marked by regulation, whereas other state functions such as redistribution or macro-economic stabilization do not play a significant role (Majone 1996, 2005, 2009). Because of this regulatory dominance, Majone had defined the EU in earlier publications as an emerging regulatory state (Majone 1996).

Stefano Bartolini (2005a), more explicitly than Majone, conceptualizes the EU as an emerging political order that historically transcends the nation state, but does not have an antecedent in earlier historical phases (see also Caporaso 1996). He views the nation state as a particular form of political order pertaining to a certain phase in the evolution of state-building in Europe. Bartolini conceptualizes European integration 'as a process of territorial and functional boundary transcendence' (Bartolini 2005a: xii). He introduces three conceptual tools for the analysis of the EU: centre-formation, system-building, and political structuring. 'Centre-formation' refers to the process of integration and the pooling of significant political powers at the European level. 'System-building' refers to whether the EU is capable of producing loyalty; that is, 'structures and processes of system maintenance represented by cultural integration, social sharing institutions, and political participation' (Bartolini 2005: xii). 'Political structuring' focuses on 'the institutionalization of conflict lines within the newly devised boundaries and borders of the EU' (Bartolini 2005: xii). Bartolini analyzes the extent of centre-formation, system-building, and political structuring by using Hirschman's concept of exit and voice. He clearly identifies a far-reaching process of centre-formation in the EU which, however, is out of balance with system-building and political structuring. That is, he ascertains significant differentials in boundary transcendence. While economic and legal integration proceeds rapidly and the corresponding boundaries of the nation states are easily removed, those referring to political processes and societal structures clearly persist.

Ulrich Beck and Edgar Grande (2007) also view the EU as a political system that differs fundamentally from the nation state and marks a new phase in the evolution of political rule. They start their book with a fervent critique of what they call 'methodological nationalism'; that is, a way of theorizing or conceptualizing the EU within the categories of the nation state (Beck and Grande 2007: 11–27, see also Rosamond

2008). In contrast to these approaches, they characterize the EU as a cosmopolitan empire. Such an empire, however, differs greatly from modern and pre-modern empires, in particular, because its expansion is not based on force but, rather, on voluntary accession of ever more states. The cosmopolitan empire of the EU, according to Beck and Grande, is marked by asymmetric integration and thus displays a centre-periphery structure. Further core characteristics are a variable territorial structure, a multi-national social structure, integration through law, cooperation and consensus, horizontal and vertical institutional integration, as well as forms of complex sovereignty (Beck and Grande 2007: 50–69). In terms of its systemic structure, the authors conceptualize the EU as composed of both intergovernmental cooperation and supranational integration.

Although the approaches outlined above are highly diverse with regard to their theoretical premises, analytic tools and empirical findings, they nevertheless share some common assumptions. First, scholars that conceptualize the EU as a whole emphasize its state-like system of rule, yet without equating the Union with a nation state. Many scholars view the EU as a political formation that indicates an emerging new stage of state-building that follows the phase of the nation state. Furthermore, scholars emphasize certain imbalances and also inconsistencies in the political system of the EU. Bartolini is most clear on this point when he claims that centre-formation is out of balance with system-building and political structuring. Majone's concept of a European Union, primarily focused on regulation, also indicates imbalances in the exercise of political rule. Beck and Grande point to imbalances when speaking of asymmetric integration and a centre-periphery structure. Moreover, all these authors conceptualize the EU as a composite system, combining supranational and intergovernmental features which, in turn, stand for territorial, functional, or corporate and electoral structures of representation. Finally, most authors see the EU as a political system that differs from nation states by virtue of its comparatively weaker institutional foundations, its limited and asymmetric powers and competences, and its specific modes of governance. Most of these assumptions are shared by many other scholars as well, even though they do not elaborate a complex theoretical or conceptual edifice.

Overall, we can conclude that the most recent stage of theorizing the EU has resulted in a broad consensus on certain basic issues. Thus, the EU is conceived as a political system that partly transcends the nation state and builds on specific institutions that represent the nation states, the peoples of Europe, as well as the interests of the Union as a whole. Furthermore, the Union is seen as marked by asymmetries, unclear boundaries, and a comparatively weak institutional structure as well as a low degree of what Bartolini calls 'system-building' and 'political structuring'. In the next section, I will combine these findings into a heuristic concept of the EU that will provide an analytical guideline for the empirical chapters of the book.

## The EU: a dualistic, bicephalous political system

The foregoing sections highlighted how political scientists theorize European integration and the EU as a political system. Scholars have presented a wide variety of explanations for the origins and development of the European Union, the institutional structure of the emerging polity, and the power relations among the most relevant institutions and actors. Furthermore, they have compared the EU with past and present forms of political order and, thus, defined the contours of an emerging *sui generis* order. Despite this wide variety of approaches, we can draw some general conclusions from the theoretical strands presented above and combine their insights into a heuristic concept of the dynamics of European integration and the EU as a political system.

First, most scholars agree that the European Union is a mixed or hybrid system, consisting of a combination of supranational and intergovernmental institutions. The supranational institutions – the Commission, the Court and the Parliament – generally act in the interest, or from the perspective, of the Union as a whole; the intergovernmental institutions – the Council and the European Council – represent the member states or, more precisely, national governments. Accordingly, the supranational institutions tend to push forward European integration and generally promote common action. The intergovernmental institutions, by contrast, serve to define and defend national interests and, through intergovernmental bargains, determine the common denominator so that collective decisions are taken and progress in integration is made.

Furthermore, scholars agree that the powers of the European institutions are distributed in an anomalous way. The intergovernmental institutions, the Council and the European Council, hold the power of decision-making in both primary and secondary law (Treaty amendments and law-making) and derive these powers from the sovereignty of the member states. However, the Council shares the law-making powers with the EP. The supranational institutions, by contrast, have only delegated powers at their disposal, as laid down in the Treaties. The Commission has an exclusive right to propose legislation, and it also commands certain executive powers. The Court has the powers of judicial review of all legislative and executive acts of the Union. The Parliament holds legislative and budgetary powers, which have been significantly expanded over time, as well as supervisory powers with regard to the Commission. Looking only at the formal distribution of powers, it might seem that the Councils are the decisive actors in European integration – as, in particularly, liberal intergovernmentalism claims. However, most scholars agree that the supranational institutions have a great deal of discretion at their disposal. Thus, the Commission acts as agenda setter, shapes the procedures of decision-making, and often proposes or builds compromises in order to achieve a final consensus. In sum, the Commission possesses *procedural power*. The Court, through its rulings, engages in 'judicial politics' (Hix 2005a) that by far transcend the intentions of the member states; the assertion of the supremacy and direct effect of European law are cases in point (for details, see Chapter 4). The Parliament shares legislative powers with the Council and may veto any proposal of the Commission. In sum, the supranational institutions have much discretion at their disposal which they can use, under certain conditions, to push forward integration beyond the declared objectives and aggregated will of the member states.

This configuration results in a dynamic interaction between the supranational and the intergovernmental institutions, where each side strives to expand and maximize its power, and to influence or contain the power of its counterpart. The supranational institutions rely on an extensive use of their powers, as they cannot contain the power of the Councils in real terms. However, they can act in such a way that the Council is constrained in exercising its decision-making powers. Thus, the Commission, by launching proposals that reflect a rational and functional logic, and by building alliances with other, supra- or transnational actors and institutions in their support – for example, the Parliament, the European Round Table of Industrialists, the unions – can pressurize the Council to adopt its proposals. The Court, as an independent judiciary, can pass undesired judgements that the Council cannot reject. At best, the Council in such cases can use its legislative powers to amend the law. The Parliament with its veto-power can block legislation or, else, threaten to veto legislative acts in order to achieve compromises that are nearer to its preferences than those of the Council. In sum, the supranational institutions, when using their formal powers and competences to a maximum, can significantly constrain the Councils' room to manoeuvre, even though it is the Councils that hold the topmost powers in decision-making. In addition, the Council and the European Council are also severely constrained in exercising their extensive powers because of internal dissent. With, at present, 28 member states and highly diverging national interests and preferences, building an overarching consensus is difficult, particularly in those cases where unanimous decisions are required.

However, the Councils are not helpless in face of the supranational institutions. On the contrary, they have powerful instruments at hand to contain the discretion of their counterparts. Besides their powers in policy decisions, the Councils hold the exclusive right to adopt or amend the Treaties. In other words, they can alter the institutional setting of the EU.

Throughout the history of European integration, they have made extensive use of these powers, as the following chapters will show in greater detail. However, the Councils never formally diminished the role of the supranational institutions. In the case of the EP, they have even significantly expanded its competences over time. Pushing back the position of the supranational institutions would have undermined the credibility of member states' commitment to European integration. Instead, the Councils chose to contain the powers of the supranational institutions by strengthening their own position within the European polity. The most important step to this end was the establishment of the European Council as the supreme authority in the EU (for details, see Chapter 4). In addition, a series of other, less visible institutional changes were implemented in order to strengthen the intergovernmental dimension of the Union. On the whole, these changes weakened the influence of the supranational institutions, particularly the Commission, by indirect means.

This leads us to the conclusion that the supranational and the intergovernmental institutions are entangled in struggles for power and influence in the EU. However, we should not imagine these power struggles in concrete terms. On the contrary, on the surface, European institutions interact in a harmonious and consensual way. Instead, the relationship among these institutions is marked by a structural conflict, which results from the different functions that these institutions perform in the EU. As said, the supranational institutions represent the interests of the Union as a whole, whereas the intergovernmental institutions represent diverging national interests and preferences, which, after extensive bargains, may result in collective decisions and actions. Thus, the conflicting relationship between these institutions reflects the need to mediate between the conflicting interests underlying European integration. It is only through mediation between these interests that European integration can be moulded in such a way that it reflects both the common interests of the member states and, as much as possible, their individual preferences and interests. In other words, the conflicting relationship between intergovernmental and supranational institutions and the continuous mediation between the interests and preferences they represent serves to shape integration in such a way that common projects and actions are, as much as possible, compatible with the diverging economic, political, and social conditions in the member states.

The Councils and the Commission are at the heart of European decision-making, and therefore also at the centre of the structural conflict between the supranational and the intergovernmental institutions. The Court as an independent judiciary is not involved in decision-making; it exercises its influence on integration through judicial review and, thus, in an indirect manner, although often with far-reaching consequences. The Parliament is included in legislative decision-making, but it does not possess the powers to propose legislation, or to structure procedures and institutions outside its realm. Therefore, in spite of its far-reaching competences, the EP is not in a position actively to shape integration. By contrast, the Commission has a much broader role, as it has a monopoly in launching legislative and policy proposals. Furthermore, through its activism, it plays a pivotal role in all processes of decision-making and, to a great extent, it can structure these processes. Finally, the Commission engages in institution-building, although often in an informal or under-formalized manner. In sum, the Commission is the most important and powerful counterpart in relation to the Councils. Hence, the Councils, when strengthening their role in the European polity, above all seek to contain the power position and activism of the Commission.

In conclusion, we can state that the combination of supranational and intergovernmental institutions characterizing the EU reflects the conflicting interests that underlie European integration: on the one hand, the desire to build the conditions for and engage in joint problem-solving; on the other hand, the need to mould this process in such a way that it is compatible with the existing economic, political, and social systems of the member states or, at the very least, to minimize the costs of integration for the individual states. Consequently, the EU is marked by a structural conflict, represented by two types of institutions that strive to maximize their power and influence on integration, or to contain the power position of their counterparts. It is true that, initially, national governments only delegated certain powers to the European institutions. Yet, over time, these institutions have gained a certain degree of autonomy, which enables them to counter the Councils. Furthermore, the powers delegated to the supranational institutions are irrevocable, at least as long as the member states are willing to maintain the EU as a political order that serves to solve problems they cannot solve on their own. I therefore conceptualize the EU as a dualistic or bicephalous system. The EU displays a dualistic institutional structure as it does not fit into clear-cut systemic categories of either supranationalism or intergovernmentalism. When speaking of a dualistic system, I refer to the nature of the EU as consisting of both supranational and intergovernmental institutions, which serve to represent two categories of interests and to mediate between them. When speaking of the EU as a bicephalous system, I refer to the power structure within the EU. As we have seen, power in the EU is divided between the supranational and the intergovernmental institutions, and both sides strive to maximize their powers at the expense of the other. Although this is valid for all supranational institutions, we can state that, in terms of power relations, it is the Commission and the Councils that are at the heart of these power struggles even though, on the surface, the Commission acts as an agent of the Councils or the member states. Hence, the Commission and the Councils represent most clearly the heads of the EU's bicephalous institutional structure.

## Conclusion

In this chapter, we have examined various theoretical strands that attempt to explain the origins and dynamics of European integration and the political system that emerged from this process. The scientific debate started with a clear dichotomy between neofunctionalists and intergovernmentalists. Whereas the first assumed that supranational and transnational actors push forward a process of functional spill-over, the latter emphasized the role of governmental actors, represented through the Council and the European Council, which promote and shape, but also stall, integration. Besides these two dichotomous concepts, a third, federalism, played a certain role in capturing the nature of the emerging European polity. However, this approach provided a vision of a future polity, rather than an explanation of what actually came into existence. By contrast neo-functionalism and inter-governmentalism provided explanations for the actual processes of integration. Neo-functionalism clearly reflected the initial phase, when the Communities were founded and rapidly consolidated, whereas inter-governmentalism increasingly gained ground after the process entered into a phase of stagnation.

The sudden and unexpected re-launch of integration from the mid-1980s onwards also contributed to a re-launch of integration theory. First, scholars revisited intergovernmentalism and neo-functionalism and attempted to adapt these approaches to the changed state of inte-gration. In the longer run however, scholars opened up new theoretical avenues by drawing, first, on new institutionalism and, later, on social constructivist approaches. Thus, they transcended the theoretical dichotomy by acknowledging both the power of national governments in moulding integration *and* the ability of supranational institutions to shape this process to a great extent.

When, after the turn of the century, the Union continued to expand its membership and to deepen integration, a renewed interest emerged in defining the system as a whole. These approaches span from a general notion of a system *sui generis*, or simply a political system, via a specific form of federation, to a mixed and unbalanced system, as well as a cosmopolitan empire. In spite of these differing approaches, scholars share some general assumptions on the EU. They see the Union as a new political order beyond the nation state, consisting of a mixed set of insti-tutions that represent diverging political forces underlying integration.

Against this background, I define the Union as a dualistic, biceph-alous system. This definition refers to the combination of supranational and intergovernmental institutions, and to the structural conflict that characterizes their relationship. As many other scholars of the EU, I assume that the supranational institutions have much discretion at their disposal, so much that they are powerful actors in their own right and can form an effective counterweight to the dominant position of the Councils in formal terms.

Despite theoretical progress achieved thus far, a number of issues remain disputed. Definitive conceptualizations of the EU as a political system – its formal institutional structures and informal arrangements, its procedures of decision-making and policy implementation, as well as its regulatory or other capacities of political steering – have not yet emerged. Furthermore, certain questions concerning the process of integration remain unanswered. Is the EU still evolving and, therefore, in a transitional stage towards a different, definitive form? Will such a definitive form coincide with one of the well-known types of political order (e.g. federations), or will it constitute a completely new type? Or, is the dualistic institutional structure of the EU, as it has developed through 'integration by stealth' (Majone 2005, 2009), its core characteristic and, thus, the definitive form of post-national statehood? Another set of questions refers to the relationship between the EU and the member states. Is the EU, in itself, a political system independent of the member states, or is it only capable of existing and evolving in symbiosis with national political systems? Will the EU transcend the nation states and make them obsolete in the long run, or will it transform them into parts of a complex multi-level system, or a true federation?

The outline of the academic debate on European integration and the EU as a political system has highlighted certain, undisputed features of the EU. It has also resulted in a series of questions that, by no means, have been (or can be) answered in the short term. I do not claim to offer definitive answers to these complex questions. Nonetheless, these questions, as well as the findings on the nature of the EU presented above, provide a heuristic framework that guides and inspires the empirical parts of this book. In the following chapters, we will examine in more detail how the EU's institutional structure has evolved over time; how the individual institutions act and interact or, under certain conditions, counteract each other; and what outcomes – achievements, as well as shortcomings – they produce.

# Chapter 2

# Building the European Union: Supranational Dynamics and Intergovernmental Configurations

This chapter, together with Chapter 3, analyzes the evolution of European integration. These chapters view integration as a dynamic process, driven by a variety of forces and actors that, through their interactions, build and shape the institutional structure of the European Union. For analytical purposes, I divide the history of European integration into four phases (see also Gillingham 2003). For practical purposes, I have chosen to present this history in two separate chapters. This chapter looks at the first three phases, which were instrumental to building the European polity in its multifaceted dimensions and in its unique combination of intergovernmental and supranational institutions. In contrast, Chapter 3 considers only the fourth phase, where the Union has already evolved into a full-blown, mature polity. During this fourth phase, the EU continues to evolve in terms of its size, its institutional structure, and its decision-making procedures. However, these changes generally serve more to expand, consolidate, and diversify the existing system than to bring about a fundamental transformation of it. Accordingly, a close look at the respective evolutionary processes will highlight the continual dynamics of system-building beyond the nation state that characterizes the EU.

If we turn our attention to the history of European integration, we find that the first and third phases are primarily characterized by supranational dynamics, whereas the second and fourth phases are dominated by intergovernmental configurations. It should be emphasized, however, that in each phase the tension between these contradictory dynamics and the interactions among the corresponding institutions and actors determine the pace and scope of integration (see also Chapter 13).

In this chapter, we explore the historical process of building the European Union as an emergent political order beyond the nation state. We begin in the 1950s and consider various stages through to the 'mature' EU of the 1990s. In this process, we learn that the Union did not evolve in a straightforward and linear manner, following a specific plan or concept. Rather, it unfolded through a piecemeal process of institution-building, shaped by the varying responses of European leaders to internal dynamics and external challenges. The overall process is marked by a 'stop-go character' (Sandholtz and Zysman 1989: 99); that is, accelerated integration alternated with stagnation. The first and the third phases were marked by accelerated integration, whereas the second phase was dominated by stagnation. During accelerated integration, supranational dynamics played a pivotal role, often fostered by actors and institutions at the European level. In those phases, the European Commission in particular exercised forceful leadership (Sandholtz and Zysman 1989; Sandholtz and Stone Sweet 1998). In contrast, the stagnation phase was dominated by intergovernmental configurations. This means that member states' preferences and choices dominated the agenda. As a result, this phase was marked by fundamental conflicts among national governments, as well as blockades in decision-making and weak compromises (Moravscik 1991, 1998). Nonetheless, we will see that the stagnation phase was of paramount importance for building the European polity, as stalemates and a lack of consensus among the member states ultimately led political leaders to explore new directions in European integration. As national governments often resisted further integration projects, progress could be achieved only by expanding and diversifying the institutional structure of the EU and its decision-making practices in favour of the intergovernmental dimension of the system. Thus, the overall process of European integration resulted in the steady building of a new political order beyond the nation state that is characterized by both supranational and intergovernmental features.

## Founding the European Communities under a model of supranational integration

The European Union, viewed as a specific form of structured cooperation between nation states, is essentially a product of the postwar era. In the aftermath of World War II, the creation of an array of international organizations and other forms of interstate cooperation scored high on the political agenda – not only in Europe, but also in the United States (US). Political elites hoped to contain conflicts between nation states by creating structured forms of intergovernmental – and, to a lesser degree, supranational – cooperation. The underlying objective was to create a new, more peaceful world order. In the economic realm, this resulted in concepts to foster market integration and the regulation of selected sectors on a European scale. In the political realm, the goal was to create collective security structures and corresponding functional organizations to help resolve transnational problems and thereby prevent interstate conflicts. These steps were advocated not only by political elites, but also by opposition movements. During World War II, European-wide resistance movements against fascism launched extensive proposals for supranational integration, which subsequently influenced postwar political debates (Lipgens 1986). In addition, academics expressed normative theories that highlighted the importance of creating an array of transnational organizations to serve various functional needs (Deutsch *et al.* 1957; Mitrany 1966).

However, the actual creation of these institutions in postwar Europe was not an easy task. National interests soon proved to be stronger than the political will for integration (Milward 1984, 2000, Dinan 2004a). Consequently, neither the ideas of the resistance movements that called for the creation of a federal state in Europe (Lipgens 1986: 19–188), nor the moves towards close economic and political cooperation that were so vigorously advocated and supported by the US, fully materialized (Milward 1984, in particular: 90–125). The US concepts, bolstered by substantial financial assistance through the Marshall Plan, did lead to the foundation of several international organizations, including the Organization for European Economic Cooperation (OEEC) in 1948 (later renamed the Organization for Economic Co-operation and Development: OECD) and the Council of Europe in 1949. However, these organizations could never assume a leading role, as they focused on limited and highly specialized tasks. It was only in the 1950s that the cornerstones for European integration were laid.

The euphoria surrounding the uniting of Europe and the move towards new forms of cooperation died down in the early 1950s. Only small groups of highly committed citizens continued to discuss comprehensive proposals for transnational integration. Instead, more specific ideas about partial integration emerged. One concept for partial integration was the Schuman Plan, put forward in 1950. The plan provided for the integration of only two economic sectors: coal and steel. This limited focus was, however, important because these two sectors were of vital importance as they produced raw materials for nearly all manufacturing industries (Milward 1984: 380–420). The Schuman Plan did not correspond to the basic ideas and preferences regarding interstate cooperation of the individual states (Dinan 2004a: 37–41). In fact, it mirrored the French preference for a certain degree of *state dirigisme*, whereas the Federal Republic of Germany primarily favoured the creation of a free trade regime (Gillingham 2003: 23–8). Despite their differences in approach, a general consensus was quickly reached among a small group of European states. Thus, France, Germany, Italy, Belgium, the Netherlands, and Luxembourg agreed to the formation of the European Coal and Steel Community (ECSC). Importantly, the United Kingdom preferred to remain on the side-lines (Dinan 2004a: 46–57).

The plan's architect, Jean Monnet, envisaged the creation of a High Authority that would be granted significant regulatory and decision-making powers over both sectors. However, after difficult negotiations among the cooperating partners, his concept of supranational integration was significantly watered down by adding institutional elements of an intergovernmental organization (Dinan 2004a: 51). Thus, although the High Authority was granted extensive executive powers, additional institutions were created to help exercise political control. There was a Council of Ministers (representing the member states), a Parliamentary Assembly (made up of delegates from national parliaments, and endowed with advisory and limited oversight functions), and a Court of Justice (to clarify legal disputes). Most observers at the time and in the following years referred to the ECSC as an emerging supranational system (see, e.g., Haas 1958; Lindberg and Scheingold 1970: 14–23). In fact, even with the extensive competences of the High Authority, its basic institutional structure already displayed the hybrid nature of the later Communities.

There was an underlying intention to extend the ECSC's organizational form to other sectors and policy areas. However, the debates were again wrought with competing models of integration – specifically, the creation of a common market versus the establishment of a comprehensive political union. In the early 1950s, a majority of the original six member states favoured the establishment of a comprehensive political union. This led to a plan to create a European Defence Community (EDC), a concept that the USA strongly supported (Gillingham 2003: 29–33; Dinan 2004a: 57–64). The idea was to unite the military potential of the participating states under common command. The six ECSC member states signed a respective Treaty (1952) while, once more, the United Kingdom did not show any interest in the project. However, the Defence Treaty failed to be ratified by the French National Assembly (1954), as the Assembly expressed concerns over the loss of national sovereignty. In the meantime, surrounding political circumstances had changed and the idea of a defence union had lost much of its overall appeal. By the mid-1950s, the North Atlantic Treaty Organization (NATO) – a transatlantic defence alliance under the leadership of the US, and with a strong supporting role for the UK – had acquired a dominant position. In 1954, a group of European states created the Western European Union (WEU), to bring the Federal Republic of Germany (FRG) into a common defence structure (Brown Wells and Wells 2008). While this was an important step, the WEU was not able to fulfil the tasks envisioned under the defence community. After the failure of the EDC, all ambitious projects to create a political union in Europe were off the table for many years.

Instead of the defence union, in the mid-1950s the ECSC member states focused on expanding their project of economic integration (Milward 2000). Two main options were explored: the creation of a European Economic Community (EEC) in the form of a customs union, and the creation of an organization for the peaceful use of nuclear energy (European Atomic Energy Community: EAEC, or abbreviated to EURATOM). While Germany favoured the customs union, France advocated the EURATOM concept (Gillingham 2003: 43–5; Brown Wells and Wells 2008: 35). The EURATOM option appeared to face fewer obstacles from existing powerful institutional structures in the member states, as it involved cooperation in an entirely new economic sector. Unsurprisingly, the UK rejected both proposals as too supranational. Instead, the UK intensified its vision for minimal integration by increasing efforts to create a free trade zone (Gillingham 2003: 34–8). Despite significant differences in opinion, the ECSC members succeeded in forging a compromise (Gilbert 2003: 62–9). After a relatively short phase of negotiations, they signed the Treaties of Rome (1957) to create both the EEC and EURATOM. The Treaties went into effect on 1 January 1958 (Dinan 2004a: 64–79).

The institutions of both these new Communities were essentially modelled after those of the ECSC. However, instead of the High Authority, a European Commission (EC) was now established. The Commission enjoyed far fewer powers than the High Authority (Dinan 2004a: 77). The UK reacted to the foundation of the Communities with the creation of the European Free Trade Association (EFTA), encompassing seven countries: Austria, Denmark, the UK, Norway, Portugal, Sweden and Switzerland. Thus, by the end of the 1950s, Europe was home to two competing systems of interstate cooperation. These two organizations did not begin to cooperate amongst themselves until a much later point in time. In 1991, they created an internal market, the so-called European Economic Area (EEA). In the long run, the European Communities have proven to be the more sustainable project, with their encompassing model of integration and inherent, yet limited, supranational dynamics (Milward *et al.* 1994).

The early years of the EEC passed without any major conflicts. The integration objectives stipulated in the Treaties – in particular, the dismantling of national tariffs and the creation of a customs union – materialized even more quickly than anticipated. Moreover, the broad concept of market integration proved to be a great success (Gilbert 2003: 86–8). Begun during a phase of strong economic growth, market liberalization provided favourable conditions for expanding firms and markets. As a result, all six founding states of the Communities benefited enormously from the common market. Over the course of several years, these states achieved extraordinarily high growth rates or, in the case of Germany, even an 'economic miracle'. Based partially on these successes, the UK applied to join the Communities in 1961 (Dinan 2004a: 97–102). This first application, however, was categorically rejected by then French President Charles de Gaulle.

Drawing on the success of the early years, the six members of the EC concentrated on quickly completing steps towards further integration, especially in the area of economic policies. In the early 1960s, they removed additional barriers to free trade and adopted a common agricultural policy (CAP) in order to adapt this sensitive sector to liberalized markets (Milward 2000: 224–317).

By the mid-1960s, however, this impressive development suddenly slowed. In particular, France, under President de Gaulle, began a vigorous defence of its national interests. Fundamental differences between France and the other member states emerged over issues such as the CAP and the accession of the UK. France also refused to accept the transition to majority voting in the Council of Ministers, even though this was envisioned in the Treaties. When the other member states refused to give in to France's demands, the French government turned to an 'empty chair politics' that lasted from July 1965 to January 1966. During this time, the French government boycotted all meetings of the Council of Ministers, refusing to send any ministers to the meetings, thus effectively blocking all decisions (Gillingham 2003: 68–71).

This stalemate could only be overcome when the other partners relented and agreed to a new compromise. The resulting so-called 'Luxembourg Compromise' stated that, despite a general move towards majority voting, if a member state considered its vital national interests to be at risk, decisions in the Council of Ministers should still be taken unanimously (Dinan 2004a: 107–8). In effect, this compromise granted a *de facto* veto power to every member state. The unanimity rule remained the general mode of decision-making in the Council. In the following years, not only France, but also many other member states made excessive use of their veto power. This is evidence that the Luxembourg Compromise not only served the interests of France or those of President de Gaulle. It also reflected the will of all member states to maintain control over the course of integration.

The Luxembourg Compromise is generally seen as a fundamental turning point in the process of European integration (Gilbert 2003; Gillingham 2003; Dinan 2004a). It ended the initial path towards integration that had been marked by a clear commitment to create supranational institutions. Instead, it initiated steps towards improving intergovernmental decision-making and control. It also terminated the early phase of accelerated integration and gave way to a long phase of stagnation, characterized by dissent among the member states. We may assume that this first turning point in the process of European integration was not only caused by the stubborn attitude of President de Gaulle, but also constituted a response to changed circumstances that, in turn, high-lighted the weaknesses of the initial integration path.

Circumstances had, indeed, changed. First, early integration steps had been laid down in the Treaties and thus were sustained by a strong political will to build the foundations of close cooperation. However, once further integration steps were proposed, the initial consensus was no longer sufficient to sustain the momentum. Second, the early phase of integration primarily focused on the creation of the common market. Lacking a clear consensus among the member states, attempts to integrate other policy areas that would require a stronger regulatory policy for the Communities resulted in the stagnation of the integration process. Third, the first signs of a looming economic crisis partially legitimized giving priority to national interests over common goals. Overall, in these changed circumstances, the careful consideration of national interests proved to be of vital importance.

Against this background, the Luxembourg Compromise may also be seen as an adjustment of the EC to changed and more complex needs and, therefore, as the first institutional reorganization of the European polity. By enhancing the procedures for intergovernmental decision-making and consensus-building, the Communities were prepared to widen their membership and deepen integration.

## Restructuring the European Communities under improved intergovernmental control

Despite the difficulties outlined above, the 'Community of Six' continued on its path towards increased integration throughout and beyond the 1960s. One of the first steps taken by the member states was to adopt the Merger Treaty (signed 8 April 1965 and coming into effect on 1 July 1967), which combined the executive bodies of the three Communities – the ECSC, EEC, and EURATOM – into a single institutional structure, thenceforth named the European Communities (EC). This reform, to a degree, strengthened the position of the European Commission, as it now could intervene in a broad range of policy areas. After de Gaulle's resignation in 1969, and after a coalition government led by the social democratic party assumed power in Germany, heads of state or government discussed comprehensive plans to create an economic and monetary union (Gilbert 2003: 120–8; Gillingham 2003: 87–9; Dinan 2004a: 126–34; Brown Wells and Wells 2008). These plans envisaged not only a single currency, but also a common economic policy. Furthermore, they envisioned a regional policy with the aim of alleviating economic disparities in the member states, which could otherwise be aggravated by a monetary union.

However, these ambitious plans were difficult to realize. They failed, mainly, because of the enormous differences in interests and preferences among the member states. More importantly, the first signs of crisis, heralding the end of an extraordinarily long period of economic growth and prosperity loomed large. As a consequence, the economic weaknesses of the individual member states and the structural disparities that existed among them became increasingly apparent. These economic disparities, in turn, exacerbated the political differences among national governments (Gilbert 2003: 132–3).

The member states of the EC initially responded to the emerging crisis by adopting national strategies. They attempted to tackle the new situation with more vigorous macro-economic and demand-driven policies, and neo-protectionist measures. These involved a systematic recourse to non-tariff trade barriers, such as the introduction and strict implementation of technical standards, and a preference for national providers in public procurement. Through these protectionist measures, many of the accomplishments of the common market were systematically undermined (Gillingham 2003: 106–20).

The process of integration took a new turn when the six founding members agreed to implement the first enlargement of the EC (Dinan 2004a: 134–45). In 1973, after a relatively short negotiation phase, the UK, Ireland, and Denmark joined the Communities. Norway had also applied for membership, but withdrew its application in 1972 after a national referendum on membership failed to pass. This first enlargement had far-reaching consequences for the Communities. In economic terms, the new members were in a difficult phase of development (Ireland) or restructuring (the UK). Furthermore, the political elites in Denmark and, particularly, the UK were much less integration-minded than those of the original member states. This resulted in further political differences that significantly hampered decision-making in the Council and slowed down the integration process as a whole (Geary 2012: 17–18). Academics and political elites alike were quick to note that widening the EC could seemingly only be realized at the expense of deepening integration (e.g. Pinder 1991: 51).

Many observers assume that the dissent among the member states after the first enlargement of the EC led to a long phase of stagnation. In fact, these differences of opinion actually provided the stimulus to promote integration in a manner different from that which was originally envisaged. Following enlargement, the institutional structure and the decision-making procedures of the EC were rearranged and refined. This resulted in a stronger intergovernmental dimension of the European polity. Furthermore, new policies were initiated and implementation strategies were designed to take differences among the member states into account (see Chapter 8). Finally, the member states prioritized more flexible and informal processes of integration over those that were anchored in clearly defined institutional structures. An example of this is the establishment of the European Council as an additional layer of inter-governmental decision-making. Initially, heads of state and government convened summit meetings on an *ad hoc* basis, in order to build, refine, and, above all, facilitate consensus-building among them. Thus, the Hague Summit of 1969 and the Paris Summit of 1972 resulted in major decisions to further integration (Geary 2012). In 1974, heads of state or government institutionalized the summits as scheduled meetings, in order to create a permanent forum for consultations and decision-making (Werts 2008). Over time, the summits figured as European Councils and developed into an additional, supreme decision-making body in the EU (Nugent 2010: 177). The European Council serves to find solutions to conflicts that the Council of Ministers cannot resolve and to make the key decisions that set out the objectives, further course, and direction of European integration (see Chapter 4).

Other important steps to restructure the European polity followed over the course of the 1970s. One such step consisted in considerably strength-ening the status of the European Parliament (Lord 2004: 151–2; Ritt-berger 2005). In 1970 and 1975, important budgetary powers were assigned to the Parliament, after the Communities were granted their own financial resources. The Parliament was able to use its powers of consent to the non-obligatory expenditures of the EC either partially to expand or contain the political activities of the Commission. In 1977, after more than 10 years of vigorous demands of the Parliament, the Council finally introduced direct elections to the EP. The first direct elections took place in 1979. This constituted a major step in creating a direct link to the citizens of Europe. More importantly, though, it contributed to an increased professionalization of the Parliament. Whereas the members of the EP (MEPs) were previously both national and European parliamentarians, with the introduction of direct elections, MEPs held only one role. Instead of being, first and foremost, parliamentarians in national chambers, they could now actively pursue new initiatives at the European level. As may be anticipated, the EP soon became an important player in the European polity, fostering integration in a number of ways.

Furthermore, in the framework of the increasingly heterogeneous Communities, the *policy functions* of the EC were significantly expanded and reformed (see Chapter 8). In 1975, a European regional policy was established that was aimed primarily at alleviating the economic dispari-ties between 'rich' and 'poor' member states. Furthermore, the Social Fund, which had existed since the foundation of the ECSC, was trans-formed into a tool to allow targeted interventions in the European labour market through vocational training. Finally, a series of directives on equal rights for men and women in the labour market were adopted. Although these new activities were geared towards processes of economic modernization, they also entailed a social component. These new or reorganized policy areas were based only on Council decisions; a definitive transfer of formal powers to the European level through Treaty amendments did not take place until much later, as will be revealed.

Finally, after taking steps in 1972 to fix exchange rates within a given margin of fluctuation, in the late 1970s, the European Monetary System (EMS) was introduced (Gilbert 2003: 138–45; Brown Wells and Wells 2008: 35–7). The most impressive aspect of the EMS was its flexibility. Depending on the economic performance and political options of a member state, the band within which an exchange rate could fluctuate varied. It was also possible for a state to choose to remain outside the EMS altogether. By allowing for this flexibility, the EMS formed the first prominent case of differentiated integration (Kölliker 2006; Leuffen *et al.* 2012: 145–7). Overall, the policies established in the 1970s were hardly steps towards rapid supranational integration. Rather, they provided mechanisms for loosely connecting differently structured states (i.e. EMS), and strategies to reduce or compensate for economic disparities among member states (i.e. regional and social policy).

These significant steps in the process of integration were barely noticed by the wider public. Instead, to the majority of the public, the EC of the late 1970s and early 1980s appeared to be marked by crisis and stagnation (Dinan 2004a: 167–8). Catchwords such as 'Euro-pessimism', or even 'Euro-sclerosis', were widely used to describe the situation. European summits were dominated by conflicting interests and fundamental differences of opinion among national governments, which threatened to paralyze decision-making. In the face of a series of unsolved problems – including budgetary conflicts, the steel crisis, increasing expenses for the common agricultural policy, the aggravated economic crisis and its rapidly rising unemployment rates – some observers saw the EC as more a part of the problem than part of the solution.

Nonetheless, even against this difficult economic and political backdrop, the EC was enlarged and continually transformed, although more behind the scenes than centre-stage. In 1981, the second enlargement brought Greece into the Communities and, shortly thereafter in 1986, Spain and Portugal joined in the third round. As with so many other key decisions on integration, the Southern enlargement of the EC was not motivated primarily by an economic rationale, as both sides actually anticipated more disadvantages than advantages. Rather, it was driven largely by political motives. In particular, the political stabilization of these countries after their liberation from authoritarian rule in the mid-1970s formed a strong argument for including them in the Communities. Importantly, the Southern enlargement implied a conscious decision to move towards a community of economically unequal partners. This, in turn, implied a decision for a more comprehensive regional or 'cohesion' policy, as it came to be known, at the European level. To this end, the regional policy of the EC was reformed and the Social Fund increasingly subsumed under regional policy objectives. Both policies turned out to be powerful instruments for offering side-payments to the economically weaker member states in negotiations around the creation of the single market and, later, monetary union.

The beginning of the 1980s was also marked by a further expansion of the scope of European policies (see Chapter 8). In particular, a technology policy was established at the European level. Initiated by the Commission, this move was not welcomed by the member states. The Commission organized a round table comprising representatives of the then 12 leading European high-tech companies. In the beginning, even these top industrialists were sceptical about the Commission's project. Nevertheless, they jointly drew up a preliminary concept for a European technology policy. Ultimately, when pitted against the alliance of the Commission and the top European industrialists, the Council had no real option other than to approve the project. It could only limit the scope of the new policy by significantly reducing the foreseen budget. In the long-term, however, European technology policy has been backed by the member states, as it has served to strengthen the competitive position of Europe in relation to the US and Japan.

An increasing awareness of the weak competitive position of Europe on global markets and its economic and political fragmentation soon led to the conviction that it was essential to push forward integration (Sandholtz and Zysman 1989). As a result, at the beginning of the 1980s, there were intense debates among the European leaders over the next steps in the integration project and a corresponding reform of the EC. Initially, a variety of reform proposals was launched, but there was no broad consensus about the path that ought to be pursued (Dinan 2004a: 192–201). At the initiative of Altiero Spinelli, a committed advocate of European integration since World War II, the European Parliament was the first institution to advance a proposal for creating a European Union, based on a new Treaty (proposed: November 1981, adopted: February 1984). National governments also launched new concepts for integration (e.g. the Genscher-Colombo Plan, tabled in November 1981). At the same time, behind the scenes, leading European industrialists exercised intense political pressure on politicians to complete the single market (Sandholtz and Zysman 1989; Gillingham 2003: 237–40). A series of committees was set up to elaborate reform proposals. Yet, most of these proposals envisaged a transfer of sovereignty to the European level, which far exceeded what member states were willing to concede. The immediate outcome, therefore, was the paralysis of the '*relance européenne*' (European re-launch), even though a basic consensus over the necessity of profound reforms was emerging. The time was ripe for yet another stage in the process of European integration.

In summary, it is apparent that the phase of expansion and restructuring of the EC was primarily defined by intergovernmental configurations. First, in the 1960s, French President de Gaulle ensured the continuation of unanimous voting in the Council and blocked – or, at least, slowed down – steps towards further integration. This hurdle was not overcome by strengthening supranational integration but, rather, by improving intergovernmental decision-making and consensus-building procedures. The creation of the European Council constituted the most important step in this direction. This body added substantial authority to European decisions and provided leadership in critical situations. In addition, it facilitated consensus-building among member states and helped the systematic linking of the integration process to the policy positions and preferences of the participating states. As the experiences of the early years of integration show, this was probably the only way to overcome or contain the ever-present differences between the member states (Gillingham 2003).

Second, successive enlargements of the EC during this phase also necessitated an increase in the authority of the intergovernmental institutions and configurations. Growing economic disparities between the member states, together with political differences over the course of integration, hampered decision-making. At the same time, however, these differences stimulated the quest for new ways to overcome these dilemmas. This is particularly reflected in the creation of new Community policies. The expansion of European policy-making during this phase was driven by diverging interests among the member states. New or reorganized policies either served to compensate for economic disparities (the Regional and Social Fund) or to link highly diverse national economies in a flexible manner (the EMS). In the face of the challenges of increased global competition, only technology policy served to pursue pan-European objectives.

Third, and finally, allocating the European Parliament budgetary powers and introducing direct elections improved the position of the EP. These measures were primarily aimed at containing the power of the Commission by enhancing the Parliament's authority and control functions. In practice, however, they fostered the supranational dynamics of European integration, and thus lent support to the Commission.

The contradictory nature of some of these steps towards increased integration helps us to better understand the nature of the European polity. Even though this second phase was apparently characterized by stagnation – with dissent among the member states regularly blocking decisions and, thus, the integration process as a whole – it was this same period that set the stage for the later revival of integration (Gillingham 2003; Dinan 2004a: 167–201). Besides the improvements described above, all of which helped to mitigate the differences among the member states, several other changes fostered or facilitated a re-launch of integration, too. The supranational institutions of the EC, through their actions and their means of operating, were instrumental in preparing the groundwork for the renewal of the project of integration. The Commission refined its strategies to bring about consensus in the Council of Ministers; for example, by using small-scale experiments to create *'faits accomplis'*, or by forming alliances with external actors such as the European Round Table of Industrialists, or even utilizing both strategies at once. The performance of the Parliament quickly evolved as the institution made use of, and even exceeded, its formal powers. The jurisdiction of the European Court of Justice (ECJ) strongly promoted the logic of supranational integration (Alter 2001, 2009). These actions and the corresponding achievements of the supranational institutions of the EC – which were less visible and, thus, initially less understood by academics – sustained the subsequent spectacular leap forward in European integration.

In conclusion, we can see that the dynamics and direction of European integration during this phase were largely shaped by the interplay between intergovernmentalism and supranationalism, and the power relations between the respective institutional actors. Intergovernmental decision-making and consensus-building took centre-stage and was significantly enhanced by the creation of new formal institutions. However, behind the scenes, the activities and performances of the supranational institutions set the stage for further integration.

## Re-launching supranational integration

A new era in European integration began in 1985 when Jacques Delors assumed office as President of the Commission (Gillingham 2003: 149–51). This era was dominated by supranational dynamics, which led to significant progress in both economic integration and political institution-building. Nonetheless, these steps were not without controversy among the member states. The result was a large discrepancy between the proposals launched and the reforms actually implemented.

The new Commission, under the leadership of Delors, successfully bundled various initiatives and activities to reform the EC in two core areas: a project for economic integration and a project to strengthen political union. The former provided for the completion of the internal market by 1992. The latter envisaged far-reaching institutional reforms and changes to the EC's decision-making procedures. The Commission was especially successful in presenting these projects as inherently linked to each other (Gilbert 2003: 169–74; Dinan 2004a: 206–23).

The foundations for the project of economic integration were laid down in a White Paper, drawn up by Commissioner Lord Cockfield. The White Paper addressed all that was necessary for the completion of the single market (presented on 14 June 1985; see European Commission 1985). It listed nearly 300 proposals for directives and regulations that would remove the remaining barriers to the free movement of goods, capital, people, and services. In addition, the White Paper provided for the harmonization of regulations in the member states. The barriers to the so-called 'four freedoms' were not so much 'still existing' but, rather, new ones that the member states had only set up during the 1970s. As part of their national strategies for crisis management, member states had turned to protectionist measures, including setting different technical norms and standards, privileging national providers in public procurement, and providing (indirect) subsidies for public and private firms.

In view of the declining competitiveness of Europe in globalizing markets, a basic consensus on the ambitious programme for completing the single market emerged relatively quickly (Brown Wells and Wells 2008: 37). In fact, a consensus on further market integration had already been in place; but Delors transformed this vague idea into concrete proposals for implementation. The pressure on politicians to take swift decisions increased as leading industrialists at both the European and national levels pushed strongly for the realization of the project (Sandholtz and Zysman 1989; Gillingham 2003: 237–40). In order to facilitate the necessary decisions, the Commission mandated two comprehensive and detailed studies. The first study highlighted the advantages of the single market, using impressive growth statistics (Cecchini Report, see Cecchini 1988). The second investigated the potentially unequal economic impacts on the member states, but judged these to be negligible, if the corresponding political measures were taken (Padoa-Schioppa Report, see Padoa-Schioppa 1987). These studies, in particular, triggered a heated public debate on the pros and cons of the single market. Meanwhile, private firms recognized the possible advantages of the single market. As a consequence, an 'integration euphoria' that facilitated the implementation of the project, spread rapidly.

The reform of the institutional structure of the EC turned out to be a more complicated matter. However, there was, at the very least, a minimal consensus around certain issues. On a proposal of Commission President Delors, a Treaty amendment was adopted: the so-called Single European Act (SEA). The SEA implied somewhat minor innovations that, taken together, formed essential stepping stones for subsequent reforms (for the origins of the SEA, see Sandholtz and Zysman 1989; Moravcsik 1991, 1998; for an assessment of the SEA, see Keohane and Hoffmann 1991; Gilbert 2003: 180–3). The centrepiece of the SEA was the extension of qualified majority voting in the Council of Ministers in numerous areas – in particular, those that pertained to the completion of the single market (Brown Wells and Wells 2008: 37). Furthermore, the SEA significantly enhanced the legislative powers of the European Parliament by introducing the so-called 'cooperation' procedure. This procedure provided for two readings of legislative proposals. This gave Parliament a stronger, though not decisive, voice in legislation. It could thus not be entirely ignored by the Commission and the Council of

Ministers (for details, see Chapter 5). The Parliament subsequently made extensive use of these new opportunities. However, the procedure applied only in a limited number of issues, primarily those pertaining to single market regulation.

The SEA also enhanced the role of the Commission, particularly in its policy-making functions. The Treaty designated a series of policy areas as responsibilities of the EC. These areas were previously reliant on Council decisions only. In particular, the SEA now explicitly mentioned regional policy, technology policy and environmental policy as the purview of the EC (see Art. 23, 24, and 25 SEA, referring to Art. 130 a–e, 130 f-p, 130 r-t TEC-M; now Art. 174–178, 179–190, and 191–193 TFEU). This underscored the enduring nature of the transfer of powers to the EC.

In order to compensate for potentially negative effects of integration, national governments sought political solutions at European level. For example, the EC responded to the expected increase in economic disparities as a consequence of the single market by doubling the financial resources of the Structural Funds and thoroughly reforming the related procedures of policy-making (decision taken by the European Council in 1988; Gillingham 2003: 262–3). Furthermore, it at least recognized the possible increase of social inequalities in the single market as a political problem. Consequently, the Commission made sure that strengthening the 'social dimension' of the Community was on the agenda as a necessary complement to economic integration (Dinan 2004a: 225–9).

The expanded agenda of the Delors Commission appeared to confirm what neo-functionalists would refer to as the spill-over dynamics (see Chapter 1). However, the Community's capacity for consensus-building had apparently now come to an end. Social policy issues, in particular, triggered significant conflicts in the following years, as especially the UK rejected any further European involvement in this area outright. Nevertheless, the Commission succeeded in winning over 11 of the 12 member states for a basic commitment to social affairs. This resulted in the adoption of the Social Charter (1989) and an Action Programme building on this (Leibfried 2010: 262–4). Although not legally binding, these initiatives implied that the member states could hardly deny, or avoid any commitment to, social policy in later phases of decision-making.

The harmonization of taxation, a policy area closely linked with the single market, proved to be another conflict-ridden issue to which there appeared to be no satisfactory solution. The differences between the taxation systems of the member states are particularly pronounced and making the necessary adjustments would have been a huge burden for some member states. National governments could reach an agreement only on a gradual approximation of the rates of value added taxes (VAT) (Genschel 2007).

By far the most ambitious endeavour that the Delors Commission launched in the wake of the single market project was the creation of an economic and monetary union (EMU). Whereas Delors viewed EMU as the culmination of the single market, the project met strong resistance from the member states. It was not only rejected by the UK, but also the governor of the German Bundesbank was highly reluctant (Brown Wells and Wells 2008: 39). However, the Kohl government eventually decided to support the promotion of the monetary project. It is generally assumed that this step was motivated by pressures emanating from the rapid and unexpected changes in Central and Eastern Europe, and as a means of winning over France as an ally for German reunification (e.g. Gillingham 2003: 235). Other authors, however, stress that the German Chancellor Kohl had already committed to a significant deepening of integration, including a commitment to the creation of EMU (Brown Wells and Wells 2008: 41). In December 1990, an Intergovernmental Conference (IGC) was convened to draw up and negotiate the details of the monetary project (Geary 2012: 13). National governments did not acknowledge the necessary institutional reforms until the very last minute. As a result, a second IGC was convened to prepare for the creation of a political union.

As is so often the case in the history of European integration, these two projects were pursued at different rates and with different scopes (Ross 1995). Technical experts, specifically the governors of the national central banks, made the preparations for EMU, and they could thus proceed quickly. However, the political union was a diffuse and controversial project characterized by dissent among the member states (see Ross 1995; Gilbert 2003: 203–4; Gillingham 2003: 269–84; Brown Wells and Wells 2008: 39–41). While the experts found feasible solutions for disagreements with regard to economic and monetary union, negotiations among national governments over political union continued at the highest levels until the very last minute. Finally, the European Council in Maastricht struck a compromise and adopted the Treaty on European Union (on 9/10 December 1991, signed on 7 February 1992). It is no surprise that this second important treaty revision, 'one of the greatest milestones in the history of European integration' (Dinan 2004a: 233), is defined by imbalances.

EMU constituted the core of the Maastricht Treaty. The project was to be implemented in a three-stage procedure (for the origins of the Treaty, see Ross 1995; for an assessment of the Treaty, see Dinan 2004: 245–64). In contrast to the envisaged monetary union of the 1970s, the actual project required only the creation of a common currency and the establishment of an independent central bank at the European level. The corresponding economic harmonization remained the responsibility of the member states. This did not mean that the member states were entirely free to act as they chose. On the contrary, clear guidelines, called the 'convergence criteria', were set out for the economic and fiscal performance of those states that hoped to participate in monetary union. The criteria set strict standards for the inflation rate, the long-term interest rate, the gross annual government deficit, and the gross government dept in relation to the gross domestic product (GDP). In addition to their concrete demands, the criteria also set strict parameters for a broad array of national policies, including fiscal and macro-economic policies and, in the long run, the whole spectrum of social policies and welfare state measures (Scharpf 1999). Notwithstanding these constraints on policy-making at national level, the following years saw a race among individual states to comply with the criteria and demonstrate their readiness to participate in the new project.

Monetary union, as with the EMS before it, was a project of differentiated integration or 'variable geometry'. The decision about who could participate was based on whether member states met the convergence criteria. This implied that participation in the project primarily depended on the capabilities and options of the respective governments. However, the actual decisions on the participants were largely induced by political criteria, rather than strict economic parameters, as several countries were admitted to the Euro-zone even though they had not fulfilled all criteria.

In terms of institutional reform, the Maastricht Treaty was far less successful, although the Delors Commission had tabled far-reaching proposals (Ross 1995; Gillingham 2003: 278–84). However, the reforms that were achieved constituted significant modifications to the institutional structure and procedures of decision-making of the EU (Dinan 2004a: 249–58).

Some of the modifications appeared to be more rhetorical than substantive. For example, the European polity was renamed the European Union, while the former Communities now constituted the European Community, or the first pillar within the Union (see Chapter 7). Moreover, there was an expressly declared commitment to further integration and to the principle of subsidiarity. Other institutional changes were, however, more substantive. Although some of these initially appeared only as minor incremental steps, in the long run they triggered considerable dynamics of integration. The introduction of the co-decision procedure for certain issues in the European Parliament is a case in point. The co-decision procedure provides for three readings of legislative proposals, and a conciliation procedure if there remains disagreement between the Council and the Parliament. It also gives the Parliament the power to veto a legislative proposal. Although the procedure did not grant Parliament a legislative status equal to that of the Council, it did extend its leverage on the substance of European legislation significantly (see Chapter 5). The Maastricht Treaty also gave the Parliament the power to confirm (or reject) the incoming College of Commissioners. Furthermore, it greatly extended majority voting in the Council of

Ministers, mainly to those issues where co-decision applies. Finally, the Treaty formally recognized the European Council as the highest decision-making authority of the Union.

The most spectacular – and, in the long run, most significant – step was an agreement to increase European cooperation in a wider array of policy areas, including Common Foreign and Security Policy (CFSP), and Justice and Home Affairs (JHA). Despite being brought into the folds of the European Union, both these areas remained under the exclusive responsibility of intergovernmental bodies and were thus placed outside the influence or control of the Commission, Parliament, and Court of Justice. The designation of these two areas as the second and third pillars (for CFSP and JHA, respectively) clearly signalled that the Union was pursuing a new approach to integration (see Chapter 7). This was reinforced in the decision to define the entire European Community, as it had existence thus far, as the first pillar of the new Union. During the negotiations on the Maastricht Treaty, the image of the European Union as a temple built on three pillars was frequently invoked and illustrates the co-existence of two forms of integration under a common institutional roof. While the first form of integration was characterized by a high degree of supranational influence, the second was governed by intergovernmental cooperation.

Furthermore, the Treaty of Maastricht included several new provisions whose scope and impact only became visible over time. First, it introduced European citizenship to connect citizens of the member states directly to the Union. Although this provision does not entail any significant rights, it has changed citizens' expectations and, to a degree, has facilitated the emergence of a European identity. Second, the Community, and thus the Commission, was granted powers in new policy areas. Although these refer mostly to narrowly or vaguely defined responsibilities such as education and vocational training, culture, public health, consumer protection and trans-European networks (Titles VIII-XII TEC-M), they have paved the way for embarking on new activities. Third, the Treaty established a new advisory body: the Committee of the Regions (CoR). In this advisory body, the sub-national level has been granted a voice in European decision-making for the first time, albeit only advisory (see Chapter 9). Finally, the Maastricht Treaty made provisions for a common social policy. This time a procedural 'trick' served to circumvent UK opposition. A 'social protocol', allowing for European legislation in matters of social policy, was appended to the Treaty and signed by all member states except the UK (see Chapter 10; Falkner *et al.* 2005).

The Maastricht Treaty was signed in February 1992 and, taken as a whole, marks the apex of an accelerated phase of integration (Geary 2012: 19). The adoption of the Treaty also heralded a new phase of integration, characterized by more heterogeneous developments.

However, soon after the adoption of the Treaty, the divisions in the common European house became more visible than ever before. Member states ratified the Treaty on European Union with difficulty and only after significant delays (Dinan 2004a: 258–62). In Denmark, citizens initially voted against the Treaty in a referendum (June 1992). In France, a referendum barely obtained the necessary majority (September 1992). Only with major concessions in the form of opt-outs (in particular, for the UK and Denmark) or compromises (in Germany, where the federal government allowed the *Länder* a voice in certain Council negotiations) was it possible to gain the approval of national parliaments and the electorates. However, even after the ratification of the Maastricht Treaty, the fissures in the European house remained visible. The citizens increasingly showed themselves to be sceptical or deeply divided, and the overall mistrust towards integration grew.

This situation worsened because of monetary union, a project that was difficult to implement effectively. The enormous costs and burdens that the project imposed on the member states undermined the consensus surrounding the project itself. The arduously negotiated consensus withered away even in other policy and issue areas. Whatever issue was on the table in political debates, the diverging interests and preferences of the member states blocked decisions.

Besides these internal matters, external factors also posed entirely new challenges to the Union. The end of the Cold War led to the fundamental transformation of the Central and Eastern European countries (CEECs) and the collapse of the corresponding block constellation. It also placed the Union under enormous pressure to take action. German reunification – and, thus, the integration of the former German Democratic Republic (GDR) into the European house – was, relatively considered, the least complicated step that the Union had to manage in this context (Gilbert 2003: 198–203). The Delors Commission prepared the ground for the smooth accession of the GDR to the EU by declaring the accession completed with German reunification (3 October 1990). In addition, the Commission quickly put forward concrete solutions for the related adjustment problems; for example, the creation of additional seats in the EP, or the increase of the financial allocations under the framework of cohesion policy.

A response to the upheaval in the other states of the former Eastern bloc proved to be more difficult. By 1989, even before the political transition in these countries, the Commission had set up an assistance programme for Poland and Hungary (PHARE). As soon as the transition process set in, in Poland and Hungary as well as other countries of the Eastern bloc, the Commission was able to achieve swift expansion of its assistance programme to all these countries. In addition, it set up a special programme known as TACIS for the republics of the former Soviet Union. Both PHARE and TACIS provided for partnership and cooperation agreements with the transition states. However, with the exception of Russia, these states aspired to more far-reaching objectives and agendas, as they forcefully pushed for full membership in the EU. Since the Union was unable to answer their demands with an attractive alternative, it increasingly came under pressure to accept Eastern enlargement (Gilbert 2003: 237).

The collapse of Yugoslavia and the resulting Balkan wars posed another major problem to the Union, challenging not only its common foreign and security policy, but also its limited capacity for action (Gilbert 2003: 251). Given the enormous expectations on the Union, these actions were largely insufficient or ineffective. It became clear that the EU would have to search for new solutions, if integration were to proceed even in the face of such profoundly complex problems in the immediate neighbourhood. However, deep divisions among the member states made concrete steps increasingly difficult to implement (Gillingham 2003: 314).

Overall, the period of accelerated integration beginning in 1985 must be viewed as a dynamic period. Economic integration was 'completed' with the creation of the single market and the preparation of EMU. Although the EC as a political system was not fundamentally transformed, the Single European Act and the Treaty of Maastricht brought about decisive reforms. These Treaty revisions further developed and refined the institutional structure of the EU and enhanced, rationalized, and democratized its decision-making procedures. Furthermore, a series of policy areas and corresponding powers were transferred to the European level, even though they were rarely triggered by the spill-over dynamics of economic integration.

These developments, advanced by a very active Commission under the presidency of Delors (Brown Well and Wells 2008; Geary 2012; Tömmel 2013), may be interpreted as a result of the increased momentum of supranational integration. The shift towards majority voting in the Council of Ministers, the significantly enhanced role of the Parliament in the legislative process, and the incorporation of an array of external actors into decision-making might confirm this position. However, such an interpretation only sheds light on one side of the coin. The progress made in supranational integration was accompanied and supported by refined procedures and practices of consensus-building in intergovernmental arenas. Thus, the method of integration was transformed so as actively to tackle the problem of persisting differences among the member states. At first, it appears that it was the large-scale IGCs, and the subsequent Treaty revisions, that were responsible for refining and differentiating the procedures of consensus-building between the member states and other actors and constituencies (Moravcsik 1998). In structural terms, however, it was the increased flexibility and diversification of the mode of integration that facilitated further progress. In this context, it is particularly helpful to remember the diverse forms of 'opting-out', the special clauses for individual member states, the adoption of integration steps below the level of formal Treaty provisions (Social Charter, Social Protocol) or outside the Treaties (Schengen Agreement, see Chapter 7), and finally codified forms of differentiated integration (monetary union). All these approaches include only a certain number of member states, while others remain outside the process (Leuffen *et al*. 2012; Avbelj 2013). The enhanced supranationalism on centre-stage is thus complemented by differentiated forms of intergovernmentalism, mostly behind the scenes.

Furthermore, the creation of distinctive pillars by the Treaty of Maastricht led – for the first time in the history of the EU – to the institutional separation of two different models of integration: one primarily driven by supranationalism and the other organized under intergovernmental auspices. Even though forms of intergovernmental cooperation existed before the adoption of the Maastricht Treaty, it is only with the establishment of the Union that intergovernmental cooperation was formally acknowledged by Treaty provisions and incorporated into the structure of the European polity. This meant that the political will to integrate the corresponding policy areas under the European umbrella now existed. However, the political will was not strong enough to enhance the supranational dynamics of integration. Consequently, since Maastricht, integration has taken place through the centralization of powers and decision-making at European level, and *also* through structured forms of intergovernmental cooperation.

## Conclusion

This chapter has outlined the history of European integration from its beginnings in the 1950s to its advanced form in the 1990s. This history started in the postwar era with initial cooperation among six European states. They founded three Communities that served to create a common market and to integrate selected economic sectors. The institutional setting of the Communities allowed for stable intergovernmental cooperation with the support of strong supranational institutions. After these initial successes, however, integration soon stalled, primarily due to major dissent among the member states. This resulted partly in stagnation, but also partly in shifts in the direction of the integration process. The membership of the three Communities was enlarged, new policy areas were added, and, most importantly, the intergovernmental dimension of the emerging polity was strengthened. After these transformations, supranationalism could once more expand its influence on integration. This resulted in further enlarging the Communities, completing the single market, creating EMU and undertaking two fundamental Treaty revisions, which re-introduced majority voting in the Council and improved the EP's voice in legislation. Yet, at the same time, a new path towards integration in the form of the second and third pillars further strengthened intergovernmental decision-making and control.

The outcome of this three-stage process is a new political order beyond the nation-state, one that rests on a unique combination of institutions. These institutions, on the one hand, predominantly foster the European cause and supranational dynamics; on the other hand, they embody intergovernmental bargaining processes and enable mediation of diverging interests among the member states.

The historical overview presented in this chapter has highlighted several of the characteristics of European integration. We have seen that the integration process does not proceed in a linear manner, following set guidelines or a clearly defined concept. Instead, phases of accelerated integration alternate with phases of stagnation. During phases of accelerated integration, supranational dynamics prevail; in phases of stagnation, intergovernmental configurations dominate, along with difficulties in compromising among the member states. Furthermore, European integration is a *selective process*. Although manifold and far-reaching reform projects are launched in every phase, national governments adopt only a fraction of them, so the process of integration proceeds only in certain issue areas, while others lag behind. This, in turn, implies that European integration is an *asymmetrical process*. While the regulation of the economy (and, particularly, the single market) is to a great extent achieved by the EU, other policy areas and issues (such as social policy, or the 'high politics' of peace and security issues, and foreign policy more generally) pose major obstacles to integration.

This chapter has also illustrated that integration results from the aggregated preferences and choices of the member states (Moravscik 1991, 1993, 1998). At the same time, however, the activities of the supranational institutions and actors – in particular, the European Commission – have played an important role in fostering integration (Sandholtz and Zysman 1989; Sandholtz and Stone Sweet 1998; Alter 2001, 2009; Pollack 2003). In addition, external factors and constellations have exercised significant influence on the course of the process. In Chapter 3, we will learn how these institutions, forces, and factors have influenced and shaped the most recent phase of European integration and polity-building.

# Chapter 3

# Consolidating the European Union: Enlargement, Deepening Integration and Crisis Management

This chapter analyzes the most recent phase of European integration and the ongoing process of system-building. By the 1990s, the European Union could be considered a mature polity. However, it still continued to enlarge its membership and transform its institutional structure and procedures of decision-making in response to newly emerging external challenges and persistent internal deficiencies. Moreover, since 2008, the Union has been seriously affected by the international financial crisis and the sovereign debt crisis of its member states, resulting in a deep crisis of the Euro. These crises have called into question the architecture of monetary union and have triggered a series of institutional, procedural, and regulatory adjustments in the monetary sphere. Yet, these adjustments did not result in formal Treaty amendments, as this would have provoked further dissent among the member states. Thus, the most recent phase of European integration is characterized by formerly unknown challenges that are placing the Union and its political leaders under enormous strain.

As early as the 1990s, and shortly after the adoption of the Maastricht Treaty, the EU came under increased pressure to enact further reforms. These pressures emanated, on the one hand, from the challenges of the post-Cold War era and, on the other hand, from problems inherent to the Union's institutional structure. Externally, it was the prospect of Eastern enlargement that put pressure on European leaders to initiate the next steps towards integration. This, in turn, aggravated the internal problems and deficiencies. The cumbersome procedures of decision-making, the veto rights of the member states and, generally, the arduous processes of consensus-building in the Councils acted as particularly high barriers to the effective governance of a significantly enlarged Union. Thus, institutional reforms that would redefine the powers and competences of the EU's institutions and redistribute the voting weights of the member states were placed especially high on the political agenda. The overall objective was to tackle both issues – the challenge of Eastern enlargement and the Union's weaknesses in deci-sion-making – and, at the same time, preserve the dominance of the intergovernmental institutions. For the first time in its history, the EU had to implement an enlargement of an unparalleled magnitude, while simultaneously striving to deepen integration.

These competing challenges led the EU initially to take only small, cautious, incremental steps towards further integration. In the longer run, though, European leaders, once again, changed the model of inte-gration. In face of major enlargements, reforms now needed to take the increasing differences among the member states into account. This resulted in a further strengthening of the intergovernmental dimension of the European polity and in Treaty provisions to allow differentiated forms of integration. Overall, during this phase the EU evolved into a much larger polity, but one with more internal differentiations; it was thus vested with stronger intergovernmental institutions and corre-sponding procedures of decision-making.

After accomplishing Eastern enlargement and adopting the Lisbon Treaty, the Union appeared to be entering a consolidation phase. However, it was suddenly hit with a deep financial and sovereign debt crisis. Initially, the Union reacted only slowly and reluctantly to these new challenges. However, over the course of several years, it enacted a series of measures that would hopefully stabilize the Euro and the highly-indebted member states, and would improve the institutional architecture of monetary union. These innovations, mostly adopted by the heads of state or government of the Euro-group, further enhanced the intergov-ernmental dimension of the EU and deepened differentiated integration. An end to this crisis is not yet in sight. On the contrary, from the economic sphere the crisis swept over to the political sphere, calling into question the achievements of European integration and exacerbating Euro-scepti-cism, particularly in those states most affected by the crisis. Thus, the economic and financial crisis triggered a political crisis whose impacts might once more provoke a change in the direction of integration.

## Cautious incremental steps

### Preparing Eastern enlargement

The Union made a cautious incremental step towards greater integra-tion in 1995, when it undertook the fourth round of enlargement (Dinan 2004a: 268–71). One of the motives for this step was to increase the number of economically well-developed and wealthy Western European states, and, in this way, strengthen the Union as a whole before Eastern enlargement. Accordingly, following positive referenda, Sweden, Finland and Austria joined the European Union in 1995. The negotiations proved to be arduous because the governments of the candidate states had to balance their explicit commitment to accession with diverging interests of certain constituencies and the sceptical attitudes of their citizens. In Norway, the fourth candidate state, a failed referendum forced the government to retreat from its plans of membership, even though the accession negotiations had been completed. Overall, however, this fourth round of enlargement was comparatively unproblematic. The new member states had already reached a high degree of convergence with the principles and rules governing the EU as a result of their membership in the European Economic Area (EEA). The EEA was created in 1991 in order to integrate the EFTA-states into the single market of the EU. At that time, EFTA comprised seven states, including the three candidates for EU accession. This implied that these states had, to a great extent, already adopted most of the rules of the EU's single market.

In contrast, it was much more difficult to achieve a common position among EU member states in the accession negotiations of the CEECs (Dinan 2004a: 271–9). One reason was that the disparities in political and economic terms between these countries and the EU-15 formed a major obstacle to rapid integration (Gilbert 2003: 237). Moreover, there were significant differences in preferences among the EU member states and within individual constituencies about Eastern enlargement. While the Northern member states generally welcomed Eastern enlargement, the Mediterranean members assumed a much more reserved position. In addition, workers and trade unions throughout the Union feared competition from labour migrants of the accession states, and worried that this might eventually result in social dumping. In spite of these diverging views and preferences, a plan slowly emerged to help prepare the transformation states for accession to the EU (Gilbert 2003: 237–41, Dinan 2004a: 271–9). The first step consisted in concluding association agreements: the Europe Agreements. These agreements provided for trade liberalization and for political cooperation and assistance during the transition phase. At the same time though, the Union set the membership bar quite high. As early as June 1993, the heads of state or government formulated clear criteria for membership at the Copenhagen Summit. The core requirements of these 'Copenhagen criteria' were: stability of institutions to guarantee democracy, the presence of a functioning market economy, and the ability to take on the obligations of EU membership.

The European leaders also set high hurdles for themselves. They declared that Eastern enlargement should only take place after integration had been deepened; that is, after a fundamental reform of the

Union's institutions and decision-making procedures (Gilbert 2003: 241). Their primary objective in doing this was to ensure the Union's capacity to act with a much larger number of member states.

Yet, a necessary step before proceeding to tackle such a fundamental reform was to nominate a President of the Commission by the end of 1994. Heads of state or government had difficulties agreeing on a candidate for this position. After Delors, they clearly preferred a personality who would not interfere too much in their domestic affairs. Finally, after lengthy negotiations and vetoes against two candidates, they nominated Jacques Santer, then Prime Minister of Luxembourg. This choice reflected a rather defensive attitude towards uniting Europe (Tömmel 2013). The Parliament gave Santer its vote of consent by only a very small majority. For his part, the new President did not announce spectacular steps towards further integration, but promised only 'doing less, but doing it better' (Cini 2008: 117–18).

In the meantime, mistrust among citizens with regard to European integration had risen to an all-time high. This became particularly evident in the run-up to the creation of EMU (Gilbert 2003: 228–30). Most governments of the member states were engaged in a race to fulfil the convergence criteria in order to participate in monetary union. This often meant making tough decisions on fiscal austerity and deep cuts in the social safety net. Although new debates were flaring up over the 'Esperanto currency' (a term coined by the German Finance Minister of that time), European leaders adhered to the schedule for establishing EMU. In January 1997, they officially set up common monetary institutions. In January 1999, they introduced the Euro as a parallel currency to those of the member states and, in January 2002, the Euro became the exclusive means of payment in the countries of the Euro-zone. Contrary to initial expectations, it was not only seven or eight member states that qualified for monetary union, but eleven. In 2000, the twelfth member of the Euro-zone, Greece, was admitted. As Gilbert and many other observers concluded: 'the decision was ultimately political, not economic' (Gilbert 2003: 234). The first project of differentiated integration anchored in the Treaties exercised strong pressures on highly-indebted countries to reorder their public finances and to realign their economic and social policies accordingly. It also exercised substantial pressure on *all* member states that they eventually take part in this integration step (for more details, see Chapter 7).

In 1996, the heads of state or government, amid increased pressures from numerous countries for rapid accession, and facing a further decline in support for the European project among citizens, convened an IGC for a revision of the Treaties. The declared aim of this IGC was to elaborate proposals both for a more democratic and transparent system, and for a more rational and efficient institutional structure, in order to ensure the Union's capacity to act with 25 members, or even more.

A host of reform proposals and suggestions for smaller or larger steps towards integration were presented to the IGC. The Commission, the Parliament, governments of the member states, the Committee of the Regions, sub-national administrative units, as well as a broad range of interest associations and non-governmental actors, drew up position papers, opinions, and proposals for Treaty amendments (Dinan 2004a: 284). Yet, even here, national governments could reach, at best, minimal compromises and agree on minor, incremental steps towards reform. Once again, they postponed fundamental institutional innovations to the future.

Finally, in June 1997, the Amsterdam Summit successfully negotiated a revision of the Treaties (Dinan 2004a: 285–7). It will come as no surprise that this revision hardly corresponded to the original grand expectations. The incremental approach resulted in a consistent enhancement of the powers, authority, and capacity for action of the European institutions, but not in an improvement of their transparency or democratic accountability. Instead, it further reinforced the 'interlocked' nature of the European polity (for the origins of the Amsterdam Treaty, see Moravcsik and Nicolaïdis 1999; for an assessment of the Treaty, see Neunreither and Wiener 2000).

## Amending the Treaties

The Treaty of Amsterdam offered significant improvements to the EU's institutional architecture and decision-making processes, but it did not remove the hurdles for Eastern enlargement. Importantly, it expanded the co-decision procedure from 15 to 38 areas. This clearly strengthened the legislative role of the Parliament and put it on a *de facto* equal footing with the Council in these areas (Tsebelis and Garrett 2001). At the same time, the Treaty significantly streamlined and simplified the procedure in an attempt to improve the efficiency of decision-making (Art. 251 TEC-A; for details, see Chapter 5). Furthermore, the Treaty largely repealed the cooperation procedure that had been introduced in the SEA. In retrospect, this appears to have been only a stepping stone towards a more powerful role for the Parliament. Finally, the Amsterdam Treaty gave Parliament the mandate to draw up proposals for Europe-wide elections (Art. 190(4) TEC-A). Such elections could increase the legitimacy of the Parliament and bring it closer to the citizens, as elections would no longer be held individually in each member state according to national rules, procedures, and party systems. This shift could, moreover, trigger the emergence of a genuinely European party system. However, to date, the Parliament has not adopted a decision on this issue, even though elaborate proposals for a Europe-wide election were already made public in 2010 (Duff 2010).

The Amsterdam Treaty strengthened the position of the Commission marginally – in particular, the role of the Commission President. It assigned the President a role in selecting the Commissioners (Art. 214(2) TEC-A), as well as 'broad discretion in the allocation of tasks within the college' (TEC-A Final Act, Declaration nr. 32). With regard to the Council of Ministers, the Treaty expanded qualified majority voting, albeit only in certain issue areas. Furthermore, the Treaty upgraded the role of national parliaments in European decision-making, although this was only laid down in a protocol to the Treaty.

The Amsterdam Treaty also included new responsibilities in two important policy areas, employment and social policy. In the case of social policy, 'only' the consent of the UK was required to include the respective protocol agreed on in Maastricht into the Treaty (Title XI TEC-A). This consent was easily given by British Prime Minister Tony Blair, who clearly advocated a European social policy after the electoral victory of the Labour Party in May 1997. With regard to employment policy, however, national governments had to adopt an entirely new chapter in the Treaty (Title VIII, Art. 125-130 TEC-A). Remarkably, they agreed to subject employment policy and certain aspects of social policy (equal opportunities), which had been highly contentious issues for a long time, to qualified majority voting (Art. 137 and 141 TEC-A).

All Treaty revisions outlined above pertain to the first pillar of the Union and enhance, to a greater or lesser degree, all European institutions in their capacity to act. In this sense, these provisions reinforce, in principle, the supranational dynamics of integration. However, the Amsterdam Treaty also enhanced the Union's capacity to act in the second and third pillars, thus clearly strengthening the intergovernmental dimension of the European polity (see Art. 11-28, and 29-42 TEU-A). For the second pillar, in particular, the Treaty established a new position of High Representative for the Common Foreign and Security Policy (HR). The person holding this position will, simultaneously, act as High Representative and Secretary-General of the Council. Heads of state or government rejected the Commission's demand to mandate a Commissioner with the function of HR. The Treaty also established a new 'policy planning and early warning unit' within the General Secretariat of the Council (see TEC-A Final Act, Declaration on the establishment of a policy planning and early warning unit). The unit is designed to support the High Representative by providing analyses of international developments and drawing up policy proposals. This institutional innovation clearly side-lined the Commission's role in European foreign policy. Overall, the Amsterdam Treaty consolidated the pillar structure and, thus, confirmed the institutional separation of the two models of integration first introduced with the Treaty of Maastricht.

The most spectacular provision in the Amsterdam Treaty was the introduction of a concept of differentiated integration. The Treaty provided that a group of states could take steps towards 'closer cooperation' within the EC (Art. 11 TEC-A). These provisions allowed certain member states to act as an *avant garde* in European integration. Such activities were already *de facto* in place; for example, in the Schengen Agreement of 1985 (Kölliker 2006; Leuffen *et al*. 2012). However, the Schengen agreement falls outside the formal institutional framework of the EU. By incorporating the 'closer cooperation' into the Treaty, a group of member states wishing to embark on new integration steps could draw on EU resources to meet their goals. Consequently, the integration process could move forward even without consensus among all member states. The Treaty, however, put certain restrictions in place. Although the Council of Ministers could decide on 'closer cooperation' by qualified majority, a single member state – specifying reasons – could block a majority decision with a veto (Art. 11(2) TEC-A).

Overall, the Amsterdam Treaty reflected a slowdown in the momentum of integration, as it involved only minor steps towards reform. At the same time, however, the Treaty paved the way for a new direction in European integration. The gradual consolidation of the institutions of the EU and the incorporation of additional actors into the process of decision-making (.e.g. the national parliaments) generally reinforced the interwoven character of the European polity without significantly strengthening its core institutions. The support for various forms of 'closer cooperation' in the Treaty implied that further steps towards integration were no longer dependent on a consensus among all member states. Instead, the dynamics between leaders and laggards in the European arena would determine the future pace of integration. Both trends originated in earlier phases of integration but they had not been systematically pushed forward and underpinned by Treaty regulations.

With the adoption of the Amsterdam Treaty (signed 2 October 1997, effective as of 1 May 1999), the Union was still far from achieving the institutional reforms necessary to prepare for Eastern enlargement. Nevertheless, concrete steps to this end were soon taken. During the preparations of the Amsterdam Summit, the Commission recommended opening accession negotiations with five CEECs (the Czech Republic, Estonia, Hungary, Poland, Slovenia) and one Mediterranean state (Cyprus). At the same time, it presented 'Agenda 2000', a document that outlined the fundamental reforms necessary for preparing for Eastern enlargement (European Commission 1997). The Agenda identified the restructuring of the common agricultural policy and the Structural Funds, together with a pre-accession strategy for the candidate states, as the most important steps towards this end (Gillingham 2003: 319–20). After tough negotiations over the reform proposals, largely fuelled by major distributional conflicts, the European Council in Berlin adopted

Agenda 2000 (March 1999). Earlier in Luxembourg (December 1997), the European Council had accepted the Commission proposal to open accession negotiations with five CEECs and Cyprus. Under pressure from the European Parliament and from those countries that were excluded from the first round of negotiations, the Council decided shortly afterwards (at the Helsinki Summit, December 1999) to open accession negotiations with all states aspiring to membership. These were, in addition to the six mentioned above: Bulgaria, Latvia, Lithuania, Romania, the Slovak Republic, and Malta.

Progress was also made in areas other than enlargement. In the summer of 1999, the European Council reached an agreement on the concept of a 'European Security and Defence Identity' (ESDI) (Gilbert 2003: 250–1; Howorth 2007). It envisioned the deployment of EU defence forces on the basis of national contingents, working in close cooperation with the WEU and NATO. Thus, a consensus finally emerged on an issue that had, for a long time, been the subject of highly controversial debates among member states.

The elaboration and adoption of a European Charter of Fundamental Rights in 1999/2000 marks another significant step towards deeper integration (Alonso Garcia 2002). One objective underlying this step was to bring the EU closer to the citizens. At the same time, the Charter was also aimed at clearly defining the principles around any further enlargements of the Union including, for example, respect for human rights and the protection of minorities. The procedure used in drawing up the Charter is noteworthy. For the first time in the history of the Union it was not an IGC, but a Convention that elaborated the text (Deloche-Gaudez 2001). The Convention consisted of representatives of all EU institutions, as well as delegates of the member states. The Charter of Fundamental Rights, solemnly proclaimed during the Summit of Nice (December 2000), forms a milestone in the history of European integration for two main reasons. First, the procedure for its elaboration increased the legitimacy of decision-making. Second, the content of the Charter was path-breaking, as it referred to fundamental *individual* rights. In this respect, it could form a core element of a future European constitution.

Despite – or, perhaps, because of these considerable steps towards integration – Euro-scepticism continued to spread (Hix 2008: 52–7). It increased even further when, in 1999, the Commission – or, more precisely, individual Commissioners – were accused of mismanagement and fraud (Gillingham 2003: 320–3). After heated debates in the European Parliament, where MEPs were determined to exercise their powers to a maximum by threatening with a motion of censure, the Santer Commission collectively resigned (Schön-Quinlivan 2011: 57–63; see also van Miert 2000: 353–63). In autumn 1999, a new Commission took office under the Presidency of Romano Prodi, former Prime

Minister of Italy. The Prodi Commission, as with the Santer Commission before it, was unable to reach the prestige of the Delors College (Gillingham 2003: 329–34; Cini 2008; Tömmel 2013). Its ability to act was hampered by national governments, who not even in this crisis situation were willing to delegate too much power to the EU.

Despite significant achievements, the institutional reforms of the Union that were necessary to prepare for Eastern enlargement had not been tackled by the turn of the millennium. Consequently, European leaders convened yet another IGC to deal with the 'leftovers' of Amsterdam (Gillingham 2003: 334–40, Dinan 2004a: 287–9). The most salient issues in this context were a new system of weighted votes in the Council of Ministers, downsizing the Commission, and the redistribution of seats in the European Parliament. After a year of preparations, the Summit of Nice negotiated Treaty revisions in December 2000. However, the resulting Treaty of Nice also failed to fulfil expectations (for the Treaty of Nice, the negotiations, the final outcomes and an assessment, see Gray and Stubb 2001; Yataganas 2001; Sbragia 2002; Gilbert 2003: 243–4).

The reform of the system of weighted votes in the Council of Ministers was primarily in the interest of the large member states. Eastern enlargement involved almost exclusively small states that would have been heavily over-represented with the 'old' formula of weighted votes. After arduous and extraordinarily turbulent negotiations, the Nice Summit reached a consensus on a shift in the weighing of votes in favour of the large member states. The Treaty stipulated that the votes of the large member states were to multiply on average by the coefficient 2.9, whereas those of the smaller states by only 2.0. However, this rule was not universally applied. The votes of Spain were multiplied by 3.4. Poland sought, and was finally able to obtain, the same number of votes as Spain (*de facto* 27 as compared with the 29 of the large member states) and, thus, solidified an even more disproportionate weight in the Council than Spain, as it has much fewer inhabitants. The Treaty of Nice stipulated two additional conditions for a qualified majority in order to confirm the power of the larger and, indeed, most important 'old' member states. First, a positive vote had to represent more than half the number of all member states and, second, it had to represent 62 per cent of the Union's population. The population-based rule was mainly a concession to Germany, which could not achieve a higher voting weight than the other large member states.

In terms of the size of the Commission, the member states could not reach a consensus. Particularly, the smaller states were forceful in their claim to representation in the College of Commissioners. As a result, despite demands for greater efficiency, the Council decided that the number of Commissioners could increase to a maximum of 27. In order to accommodate a larger number of accession states, the large member states were willing to cede one of their two seats in the Commission. This compromise was sufficient to accommodate the 12 candidate states still involved in accession negotiations at this time (December 2000).

The decision to limit the maximum number of seats in the European Parliament at 700, as laid down in the Amsterdam Treaty, could not be maintained with Eastern enlargement. Consequently, European leaders agreed on a distribution of seats that reduced the proportion of seats held by the current members, so as to make room for the accession states. At the same time, however, the weight of the larger states was increased, so that the number of their seats would better reflect the size of their population. This, in turn, meant that the total number of seats in the EP would exceed the 700 ceiling after Eastern enlargement.

While the Nice Treaty was at least partially successful in restructuring the institutions, the necessary reform of the decision-making procedures lagged far behind expectations. The Treaty extended majority voting in the Council of Ministers to 24 cases, but granted the Parliament co-decision powers in only seven cases. Hence, the European Council clearly rejected the Parliament's claims for attaining co-decision in all legislative matters and, thus, a role as a fully-fledged co-legislator, at least for the time being.

In contrast, the Nice Treaty enacted the facilitation of the procedure of 'closer cooperation', now labelled 'enhanced cooperation', with surprising ease. It abolished the veto option for individual member states, and set the minimum number of participants in 'enhanced cooperation' at 8. Thus, the Treaty, in fact, maintained the provisions agreed in Amsterdam, which, in a 15-member Union, had required the participation of more than half of the member states, or at least 8. However, following enlargement, the threshold of 8 states would mean that a group of less than one third of the member states could embark on a process of enhanced cooperation.

Unsurprisingly, the usual widespread criticism accompanied the adoption of the Nice Treaty (Dinan 2004a: 288–9). However, the European leaders, at least, believed that they had taken the steps necessary to set the course for Eastern enlargement. Although they did not achieve major reforms of the institutional structure of the EU, they readjusted the relative political weight of the individual states, officially in favour of the larger states but, *de facto*, in favour of the 'old' members of the EU. The new Treaty was ratified without any delays and came into force on 1 February 2003.

In conclusion, we can see that national governments reacted reluctantly, at first, and, later, cautiously to the exponentially increased challenges of the last decade of the twentieth century. They did not have a clear plan in light of the pressures from the CEEC to join the EU; neither did they know how to accommodate dramatically declining public support for further integration. It was only after initial delays that they embarked on a minor enlargement that strengthened the group of the 'rich' countries, as well as specific incremental steps towards reform that were codified in Treaty amendments. The Commission – still under Delors and, later, Santer – was also more cautious in presenting new projects; its activities focused mainly on adhering to the projects that were scheduled earlier (EMU), or in initiating minor reforms in order to achieve inevitable advances (Agenda 2000). However, within this stalemate, some achievements stand out, and these later formed the stepping stones towards major progress in integration. The Charter of Fundamental Rights and the establishment of a Convention for drawing it up, the decision to start accession negotiations with 12 neighbouring states, and the creation of a military dimension of the EU were all significant achievements. In addition, the Treaty amendments entailed a number of regulations that could later be transformed into true innovations including, for example, the extension of majority voting in the Council and co-decision for the Parliament, the change of the system of weighted votes in the Council, and, particularly, the concept of 'enhanced cooperation'.

## Changing parameters in integration

### Implementing enlargement and elaborating a Constitutional Treaty

Building on the small successes achieved in the Treaty of Nice, the Union quickly moved forward with enlargement. Accession negotiations with six countries had begun in March 1998. In February 2000, they were expanded to the six remaining candidate countries. The 29 chapters that were originally opened for negotiation were partly concluded during 2001, but a number of problems were still looming (Avery 2004). Difficulties were especially prevalent in agricultural and environmental policy, as well as the free movement of workers. Furthermore, although several of the accession states had accepted the demands and requirements of the EU without any reservations, others had expressed significant objections. The most disputed issue between the Union and the candidate states was a clear target date for accession (Avery 2004). The Union was reluctant to set a specific date and left it open for as long as possible. On the one hand, it felt that it was not really ready to admit the new members. On the other hand, the EU did not want to lessen the pressures on the candidate states to conform to its conditions. In the end, a decision to extend the transition periods after enlargement alleviated several of the concerns of both Union and candidates. Only once the negotiations were nearing their end, in 2002, did the EU set 1 May 2004 as the definite date for enlargement. With this decision, the pendulum of European politics once again shifted towards deepening integration.

The Treaty of Nice also had 'leftovers' that required another Treaty revision in order for them to be addressed. This revision was expected to take place by 2004, the last possible date before Eastern enlargement. Remarkably, for the first time in the history of the EU, member states did not elaborate the Treaty revision through an IGC. Instead, they entrusted a Convention with this task. The Convention consisted of delegates from both European institutions and member states' legislatures and executives (Dinan 2004a: 296). A Convention had proven successful in drawing up the European Charter of Fundamental Rights, and the Union hoped that this success could now be repeated (Deloche-Gaudez 2001).

The Convention on the Future of the European Union, inaugurated on 28 February 2002, was entrusted with the goal of elaborating proposals for a fundamental Treaty reform (Dinan 2002). It consisted of 15 delegates of member states' governments, 30 deputies of the national parliaments, and 16 deputies of the European Parliament. A further 13 government members and 26 parliamentarians from the accession states were also included. Besides the representatives from the 12 accession states, representatives from Turkey as a candidate for accession were also allowed to participate. Finally, the Commission was allocated two of the total 105 members of the Convention (Dinan 2004a: 296). The three members of the Convention missing in this total number are its President and two Vice-Presidents, who were directly appointed by the European Council.

The establishment of the Convention was heralded as an important step towards the further democratization of the EU (see, e.g., Reh 2008 and the literature discussed there). Indeed, more than two thirds of its 105 members, or 72 individuals, were directly elected parliamentarians. However, only 18 of its representatives (i.e. less than one fifth) were delegates of European institutions. In other words, the Convention was dominated by present and future member states and, thus, remained firmly anchored in the intergovernmental dimension of the European polity.

The European Council, via its Laeken Declaration (Laeken Summit of December 2001) entrusted the Convention with a comprehensive and difficult task (Dinan 2002; Magnette 2005a). The Convention was charged with drawing up proposals for a Treaty reform which would prepare the Union for the future by increasing the efficiency, transparency, and democratic accountability of its institutions and decision-making procedures. The Convention was also charged with more clearly defining the specific powers designated to the European and national government levels. It was furthermore expected to present a proposal for a European Constitution. In short, it was 'faced with tricky reform issues, which the heads of state or government ... had not been able to solve before' (*Frankfurter Rundschau*, 28 February 2002: 8, translation by author). Despite initial low expectations, the Convention was able to solve several of the 'tricky reform issues'. After an intense and highly controversial six-month period of deliberation, the Convention presented a Draft Constitutional Treaty (DCT) (Crum 2004; Dinan 2004b). Contrary to its initial mandate, the Convention did not draw up several alternatives but, rather, only one Draft Treaty, thus significantly constraining the choices of the Council. The Convention added additional weight to its proposal by explicitly warning the governments of the member states not to reopen Pandora's box, as this would likely undermine the ability to reach a final decision.

It was certainly necessary to warn the governments so emphatically, as the Convention had designed a Draft Treaty that proposed solutions to a number of long-disputed issues. The proposals clearly exceeded what member states were ready to concede (Dinan 2004b). Indeed, presenting the Draft Treaty as a 'constitution' already went beyond what national governments wanted, as this served to emphasize the state-like character of the EU (Crum 2004). A proposal for the complete incorporation of the Charter of Fundamental Rights into the Constitutional Treaty without modifications also went far beyond member states' aspirations. They feared that such a step could create a 'Europe of the citizens' and would, once again, emphasize the state-like character of the Union. However, the most spectacular reforms were reflected in the proposals for the substantial modification of the EU's institutional structure and decision-making procedures (Crum 2004; Dinan 2004b, 2005). The Convention put forth the following proposals:

- Reducing the size of the Commission to 15 members.
- Election of the Commission President by the Parliament on a proposal by the Council.
- Abolishing the rotating Council Presidencies and replacing them with a system in which the Presidency is set for a term of two-and-a-half years.
- Creating the position of a European Foreign Minister, who would act as the Chair of the Foreign Affairs Council and, at the same time, as Vice-President of the Commission.
- Upgrading the role of the Parliament to an equal co-legislator, by making the co-decision procedure the regular legislative procedure.
- Abolishing the pillar structure of the Union.

Even more spectacular was the Convention's proposal for a modified voting procedure in the Council of Ministers. The proposal sought to do away with the weighing of votes. Instead, every member state, whether large or small, would have just one vote, and decisions would only be taken with an absolute majority of the Council members. To accommodate the concerns of the larger member states, the positive votes were required to represent at least 60 per cent of the Union's population. Furthermore, the Convention proposed significant relaxation of the conditions for initiating the procedure of 'enhanced cooperation'.

Given the scope of these reform proposals, one may have expected heated debates over the pros and cons of the Convention package. Interestingly, this did not occur. Some of the large and important member states, particularly France and Germany, quickly supported the Convention and declared that the proposed reform package should be adopted in its entirety. Otherwise, they argued, the revision of the Treaties would fail. It was largely Spain and Poland, as the two countries that had the most to lose, that vehemently opposed the Convention proposals. Both were particularly concerned about the abolishment of the principle of weighted voting in the Council. As the smallest of the large states, they were concerned about losing the privileges they had gained with the Treaty of Nice. Partially because of their fierce opposition, the Brussels Summit at the end of 2003 failed to adopt the Constitutional Treaty (Dinan 2004b). This failure must also be partially ascribed to the Italian presidency and the half-hearted conduct of negotiations by Prime Minister Berlusconi, known for his Euro-sceptic mindset. Objections by other actors behind the scenes may also have played a role. In any event, the EU missed a unique chance to deepen integration before the enlargement by the 10 new member states was set to take place (on 1 May 2004). Although the candidate countries had participated in the deliberations of the Convention, the 'old' member states anticipated that the accession states would raise more explicit objections to the proposed reforms, once they had gained full membership, especially if such proposals constrained national sovereignty.

Surprisingly, the member states of the enlarged Union quickly reached a consensus. The decisive breakthrough came in Brussels in June 2004, almost immediately after the euphoric celebrations of the historic Eastern enlargement and shortly after the successful elections to the incoming European Parliament. Under the direction of the Irish Presidency, the now 25 heads of state or government unanimously adopted the Draft Constitutional Treaty for the European Union. Although, in particular, the smaller member states were satisfied with having achieved some concessions in the final negotiations, for the most part, the European Council did not significantly dilute the Draft put forward by the Convention, as many hasty commentators had feared.

The most crucial modifications to the Convention proposal were as follows (see Dinan 2005):

- A reduction of the number of Commissioners to two thirds of the number of member states; the introduction of this modification was postponed to the year 2014.

- A president of the European Council elected to a term of two-and-a-half years; all other Council formations would maintain the principle of six-month rotation.
- Majority voting in the Council of Ministers required at least 15 positive votes which had to represent at least 65 per cent of the population of the Union. A minimum of four states could form a blocking minority.

Overall, these modifications of the Convention proposal slightly strengthened the political weight of the member states, especially in the Commission and Council. These changes were particularly important for the smaller states.

The adoption of the Draft Constitutional Treaty marked an achievement that the previous Treaty revisions had not been able to accomplish: a fundamental restructuring of the institutions of the EU and its decision-making procedures. The provisions of the Constitutional Treaty enhanced the Union's capacity to act, and even improved its democratic legitimacy to a certain extent. However, enhancing the Union's capacity to act was not accomplished by strengthening the supranational dimension of the Union. Instead, it improved the ability of the Councils to take decisions and, thus, to increase their authority and leadership role in the enlarged EU. This, in turn, severely constrained individual member states, or groups of member states, to act as veto-players (Tömmel 2010).

In the academic literature, analysts generally recognize that management of the situation by the Convention was responsible for the spectacular breakthrough in deepening integration. Many observers assume that the Convention achieved these impressive results because its deliberations took the form of 'arguing' (i.e. putting forward sound and convincing arguments) rather than 'bargaining' (i.e. striving for maximum advantages through negotiations) (Magnette 2005a; Risse and Kleine 2007; Reh 2008). Furthermore, former French President Valérie Giscard-d'Estaing, as Convention President, is credited with having been a driving force behind this success (Dinan 2004b; Kleine 2007; Tsebelis and Proksch 2007). At the same time, however, these results were achieved because, early on, the Convention method neutralized potential veto-players among national governments (Tömmel 2010). During the subsequent IGC, these veto-players barely had a chance to dismantle the tightly-laced package and alter its substance.

However, we cannot explain the historic achievement of reaching an agreement on a Constitutional Treaty merely as the result of the internal dynamics of European integration. The pressures emanating from external challenges linked to the end of the Cold War also provoked an improvement in the Union's capacity to act. Yet, such improvements could not be implemented overnight. In fact, in the first few years after the adoption of the Maastricht Treaty, European leaders generally displayed a defensive attitude and a tendency towards, at best, cautious incremental changes. Both the widening (Eastern enlargement) and deepening (Treaty reform) projects gained momentum only when the accession candidates knocked ever harder on the Union's door. This then involved not only expanding the Union in quantitative terms, but also restructuring its qualitative dimension. In particular, the idea of 'enhanced cooperation' (which allows for differentiated integration) and the reform of the EU's institutional structure and decision-making procedures (which facilitate collective action) were significant steps in response to external challenges. However, these steps, if implemented, could transform the EU into a union of unequal partners (Gillingham 2003: 410–13).

### Accomplishing reform: the Lisbon Treaty

The Constitutional Treaty had just been agreed (June 2004), when yet another controversial issue was added to the EU's agenda: appointing a new Commission (Dinan 2005). The member states, against everyone's expectations, quickly reached consensus on Portugese President José Manuel Barroso. The designated Commission President had close ties with the European Peoples' Party that had, after the elections in June 2004, once again proven to be the strongest political force in the EP. He was also seen as a consistent advocate of neo-liberal policies. Since Barroso was not considered a particularly strong candidate, his designation also dispelled fears about an overly-independent Commission. However, the process of nominating the College of Commissioners was not without conflict. Again, the EP drew on its right to approve the entire Commission, this time more powerfully, by questioning the qualification of individual candidates for office (Spence 2006a: 37; Westlake 2006: 267–8). As a result of the Parliament's scrutiny, Italy and Latvia had to withdraw their candidates and appoint others. In addition, Barroso was compelled to redistribute some of the portfolios and responsibilities of the designated Commissioners. While the Parliament was able to strengthen its position, the Commission was weakened by this process (Dinan 2005: 52–4).

However, the success of the quick agreement on the Constitutional Treaty turned out to be short-lived. Difficulties arose with the ratification of the Treaty at the national levels. In some states, national parliaments were able to approve and ratify the Treaty; in others, a referendum was necessary. It was particularly difficult to anticipate the outcome of the referenda. In 18 member states, the Constitutional Treaty was successfully ratified by the national parliaments. The referenda were less consistently positive. In Spain and Luxembourg, the majority of citizens voted in favour of the Treaty; in France and the Netherlands, citizens clearly rejected the project (Taggart 2006; Startin and Krouwel 2013). In the UK, the government did not even formally schedule a referendum because of concerns that the result would be a resounding 'no'. Other member states that had planned to hold a referendum hesitated after the negative votes in France and the Netherlands. The clear rejection of the Constitutional Treaty by the citizens – in particular, in two founding member states of the EU – and the omnipresent scepticism among those who were not given the chance to voice their opinions in a referendum, evoked a deep crisis of the EU. Once again, it became evident that, even in an enlarged Union, integration was not slowed down because of the differences among the member states but, rather, because of the deep divide between integration-minded elites and an increasingly sceptical public. As a result of the failed referenda, the European Union's constitutional project had to be postponed. The European elites proclaimed a 'period of reflection' (Dinan 2006: 64). There were, after all, enough other controversial issues that required attention.

One issue that loomed large was the decision on the 'financial perspective' of the EU for the period 2007–2013. This involved drawing up a multi-annual spending programme. Decisions on multi-annual spending have wide-spread consequences for European policies – in particular, in distributive policy areas such as agricultural and cohesion policy. It is thus not surprising that this was a controversial issue that generated major disputes (Dinan 2006).

Interestingly, despite expectations, the primary divisions were not along the lines of West and East, or old and new member states. Rather, the biggest disputes were among France, Germany, and the UK. France mainly sought to secure its agricultural subsidies, while the UK strongly advocated spending to foster innovations in research and technology. The UK also tried to secure the continuation of the British rebate that it had received since the early 1980s in order to balance its position as net-payer to the budget. Germany, as a net contributor, and arguing that it had to comply with the criteria of the Stability and Growth Pact (SGP), tried to reduce the overall budget of the Union as much as possible. By the end of 2005, the European Council finally agreed on a compromise, calling for concessions from all parties.

Following the decisions on the multi-annual spending programme, enlargement was once again on the European agenda. In October 2005, the European Council decided to open official accession negotiations with Croatia and Turkey. This was decided despite persistent scepticism in many member states and despite the still unsolved Constitutional crisis. Even with these unresolved issues, most of 2006 was characterized by 'business as usual' (Dinan 2007). Laws were adopted, agreements with third-countries were signed, monitoring reports on various policies and projects were elaborated, and Green and White Papers were discussed. On 1 January 2007, Romania and Bulgaria joined the EU as scheduled, although doubts remained as to whether they had actually fulfilled the accession criteria.

No attempt to return to the Constitutional Treaty was made until Germany took over the Presidency in the first half of 2007. Under the premise of setting a schedule for launching Treaty revisions, the German Presidency initiated extensive steps towards reform (Maurer 2008). First, the 'Berlin Declaration', proclaimed on the occasion of the fiftieth anniversary of the EC/EU on 25 March 2007, prepared the way for renewed reform. In addition to the flowery phrases, the signatories sent a serious message of political will to conclude the constitutional reform before the parliamentary elections in 2009. Shortly thereafter, at the European Council held in June 2007, European leaders adopted a mandate for the revision of the Treaties. Dinan comments that 'the German Council Presidency ... decided, in effect, to negotiate the IGC before it would officially begin' (Dinan 2008: 75). However, negotiations leading up to the mandate did not run smoothly. Poland was strongly opposed to the proposals, especially to the new rules to facilitate majority voting. In the end, Poland's President had little choice but to conform to the will of the vast majority of the member states (Dinan 2008: 78–9). The final mandate included the details of the envisaged Treaty revision, so that the subsequent IGC could not decide any less than this (see Council of the EU, IGC Mandate, No. 11218/07, Brussels, 26 June 2007). At the same time, politicians tried to downplay the range and scope of the reform by avoiding the term 'Constitutional Treaty'. Instead, they expressed their aims as adopting a 'Reform Treaty'. French President Nicolas Sarkozy downplayed the reform even further by speaking of a 'mini-treaty'.

The renewed Treaty revision project was not only different in name; the mandate itself defined a number of modifications for revising the Draft Constitutional Treaty (see Council of the EU, IGC Mandate, No. 11218/07, Brussels, 26 June 2007, and Dinan 2008). First, it stripped the Treaty of all elements that made the EU appear to be a state-like polity. It removed references to an anthem and a flag, replaced the term 'law' with the well-known 'directive' and 'regulation', and renamed the proposed Foreign Minister the 'High Representative of Foreign Affairs'. Furthermore, the mandate stipulated that the Charter of Fundamental Rights of the European Union would be maintained as a separate treaty even though it would remain binding for all member states except the UK. Finally, the mandate divided the remaining text of the Constitutional Treaty back into two Treaties, as they have been the norm since the adoption of the Treaty of Maastricht. Accordingly, there was a Treaty on European Union (TEU), which contained the general regulations regarding the European polity. The second Treaty, named the Treaty on the Functioning of the European Union (TFEU), was conceived to replace the former Treaties on Establishing the European Communities (TEC). Separating and partly renaming the Treaties indicates a hierarchical relationship between them. The status of a constitution can be attributed at most to the TEU as well as the Charter of Fundamental Rights, whereas the TFEU only refers to secondary issues of decision-making and policy implementation.

The mandate made no major modifications to the Constitutional Treaty in terms of the institutional structure of the Union (see Council of the EU, IGC Mandate, No. 11218/07, Brussels, 26 June 2007; and Dinan 2008). It only slightly altered the procedure for majority voting in the Council of Ministers and postponed the introduction of this new scheme until 2014. Moreover, until 2017, a member state can request that the old voting procedure apply. Furthermore, the procedure increased the minimum number of states required to block decisions from four to five, a regulation that particularly benefits the smaller members of the EU. The procedure of 'enhanced cooperation' was reconfirmed and the required threshold of participating states was slightly increased from eight to nine. However, this increase only keeps pace with the 2007 enlargement. The mandate also slightly improved the role of the national parliaments in European decision-making.

With a few exceptions, these modifications are primarily cosmetic. If it can be said that any substantive changes at all were made, they were aimed at strengthening the position of individual states, and at improving the links and feedback mechanisms between the European level and the member states. It is noteworthy, however, that no real fundamental changes to the Constitutional Treaty were made. At most, some of the contested issues were resolved by postponing the date of the entry into force of the new rules.

With these issues already agreed in the mandate for reform, the course was clearly set for the ensuing IGC to be held under a Portuguese presidency. The European Council soon reached a final decision on the Reform Treaties in October 2007 (Dinan 2008). On 13 December of that year, heads of state or government solemnly signed the amendment on the EU Treaties in Lisbon. The Reform Treaty, as it was called at that time, was soon renamed after the location of its conclusion: the Lisbon Treaty. European leaders had succeeded in implementing the reform in time, so that ratification could be completed by January 2009; that is, before the elections to the European Parliament in June of that year.

Given the previous experience with the failures to ratify the Constitutional Treaty, several governments decided against a national referendum on the Lisbon Treaty. They argued that the Lisbon Treaty entailed only minor revisions to the existing Treaties, so explicit public consent was not required. Only the Irish government, according to its own constitutional rules, opted for a referendum. Once again, political elites pushed European integration forward, while pretending that the Lisbon Treaty represented a significant back-pedalling of the Constitutional Treaty.

However, as has happened so often in the history of European integration, events did not unfold as expected. In the referendum on 12 June 2008, a majority of the Irish citizens voted against the Lisbon Treaty (Dinan 2009). Once again, the progress made towards deeper integration ended in stalemate – if not crisis – for the EU. Interestingly, this time the reaction of European elites was different. They did not hesitate to blame Ireland for preventing a Union of 450 million citizens from reaching its goals. Ironically, the opposition forces in Ireland had encouraged people to vote against the Lisbon Treaty by arguing that Ireland, as the sole country in which a referendum was held, had the responsibility to vote on behalf of the 450 million citizens of the EU who were not given a chance to express their voice. Even though the deadline for ratification by January 2009 could now no longer be met, the EU maintained pressure on Ireland to hold a second referendum. The pressure on Ireland was increased by relatively quick parliamentary ratifications of the Lisbon Treaty in most of the member states, including the UK. Renewed negotiations offered some concessions to the Irish public. The concessions contain a declaration that the EU will not interfere in salient issues of Irish domestic policy, including family legislation and Ireland's neutrality in international affairs (Dinan 2009). The Irish government decided to hold a second referendum in November 2009 (Dinan 2010a: 95–6). This time, the Treaty was passed by a majority of the voters. However, the Union's would-be image of a democratic polity, responsive and accountable to the preferences of its citizens, was once again severely damaged. Other member states – in particular, Poland and the Czech Republic – still objected to the ratification of the Lisbon Treaty. Eventually, their reservations were also overcome and the Lisbon Treaty came into force in December 2009, following ratification in all 27 member states (Dinan 2010a).

## Tackling the financial and sovereign debt crisis

The Union appeared to enter a period of calm, following the adoption of the Lisbon Treaty. The new Treaty was seen as a final step in a long phase of Treaty amendments, beginning with the Single European Act in the mid-1980s. With no significant unresolved 'left-overs', the Lisbon Treaty would serve as the constitutional basis of the Union for a long period to come.

In June 2009, a new Parliament was elected, and even though Eurosceptic parties were able to increase their political weight a little, the overall composition of the EP did not change significantly (Dinan 2010a: 101–8). The same could be said of the incoming Commission. Despite critical voices in the EP and only 'lukewarm' support by national governments, Commission President José Manuel Barroso was nominated for a second term (Dinan 2010a: 108–9). Continuity was also reflected in the fact that 14 Commissioners were reappointed by their national governments. In December 2009, the European Council formally nominated Herman van Rompuy as its first permanent President and appointed Catherine Ashton as the High Representative for Foreign and Security Policy (Dinan 2010a: 99–100). With these nominations, the Union further strengthened the intergovernmental capabilities to act. Finally, the politics of enlargement continued, but did not dominate the agenda. In July 2013, Croatia joined the EU as its 28th member, and other states of the former Yugoslavia slowly advanced along the arduous path towards membership.

Things, however, did not stay as calm as expected. Shortly before the final ratification of the Lisbon Treaty in 2008, the financial crisis originating in the US cast a dark cloud over the EU (Menendez 2013: 499–500). In October of that year, the American mortgage system crashed, leading to the collapse of the US based Lehmann Brothers investment bank. The crisis had serious implications for the European banks, many of which are closely intertwined with the American banking and financial system. The member states responded to these events by individually bailing out the banks that were considered to be important to the whole financial system. This meant that states had to spend enormous amounts of public finance – tax-payers' money – to save their banks from bankruptcy. As a consequence, sovereign debt levels increased to unusual levels in most of the EU's member states. This, in turn, undermined the credibility of the Stability and Growth Pact (Dinan 2010a: 112). Still, it appeared that, for the time being, the crisis was contained. There were also small cautious attempts to tackle the financial crisis through joint measures at the European level where political leaders and experts discussed various options for stricter financial market regulation. However, because of the fundamental disagreement among the Union's member states, only a few small steps in this direction were taken (Menendez 2013: 502).

In October 2009, signs of a second, more enduring crisis suddenly loomed. During this month, the newly elected Greek government headed by socialist Prime Minister Giorgos Papandreou announced that his country's public debt to GDP ratio amounted to 12.8 per cent, not the 3.6 per cent the previous conservative government had asserted. This figure was later corrected up to 13.6 per cent (Featherstone 2011: 199). Obviously, the Greek government could no longer repay its enormous debt and Papandreou applied to the EU for support.

In the European Council and the Council, the national governments responded only slowly to Greece's request. It seems that they did not initially grasp the gravity of the problem and, once they did understand the severity, they were reluctant to embark on highly unpopular support measures (Dinan 2010a; Featherstone 2011). This was especially true for German Chancellor Angela Merkel, who delayed any decision about a loan to Greece because of the elections in North-Rhine Westfalia looming in May 2010 (Paterson 2011). Partly because of these delays, financial markets lost confidence in Greece's capacity to repay its debt and interests rates increased enormously, thus aggravating the crisis. Nevertheless, in May 2010 the European Council agreed on a rescue scheme for Greece. The plan envisaged providing extensive loans to the Greek government, while imposing strict terms for cutting public expenditure and implementing fundamental reforms. To this end, with the support of the International Monetary Fund (IMF), the Union established the European Financial Stability Facility (EFSF) as a provisional instrument to provide financial support to debtor states (Gocaj and Meunier 2013).

Soon afterwards, it became clear that not only Greece, but also a number of other members of the Euro-group were having difficulties coping with their massive debt (Menendez 2013: 504). This applied to Ireland, where the recent bail out of the national banks had sharply increased sovereign debt. For different reasons, the Mediterranean member states also faced severe economic problems that placed public expenditure under enormous strain. Rating agencies downgraded the status of these countries and financial markets reacted with sharp increases in interest rates. At this point, political leaders realized that the sovereign debt crisis was not limited to Greece, but had contagious effects on other countries. Accordingly, the crisis quickly escalated to a Euro-crisis requiring swift action.

Although they were not especially quick, the governments of the Euro-zone members and, to an extent, the Union as a whole did respond to the escalating crisis with a series of new measures. These involved small incremental steps, but also some completely new avenues of EMU governance (Hodson 2012a). As early as 2010, the governments amended the procedures for fiscal surveillance in the member states, a process they termed a 'European Semester'. The European Semester involves an annual European-level examination of the member state budgets even before they are discussed and adopted by national parliaments. Both the Commission and the Council may issue non-binding recommendations to the national governments (Hodson 2012a: 186–7). When the European Semester was adopted, the national governments rejected more far-reaching proposals that foresaw quasi-automatic sanctions in cases of violations of the SGP.

However, these measures were not sufficient to diminish the crisis. Greece continued to use extensive loans from the EFSF. Ireland and Portugal also applied for support. Spain and Italy appeared to be in need as well but, for the time being, rejected any assistance in order to avoid the accompanying austerity measures. In light of the increasing demand for assistance, the European Council decided in February 2011 to establish a permanent rescue scheme for highly-indebted states: the European

Stability Mechanism (ESM) (Gocaj and Meunier 2013). The European Council was required to implement a slight Treaty change by adding an annex to Art.136 TFEU (Hodson 2012a: 188) in order to give the ESM a legal basis. In November 2011, the so-called 'six pack' entered into force, a set of five regulations and one directive for reinforcing the SGP and improving the governance of the Euro-zone. Four of these regulations focus on reform of the SGP and envision almost automatic sanctions in case of non-compliance with its rules. The remaining two legislative acts regulate the surveillance of excessive macroeconomic imbalances among the member states (Leuffen *et al*. 2012: 151). Finally, in December 2011, the member states – with the exception of the UK and the Czech Republic – adopted the European Fiscal Compact (EFC). This is a new Treaty requiring strict fiscal austerity by the signatories. This new Treaty on Stability, Co-ordination and Governance (TSCG), as it is officially called, requires member states to translate their commitment to the SGP into national law; the Commission is entitled to monitor compliance with these laws and the Court of the EU can be referred to in case of violation of the Treaty (Hodson 2012a: 189).

Yet, in spite of these far-reaching measures, financial markets did not settle down to any great extent. The crisis continued to threaten the stability of the Euro and, with it, unsettled the political stability of the Union as a whole. It was only at the end of 2011, after Mario Draghi had assumed office as the third president of the European Central Bank (ECB), that the situation improved slightly. One of Draghi's first moves was to provide low-cost loans to recapitalize European banks in order to prevent another systemic crisis in the banking sector (Hodson 2012a: 184). Then, in 2012, he announced intentions to buy an unlimited number of government bonds of indebted and struggling states. Earlier proposals to alleviate the crisis by buying such bonds or issuing Euro-bonds had been outright rejected by national leaders, particularly German Chancellor Angela Merkel (Paterson 2011). However, Draghi's announcement sufficiently calmed the financial markets and partially restored confidence in the EU's ability to rescue the Euro and the highly-indebted states. This, in turn, created room to manoeuvre in order to embark on more long-term steps that would improve the governance of the EMU.

The most important step towards improving the governance of the EMU is the project to create a banking union; that is, an institutional and procedural arrangement that would allow European and national monetary institutions to phase out or close down banks in severe difficulties, rather than requiring national governments to bail these banks out with taxpayers' money. Discussions and the first steps towards implementation had already begun in 2010. However, the proposal provoked major dissent among the member states, which prevented them from taking any strong actions. The large member states, in particular, were and remain quite opposed to any major interventions in their banking sector. Nonetheless, the sovereign debt crisis in Cyprus, which emerged in 2013, really highlighted the importance of regulating the dissolution of banks. In the meantime, the Commission has put forth a directive, together with a regulation, to establish a banking union. Its proposal would allocate extensive powers to the European level, while also drawing the national authorities into the procedure (see European Commission 2012a). A basic decision by the European Council has already been made on these proposals.

Overall, during the last few years, the European leaders have implemented a number of new and, in some cases, far-reaching measures in order to tackle the financial and sovereign debt crisis. Whether these activities will result in enduring success, currently remains unanswered. Scholars from various disciplines have strongly criticized both the initial institutional arrangements that govern EMU, as well as the recently adopted measures aimed at overcoming its weaknesses. They blame the asymmetry that results from European-led monetary integration combined with national responsibility for fiscal and macro-economic stability. These characteristics have underpinned the governance of EMU since its inception (e.g. De Grauwe 2013). Moreover, critics also point to the inconsistency and the ineffectiveness of the actual measures taken to remedy the crisis (e.g. Menendez 2013). In addition, they question the legality of these measures (e.g. Joerges 2012). Many scholars therefore expect that the crisis will endure and Europe's economy will undergo a deep recession.

The crisis, together with the steps taken to try to mitigate it, has had strong repercussions beyond the obvious monetary, fiscal, and broader economic implications. They have had a strong impact on European politics as a whole and the political system of the EU. There has been a slow but steady shift in the balance of power within and among the European institutions and also among the member states. First, the responses to the crisis have increased the voice and authority of the European Council in decision-making. Within the European Council, there has been an increase in the role of the Euro-group which, in turn, has strengthened differentiated integration (Puetter 2012). Second, the Economic and Financial Affairs Council (ECOFIN), and particularly the Euro-group ministers, have become increasingly important, while the role of the General Affairs Council has decreased (Dinan 2011: 104–5). Third, the Commission has been relegated to a minor role, even though it gained a few additional competences in monitoring compliance to the SGP. Fourth, the ECB's mandate has been expanded, partly by charging it with new tasks, but also through its own decisions, which actually transgress the original mandate of the institution. Furthermore, the political weights among the member states have shifted considerably. Large EU members have been able to increase their power over small states; Northern members over the Southern, and creditors over debtors.

According to some observers, Germany has transformed into a hegemonic power, albeit a 'reluctant hegemon' (Paterson 2011). With these shifts, the basic principle of formal equality of all member states regardless of their size, that has underlined European integration since its inception, is being increasingly challenged.

Moreover, the financial and sovereign debt crisis threatens to spillover into a political crisis for the EU. The hard austerity measures imposed on the citizens of the debtor states; the high costs for the creditor states, which could undermine their economic and fiscal stability; and the fact that there is no real end in sight, despite multiple attempts to solve the issues, are all factors that could take a political toll on the Union. In fact, the dimensions and scope of the crisis are not yet fully visible. As Tsoukalis remarks, 'the political and social consequences of financial crises usually follow with a time lag. In Europe, they do not respect national borders, and this is complicating matters further' (Tsoukalis 2011: 26). What is, however, already visible at the member state level is an enormous loss in confidence in the European political institutions – and, to a lesser extent, also in the national political institutions. There is a significant increase in Euro-scepticism; a rise of populist and Euro-sceptic parties – mostly, but not only, on the extreme right of the political spectrum; as well as a general political destabilization within the debtor states (Featherstone 2011; Menendez 2013).

If we attempt to draw together some conclusions about the latter half of the fourth phase of integration, we can see that European integration proceeded with rapid strides, but certainly not without major hurdles. The Union completed an enormous enlargement, nearly doubling its membership. At the same time, it succeeded in implementing an extensive Treaty reform, even though there were significant delays. Furthermore, the Union has tackled the financial and sovereign debt crisis, which, while not to date resolved, is at least contained. Throughout this period, the intergovernmental institutions have taken the lead in consolidating the European polity. This does not mean, however, that the member states have always agreed. On the contrary, the divisions and dissent were as pronounced as ever and, in some cases, even stronger. The enormous enlargements of the past decade, in conjunction with the highly controversial issues that had to be settled during this period, have multiplied the differences in national interests. However, during this phase, the dissent among the member states has not led to overall stagnation, as it did during the second phase of European integration (see Chapter 2). Strong external pressures contributed to joint action, or even unity, as we saw in the case of Eastern enlargement and in the responses to the financial and sovereign debt crisis. In addition, new institutional and procedural arrangements, including the establishment of the Convention; some provisions of the Lisbon Treaty; and the increased use of differentiated integration have either reduced Council bargains to a few, salient issues, or have improved the authority of the Councils and their capacity to act.

Nonetheless, the citizens of Europe, with their widespread scepticism towards widening the Union and deepening integration, have presented a major stumbling block for the activism of European elites. In light of the financial and sovereign debt crisis and the limited capacity of the Union to resolve it, political support for European integration is rapidly withering away. In the future, widespread Euro-scepticism might not only form a stumbling block delaying integration, but may become a major destabilizing force in the European polity.

## Conclusion

In conclusion, we see that the entire fourth phase of European integration is characterized by reinforced intergovernmentalism. In other words, there has been an increased dominance of the national governments and elites in building the Union and in determining its politics and policies. However, the pace and scope of integration have largely been determined by external challenges, rather than any explicit commitment by these elites. During the first part of this phase, national governments were very cautious in their reactions. They reluctantly implemented only small, incremental steps. This was the case both for the Eastern enlargement and the adoption of corresponding Treaty amendments. It was only during the second part of this fourth phase that national governments, driven by external pressures and demands, undertook a fundamental revision of the Treaties and an unparalleled enlargement. Yet, even these measures were only accomplished in fits and starts. This time, it was primarily the scepticism of the European publics that contributed to the stalemate. Many European citizens were displeased with both Eastern enlargement and the proposed European constitution. However, only a few were given the opportunity to voice their dissent through a formal referendum. As a result, European leaders could only widen the Union and deepen integration at the expense of public support. A similar pattern was visible during the most recent period of integration, mainly marked by responses to the financial and sovereign debt crisis. After a few initial and generally cautious steps, the intergovernmental institutions, supported by the ECB, enacted a series of new measures and regulations aimed at containing the crisis. Here, the price was even higher than ever before. A deep distrust about the EU has spread among European citizens, first in the debtor countries, but increasingly it is also taking hold in the creditor states.

Remarkably, other than in the second phase, the process of integration did not slow during the fourth phase of European integration. This difference is a result both of the enormous pressure of external challenges and of the fact that the European polity is now endowed with a more sophisticated spectrum of intergovernmental institutions to facilitate consensus-building. As a result, the process advanced, *even though* the supranational driving forces were clearly weakened. Moreover, national governments used the opportunity of the inevitable enlargement to further improve intergovernmental decision-making in the EU. Thus, in contrast to the 1970s, the EU was now able to combine extensive enlargement with significantly deeper integration. The extent of these changes became quite evident during the financial crisis, when particularly the European Council took the lead in all major decisions.

However, deepening integration through measures that generally strengthen the intergovernmental dimension of the EU has also led to an overall change in direction. The large and, particularly the 'old' member states of the Union have demanded a greater weight in decision-making, which would allow them to take a stronger leadership role. Hence, a number of revisions to the existing Treaties – elaborated, first, in the Constitutional Treaty and then maintained with the adoption of the Lisbon Treaty – were aimed at significantly enhancing the role of the large and 'old' member states (Tömmel 2010). These changes, in turn, reduced the influence of the smaller member states, particularly the accession states, which are nearly all 'small states'. The activities deployed in response to the financial crisis served to translate these provisions into daily practice. The financial crisis also offered ample room to reducing the voice of certain member states through differentiated forms of integration.

Euro-scepticism expressed by the citizens, even in previously integration-minded countries, may in the future prove to be the largest obstacle for further integration. In face of these challenges, European integration might enter a new phase, marked by differentiated forms and varied degrees of participation in integration projects. This may finally result in a multi-speed Europe.

If we take the process of European integration as a whole, we can conclude that the entire process is defined by the characteristics outlined in the conclusions of Chapter 2. In all stages, integration evolves through ups and downs with periods of accelerated integration tending to alternate with periods of relative stagnation. Furthermore, the driving forces of European integration tend to alternate between those pushed by intergovernmentalism and those that advance supranational dynamics. Moreover, there appears to be a strong discrepancy between the elaborate plans for major steps towards further integration and the reality of the rather small, incremental changes. Finally, the process as a whole displays a clear imbalance between those integration projects to which the European leaders can readily agree, such as economic regulation, and those for which a consensus is generally lacking. We can conclude that these four characteristics form the structural features of the process of integration.

Obviously, these four features are highly interdependent. Phases of accelerated integration not only go hand-in-hand with forceful supranational dynamics, but also with generally selective steps towards integration, mainly in the economic domain. Phases of apparent stagnation, in contrast, are characterized by the dominance of intergovernmental forces, and by transforming the approach towards integration. The fourth stage of integration is a bit of an exception to this rule. Only the first part of the phase was marked by a slowdown in integration, whereas its second part clearly displays strong integration steps that were advanced mainly by the intergovernmental institutions and actors. The discrepancy between ambitious projects and their actual implementation accompanies all phases to some degree.

Taken together, these phenomena of European integration constitute a steady process of system-building at the European level, in spite of the repeated shifts in the path. Thus, building the European polity is not a linear process that follows specified goals, defined designs, or clear visions for the project: in practice, objectives, designs, and visions – if elaborated at all – regularly fail to materialize, or prove to be impossible to implement. Hence, the evolution of the EU as a new political order beyond the nation state is frequently hampered by structural constraints. This initially leads to stagnation. However, over time, stagnation can form the starting point for redirecting European integration, and thus transforming and diversifying the original design of the polity. Newly emerging external challenges can also trigger or further reinforce these shifts. Hence, the 'stop-go character' (Sandholtz and Zysman 1989: 99) of the process actually mirrors the alternating phases of accelerated integration in limited policy areas with apparent stagnation which, however, results in a transformation of the model of integration. Both these dynamics of integration successively transform the institutional structure of the European polity, as well as its decision-making procedures.

Furthermore, we can see a further transformation: that of the mode of capitalist regulation as a more long-term, but decisive, factor shaping European integration. Starting in the 1930s, a new mode of regulation emerged, which was defined by increased state interventionism and associated, at least since the 1950s, with Keynesian principles of macroeconomic steering. In the 1970s, this mode of regulation reached its limits in the Western industrialized world. Since then, a process of long-term transformation, aimed at reducing state intervention and liberalizing markets, has taken hold not only nationally, but also on a global scale (Streeck 2013). The most dramatic change in the course of integration, the re-launch of the European project in the mid-1980s, is clearly connected to a choice for a neo-liberal – and, thus, an increasingly transnational – regulation of the economy. This shift may be considered an integral part and expression of a fundamental transformation of the capitalist mode of regulation (Jessop 2003: 204–10).

In conclusion, we must bear in mind that European integration is a process the dynamism of which results from the tension between inter-governmentalism and supranationalism. If a supranational development takes place in limited policy areas, based on a consensus among the member states, in turn, this triggers a tendency towards enhancing inter-governmentalism. This results, first, in improving the corresponding institutional structures and procedures of decision-making and, then, in establishing policies that can accommodate the divergent interests of the member states. This leads to a form of integration which incorporates these differences into the development and structure of the European polity, by envisaging flexible, variable, or differentiated forms of integration. However, each of these steps either serves to reinforce the supranational dynamics of integration, or sets the conditions for them to evolve. Consequently, they give impetus to the gradual and successive transfer of policies and powers to the European level. In addition, they evoke the evolution of decision-making procedures that incorporate an increasing number of actors and which cannot be exclusively controlled by national governments. Finally, they trigger an – apparently inherent – evolutionary dynamic of the European polity. This dynamic seems difficult to slow down or thwart, not least because of the influence of external factors and long-term developmental trends.

Overall, the processes described result in a European-level system that neither replicates national political systems in a supranational form, nor represents a specific model of an international organization. Instead, the EU is best viewed as a political system in which intergovernmental and supranational components are increasingly intertwined and condensed to form a new, dualistic structure. The following chapters analyze this structure and its components in greater depth.

# Chapter 4

---

# The Core Institutional Structure

In the previous chapters, we saw that the political system of the EU unfolded through an ongoing process of institution-building. This led to the emergence of a political order based on both supranational dynamics and intergovernmental configurations. In those chapters, however, we did not analyze this institutional structure in great detail. So, in this chapter we will turn our attention to an in-depth analysis of the core institutional structure of the EU, comprising five primary institutions: the Commission, the Council, the European Council, the Parliament, and the Court of Justice. Four of these institutions were established when the European Communities were founded. These four can be seen as forming the solid core of the European polity. This is not to say that these institutions have never altered their structure and performance. On the contrary, they have significantly grown in size, expanded their competences and scope of action, diversified their institutional structure, and improved their efficiency. Despite these changes, their position within the overall institutional structure of the EU has remained stable. In contrast, the fifth institution, the European Council, was an addition that was undertaken much later. Through a gradual process of consolidation, the European Council eventually became formalized in the Treaties. This was a massive change in the structure of the European Union. It was the heads of state or government who pushed for this change in order to ensure that they would be the ones to guide the European polity, and to provide authority and leadership. The evolution of the European Council is the most prominent example of the continuous reorganization of the EU's institutional structure. As such, an analysis of this institution would also fit well into Chapter 7, which considers the institutional diversification of the European polity. However, because of the significance of the European Council as the supreme authority within the EU, and thus as one of its core institutions, it is analyzed here.

Before turning to the individual institutions of the EU, let us first consider the Union's architecture; that is, how the central institutions are organized in relation to one another. Clearly, this institutional organization is different from other well-known forms of political order, even though it does share some characteristics with them. If we compare the EU to international organizations, we see similarities in the significance of the intergovernmental institutions (the Council and the European Council) within the system. However, in contrast to international organizations, the EU has also a set of supranational institutions (the Commission, the Parliament and the Court) with extensive powers. When we compare the EU to national political systems, we notice that there is a far greater fragmentation of political power among many different institutions. Furthermore, unlike nation states, the Union is defined by the absence of a government or a concentrated locus of executive power. It also lacks a clear separation of powers among its institutions. Thus, the Commission and the Council each hold both legislative and executive powers. However, as with many nation states, the Union has two legislatures – the Council and the Parliament, as well as an independent judiciary – the Court of Justice. Hence, it is clear that the institutional architecture of the EU rests on a unique combination of institutions from both the intergovernmental and the supranational or state-like spectrum. It is thus different from both international organizations and national political systems, yet it also shares some characteristics with these well-known forms of political order. For this reason, I conceptualize the EU as a dualistic system that is characterized by supranational institutions – which serve, first and foremost, to promote or safeguard integration; and by intergovernmental institutions – which steer this process in a direction that is compatible with the interests and preferences of the member states.

In the following sections, I present each institution in greater detail. This includes an analysis of their composition, organizational structure, competences, and their powers. The analysis will highlight the specific role of each institution in the European ensemble, and also the contradictions that characterize each of them. Taken together, this will accurately describe the core institutional structure of the European polity. The following chapters then further elaborate on this image by focusing on the modes of decision-making and interaction among and within the European institutions (Chapters 5 and 6), as well as the diversification of the EU's institutional structure (Chapter 7).

## The European Commission

### Institutional structure and internal organization

According to the Treaties, 'the Commission shall promote the general interest of the Union and take appropriate initiatives to that end' (Art. 17(1) TEU-L). The European Commission is set up as a collegial body:

the College of Commissioners. Since the accession of Croatia in June 2013, it has comprised 28 members. Until recently, the Commission was formed, to a certain extent, according to the principle of proportionality, where the smaller member states were each allocated one Commissioner, while the larger states (Germany, France, Italy, Spain, and the UK) were entitled to two Commissioners each. This format was altered in the Treaty of Nice, in which the principle of 'one Commissioner per country' was adopted (Art. 213 TEC-N). This 'equal' distribution of Commissioners was first applied after the 'big' enlargement in 2004; however, it is doubtful whether it will be sustained. The Lisbon Treaty stipulates that 'the Members of the Commission shall be chosen on the basis of a system of rotation established unanimously by the European Council' (Art. 244 TFEU). The Treaty envisages introducing this rotational system by 2014 (Art. 17(5) TEU-L). This was a controversial point and, after the failure of the Irish referendum on the Lisbon Treaty, the member states agreed to maintain the principle of one Commissioner per country, at least for the time being (Dinan 2010b: 153–4). This decision was a concession to Ireland, but obviously it also suited the other states, particularly the smaller members of the EU.

As a collegial body, the Commission takes collective decisions which, as a rule, only require the consent of a majority of its members (Art. 250 TFEU). The Commission is chaired by a President, who is supported in his work by five vice-presidents. According to the Treaties, the role of the President is that of a *primus inter pares*; that is, first among equals. However, over time, the President has taken on an increasingly prominent position. There are several factors that have contributed to this shift. First, it may be attributed to the Commission's role as a policy initiator (see Chapter 5). Moreover, it results from the personality of the President and from the increasing tasks that the Commission has taken on, not only within the Union, but also in other institutions and organizations. Thus, Jacques Delors was an outstanding President who significantly expanded the function of his office. This subsequently contributed to Treaty amendments (Tömmel 2013a). The Treaty of Amsterdam formally affirmed this position of the President for the first time by assigning him a role in the selection of the Commissioners and defining his leadership more clearly (Art. 214 TEC-A). The Treaty of Nice gave the President the right to ask a Commissioner to resign, but linked this to the approval of the whole College (Art. 217(4) TEC-N). The Lisbon Treaty finally stipulates that the President may request a Commissioner to resign without the approval of the College (Art. 17(6) TEU-L).

In the past, members of the Commission were appointed by the governments of the member states 'by common accord' for a term of five years (Art. 214(2) TEC-N). First, the Council nominated a President; the remaining Commission members were then nominated following consultations with the newly designated President. Beginning with the

Treaty of Maastricht, the Parliament was given a role in the process in which it is asked for a vote of approval (or rejection) on both the President and the entire Commission. This procedure was first applied in 1995. The Treaty of Lisbon fundamentally altered the procedure by stipulating that the European Council 'shall propose to the European Parliament a candidate for President of the Commission. This candidate shall be elected by the European Parliament' (Art. 17(7) TEU-L). Then 'the Council, by common accord with the President-elect, shall adopt the list of the other persons whom it proposes for appointment as members of the Commission. They shall be selected, on the basis of the suggestions made by Member States' (Art. 17(7) TEU-L). Thus, the designated President also has a voice in the appointment of the Commissioners, in order to ensure that a 'collegial body' is formed that is able to work effectively together.

For the most part, the member states are the central actors in the appointment process of the Commission, which helps to ensure them substantial power over this institution. However, individual national preferences and choices are constrained by the necessity of reaching compromises among governments. The nomination of Jacques Santer in 1994, after two candidates had been vetoed, illustrates this constraint. Additional constraints result from incorporating Parliament into the procedure. Although initially the Parliament did not play a decisive role, it could at least trade its approval in exchange for concessions or promises from the incoming Commission to take its preferences into consideration (Lord 2004: 139–43). In some cases, it even succeeded in rejecting a nominated Commissioner, as it did in the case of the incoming Barroso Commission in 2005 (Spence 2006a: 37; Westlake 2006: 267–8). According to the Lisbon Treaty, the Parliament is entitled to elect the Commission President. In practice, this implies that the Parliament has a veto power over any candidate proposed by the European Council. However, the EP attempts to influence the choice of the European Council by proposing possible candidates itself. Further constraints over the member states' powers were first introduced in the Treaty of Nice. This Treaty stipulated that both the President and the Commissioners are to be appointed by the Council by qualified majority (Art. 214(2) TEU-N). This rule effectively removed the veto rights of member states and ensured that individual states could no longer dominate or even block the procedure.

The Commissioners are each assigned a certain area of responsibility which, although it is tempting at first glance, should not be equated with the portfolio of a minister at national level (Spence 2006a; Nugent 2010: 105–8). The differences result, first, from the asymmetrical spectrum of responsibilities of the EU. Most of the responsibilities refer to economic issue areas (see Table 4.1). However, these areas are highly differentiated and thus assigned to a number of Commissioners. In addition, the regulatory effort required to fulfil these tasks is unequally distributed, and many of the tasks are of a somewhat technical nature. Finally, the portfolios of the Commissioners can hardly be compared with those of ministers, as the Commissioners are not granted the exclusive political responsibility for them. Instead, their competence is limited to the preparation of decisions in technical and substantive terms, while the actual decisions are taken by the College of Commissioners. Due to the increase in the number of Commissioners following successive enlargements, the scope of responsibilities of the Union had to be divided into progressively smaller areas, in order to assign every Commissioner a specific portfolio.

The assignment of portfolios is the responsibility of the Commission President, who sometimes has to perform a difficult balancing act. The candidates must be suited for office, the assignment of responsibilities must rotate among the member states, and the prestige of the respective responsibilities has to correspond to the power position of the member states (Spence 2006a: 34–8). As such, it is no surprise that the assignment process often comes down to a 'horse-trade' between the member states and the designated Commission President (Dinan 2010b: 131–2). The Parliament adds to this by using its vote of consent to the Commission as a whole as a means of scrutinizing the qualifications of individual Commissioners (Spence 2006a: 39; Westlake 2006: 267–8). As the 2005 investiture has shown, the Parliament does not shy away from refusing to give its approval to disagreeable candidates.

According to the Treaty, the Commission 'shall be completely independent' and Commissioners may 'neither seek nor take instructions from any Government or other institution, body, office or entity' (Art. 17(3) TEU-L). This requirement is not always easy to uphold in practice. Nonetheless, it appears that holding office as a Commissioner sooner or later leads to a convergence of 'European' attitudes among the members of the College. These tend to predominate over loyalties to their countries of origin. Famous cases of Commissioners who had a distinctly different attitude than the government of their country of origin offer evidence of this. Thus, Lord Cockfield, serving as Commissioner during the first Delors Commission (1985–88), advocated different positions than those of the Thatcher government in numerous cases. The government reacted by not appointing him for a second term (Nugent 1994: 87). There is also no lack of counter-examples. In the past, the larger member states have facilitated the independence of the Commissioners from their home government by often delegating one of the two Commissioner's allocated to them from the opposition parties. However, as the principle of 'one state, one Commissioner' is now the rule, this possibility no longer exists.

The Commission is supported by an administrative service that is currently divided into 33 Directorates-General (DGs) (see Table 4.1) and 11 special services. Their number has increased significantly over time, together with the increase in the policy portfolio of the EU and the

Commission's scope of action. The DGs are organized according to issue areas; this leads to their diversity in terms of size and importance. The majority of the DGs refer to a policy area of the EU; yet, a number of DGs deal with administrative issues (e.g. Budget, Interpretation and Translation), or have a cross-sectional function (e.g. the Secretariat General). Generally, each Commissioner is assigned one larger, or, occasionally, two smaller related Directorates-General. Since the 'big'

**Table 4.1**  *Directorates-General of the European Commission, 2013*

| *Directorates-General* | *Acronym* |
|---|---|
| Agriculture and Rural Development | AGRI |
| Budget | BUDG |
| Climate Action | CLIMA |
| Communication | COMM |
| Communications Networks, Content and Technology | CNECT |
| Competition | COMP |
| Economic and Financial Affairs | ECFIN |
| Education and Culture | EAC |
| Employment, Social Affairs and Inclusion | EMPL |
| Energy | ENER |
| Enlargement | ELARG |
| Enterprise and Industry | ENTR |
| Environment | ENV |
| EuropeAid, Development and Cooperation | DEVCO |
| Eurostat | ESTAT |
| Health and Consumers | SANCO |
| Home Affairs | HOME |
| Humanitarian Aid | ECHO |
| Human Resources and Security | HR |
| Informatics | DIGIT |
| Internal Market and Services | MARKT |
| Interpretation | SCIC |
| Joint Research Centre | JRC |
| Justice | JUST |
| Maritime Affairs and Fisheries | MARE |
| Mobility and Transport | MOVE |
| Regional Policy | REGIO |
| Research and Innovation | RTD |
| Secretariat General | SG |
| Service for Foreign Policy Instruments | FPI |
| Taxation and Customs Union | TAXUD |
| Trade | TRADE |
| Translation | DGT |

*Source:* European Commission 2013a.

enlargement of 2004, the number of Commissioners has surpassed the number of DGs. This meant that, in some cases, Commission members had to share the responsibility for a DG. As a consequence, the number of DGs was recently expanded from 23 to 33, by dividing existing DGs or by transforming special services into DGs.

In addition to the DGs presented in Table 4.1, the High Representative for Foreign Affairs and Security Policy, who simultaneously acts as Commissioner and President of the External Affairs Council, has a specific service at its disposal: the European External Action Service (EEAS). The EEAS consists of both Commission and Council civil servants, as well as diplomats from the member states. It is, thus, more than just a Commission-specific service. Currently, the administrative service of the Commission comprises nearly 27,000 employees (including the translation service). Contrary to many claims, this is actually quite a small number when understood in relation to its responsibilities (see Chapter 11). In fact, the constantly expanding responsibilities of the Commission require the increasing delegation of tasks to other institutions and actors, mostly within the member states (see Chapters 9 and 10).

## Powers

The powers of the Commission can be divided into three categories:

1 Legislative powers.
2 Executive powers.
3 Representative functions.

The *legislative powers* of the Commission primarily include its right to initiate the process of legislation. The Commission drafts and elaborates all legal acts of the Union (Art. 17(2) TEU-L). The Council may not take action except with a proposal from the Commission. However, the Council and the Parliament can request that the Commission formulate a legislative proposal in a specific issue area (Art. 225 and 241 TFEU). The Lisbon Treaty even makes it possible for collective action by one million EU citizens to petition a Commission initiative (Art. 11(4) TEU-L). The Commission's right of initiative also encompasses the right to withdraw a proposal at any stage of the legislative process and, thus, to prevent a Council decision from taking a direction that the Commission would not endorse. The right of initiative therefore actually gives the Commission a broad scope of action. It allows the Commission to shape both the substance of legal texts, and the tools and procedures to elaborate and adopt them (see Chapter 5). Furthermore, the right of initiative allows the Commission, in essence, to determine the agenda of the Council. It even provides ample opportunities to push the process of integration forward, sometimes further than the Council might want. Besides the right to initiate legislation, the Commission may also adopt minor legal acts on its own, such as communiqués, recommendations, and decisions. It can even issue regulations in support of the exercise of its executive tasks. Such regulations can have far-reaching implications, as the case of the liberalization of telecommunication proves (Schmidt 2004).

The *executive powers* of the Commission mainly involve the implementation of legislative decisions that have been adopted by the Council and the Parliament, as well as the implementation of other policy decisions taken by the Council and the European Council. Furthermore, the Commission monitors the implementation of European legislation and other decisions in the member states, insofar as the member states are responsible for it. Yet, the Commission does have fairly direct executive powers with regard to the single market and competition matters. Its tasks in these areas range from ensuring the implementation of the respective European legal framework to monitoring compliance with the competition rules. The latter responsibility includes fighting monopolies and cartels, as well as unjustified state aid, and controlling mergers and acquisitions (see McGowan 2005; Cini and McGowan 2008; Lehmkuhl 2009; Wilks 2010). Furthermore, the Commission fulfils a broad range of executive functions, including the administration of various funds and financial instruments (e.g. Agricultural Funds, Structural Funds, as well as smaller-scale or pilot programmes in diverse policy areas). Although the implementation of the related projects and programmes is actually the responsibility of the member states, the Commission plays a significant role by taking decisions about the distribution of subsidies and an array of accompanying measures.

The *representative functions* of the Commission pertain primarily to foreign affairs and, especially, the external trade relations of the EU. In addition, the Commission represents the Community or the Union in accession or association negotiations with third countries, as well as in international organizations. Although the Commission must initially be vested with a Council mandate, it can then act largely independently within international organizations, at least insofar as external trade issues are concerned.

In summary, the Commission appears to be a unique institution marked by a number of contradictions. It is vested with extensive legislative and executive powers, but it can only exercise them in cooperation with the Council and the Parliament, a constellation that significantly constrains its potential power. It is designed to be a highly-independent institution, as the member states may not give it instructions and the Parliament cannot exert extensive control over it. Nevertheless, due to its incomplete powers, it is dependent on the member states in two ways. In the legislative process, it is dependent on the decisions of the Council (and, increasingly, also the European Parliament). In the process of policy implementation, it is dependent on the performance of the governments and administrations in the individual member states.

## The Council

### Institutional structure and internal organization

The Council of Ministers – or the Council of the European Union, as it has been called since the Treaty of Maastricht – is one of the EU's legislatures. Since the Treaty of Lisbon came into force, it shares this legislative function with the Parliament (Hayes-Renshaw and Wallace 2006; Nugent 2010: 139–60). However, besides its legislative powers, it decides also on major and minor policy issues and, when necessary, also on fundamental matters in European affairs. The 28 current member states are equally represented in the Council of Ministers. Each state has one representative who is, as a rule, a national-level minister or deputy minister with corresponding competences (Art. 16(2) TEU-L). Hence, large and small states have equal representation, even though, as we shall see, their votes are weighted differently (see Table 4.2).

In practice, the Council consists of an array of Councils. First, the foreign ministers of the member states convene in two formations, the General Affairs Council, and the Foreign Affairs Council, according to the issues at hand (Art. 16(6) TEU-L). These Councils are, respectively, responsible for fundamental issues concerning European integration, and foreign policy. In addition, there are a number of specific Councils consisting of the ministers for various portfolios that deal with the respective policy areas. The most important of these Councils, and one that has a long history, is the Economic and Financial Affairs Council (ECOFIN). This body has been involved in determining the fate of the EC since its inception. Beginning in the 1990s, ECOFIN has been in charge of creating and monitoring EMU (for details, see Chapter 7). Another long-standing Council, formed in the early years of the Community, is the Agriculture and Rural Development Council. Other Councils – such as those for Environment, Transport, or Spatial Planning – emerged more recently, as corresponding policy areas were increasingly Europeanized. By the end of the 1990s, the number of Council formations had risen to 22, covering the entire spectrum of national ministries and the related policy areas (all figures obtained from: Council of the European Union 2013a). In face of this growth, heads of state or government attempted to rein in the uncontrolled expansion of the Council configurations. In June 2000, they decided to reduce the number of Councils to 16; in June 2002, they further reduced it to 9. Since the Lisbon Treaty has come into force, the Council has convened in 10 formations, as shown in Table 4.2.

Table 4.2    *Council formations, 2013*

| |
|---|
| General Affairs |
| Foreign Affairs |
| Economic and Financial Affairs |
| Justice and Home Affairs |
| Employment, Social Policy, Health and Consumer Affairs |
| Competitiveness (Internal Market, Industry, Research and Space) |
| Transport, Telecommunications and Energy |
| Agriculture and Fisheries |
| Environment |
| Education, Youth, Culture and Sport |

*Source:* Council of the EU 2013a.

The most important Councils convene nearly every month in Brussels, except for three months of the year, when they hold their meetings in Luxembourg. This last provision is a concession to national governments who, in the early years of integration, requested that meetings and common institutions be dispersed across the member states. The other Councils meet only several times a year. The Presidency of the Council is assigned to one member state for a period of six months (Art. 16(9) TEU-L and 236 TFEU). Only the Foreign Affairs Council is an exception to this rule, as it is permanently presided over by the High Representative for Foreign Affairs. Originally, the sequence of the rotating Presidency was based on alphabetical order. However, with successive enlargements, it is increasingly being modified to allow the Presidency to swing between small and large states, as well as old and new members (Hayes-Renshaw and Wallace 2006: 139). In order to ensure a degree of continuity despite the short duration of the Presidency, a troika system was established. In the troika system, the previous and subsequent Presidencies support the current Presidency in its activities. This solution was considered to be preferable to lengthening the term of the Presidency, as a longer term would mean that each state would only rarely have a turn at holding the Presidency. The Convention launched the proposal to assign the Council Presidency to a member state for at least one year by means of an electoral procedure (Crum 2004). This proposal, however, was not accepted by the governments of the member states. They favoured a modified troika principle, which would entrust a group of three states with a joint presidency for 18 months. Yet, even this modified proposal was not included in the final version of the Lisbon Treaty.

The Council is supported by a Secretariat General in Brussels that employs about 3500 civil servants. Its civil service is much smaller than that of the Commission. A large share of the civil service is employed in translation services, so the number of officials dealing with substantive issues is quite small, particularly in comparison with the number of Commission officials. The Secretariat General prepares the meetings of the Council and its committees, as well as their decisions; it also takes care of all the administrative matters related to the meetings (translations, and so on) (Hayes-Renshaw and Wallace 2006: 101–4).

Furthermore, a Committee of Permanent Representatives – known as COREPER, drawing on the French acronym – acts as a comprehensive support structure to the Council. Moreover, every member state has a Permanent Representation (PR) to the EU in Brussels. Each of these bodies is comparable to an Embassy. The members of the various national PRs work together in COREPER, essentially creating a Council *en miniature*. Together, they prepare all the decisions of the Councils. Over time, the number of staff of the PRs has increased significantly, together with the expansion of the competences and activities of the European polity, and the workload of the Councils. Germany's PR is the largest, with 138 staff members; the PR of Luxembourg amounts to 31 civil servants (Lewis 2012: 321). The Committee of Permanent Representatives is divided into two parts, COREPER I and COREPER II. While COREPER I deals primarily with economic and adjacent policies, COREPER II focuses on political issues in a more narrow sense (i.e. foreign policy), but also deals with major integration initiatives (Lewis 2012: 319). Accordingly, COREPER I is designated as the 'technical committee' and COREPER II as the 'political committee'. As a rule, COREPER I consists of the Deputy Permanent Representatives, while COREPER II is run by the Permanent Representatives of the member states to the EU. The work of COREPER is, in turn, prepared either by working groups, or by parties that are set up for individual policy or issue areas. These working groups usually consist of staff from the PRs; they sometimes also include civil servants from national ministries. In 2013, there were 213 of these working groups (including subgroups) (Council of the European Union 2013b). According to Häge (2012: 23), their number has significantly decreased from 298 in the year 2000 and 254 in 2005. Häge ascribes this decrease to a process of rationalization that resulted in the abolition of some groups and the consolidation of others. It, furthermore, represents the need to bring the working groups in line with the reduced number of Council formations (Häge 2012: 23). In any event, the decreased number of the working parties is not a sign of their reduced importance but, rather, indicates efforts to improve their efficiency. Interestingly, the number of working parties diverges considerably across Council formations and, thus, policy areas. Agriculture and Fisheries has the lead with 81 groups and subgroups, followed by Foreign Affairs with 36, Justice and Home Affairs with 19, and General Affairs with 18 groups. Council formations referring to Employment or Environment are only supported by 4 and 2 groups, respectively (all figures obtained from: Council of the European Union 2013b). The number of working parties thus not only reflects the workload of different Council formations, but also the extent to which the respective issue areas are contested among the member states.

## Powers and voting procedures

The responsibilities of the Council are relatively clearly defined: it is one of the two legislative bodies of the EU. However, the legislative role is restricted to a certain extent as the Council can only take action on a proposal of the Commission, though, as we saw above, it may call on the Commission to make such proposals (Art. 241 TFEU). Furthermore, since the introduction of the co-decision procedure in the Treaty of Maastricht, and its subsequent transformation into the ordinary procedure of legislation through the Lisbon Treaty, the Council is further restricted. The ordinary legislative procedure constrains the Council to pass laws only with the approval of the Parliament (see Chapter 5). The Council is, moreover, responsible for coordinating the economic policies of the member states, a function that has been significantly upgraded with the Treaty of Maastricht and the establishment of monetary union. The Treaty enables the Council, following the Commission issuing 'warnings', to give 'recommendations' to the member states, and even to impose sanctions in cases of non-compliance (Art. 121(4) and 126(11) TFEU; see also Verdun 2009). The Council also has the power to make appointments to some of the European institutions, including the European Economic and Social Committee (EESC), the Committee of the Regions (CoR), and the European Court of Auditors (ECA). Furthermore, it has budgetary authority, in that the Council draws up the budget on a proposal of the Commission which must, however, be approved by the Parliament. Finally, the Council is the institution that concludes agreements with third states or international organizations (Borchardt 2010: 57).

The voting procedures in the Council, although fairly clearly defined, are rather complicated (Borchardt 2010: 59–61). The Council takes decisions by simple majority, with every state having one vote. However, this procedure applies only in those areas where the Treaties do not explicitly specify a different procedure. Yet, in most cases, the Treaties specify otherwise. Currently, qualified majority voting applies to most policy areas, and unanimity is required for certain sensitive areas – in particular, those that affect fundamental issues or vital interests of the member states. In the original EC Treaties, it was assumed that, after a certain transitional period, qualified majority voting would become the norm. However, the 'empty chair politics' of French President De Gaulle in the 1960s meant that unanimity was the general rule for a long time It was only with the adoption of the SEA (1986) that qualified majority voting was significantly expanded. This marked a fundamental turning point in the process of integration (see Chapter 2).

Ever since the founding of the Communities, whenever qualified majority voting has been required, the votes of the member states have been weighted (Art. 205 TEC-N), so as to roughly approximate the population of the member states (Table 4.3). In the past, the large states had 10 votes each, whereas the smaller states were given between 2 and 5 votes. The Treaty of Nice shifted the weighting in favour of the large member states, as the Council anticipated that there would be an over-representation of the smaller states as a result of Eastern enlargement (Table 4.3). In strictly formal terms, even this system privileged the small states. On the one hand, one could argue that this was necessary in order to protect their vital interests. On the other hand, the idea of weighted votes (as opposed to the principle 'one country, one vote' prevalent in international organizations) can also be seen as a means of protecting the interests of the large states, since it is difficult for the small states to out-vote the large ones. When Croatia joined the EU in 2013, it was assigned 7 votes (Table 4.3). This increased the total votes to 352. Since that time, 260 votes (or 70 per cent) have been required for a qualified majority. Conversely, a positive decision can be prevented with 92 votes. Thus, in order to form a blocking minority, at least three large and one small, or four or more larger and smaller states are needed.

However, the Lisbon Treaty outlines a fundamentally modified voting system. According to these provisions, every member state has just one vote. A qualified majority is reached when the positive votes represent 55 per cent of the member states, constituting at least 15 states, and 65 per cent of the population of the Union (Art. 16(4) TEU-L and Art. 238(3) TFEU). Conversely, a blocking minority must represent at least 35 per cent of the Union's population plus one additional member state. These provisions come into effect in 2014; they significantly lower the threshold for qualified majority voting and, thus, are anticipated to facilitate decision-making in the Council.

Overall, the voting procedures in the Council of Ministers reflect a difficult trade-off between purely intergovernmental principles ('one country, one vote', but also the *de facto* veto of one state in the case of unanimous decisions) and more efficient decision-making in the interest of a well-functioning and swiftly acting Union (majority voting, weighting of the votes, taking into account the size of a state in terms of population). While intergovernmental principles dominated in the early phases of integration – and, in particular, after the intervention of De Gaulle in the 1960s – they were steadily pushed back by the successive Treaty revisions in favour of more efficient modes of decision-making. Nevertheless, even the simplified voting procedure, as stipulated by the Lisbon Treaty, will require sophisticated techniques of forging compromises and consensus (see Chapter 6).

Table 4.3    *Voting weights in the Council of the European Union, 1995–2014*

| Member state | Votes per state 1995–2004 | Votes per state 2004–2014 |
|---|---|---|
| Germany | 10 | 29 |
| France | 10 | 29 |
| Italy | 10 | 29 |
| United Kingdom | 10 | 29 |
| Poland | – | 27 |
| Spain | 10 | 27 |
| Romania | – | 14 |
| Belgium | 5 | 13 |
| Czech Republic | – | 13 |
| Greece | 5 | 12 |
| Hungary | – | 12 |
| Netherlands | 5 | 12 |
| Portugal | 5 | 12 |
| Austria | 4 | 10 |
| Bulgaria | – | 10 |
| Sweden | 4 | 10 |
| Croatia | – | 7 |
| Denmark | 3 | 7 |
| Finland | 3 | 7 |
| Ireland | 3 | 7 |
| Lithuania | – | 7 |
| Slovakia | – | 7 |
| Cyprus | – | 4 |
| Estonia | – | 4 |
| Latvia | – | 4 |
| Luxembourg | 2 | 4 |
| Slovenia | – | 4 |
| Malta | – | 3 |
| EU Total | 87 | 352 |
| Qualified Majority | | 260 |

*Sources:* 1995–2004: Art. 205(2), TEC-A, 2004-2014: TEC-N, Declaration on the Enlargement of the European Union; Treaty concerning the accession of Croatia, Art. 20.

In conclusion, the Council of Ministers in its structure, composition, responsibilities, and procedures of decision-making appears to be a well-defined institution. On closer examination, however, its heterogeneous structure becomes apparent. This heterogeneity results not only from the increasing number of member states in the Council and the conflicting interests they represent, but also from the variety of individual Councils that deal with highly-divergent policy areas. The heterogeneity is further increased by the rotating Presidency, which allows every member state to define the agenda and profile of the Council for a short period of time.

Finally, it is reflected in the complicated decision-making procedures, which are supposed to take interests of every individual state into account, while also ensuring that integration continues to progress. Consequently, the Council, with its prominent functions in legislation and policy-making, is also an institution marked by contradictions. It does not simply have the task of deciding on the legislative proposals drawn up by the Commission. Above all, it is structured in a way that allows for differentiated procedures of weighing and mediating the often highly-divergent interests of the member states and the constituencies that the states each represent. It is therefore the dominance of national interests that shapes the institutional structure and modes of operation of the Council, while the pursuit of the common interest in promoting integration is, in the main, delegated to the Commission. However, a series of reforms – such as the introduction, expansion, and significant facilitation of qualified majority voting – indicate that the pursuit of the common interest of the member states in fostering integration is increasingly being taken over by the Council of Ministers (Tömmel 2010).

## The European Council

While four of the five institutions described in this chapter have been a part of the EU's institutional structure since the founding of the European Communities, the European Council is a true institutional innovation that has slowly developed over time. This innovation not only expanded the EU's core institutions from four to five, but altered the whole architecture of the European polity. In fact, the European Council significantly strengthens the intergovernmental dimension of the Union. More importantly, it constitutes a body that acts as the overarching authority of the entire system. However, such an institutional suprastructure was not envisaged with the original design of the EC/EU. It only emerged over time (Hayes-Renshaw and Wallace 2006: 165–7; De Schoutheete 2012: 45–6). As a result of the process of ever closer integration, European leaders recognized a need to institutionalize a high-level arena for intergovernmental bargains and consensus-building among the member states. To this end, they established the European Council through a piecemeal, incremental process. The Lisbon Treaty, for the first time, devotes an entire article to the European Council as one of the EU's institutions (Art. 15 TEU-L). This marks the culmination of this gradual evolution.

The first steps in the long process of establishing the European Council date as far back as the late 1950s. In 1959, French president De Gaulle already suggested establishing meetings of the heads of state or government every three months. The work around these meetings was to be supported by a permanent secretary. However, the other member states rejected this plan (Urwin 1993: 86). It was only after the resignation of De Gaulle that such meetings were occasionally held. Starting in 1969, summit meetings of the heads of state or government led to far-reaching decisions that contributed significantly to the evolution and advancement of European integration. For example, the Hague Summit of 1969 proposed the first enlargement of the Communities and developed a plan for a monetary union (Dinan 2004a: 129). Another summit, held in Paris in 1972, took the final decision on enlarging the EC with the UK, Denmark and Ireland, and also decided to expand European policies (Dinan 2004a: 145). The first enlargement of the EC (1973), in turn, triggered the initiative of French President Giscard d'Estaing at the Paris Summit of 1974 to institutionalize summit meetings as regular events. These meetings were established under the name 'European Council' (Dinan 2004a: 126). Initially, heads of state or government agreed on a minimum of three annual meetings; later (1985), they reduced the number of meetings to two, taking place at the end of every Council Presidency (Urwin 1993: 174). Presently, four meetings generally take place each year. Additional meetings can be convened, if necessary.

The establishment of the European Council not only improved inter-governmental decision-making, but also created 'the key EU decision-making body' (Dinan 2012: 34). It thus vested the Communities and later the Union with a true 'locus of power' (Hayes-Renshaw and Wallace 2006: 165). The status of the European Council was formalized for the first time with the Maastricht Treaty (Art. D TEU-M), a step that affirmed its role as the central authority of the Union. The Treaty states: 'The European Council provides the Union with the necessary impetus for its development' and defines the 'general political guidelines' (Art. D, TEU-M).

The authority of the European Council has been strengthened in additional Treaty modifications. Most important in this context are the provisions of the Lisbon Treaty. This Treaty, for the first time, mentions the European Council as one of the EU's institutions (Art. 13(1) and 15 TEU-L). Before, the European Council was silently subsumed under the term 'Council' and thus, in fact, defined as a specific Council formation. Accordingly, the earlier Treaties mention in different articles 'the Council, meeting in the composition of the Heads of State or Government' (see e.g. Art. 11(2), 121(2-4) and 122(2) TEC-A).

The Lisbon Treaty furthermore establishes a new position of permanent President of the European Council (De Schoutheete 2012: 48). In the past, the government that held the rotating presidency of the Council was also responsible for the European Council. Now, the President is elected by a qualified majority of the European Council for a term of two-and-a-half years, with the possibility of reappointment (Art. 15(5) TEU-L). The President is expected to be an outstanding personality (Borchardt 2010: 53). His (or, perhaps in the future, her) extensive tasks are defined in the Treaty as follows: He shall chair the meetings of the European Council and 'drive forward its work, ... ensure the preparation and continuity of its work, ... endeavour to facilitate cohesion and consensus within the European Council, ... present a report to the European Parliament after each of the meetings, ... ensure the external representation of the Union on issues concerning its common foreign and security policy' (Art. 15(6) TEU-L).

With the creation of this position, heads of state or government clearly intended to give the European Council additional political weight (Tömmel 2010). Borchardt emphasizes that the 'President of the European Council, unlike the former rotating Presidency, has a European mandate, and not a national one' (Borchardt 2010: 53). In the past, when the European Council was chaired by the head of state or government of the state that also held the presidency of all Council formations, there were often concerns that the presidency was marred by national interests. A famous and deplorable example is the European Council of Nice, which was chaired by French President Chirac, who strongly defended national interests, especially during the negotiations around the weighting of votes in the Council (Gray and Stubb 2001; Schout and Vanhoonakker 2006). Hence, the Lisbon Treaty clearly states: 'The President of the European Council shall not hold a national office' (Art. 15(6) TEU-L). Endowed with a European mandate, the President can set the agenda of the European Council, facilitate and improve decision-making and consensus-building within this body and, on the whole, improve its capacity to act (Blavoukos *et al.* 2007). Overall, as a result of these institutional changes, the European Council now, more than ever, is empowered collectively to exercise leadership in the EU, and to determine the pace and scope of integration (Tömmel 2010). This, in turn, implies that it is also empowered to contain any undesired activism of the Commission, and even to encroach on the latter's role of 'motor of integration', as we have seen from the European Council's extensive involvement in the financial and sovereign debt crisis (for details, see Chapter 7).

The European Council is composed of the heads of state or government, its elected President, and the President of the European Commission. 'When the agenda so requires, the members of the European Council may decide each to be assisted by a minister and, in the case of the President of the Commission, by a member of the Commission' (Art. 15(3) TEU-L). Before the enactment of the Lisbon Treaty, it had become common practice for the Ministers of Foreign Affairs to take part in the summit meetings also. However, after the enlargements of 2004 and 2007, this would have meant holding meetings with more than 50 delegates. This did not appear to be manageable, particularly when highly contentious issues were on the agenda. Therefore, the Lisbon Treaty envisages that ministers can attend, but this is not a requirement.

The first elected President of the European Council, former Belgian Prime Minister Herman van Rompuy, announced immediately after his nomination that, as a rule, foreign ministers should not participate in the meetings (Kietz and van Ondarza 2010).

The Lisbon Treaty also confirmed the practice that 'The European Council shall meet twice every six months' (Art. 15(3) TEU-L), or four times in a year. The Nice Summit in 2000 had decided that all regular scheduled meetings of the European Council should take place in Brussels, instead of in the country holding the presidency. This decision was taken on a proposal of COREPER, the 'power behind the Council throne' (Dinan 2001: 33). Clearly, COREPER intended not only to improve the quality of the Council's work, but also to improve its own position (Dinan 2001: 33). Starting in 2003, the European Council used to convene in Brussels, except for a few informal meetings. Since 2009, both formal and informal meetings take place in Brussels.

In summary, we see that the evolution of the European Council as the fifth core institution of the EU has been an extremely important development within the European polity. This Council has established itself as the supreme authority in the Union for both striking the final bargains in contested issue areas and providing direction and leadership to the whole integration process. The Lisbon Treaty confirmed this important position by formally including the European Council as one of the EU's core institutions. The Treaty further confirmed this importance by establishing a permanent presidency, which is intended to enhance the European Council's capacity to act and to alleviate the problems of collective action that such an intergovernmental body clearly faces (Tallberg 2006). The increased and intense activities of the European Council and its permanent President during the recent financial crisis did prove the importance of this body in coping with exceptional challenges and threats to the EU. However, in spite of the institutional innovations of the Lisbon Treaty and the ensuing forceful practice, the European Council remains torn between contradictory objectives. On the one hand, it constitutes the top-level arena for bargains among the member states; on the other hand, it aspires to provide leadership to the Union, a role that is hard to reconcile with the omnipresent intergovernmental dissent.

## The European Parliament

### Size, election procedures and organization

In the words of the Lisbon Treaty, the European Parliament is 'composed of representatives of the Union's citizens' (Art. 14(2) TEU-L). ). Previously, the Treaties defined the EP as consisting 'of representatives of the peoples of the States brought together in the Community' (Art. 189

TEC-N). Thus, with the Lisbon Treaty, the citizens of the EU are assumed to form one electorate, even though elections are still held separately in each member state (see pp. 104–5).

It is interesting to note that, although the EP gave itself this name in 1958, it was not until the Treaty of Maastricht that the name 'European Parliament' was officially accepted (Borchardt 2010: 45). Before this Treaty revision, the body's official name was Assembly. The successive enlargements of the EC/EU and the increasing significance of the EP within the European polity have led to its gradual expansion in size. The Assembly started in 1958 with 142 seats; the first enlargement led to an increase to 198, and the introduction of direct elections in 1979 more than doubled the number of seats to 410. Successive enlargements further increased the number to 518 (Southern enlargement), then 567 (German reunification) and 626 members (Northern enlargement). In the face of Eastern enlargement, European leaders perceived the need to restrict the size of the EP, but an agreement on this issue was difficult to achieve. The Lisbon Treaty finally stipulates a maximum of 750 seats plus the President (Art. 14(2) TEU-L).

However, with the most recent elections to the EP held in 2009, just before the Lisbon Treaty came into force, the Parliament encompassed 785 members, elected on the basis of specified quotas for each member state. The accession of Croatia in July 2013 brought another 12 members into the EP so, in reality, it is much larger than the Treaty of Lisbon would dictate. To rectify this, it has been necessary to revise the distribution of seats among the member states before the elections of 2014. This has been undertaken in full respect of the principle of degressive proportionality, which was also laid down in the Treaty (Art. 14(2) TEU-L; see also Duff 2010: 38–40). Degressive proportionality means that less populous states are allocated comparatively more seats than more populous states. However, this principle is not always easy to implement. Demographic change may alter the proportions between states (Duff 2010: 38). Moreover in the past, the principle of degressive proportionality has not always been strictly respected. States often bargained for more seats in relation to other states and there has been a degree of success in this strategy, as evidenced by Spain and Poland in the Nice negotiations (see Chapter 3). Table 4.4 presents the new distribution of seats for the term 2014–2019, as elaborated by the EP and adopted by the European Council.

According to this revised scheme, Germany has the largest number of members with 96 delegates. Cyprus, Estonia, Luxembourg and Malta have the fewest representatives, with only 6 members each. The over-representation of the smaller states primarily serves to ensure an appropriate size of a national delegation, which should adequately represent the entire party spectrum and participate at least in the most important Parliamentary committees (Lord 2004: 104–5).

**Table 4.4**   *Number of seats in the European Parliament by member state, term 2014-2019*

| Member state | Seats |
| --- | --- |
| Germany | 96 |
| France | 74 |
| Italy, United Kingdom | 73 |
| Spain | 54 |
| Poland | 51 |
| Romania | 32 |
| Netherlands | 26 |
| Belgium, Greece, Portugal, Czech Republic, Hungary | 21 |
| Sweden | 20 |
| Austria | 18 |
| Bulgaria | 17 |
| Denmark, Finland, Slovakia | 13 |
| Ireland, Croatia, Lithuania | 11 |
| Slovenia, Latvia | 8 |
| Estonia, Cyprus, Luxembourg, Malta | 6 |
| Total | 751 |

*Source:* European Parliament, 2013a.

The members of the Parliament (MEP) are elected for a period of five years. Although the Treaties provide for general Europe-wide elections, to date the elections have always been held separately in each member state. As a result, every country elects its own national delegation according to the existing party spectrum and national electoral procedures (Duff 2010: 58–63). For example, until 1999, European elections in the UK were based on a system of majority voting. However, this tended to return a very unequal representation where one of the two main parties always dominated and the smaller parties were not represented at all. When the Labour government took office in 1997, the UK switched to a system of proportional representation for EP elections (as of 1999). Since then, the UK has been represented by 9 parties in the EP. In 11 member states, a minimum threshold (usually between 3 per cent and 5 per cent) applies for the allocation of seats. As a result, in these countries smaller party groups have difficulties winning a seat. Of the member states, 22 constitute a single constituency. The remaining 6 states (Belgium, France, Ireland, Italy, Poland, and the UK) are divided into a number of regional constituencies. This arguably allows for a closer relationship between MEPs and their electorate.

The various electoral procedures also result in a parliamentary arena that is characterized by an extremely broad and heterogeneous spectrum of parties (Hix and Lord 1997; Hix *et al.* 2007; McElroy and Benoit 2010). In practice, closely related parties cooperate to form transnational party groups but the groups remain, nevertheless, very heterogeneous according to the different national traditions and political cultures. In an attempt to develop a more 'European' Parliament, the Treaty of Amsterdam laid down provisions for the introduction of a Union-wide electoral procedure (Art. 190(4) TEC-A). The respective proposals elaborated by the Parliament have not yet resulted in the adoption of such a procedure (Duff 2010).

The Parliament is chaired by a President, who is supported by 14 vice-presidents and accompanied by six quaestors, who hold an advisory role (Borchardt 2010: 46). This group of office-holders forms the Presidency of the European Parliament; it sets the agenda and determines the modes of procedure for the plenary meetings.

## Powers

The powers of the Parliament can be divided into five areas (Borchardt 2010: 46–50, Dinan 2010b: 252–58; Nugent 2010: 179–89):

1 Legislative powers.
2 Budgetary powers.
3 Supervisory powers.
4 Powers of consent in foreign affairs.
5 Powers of approval.

In European *legislation*, for a long time, the Parliament held only an advisory function. In practice, this meant that the Parliament had to be consulted on all proposals of the Commission and that it was offered the opportunity to give its opinions. However, the Council was by no means obliged to take the opinions of the Parliament into account. Council frequently even took decisions before the Parliament had had a chance to give its opinion. This situation changed with the SEA. Under this Treaty, the Parliament was granted, for the first time, a limited say in legislation through the introduction of the 'co-operation procedure' (Art. 189c TEC-M). This procedure provides for two readings of legislative proposals in the Parliament. If Parliament rejects or amends a proposal by absolute majority during the second reading and the Commission does not accept the amendments of the EP, then the Council can only out-vote the position of the Parliament through a unanimous decision. Otherwise, the proposal is rejected. Although this new procedure did not really grant the Parliament extensive decision rights, it did help the Parliament to gain a strong bargaining position with regard to the Council. This has proved itself to be especially true in cases where the Council was internally divided, as is so often the case. In these situations, the Parliament could achieve considerable concessions in line with its own preferences and options.

The Treaty of Maastricht further strengthened the Parliament's role by introducing the co-decision procedure (Art. 189b TEC-M). This procedure stipulates that there be three readings of legislative acts. If the Parliament rejects a proposal by absolute majority during the second reading, a Conciliation Committee, consisting of representatives of the Council and Parliament, is convened. If the Conciliation Committee cannot reach an agreement, then the Parliament may ultimately reject the proposal during the third reading by an absolute majority (for details, see Chapter 5). This procedure grants Parliament a veto power that allows it to stop, or to threaten to stop, the legislative process if it does not agree with a proposal. Thus, the co-decision procedure puts a great deal of pressure on all the involved parties to reach compromises and consensus (Corbett 2007).

Initially, both the cooperation and co-decision procedures only applied to specific policy areas. This limited scope considerably constrained the Parliament's newly acquired powers However, Parliament's legislative powers continued to grow under the Treaties of Amsterdam and Nice, which expanded the co-decision procedure to a significant number of new areas. The co-operation procedure was largely repealed. As a result, as long as the Parliament itself could reach a common position, it could exert substantial influence on legal acts in a broad array of issue areas.

The most recent Treaty revision has since transformed the Parliament into a fully-fledged legislature alongside the Council. The Lisbon Treaty stipulates: 'the European Parliament shall, jointly with the Council, exercise legislative and budgetary functions' (Art. 14(1) TEU-L). Moreover, instead of the co-decision procedure, the Treaty refers to this process as the 'ordinary procedure of legislation' and expands it to almost all legislative acts of the Union. There remain a few exceptions that are decided by the 'special legislative procedure'. Thus, after a long period of a subordinate position, the Parliament has finally acquired a position that gives it an equal role with the Council in legislative matters. However, as with the Council, the Parliament is not entitled to elaborate legislative proposals; it may only 'request' that the Commission submit such proposals (Art. 225 TFEU).

The Parliament's *budgetary powers* are also quite extensive. Since the 1970s, the European Parliament has been authorized to decide on the non-compulsory expenditures of the EC. Non-compulsory expenses comprise those that are not specified in the Treaties – including, for example, expenditures for cohesion policy, developmental policy, assistance measures for Eastern transition states and, in general, a broad range of support measures. With the Treaty of Lisbon, the EP gained the right to decide, jointly with the Council, on all expenditures of the EC

(Art. 14(1) TEU-L; and Art. 310 and 314 TFEU). This implies that compulsory and non-compulsory expenditures will no longer be considered separately (Borchardt 2010: 50) and that the EP will also decide, for example, on expenditures for agricultural policy. Parliament also adopts or rejects the annual draft budget of the Union (Art. 314 TFEU) and gives final approval to the Commission on the implementation of the annual budget (Art. 319 TFEU). As in legislative matters, the EP is now on equal footing with the Council in budgetary issues as well.

Whereas Parliament has gained far-reaching legislative and budgetary powers, its *powers of supervision and control* are comparatively weak (Westlake 2006: 267). Parliament's powers in this area are mostly directed towards the performance of the Commission. In general, Parliament is limited to indirect mechanisms of control, such as questions and hearings (Judge and Earnshaw 2003: 234–41). The Parliament is also allowed to investigate potential Commission misconduct through committees of inquiry (Art. 226 TFEU). In case of misconduct of the Commission, the Parliament can, with a majority of two thirds, pass a vote of censure that would require the Commission to resign collectively (Art. 17(8) TEU-L and Art. 234 TFEU; see also Borchardt 2010: 50). This right has never been used, but the threat of using it led to the resignation of the Commission in 1999 (Judge and Earnshaw 2003: 227–30).

The Parliament is also granted specific, though limited, *powers of consent* in external affairs. In particular, it has the right of consent to all important EU international agreements, and to the accession of new member states to the Union (Art. 49 TEU-L and 218 TFEU). These rights give the Parliament veto powers that may be used to compel other institutions to take the preferences of the Parliament into account in related treaties and agreements (Westlake 2006: 269).

Finally, the *powers of approval* of the Parliament are directed only against the European Commission. Since the Treaty of Maastricht, the Parliament must approve the incoming College of Commissioners as a whole. The Lisbon Treaty even stipulates that the EP 'shall elect the President of the Commission' (Art. 14(1) TEU-L). However, since the European Council proposes the candidate to the Parliament (Art. 17(7) TEU-L), this 'election' is only a right to approve or veto a candidate. Nevertheless, the Parliament currently seeks to predetermine the choice of the European Council by proposing candidates itself.

In conclusion, it is clear that the European Parliament has become a powerful actor in the EU's institutional setting (Hix *et al.* 2007). Beginning in the mid-1980s, Parliament's powers have steadily expanded, initially as a result of the introduction of the cooperation procedure followed by the co-decision procedure, and later with the expansion of co-decision to a larger number of issue areas. This process culminated in the Lisbon Treaty, which gives the EP the role of co-legislator along with the Council. The Lisbon Treaty also put the EP on an equal footing with the Council in budgetary matters. For the most part, the Parliament has only veto rights at its disposal. This gives it a strong bargaining position with regard to the other institutions, but does not include the opportunity definitely to shape or determine legislation and other policy projects in substantive terms. Furthermore, the Parliament is largely excluded from policy decisions of the Council that do not result in legal acts, and even more so from fundamental decisions on Treaty amendments. Compared with the other institutions of the EU, the Parliament is in a comparatively weaker position. Moreover, unlike national parliaments, the EP does not have a right to elect a government or to initiate legislation.

In practice, the successful exercise of the EP's powers depends on whether it is able to build internally consensus, in order to achieve a broad majority in its decisions. This is not always easy. As elections are not organized Europe-wide, but are conducted individually in each member state, the party spectrum is highly-fragmented. This can make it difficult to aggregate political positions on issues related to European integration. Furthermore, the Parliament is weakened in its position because of the comparatively weak trust, political support, and interest in its work of the European citizens. Thus, overall, the EP is also marked by contradictions between an increasingly powerful formal position and many institutional restrictions to exercise these powers, in practice. Nevertheless, we will see in the next chapters that the EP often succeeds in using its powers to a maximum and, partly, even transgressing them.

## The Court of Justice

The European Court of Justice (ECJ) – or, as it was renamed by the Treaty of Lisbon, the Court of Justice of the European Union – acts as the judiciary of the EU. The Court is the institution that ensures the legality of European decisions and monitors the consistent application of European law across the Union. According to the EU Treaty, the Court 'shall ensure that in the interpretation and application of the Treaties the law is observed' (Art. 19(1) TEU-L).

The Court was established by the ECSC Treaty and was later incorporated into the framework of the EEC and EURATOM. From the very beginning, the founding members have acknowledged the importance of an independent judiciary in ensuring the effectiveness of jointly agreed legislation (Borchardt 2010: 66). This, however, has meant that they have had to accept constraints on their national sovereignty. Over the years, the case law and judgements of the Court have furthered the supranational dynamics of European integration (Burley and Mattli 1993; Alter 2001, 2009; Stone Sweet 2004). Because of its independence, the position of the Court of Justice fits with the principle of the separation of powers. In this way, the Court is comparable to a national level Constitutional Court, even though the EU does not have a constitution (Dehousse 1998). At best, we might consider the Treaties as quasi-constitutional.

At present, the European Court of Justice consists of 28 judges and 8 Advocates-General, who are appointed by the governments of the member states 'by common accord' for six years with the possibility of reappointment (Art. 19(2) TEU-L). The judges are chosen from individuals whose independence is 'beyond doubt' (Art. 19(2) TEU-L). As in the other institutions, the principle of proportional representation of the member states is respected; every EU member has a judge in the Court. This provision is also advantageous because the judges are all familiar with their national legal systems and, to a degree, the language problems can be alleviated during court proceedings. The principle of proportionality among the member states is also considered when appointing the Advocates General; however, the four large member states always have an Advocate General (Germany, France, Italy, and the UK), while the other 24 member states share the remaining four positions on a rotating basis (Borchardt 2010: 69).

The Treaty on the Functioning of the EU provides for a variety of legal actions and procedures that the Court of Justice can consider (for an overview, see: European Union 2013a).

In *infringement procedures*, the Commission turns to the Court of Justice for a ruling in cases where a member state fails to fulfil its obligation under EU law (Art. 258 TFEU). Such cases usually involve the failure to transpose European directives into national law. Individual member states also have the right to bring action against other member states for Treaty infringements to the Court (Art. 259 and 260 TFEU); however, in most cases they refer the matter to the Commission, which then carries out the necessary steps.

*Actions for annulment* can be filed in order to examine the legality of EU law: if the law in question was not correctly adopted, or if it violates the Treaties, it can be nullified (Art. 263 TFEU).

*Actions for failure to act* are directed at the institutions of the EU. These actions may be initiated if the European institutions fail to take action in the areas provided for in the Treaties (Art. 265 and 266 TFEU).

*Preliminary rulings* involve cases that are pending in the member states the outcome of which is at least partially determined by Union law. In these cases, the national courts may request a preliminary ruling from the ECJ to assist them in their decision (Art. 267 TFEU). For example, a member state may ask the ECJ to rule on how the European laws on equality between men and women in the workforce are to be interpreted, if they differ from national legislation in this area (MacRae 2010). It is generally agreed that the procedure of preliminary rulings is an important means of harmonizing the interpretation of EU law across the member states. Far more than half of all procedures at the ECJ fall under this category (in 2011, it was 423 out of a total of 688 cases). However, the courts of the individual member states make use of preliminary rulings to very different degrees. In 2011, the six founding members of the EU used the procedure in a total of 216 cases: the 9 states of the Northern and Southern enlargements (1973–1995) combined for 126 cases; the 12 states of the most recent enlargements (2004 and 2007), taken together, appealed to the European Court in only 81 cases (all figures obtained from Court of Justice 2013a: 96 and 118).

In addition to these formal procedures, the European Court of Justice also deals with legal disputes between the EU institutions and its employees (Art. 270 TFEU).

Over time, the tasks of the Court of Justice have continued to increase. The Court began its life in 1953 with only four cases. This increased to 43 cases in 1958, 79 in 1970, and 433 in 1985. By the turn of the millennium, the number of cases before the European Court of Justice had reached 502 and, by 2011, the number had further increased to 679 (all figures obtained from Court of Justice 2013a: 116). This enormous increase in cases can be attributed to the steady increase in European legislation, which now covers about 30,000 legal acts. Furthermore, the successive enlargements of the Union with new member states have also contributed to the increase.

To help disperse the workload, a Treaty revision in the SEA paved the way for the creation of a Court of First Instance in 1988 (Borchardt 2010: 71). With the Lisbon Treaty, this court was renamed 'General Court'. The General Court is primarily responsible for many of the legal matters mentioned above. Only the infringement procedures and preliminary rulings are carried out by the ECJ. The ECJ, furthermore, acts as a Court of Appeal for cases that have been decided by the General Court and whose rulings have been subsequently challenged by one of the parties.

The Court of Justice and the General Court may convene either in plenary sessions, or in smaller groups of judges. To this end, fixed chambers have been created to deal with area-specific issues. As a basic principle, decisions and rulings are made by simple majority. Therefore, the number of members of the Courts, as well as the chambers, must always be an odd number.

The European Court of Justice is independent in both formal and practical terms. Its rulings are highly regarded across the Union, even if they do not conform to the preferences and interests of the member states. In fact, its judgements frequently clash with the interests of one or more – and sometimes all – the member states. The Court of Justice not only settles legal disputes, but *de facto* also sets law or casts a 'shadow of law' on European legislation through its case law and the interpretation of the Treaties. The necessarily fragmentary character of the Treaties and the indeterminate character of EU legal texts leave much room for interpretation, which the Court uses proactively (Schmidt 2011). In this manner, the Court has clearly taken on a much stronger role than was originally assigned to it (Weiler 1994; Alter 2001, 2009; Stone Sweet 2004).

During the early years of integration, in particular, the Court took several landmark decisions that established constitutional doctrines in a manner that the Treaties had not originally envisioned (Weiler 1994; Dehousse 1998; Alter 2001, Borchardt 2010). As early as 1963, the direct effect of EC law for the citizens of the Union was ascertained (Case 26/62, judgement of 5 February 1963; Van Gend and Loos). Based on this ruling, it was determined that European law confers rights and responsibilities directly on European citizens. In 1964, the Court took a ruling that declared the supremacy of EC law over national law (Case 6/64, judgement of 15 July 1964; Costa/ENEL). As a result, if there is a conflict between national and European legislation, the European law will be regarded as superior (Borchardt 2010: 117–22). Unsurprisingly, these judgements had far-reaching consequences for the entire European legal practice. They not only blurred the separation of powers between the legislature and judiciary at the European level, but also significantly constrained the sovereignty of the member states (Weiler 1994; Alter 2001, 2009). Furthermore, this case law has contributed to the establishment of an independent European legal system that, in turn, has transformed the Court of Justice. The Court has evolved from an institution that was conceptualized as a part of an intergovernmental organization to one that operates according to federal principles (Weiler 1994; Dehousse 1998; Hix and Høyland 2010: 86).

The European Court has, through its rulings, also been able to push forward integration, especially during phases of non-decision in the Council, or overall stagnation (Burley and Mattli 1993). The most famous case in this respect is the frequently cited *Cassis de Dijon* ruling (Case 120/78, judgement of 20 February 1979, *Cassis de Dijon*; see also Alter 2009: 139–58). In this case, the Court formulated the principle of 'mutual recognition'. The principle states that products produced in accordance with the legal standards of one member state may be marketed in all other member states without any restrictions, even if they do not conform to the standards of these countries. This ruling subsequently marked the breakthrough to the completion of the single market. The Commission deliberately used the principle of mutual recognition to push forward market integration (Alter 2009; Schmidt 2009). As this principle undermines all attempts to protect national markets through special regulations, member states' resistance to integration broke down. At the same time, however, due to its essentially deregulatory nature, this principle makes it impossible to protect national legal systems from European-wide harmonization (Scharpf 1999; Hix and Høyland 2010: 86). Furthermore, the ruling had extensive implications for the entire pattern of policy-making in the EU. European leaders no longer aspired to harmonize national laws and legal systems, since this turned out to be a cumbersome and almost impossible endeavour. Instead, they preferred to proceed according to the principle of mutual recognition, which shifts the burden of adjustment from the European level back to the national level (Schmidt 2009).

Despite the rulings described above, which have led to the evolution of an independent European legal order, the Court of Justice is not an authority that is formally superior to the courts of the member states. Instead, it tends to work together with the courts of the member states to form a single legal system (Bartolini 2005a: 146–7). This is particularly visible with the procedure of preliminary rulings (Alter 2001). However, since the preliminary rulings are binding for the courts at the national level and cannot be overturned by a court of appeal, the ECJ can have extensive influence on both the rulings and the overall legal systems of the member states. This puts the ECJ in a *de facto* supranational position, although in formal terms, it was not intended to play such a role.

Thus, as with the other European institutions, the ECJ is marked by contradictions. Although it is the supreme authority in the EU's judicial system, it is not superordinate to the courts of the member states in formal terms. Its decisions are binding for the member states, but in many cases the national courts make the final rulings and the ECJ does not act as a court of appeal for them. In its *de facto* law-making function, the ECJ acquires some characteristics of a constitutional court, although it was not vested with such a mandate. Instead, it was initially designed to be an international court of justice (Weiler 1994; Dehousse 1998; Alter 2009). In the literature, the Court is frequently characterized as a supranational body that triggers spill-over dynamics of integration (Burley and Mattli 1993). Indeed, the rulings of the Court have strengthened the supranational dimension of the European Union, even though the Treaties did not provide for such a development (Stone Sweet 2004).

## Conclusion

In conclusion, we can state that the institutional structure of the EU clearly deviates from well-known political orders, including both international organizations and nation states. It is different from international organizations because of the supranational powers of its institutions: the Commission's exclusive rights in legislation and monitoring powers in implementation; the Parliament's far-reaching legislative and budgetary powers; and the Court's role as a supreme judiciary in the EU. Furthermore, the legitimacy of the directly elected Parliament constitutes a major difference to international organizations. At the same time, it differs from a nation state in that there is no clear separation of powers among the EU institutions; there is no government or clear central authority providing political leadership; and there is a general lack of democratic legitimacy to the system as a whole. However, there are also some similarities with these forms of political order. Thus, even though it has been vested with some supranational powers since its inception, the EU was initially designed along the lines of an international organization. At the same time, it also displays some characteristics of federal states, including the strong role of national representatives in decision-making at European level, the directly elected Parliament, and the independent position of the Court of Justice.

The five core institutions of the EU are designed to represent either the interests of the Union as a whole, or those of the member states. Hence, they are conceived as bodies fostering supranational dynamics and impacts, or as intergovernmental arenas, adapting these dynamics and impacts to national interests and preferences. The Commission and the Council complement each other in the process of legislation and are, thus, characterized by a high degree of mutual interdependence. The Parliament shares its legislative and budgetary functions with the Council. However, representing the member states, the Council is more powerful than the Parliament in both formal and practical terms. It decides on and coordinates a wider range of EU policies beyond the realm of ordinary legislation. The institutionalization of the European Council further enhanced the pre-eminent position of the member states in all European affairs and issues of integration. The European Court of Justice enjoys an independent position that corresponds to the principle of the separation of powers within nation states.

All five institutions are marked by certain contradictions. The Commission is vested with far-reaching powers, yet it is dependent on the decisions of the Council and the Parliament in legislation and budgetary matters, and on the member states in policy implementation. The Council is a powerful actor in legislation and other policy decisions; yet, as an intergovernmental body, the Council is internally divided and constrained in the effective exercise of its functions. The same applies to the European Council, as it aspires to provide leadership and act as the supreme authority in the EU. Even so, dissent among the member states often hampers the exercise of these roles. The Parliament has acquired significant powers, putting it on an equal footing with the Council in legislation and budgetary matters. Yet, it is also internally divided, due to the fragmented party spectrum, and is only weakly supported by the electorate. The Court is the supreme authority in the EU's judicial system; that having been said, it is not superordinate to the courts of the member states in formal terms.

At this point, it might seem that the EU, because of its dualistic institutional structure and the contradictions within every institution, is constrained from taking forceful action. However, such an assumption would be mistaken. The Union often displays an amazing ability to function, in spite of its apparently 'weak' institutions. This ability results from the fact that European institutions can draw on 'strong' actors and their initiatives. In turn, this constellation of comparatively 'weak' institutions and 'strong' actors contributes to a further diversification of the EU's institutional structure, resulting in a growing spectrum of both informal arrangements and formalized, Treaty-based institutions.

# Chapter 5

# Decision-Making: Cooperation and Conflict among the Core Institutions

In the previous chapters, I outlined the basic characteristics that make up the institutional structure of the EU. Yet, in order to fully understand the position, powers, and the importance of each institution within the overall structure, we must consider how they work together and interact in the process of decision-making. In this analysis, I distinguish between three forms of decision-making in the EU, depending on their scope and political significance. First, I consider decisions around legislation and rule-making; second, I turn my attention to fundamental decisions regarding widening the Union and deepening integration; and, third, I look at those decisions that pertain to the exercise of executive powers. All of these decision-making processes are regulated by the Treaties, together with additional rules of procedure. However, these rules and regulations give broad leeway for the institutional actors to define the range and scope of their activities for themselves. These opportunities may help to streamline decision-making into an efficient and effective process. It will come as no surprise, however, they also provide an important arena for power struggles and conflicts among the relevant actors and institutions. Thus, the institutions and actors of the EU seek to expand their competences and to compete for powers to define, shape, and control the process of European integration. More generally, the institutions struggle for maximum influence with regard to their counterparts. At the same time, however, the EU's comparatively 'open' architecture, within which there are no clear hierarchies, compels actors and institutions to work towards compromises and to search for consensus. As a result, there are sophisticated procedures to temper conflicts and facilitate the ability to reach a compromise. In this chapter, I will analyze the complex – and, at times, contradictory – ways of working this brings about, in order to highlight the characteristics of

European decision-making and the role the individual institutions play in this process. The chapter will deal specifically with the interaction among the EU's core institutions as they are involved in legislative and executive functions, as well as in fundamental decisions. The Court of Justice is not considered here, as it does not take part in these processes.

## Legislation and rule-making

The main part of EU decision-making involves legislation and rule-making. Indeed, the Union has legislative competences in many policy areas, and its legislative output is considerable. It is this extraordinary competence of the European level that has given rise to the term 'Community method' (Dehousse 2011). The Community method, according to a definition by the Commission (2001), means that the European Commission alone makes legislative and policy proposals; legislative and budgetary acts are adopted by the Council of Ministers and the European Parliament; the European Court of Justice guarantees respect for the rule of law (cited by Dehousse 2011: 4; see also Wallace 2010: 91–5). Dehousse (2011: 5) stresses that this procedure is unique for two reasons: first, it gives the supranational, non-elected institutions (the Commission and the Court) an essential role in legislation and its judicial supervision; second, it also gives national governments a key role. The Community method has undergone significant changes over time, by expanding the realm of qualified majority voting in the Council and, particularly, by giving the Parliament a co-legislator role along with the Council. Thus, one could add to Dehousse's statement that the present role of the EP in European legislation is also unique. However, scholars also criticise the Community method, in particular because it does not correspond to the principle of separation of powers between legislature, executive, and judiciary; and because of the primary role that the Commission, as a non-elected body, plays in the procedure (e.g. Majone 2009).

### Legislative procedures

A wide variety of decisions make up the overall set of European legislation. These range from setting up or restructuring whole policy areas to single regulations, which might refer to detailed aspects of market regulation, product standards, or technical norms. Hence, there is a clear distinction between political decisions and decisions of an administrative or technical nature.

The actor constellation in decision-making with regard to particular policy and issue areas is highly diversified. There are essentially three core institutions that share decision-making competences. The Commission has the exclusive right to propose legislative acts or other policy initiatives. The Council and the Parliament then take decisions on these proposals. In the past, the Parliament was involved in this process of decision-making to varying degrees, ranging from mere consultation to cooperation and co-decision, including veto rights. Since the Lisbon Treaty has come into force and the ordinary procedure of legislation was introduced, the Parliament decides legislative matters along with the Council.

European legislative acts are defined in the Treaties through a specific terminology (see Table 5.1). The Treaties distinguish between five kinds of legislative acts, of which three are legally binding (Art. 288 TFEU). Non-binding recommendations and opinions may be issued by either the Commission or the Council without interference from any other EU body. While they primarily serve to express the political choices and options of the respective institutions, they may, in a later stage, be incorporated into a legislative act. In contrast, regulations, directives, and decisions are binding legal instruments. In other words, their objectives and substance must be respected by the addressees. Decisions most often relate to the implementation of policies on which agreement has already been reached, and, as with recommendations and opinions, may in certain cases be taken by either the Commission, or the Council. In any event, regulations, directives and, often, decisions are subject to the EU's ordinary procedure of legislation, or the Community method.

In the legal literature, regulations are regarded as the most rigorous form of European legislation, because they replace national law with common European norms and, thus, 'impinge furthest on the domestic legal systems' (Borchardt 2010: 88). Although this view is correct, it is in some sense also misleading. In practice, regulations usually refer to EU-policies and their implementation (e.g. the administration of the

Table 5.1   *European legislative acts*

| Legislative act | Legal status |
| --- | --- |
| Regulation | Binding and directly applicable in all member states of the EU. |
| Directive | Binding 'as to the result to be achieved', but 'leave[s] to the national authorities the choice of form and method' – directives therefore have to be transposed into national legislation. |
| Decision | Directly binding, but refers to narrow issue areas. |
| Recommendation | Not legally binding; defines certain objectives and suggests that the addressees should pursue them. |
| Opinion | Expresses a political statement or position of the respective institution on a certain issue. |

Structural Funds, or the definition of product standards) and, therefore, generally apply to more narrowly-defined issues. By contrast, directives may be viewed as less rigorous because they only define common objectives, or a 'result to be achieved' (Art. 288 TFEU). They must then be transposed into national legislation, which gives the member states a degree of discretion in their application. However, directives generally encompass fundamental political objectives, aimed at harmonization or convergence of national regulations. As a result, they can have a strong impact on national legislation and on the political logic of the member states' regulatory systems. Just one directive – for example, on equal pay for men and women – can necessitate the revision of a host of national laws in order to comply with the overall objective that has been set at European level. It is partly because of these complex repercussions of European directives on national legislation that member states so often and so systematically lag behind schedule for transposition of such directives into national law (see Falkner *et al.* 2005; Falkner and Treib 2008; Hartlapp 2009). Given the considerable scope and the potential consequences for the member states, directives should be considered the most influential legal acts in the EU, at least in a political sense. Unlike regulations, they refer to a much broader set of political objectives and, at the same time, require much more extensive revisions of national laws and norms.

In terms of the legislative process, it is first and foremost the Commission that initiates the process, although the European Council, the Council of Ministers and, since the Maastricht Treaty, the Parliament may request that the Commission launch an initiative in a certain issue area, or correct a perceived policy problem. The Lisbon Treaty even allows European citizens to bring such a request to the Commission. In this case, at least one million citizens from 'a significant number of Member States' have to support the request (Art. 11(4) TEU-L). However, it may well be that the Commission has already indicated that there is a need to act in a certain policy area, even before these formal steps are taken. In practice, it is often difficult to trace where legislation began and who first proposed the initiative. Because it has the largest set of resources at its disposal for the systematic elaboration of such proposals, we can assume that the majority of policy initiatives originate, directly or indirectly, in the Commission administration.

Once the process has been launched, the Commission works out a proposal according to its own internal procedures (for further details, see Chapter 6). After the College of Commissioners has adopted the proposal, it is forwarded to the Council of Ministers and the Parliament. Depending on the issue area at stake, either the Economic and Social Committee or the Committee of the Regions, or both, may also need to be consulted, but their recommendations are not binding (for details on these advisory committees, see Chapters 9 and 10).

In the past, the next steps varied, based on the role that Parliament was to play in legislation. Parliament held one, two, or three readings, depending on whether Treaty regulations provided for the procedure of consultation, cooperation, or co-decision.

When the *consultation procedure* applied, the Council forwarded the Commission proposal to the Parliament. The Parliament then issued its opinion; but this was not binding on the Council. However, the Commission could choose to adopt part, or all, of the Parliament's opinion and integrate it into the proposal. This then gave Parliament's opinion greater political weight. Once Parliament's opinion had been sought and the Commission had possibly revised its proposal, the Council took a final decision on the proposal and adopted the legal act. This procedure is no longer used in ordinary European legislation.

The *cooperation procedure*, introduced with the Single European Act in 1987, involved two readings in Parliament. In this procedure, the Council consulted the Parliament (first reading) and then issued a Common Position (Art. 189c TEC-M and 252 TEC-A). This did not express a definitive position of the Council; rather, it represented the most probable outcome of a future decision. The Parliament, in reaction to the Common Position of the Council, then issued its position (second reading), by adopting, rejecting or, most frequently, amending the Council's position. If Parliament adopted the Council's proposal, Council then took a final decision, in most cases by qualified majority, to pass the legislation. If, however, Parliament rejected the Common Position outright, then the Council could still adopt the legislative proposal, but only with a unanimous vote. If Parliament proposed amendments, the next steps depended on the Commission. The Commission could accept Parliament's amendments, in which case Council could then adopt the revised legislation with a qualified majority vote. If the Commission did not adopt Parliament's amendments, then the Council could only pass the legislation with a unanimous vote. With the Treaty of Amsterdam, the cooperation procedure was reduced to a few cases of legislation; the Lisbon Treaty definitively abolished the procedure.

The *co-decision procedure*, introduced with the Treaty of Maastricht (in force since 1993), significantly expanded Parliament's influence in legislation. The procedure required three readings (Art. 189b TEC-M). The initial phase of the procedure mirrored the cooperation procedure. However, following the second reading, the procedures diverged. If, after the second reading, the Council and the Parliament continued to hold divergent positions, then a Conciliation Committee was convened in order to broker a compromise. If the Committee was able to reach a compromise, the proposal went to a third reading, where it could be adopted by an absolute majority in Parliament and a qualified majority in Council. However, Parliament could also reject the proposal on its third reading, essentially exercising its veto power. The procedure was amended – and, above all, simplified – in the Treaty of Amsterdam. Thereafter, Parliament could already adopt or reject a proposal on the second reading. Moreover, a proposal was automatically rejected if the Conciliation Committee could not reach a compromise.

These procedures, which incrementally expanded the powers of the Parliament, reveal that the member states, acting through the Council, only gradually accepted the constraints on what was initially their exclusive right to decide on European legislation. Thus, in the consultation procedure, the Council could ignore the proposals of the Parliament. With the cooperation procedure, the Parliament could reject a proposal or propose amendments. Council could only ignore a rejection with a unanimous vote and, in the case of amendments, could only ignore these if the Commission chose not to adopt them. Later, the co-decision procedure gave the Parliament veto rights over any legislative proposals. It also forced the Council to engage in compromise-building with the EP through the Conciliation Committee. Yet, even in co-decision, the Council could still contain the EP's powers by applying the procedure only to specific cases. Three successive Treaty amendments (Amsterdam, Nice, and Lisbon) were needed to expand co-decision incrementally, until it now finally applies – under the new name 'ordinary legislative procedure' – to all regular EU legislative acts. As each incremental step was taken, Council slowly adapted to the increased role of the EP, so that it eventually agreed to further expand Parliament's legislative powers.

However, national leaders have still not fully empowered the EP in legislative matters, not even in the Lisbon Treaty. Besides the ordinary legislative procedure, the Lisbon Treaty also established a special legislative procedure. In this procedure, the Council acts with the 'participation of the European Parliament', or *vice versa* (Art. 289(2) TFEU). The cases where the special legislative procedure applies are all mentioned in the respective Treaty provisions. They range from certain aspects of EMU, to social policy and judicial matters, as well as dealing with citizens' rights. Moreover, they apply to the adoption of the multi-annual financial framework and to the provisions for elections to the EP. In short, the special legislative procedure applies to highly-sensitive policy areas and issues with distributive implications, as well as policies that merely envision cooperation among the member states instead of joint action at European level. Accordingly, in nearly all these cases the Council acts with the participation of the Parliament, and not *vice versa*. The Council decides by unanimous vote and only consults the EP. There are only a few exceptional cases where the actual consent of the EP is required. In contrast, in the rare cases where the Parliament acts with the participation of the Council, the EP must always seek the consent of the latter. So, in practice, the consultation procedure continues to exist. Yet, we have to recognize that it currently applies to policy and issue areas that have only recently come onto the European agenda. At the time when the consultation procedure was the norm, these policy areas were not even imagined to ever be part of European regulation. Overall, we can conclude that the powers conferred to the EP by the Lisbon Treaty constitute an enormous step forward in European integration.

At this point, the question arises why the member states were willing to empower the EP to such a degree, as this step does not fit with inter-governmentalist reasoning about self-interested actors, or with rational choice approaches that would explain institutional choices with functional considerations, or the expectation of clear benefits. In face of the shortcoming of these theoretical approaches, Rittberger (2005) has expressed an alternative explanation. He assumes that national elites, representing democratic states, perceived an imbalance between the consequentialist legitimacy (derived from the results of decisions), and the procedural legitimacy of the Union. Hence, in his view, the member states sought to remedy this imbalance by improving the procedural legitimacy of European decision-making; that is, by empowering the EP in legislation and in budgetary matters. However, we can assume that it was not only legitimacy concerns, but also the dilution of the Commission's powers in legislation that motivated this institutional choice.

At present, the EU's ordinary legislative procedure as codified in the Lisbon Treaty involves three readings (Art. 294 TFEU). If, during the first reading, the Council approves the position or amendments of the EP, the legislative act is adopted. If the Council formulates an alternative position, the proposal undergoes a second reading. The Parliament can reject the Council's position outright on the second reading without convening the Conciliation Committee, thus exercising its veto power. However, if it amends the Council's position and the Council does not accept these amendments, the proposal is referred to the Conciliation Committee. If the Committee does not reach an agreement within six weeks, the proposal is definitively rejected. If the Conciliation Committee does reach consensus and submits a joint text, both the Council and Parliament must give their consent on the third reading in order to adopt the legislative act. At all stages of decision-making, the Council may vote by qualified majority, unless it is voting on Parliamentary amendments that the Commission has rejected. In these cases, the Council has to reach a unanimous vote in order to adopt the amendments. Similarly, where Parliament votes to accept the Council's position, or to adopt the joint text of the Conciliation Committee (that is, in the first or third readings), then it takes decisions by a majority of the votes cast. However, when rejecting or amending the Council's position (second reading), it must reach an absolute majority (see Art. 294 TFEU). Figure 5.1 shows the different stages and courses of the ordinary legislative procedure, as it is currently in effect.

The Conciliation Committee consists of an equal number of delegates of the Council and the Parliament (Art. 294(10) TFEU). Usually, the

Figure 5.1    *Ordinary legislative procedure*

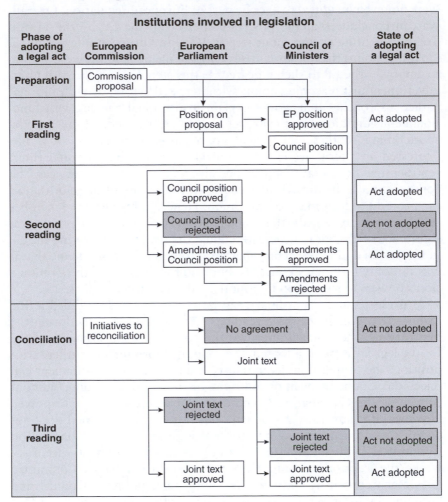

*Source:* Data from Art. 294 TFEU; see also General Secretariat of the Council 2013.

number from each delegation corresponds to the number of member states. As a rule, Parliament delegates three permanent members who, as Vice-Presidents of the Parliament, are experienced negotiators. In addition, it nominates the chair and the *rapporteur* of the relevant committees. The remaining delegates are chosen according to the political weight of the party groups in the EP. The Council is, in general, represented by the members of COREPER who are experienced and skilled in leading negotiations at European level. The Commission also holds a seat in the Committee as a mediator, but does not have the right to vote (Art. 294(11) TFEU).

The complexity of the ordinary procedure of legislation should not raise doubts about its effectiveness. Most cases do not end up in stalemate but, rather, in a legal act. And most laws are adopted on the first reading (83 per cent of cases), or on an early second reading (8 per cent). Of the legislative acts, 7 per cent required the second reading to pass, and only 2 per cent of the cases went to the conciliation procedure and a final third reading (figures for the seventh legislature, from June 2009 to February 2014, obtained from European Parliament 2014a). The effectiveness of the procedure, which functioned in much the same way under the regulations of the Amsterdam Treaty, has significantly improved over time. During the fifth legislature (1999–2004), only 33 per cent of the legislative acts were adopted on the first reading and 22 per cent on an early second reading, while 25 per cent required a second reading and 21 per cent a third reading (European Commission 2014).

One might certainly question the point of this complicated procedure which, as it is presented above, does not even consider the difficulties of decision-making within the individual institutions. However, it is important to remember that the procedure was not established by conscious design. As we have seen, it resulted from an incremental process in which the powers of the Parliament were expanded in a piecemeal fashion. The addition of a third player in European legislation – the Parliament – significantly complicated what was initially a complementary relationship between the Commission and the Council. However, this was successfully counteracted by simplifying the procedure so that, despite the possibility of three readings, it is also possible to achieve the definitive adoption or rejection of the proposal at the first or second reading (see Figure 5.1). Furthermore, additional procedures have been created in order to facilitate consensus-building in European legislation.

In particular, additional conciliation activities in the form of a Trialogue go hand-in-hand with the formal establishment of a Conciliation Committee (Farrell and Héritier 2004: 1197). Members of the Commission, the Parliament, and COREPER participate in the Trialogue. They aim at exchanging and approximating their respective positions in order to find a compromise, preferably before the Committee's first meeting. If this is not achieved, the Trialogue continues to follow the conciliation procedure. In addition to the Trialogue, technical meetings at the level of the secretariats of the three institutions may also be convened in order to try to reach a compromise. One must, however, bear in mind that, at present, the conciliation procedure is not used very often. This is partly because, in addition to the official Trialogue as outlined and acting within the framework of the conciliation procedure, an informal 'trialogue' has also been established between the first and the second reading. This informal trialogue enables the Commission, the Council and the Parliament jointly to elaborate a legal text at an early stage of the legislative process (Farrell and Héritier 2004: 1197; Rasmussen 2011; Héritier and Reh 2012). The informal trialogue is used extensively, as the numbers given (p. 000) confirm. Thus, after an initial phase during which Parliament frequently turned to the conciliation procedure, decision-making is now generally characterized by efforts to seek compromise within the framework of, at most, two readings. While this has increased efficiency, it also has its price, 'since early agreements tend to keep the decision out of the hands of the plenary Assembly' (Costa 2011: 74). In addition, 'this streamlining is reducing the transparency of Parliamentary decisions and limiting their political scope' (Costa 2011: 74, see also Reh *et al.* 2010; Rasmussen 2011; Héritier and Reh 2012).

## The implications of the legislative procedures

The complexity of the legislative procedures has far-reaching implications for all three institutions involved in the process. The delegates of each institution must screen a vast array of complex proposals tabled by the Commission, as well as amendments launched by the Council and Parliament, in order to identify consensual issues and rework conflicting matters. Furthermore, they have to reduce ambitious policy concepts and integration schemes to manageable and acceptable legal regulations. In order to fulfil these manifold tasks, the institutions closely cooperate through the informal trialogues in search of compromises. In addition, they also maintain bilateral relationships in order to build consensus.

In this context, the Commission fulfils a prominent role as a mediator for both the Council and the Parliament. The Commission is represented in all Council meetings. So, when major conflicts arise among the member states, the Commission can advance consensual solutions or amendments to the original proposal, or even package deals. The Commission also cooperates closely with the Parliament in order to achieve partial alignment of the positions of both institutions at an early stage. An intensive exchange of information takes place between the Commission and the Parliament, which can contribute to a convergence of opinions and positions, and facilitate the adoption of legal acts. In certain stages of the legislative process, the Commission is required to give an opinion on EP amendments. The Parliament and the Council also use the trialogues to identify conflicting and converging opinions and, thus, strive to align their positions. According to Farrell and Héritier (2004: 1198), early agreements in the framework of the trialogues have 'accelerated the informalization of relations between Council and Parliament'. Furthermore, empirical studies suggest that, as a consequence of these informal relations, the power relations within the EP have changed, by producing winners and, above all, losers (Farrell and Héritier 2004). Thus, Héritier and Reh (2012: 1154) conclude: 'Indeed, being at the centre of interorganisational negotiations in all policy areas seems to have brought a certain loss of open parliamentary debate, a marginalisation of rank-and-file MEPs, in particular those from small political groups and, thus, a challenge to institutional legitimacy'.

In this complex process of consensus-building among the three institutions, the powers to determine the final outcome are not evenly distributed. The Commission only has an exclusive right of initiative. Even though this right is supported by additional provisions – for example, the right to amend, and even to withdraw, a proposal at any stage in the procedure – the Commission remains constrained to the role of initiator and mediator. As such, it may influence the final outcome to a considerable degree, but not determine it. Especially if the Council and Parliament reach an early agreement, it is nearly impossible for the Commission to withdraw its proposal once the Council and the EP have built a compromise on major amendments.

The Parliament is, in principle, vested with the same legislative competences as the Council. Yet, it, too, is constrained in its ability to exercise its role as co-legislator. Although the Parliament has a power of veto at its disposal, it cannot use this power at will. First, in many cases adopting a legal act that does not correspond fully to the preferences of the EP may be preferable to having no law at all. Second, and more importantly, making extensive use of vetoes would make the EP appear to be an uncooperative player and would certainly undermine the willingness of the other institutions, in particular the Council, to embark on consensual solutions (Judge and Earnshaw 2003: 254–6). At best, the threat of a veto can result in compromises that may better reflect the EP's preferences. As a result, the Parliament must always perform a balancing act between exercising its veto power and playing the cooperative partner ready to compromise. It often chooses to cooperate, perhaps in the hope of achieving gains in another case. Nevertheless, in some cases the Parliament does not shy away from using its veto powers. However, on the whole, the Parliament cannot simply act according to its own goals and preferences but, rather, has to take strategic and tactical considerations into account at all stages of decision-making.

This is not to suggest that the outcome of decision-making depends mainly on the position of the Council. On the contrary, the reality of European decision-making shows that not only single member states, but also sometimes even the Council as a whole may be compelled to accept decisions that it did not at first favour. This apparently paradoxical outcome may result from the fact that a majority of the member states in the Council may actually prefer suboptimal legal acts over no regulation at all. It may also be the by-product of a package deal, where Council members agree to accept suboptimal legislation in one case in exchange for preferred regulation in another case. With majority voting applying to most cases of European legislation, a single member state can easily be out-voted, as can even groups of member states. Nevertheless, in spite of these constraints, the Council is often the most powerful player in European legislation, as its power not only rests on the formal regulations of the Treaties, but also on the power and position of the national governments within it.

Besides these constraints, the final outcome of any legislative process is partly determined by the abilities of the three institutions: their ability to manage the procedure successfully; to find sustainable and broadly acceptable compromises; to mobilize external actors in support of their respective positions, or to provide additional legitimacy (e.g. through the support of public opinion or strong interest associations); and, finally, by the ability to reach internal consensus.

The abilities of each institution differ. The Commission, for example, has successfully developed the first three capacities, whereas the Parliament is particularly skilful in using the first and the third. By using these capabilities, both institutions can enhance their position in relation to the Council. For the Council, and to a lesser extent the Parliament, the fourth skill is particularly important. Internal dissent not only undermines an institution's position with regard to its counterparts, but it may also be used by the other institutions to enhance their own positions. This is especially true if two of the three institutions are able to form a coalition, as the Parliament and the Commission often do. The pressure to reach compromise in decision-making thus influences the relationship *among* the three legislative institutions and, to a large extent, their *internal* relations (for further details, see Chapter 6).

The pressure to reach compromise is partly a result of the nature of the system but also, perhaps even more so, results from the conflicting interests that the three institutions represent. The most prominent and deepest divide, requiring delicate negotiations and compromise to overcome, is between the Commission and the Council. These two institutions represent, in a nutshell, the most significant and, simultaneously, most contradictory set of interests in the process of European integration. The Commission generally represents the common interest in furthering integration. In contrast, the Council embodies the individual interests of the member states, who often seek to reach decisions to maximize their own benefit or to minimize costs. In addition, the Council represents the common position of its members. The position of the Parliament, which acts as the representation of the citizens of Europe, is often nearer to the Commission's position and, thus, favours advancing the project of integration. However, when both the Commission and the Council favour powerful economic interests, the EP often takes an opposing stance. In these cases, Parliament's objectives and positions tend to reflect the collective interests of the European electorate (see Chapter 12). However, as ever more decisions are concluded early on in the process, Parliament's opportunities to exercise straightforward opposition have been significantly reduced. Thus, the final decision in European legislation often reflects the structural power position of each institution; that is, the respective interests that each institution represents.

We can conclude that decision-making and the passage of European legislation is based on complex interactions between the three legislative institutions of the Union. The formal rules that structure the procedures provide a general framework for these interactions. In practice, these interactions are characterized both by conflicts among the institutions, as they search to maximize their influence on legislation at the expense of their counterparts, and by the general necessity and the political will of each institution to reach compromise and build consensus. When there is conflict, the dividing line often runs between the Council, on the one hand, and the Commission and the Parliament, on the other. However, firm opposition of the Parliament regarding both the Commission and the Council can also occur. In any event, apart from such conflicts on major and minor issues in European legislation, all three legislative bodies forcefully engage in forging compromise and building consensus among themselves.

## Fundamental political decisions

The procedures outlined refer to European-level legislation. Other rules and procedures apply to the fundamental political decisions that relate to the act and process of integration itself, as it plays out centre-stage, as well as behind the scenes. Most importantly, these fundamental decisions take place in a much less rigid setting, allowing actors to explore new ways to deal with conflicts and achieve consensus. Moreover, these decisions are dominated throughout by the member states and the intergovernmental institutions. Thus, the Council of Ministers and the European Council are the most important players in these decisions. The Commission can launch proposals and submit preparatory papers, but whether they are taken into consideration depends on the will of the Council and the European Council. The Parliament is largely marginalized in these decisions, except for those cases where it has the right of consent. The rationale underlying the dominance of the Council and the European Council is obvious. Fundamental decisions about the nature of integration are politically much more sensitive to the governments of the member states than legislative decisions. As a result, governments are not willing to brook the permanent delegation of any real power in this area to other institutions.

The procedures surrounding fundamental decisions are most formalized in the area of enlargement (Art. 49 TEU-L). This procedure usually starts with a formal decision by the European Council to open accession negotiations with a state, or group of states, applying for accession.

While the Commission is mandated officially to lead the accession negotiations, the parameters of the mandate are defined by the Council. To a considerable degree, the accession negotiations revolve around the obligation of the candidate state to adopt the complete *acquis communautaire*; that is, the whole body of legislation enacted by the EU so far. Notwithstanding this 'hard' requirement, there is also room to negotiate the conditions of accession. It is not uncommon to make arrangements for shorter or longer transition periods, depending on the specific circumstances of the candidate state. These exceptions are intended to facilitate adaptation to the Union's rules and standards. In addition, financial resources (e.g. of the Structural Funds or other Community instruments) may be offered in order to compensate for or help a candidate country overcome difficulties in adapting.

There is, thus, a substantial amount of room for manoeuvre in the enlargement negotiations and both sides attempt to use this to their advantage. However, the Union holds the upper hand as it, by and large, sets the conditions. In accession negotiations, the Commission acts not only as a fervent promoter of the Union's general interest, but also as a mediator. However, if major conflicts arise in those negotiations between the Commission and the candidate states, the issue must be referred back to the Council, or even the European Council, for consideration. When an accession agreement is ready for adoption, the Council of Ministers must take a unanimous decision. First, however, the Parliament must grant its consent (Art. 49 TEU-L). The consent procedure (Art. 49 TEU-L and 218 TFEU), first introduced with the Single European Act (1987), gives the Parliament some degree of bargaining and even a power of veto in matters of accession. If consent is not given, enlargement cannot take place. Yet, in practice, this power can only be used to leverage minor concessions.

For decisions on major integration steps the basic parameters of which are outlined in the Treaties, such as EMU, there is a special procedure. This same procedure also applies to fundamental reforms of the Union's institutional structure, usually culminating in substantive Treaty revisions. Again, the European Council takes a basic decision on the subject. This does not imply that the whole process begins here; on the contrary, in most cases a wide variety of actors have already pushed for the implementation of specific reforms. The European Council's decision only gives a clear signal that member states agree, in principle, to a major integration step. Then a specific procedure for negotiations is set up, culminating in a 'conference of representatives of the governments of the member states' (Art. 48(4) TEU-L), usually known as an Intergovernmental Conference (IGC). Such conferences do not differ basically from the regular meetings of the European Council. However, the IGCs must be regarded as specific events with their own procedures, since they are convened for a special purpose and organized as a series of successive meetings, ending in a final marathon of negotiations (a 'night of the long knives', in EU jargon) (Christiansen and Reh 2009). This, in turn, increases public attention and the pressure to succeed.

The Commission acts as a secretariat for the IGC by compiling documents, policy proposals, and draft Treaty revisions. To some extent, however, its role is far greater than that, as the Commission itself may launch proposals (Art. 48(2) TEU-L; see also Kassim and Dimitrakopoulos 2007; Christiansen and Reh 2009: 102–7). However, the reaction of the Council to such proposals can vary. Council response may range from accepting the bulk of the Commission's proposals, as was the case with the SEA, to rejecting outright any Commission interference. Commission President Delors claimed that he had written up to 85 per cent of the Single European Act; Grant estimates that it was probably between 60 per cent and 70 per cent, which is still a large proportion (Grant 1994: 79). In contrast, when Commission President Romano Prodi ventured to launch proposals for the Constitutional Treaty, his commitment was bluntly rejected by national leaders (Tömmel 2013).

Other concerned actors can also express their views and positions on a reform proposal, or launch proposals themselves (Christiansen and Reh 2009: 111–19). This may range from an entire Draft Treaty, as elaborated in the early 1980s by the Parliament, to minor amendment proposals referring to single institutions or policy areas. Furthermore, independent experts can submit their ideas and views. Often, experts are formally commissioned to elaborate reform proposals, or reviews of such proposals. A host of this type of report on political reform were drawn up during the late 1970s and early 1980s, when the EC was in a state of crisis: the Spierenburg Report (1978); the Report of the Three Wise Men (1979); and the Dooge Report (1985). Depending on the issue at stake, special committees are set up for debating substantive problems, or negotiating compromises. For example, leading up to the negotiations on the Treaty of Maastricht, two high-ranking committees were established: one, under the Presidency of Delors, was entrusted with the task of elaborating a concept for EMU; the other was charged with elaborating proposals for a political union (Ross 1995). Particularly, the first committee put forth the general framework for much of the EMU and the steps leading to it. However, in general, the negotiations among national governments are prepared by COREPER and its working groups.

At this point, it might seem that the IGCs constitute a method for including the public in the process of elaborating major European reform projects, or revisions of the Treaties. However, this is not the case. In general, the proposals are worded in highly-detailed, specialized, and juridical terms, so that even politically well-informed citizens can barely understand them, let alone assess their implications. The IGC procedure therefore comes down to a huge consensus-building machine, in which elites and experts, isolated from the public, tenaciously negotiate on technical details and minimal steps towards reform. The document that is eventually adopted by the European Council at a summit meeting, and later ratified by the Council of Ministers and every member state, usually consists of a confusing set of minor Treaty revisions. Taken together, however, they often add up to important leaps forward in European integration (see Chapters 2 and 3).

The lack of public attention to decisions on important integration steps has led to a major change in the procedure for elaborating Treaty revisions. The Draft Constitutional Treaty, adopted by the European Council in 2004, was not simply negotiated by an IGC; a Convention was established to prepare a proposal (Crum 2004, 2008; Magnette and Nicolaïdis 2004; Kleine 2007; Risse and Kleine 2007; see also Chapter 3). The Convention method had already been applied successfully in 2000 for drawing up the Charter of Fundamental Rights of the European Union. It was hoped that a similar institution elaborating proposals for a major Treaty revision would open space for public debate of the various options and scenarios. The Convention was to include delegates from the Parliaments of the member states and the accession states, as well as the European Parliament. Two thirds of the total membership was to be from these groups, thus providing more direct democratic legitimacy to the procedure of Treaty revision. In addition to its formal members, delegates from the Committee of the Regions, the Economic and Social Committee, the social partners as well as the ombudsman were also admitted as observers to the Convention (Crum 2008: 10).

In practice, however, the high expectations around the democratic legitimacy of the Convention were only partly justified. In the end, the Convention was burdened with an enormously broad task that involved numerous 'technical' details that were hardly of interest to the wider public. As a result, major debates only emerged during the final phase of the Convention's work and during the subsequent IGC. One key debate focused on whether the Union needed a Constitution, a discussion that ignited the question of whether further integration was desirable. However, eventually, crucial decisions with regard to the Constitutional Treaty were taken by the experienced and professional elites of European integration, first, within the Convention and, later, during the IGC. The President of the Convention, Valérie Giscard D'Estaing, successfully pushed for decisions that strongly furthered integration (Kleine 2007). The ministers of foreign affairs played an important role in the final phase of the Convention debates. During the subsequent IGC, the large and the 'old' member states were particularly influential in pushing forward integration (Crum 2008). In any event, it has to be stressed that the Convention method led to a much more innovative Draft Constitutional Treaty than an IGC alone could ever have accomplished.

Ultimately, the experience of the Convention, which was apparently perceived by the member states as positive, led to the codification of the procedure in the Lisbon Treaty (Art. 48(3) TEU-L). As a result, in the future, any major Treaty revision will require that the Union establish a Convention. The Council will only be permitted to act unilaterally in an IGC in some minor cases. According to the Lisbon Treaty, the Convention shall consist 'of representatives of the national Parliaments, of the Heads of State or Government of the Member States, of the European Parliament and of the Commission' (Art. 48(3) TEU-L). Whether the heads of state or government will be represented by their ministers of foreign affairs, as was the case with the Convention on the Future of Europe, or will participate themselves even at this early stage of decision-making, remains to be seen. In any event, even though numerically under-represented in a Convention, national governments will exercise tight control over the process and, particularly, its outcome.

Overall, the Union has developed highly sophisticated procedures for taking decisions on fundamental issues of integration. These procedures increasingly include a variety of actors; yet, the Councils continue to control both the process and the outcomes. Thus, fundamental decisions, if they are taken at all, are frequently accompanied by enormous difficulties such that only minor progress is achieved. However, once adopted, these decisions have a much greater impact than one might expect given the often rather 'technical' and seemingly marginal Treaty amendments. This constellation highlights some of the paradoxes of European decision-making. Fundamental systemic reforms grow out of a series of minor, incremental steps. Decisions that have far-reaching political implications appear to be merely 'technical' details, or matters of minor importance. According to some observers, this may, over time, lead to a de-politicization of European integration issues (see e.g. Schmidt 2006; Risse and Kleine 2007). In the short term, such a de-politicization may be helpful to achieve consensual solutions. In the long run, however, the opposite could become reality, and politicization of European issues could undermine further integration. This was already apparent in the discussions around the adoption of both the Constitutional Treaty and the Lisbon Treaty (Crum 2008). These Treaties were presented as rather unspectacular steps in integration. Although the precise consequences were not readily perceived by the wider public, both Treaties evoked enormous distrust and politicization, resulting in negative referenda in France, The Netherlands and, at a later stage, Ireland (Niemann *et al.* 2008).

## Executive tasks and policy implementation

The Union also carries out an extensive range of executive tasks that are closely tied to the ever-growing and increasingly diverse spectrum of European policies. This increasing diversification and wider scope of policies, in turn, implies that a set of highly-differentiated procedures for implementing European decisions has necessarily evolved over the years. The division of responsibilities among a wide variety of actors means that policy implementation in the EU is a complex process. In most cases, the governments of the member states bear the responsibility for implementation. The governments then delegate these tasks to other public actors, and sometimes even private or non-state actors. These could include specialized authorities at state level, lower-level governments or administrations, semi-public independent agencies, as well as private or non-state organizations, such as business associations, chambers of commerce, or trade unions. Given this highly-diversified spectrum of actors responsible for policy implementation, there must be effective methods in place to direct and coordinate their activities. At the European level, a basic regulatory framework has been developed for this purpose. Furthermore, specific procedures have been established to monitor and supervise these actors. With this in mind, this section focuses on the basic decision-making patterns and underlying principles of the Union's executive tasks, as well as its coordinating and supervisory role in policy implementation. This section is not generally concerned with the details of implementation, as they are the task of the member states and may vary widely across the Union, according to the policy area, the actors involved, and the regulatory and administrative practices of each national political system.

In general, the Commission and the Council share the executive tasks of the European Union, although there is a clear division of labour between the institutions. The Council sets the framework by taking certain basic decisions, defining the rules of procedure, and establishing additional institutions. In this framework, the Commission's role and executive functions are defined quite narrowly. In spite of the division of labour between the two institutions, major conflicts regularly arise between them. The Council attempts to contain the activism of the Commission by issuing restrictive rules and establishing supervisory institutions (Pollack 2003). The Commission, for its part, strives to expand its scope of action as much as possible through both formal and informal means. This conflicting interaction is further complicated by the increasing involvement of the Parliament in decision-making. The Parliament often lends support to the Commission when conflicts about competences arise with the Council. At the same time, though, the Parliament tries to expand its own supervisory role with regard to the Commission (Lord 2004: 139–55).

The Commission performs the bulk of the executive tasks. In most cases, it acts on a mandate of the Council that is set out in a regulation. There are two types of executive tasks, those involving direct implementation, and those requiring indirect implementation (Pedler and Bradley 2006). Direct implementation refers to those areas where the Commission enjoys extensive competences, such as competition policy, agricultural policy, and the administration of the EU's financial instruments. In competition policy, for example, the Commission monitors member state compliance with the various Treaty provisions. Its responsibilities range from preventing the formation of monopolies and cartels, and the provision of unjustified state aid, to controlling mergers (Cini and McGowan 2008; Wilks 2010). In all these cases, the Commission can initiate judicial reviews. Most cases, however, are resolved with negotiations between the Commission and private firms or governmental representatives, and compromises are often reached. Although its powers in competition matters go back to the Treaty of Rome, the Commission has only been actively pursuing competition cases since the mid-1980s (Cini and McGowan 2008). This change in activities shows that, in order to carry out its executive functions effectively, the Commission needs the support of the member states, even in those areas where it has exclusive competences.

The Commission also carries out a variety of executive tasks in the area of agricultural policy. Parts of this policy – in particular, those measures that refer to rural development – have been decentralized to the member states through the agricultural reforms of the last decade (Roederer-Rynning 2010). The 2003 reform brought about the most decisive changes. Nonetheless, the Commission still performs major executive tasks in agricultural policy. Assisted by management committees (see pp. 000–00), it adopts rules about market regulations, common standards, external customs duties, and import quotas from third countries (see Council Regulation (EC) No 1234/2007 of 22 October 2007). Furthermore, it performs administrative tasks involving certain subsidy schemes. Since some of these tasks fall to the member states, and fraud is not uncommon, the Commission also exercises a supervisory role (see the Annual Reports of the European Court of Auditors).

The Commission also performs a wide-ranging and ever-increasing set of executive tasks through the various funds and financial instruments of the Union (Pedler and Bradley 2006: 237). The Structural Funds, which have evolved into a highly sophisticated policy tool and which are vested with significant financial resources, are especially important in this regard. Another area where the EU invests significant financial resources is technology policy, an area that covers a broad range of specialized programmes. In all these cases, the Commission's role involves deciding on the allocation of finances to projects and programmes, and monitoring their implementation in the member states. As part of this process, the Commission sets rules for implementation, conducts negotiations with representatives of the member states or other actors involved in policy implementation, and establishes a monitoring system based on indirect means of control. On the whole, the Commission acts as an authority that sets procedural rules and performs supervisory functions. In contrast, the actual implementation falls to the member states.

In all other areas, the Commission performs executive tasks in a more indirect manner. For example, it is responsible for monitoring the implementation of and compliance with Council decisions at the member state level. This role still involves substantial responsibilities (Pedler and Bradley 2006: 237–40). Usually, member states fulfil their obligation of transposing European directives into national legislation in a somewhat sluggish manner (Falkner *et al*. 2005; Falkner and Treib 2008; Hartlapp 2009). If it seems that states are dragging their feet, the Commission must first determine whether the deadlines for transposition have actually been breached. If they have, it may send 'Letters of Formal Notice' and a 'Reasoned Opinion' to the respective governments (Falkner *et al*. 2005: 205–8). If these measures fail to result in adequate and timely implementation, the Commission may refer the case to the ECJ. In most cases, the threat of a judicial procedure is sufficient to compel the member state to comply. As it has in competition policy, the Commission has also become more active in prosecuting cases of non-compliance. However, because of the quantity of cases, it can only proceed in a very selective manner and within certain predefined limits (Falkner *et al*. 2005; Hartlapp 2009).

As with all executives, the Commission attempts to expand the realm and scope of its own activities as much as possible. The 'open' institutional structure of the EU and its incomplete regulatory system offer numerous opportunities for such a strategy (Nugent 2001; Pollack 2003). At the same time, however, this strategy is seriously constrained by the fact that the Commission cannot act on its own, but is always dependent on the cooperation of other actors, primarily the governments of the member states. In response, the Commission has come to make extensive use of financial incentives and other indirect means to influence national policies and to expand its executive tasks beyond the realm of formal competences (see, among others, Tömmel and Verdun 2009; Sabel and Zeitlin 2010; Heidbreder 2011; Héritier and Rhodes 2011).

The Council of Ministers, for its part, attempts to offset the growing autonomy of the Commission by increasing its own role in executive affairs. In order to contain Commission activism, the Council has created a system of committees, labelled 'comitology' in EU jargon (Pollack 2003: 114–52; Pedler and Bradley 2006: 240–61; Alfé *et al*. 2008; Nugent 2010: 128–30). These committees consist of delegates of the member states, in most cases civil servants of national ministries. As with a lower-level Council, these committees monitor the work of the Commission in the implementation stage. In particular, they supervise the Commission when secondary legislation is to be adopted. Officially, the committees were established to provide advice and support to the Commission, but their supervisory role cannot be underestimated. The Commission reports that, in 2012, there were 268 comitology committees in place; their number thus roughly corresponded to that of the working parties of the Council (see Chapter 4; European Commission 2013b: 4).

The comitology system was formally established in 1987 and, in 1999 and 2006, amended by Council Decisions. Initially, three different types of committee were envisaged, varying on the issue at stake. First, *Advisory Committees* were intended only to provide non-binding advice to the Commission in administrative decisions. Second, *Management Committees* had to be heard before the Commission could adopt any measures. In the event that a Committee decision diverged from the Commission's position, the issue had to be referred to the Council. The ensuing Council decision was then binding for the Commission. Third, *Regulatory Committees* involved even closer supervision of the Commission. Again, after a negative decision of the Committee, the Commission had to submit its proposal to the Council. If the Council rejected the proposal by a qualified majority, the Commission could re-submit it in the original form, amend it, or present a legislative proposal. The latter clearly raised the hurdles for adoption (Council Decision 1999/468/EC of 28 June 1999, amended by Council Decision 2006/512/EC of 17 July 2006).

In addition to these three types of committee, an additional form was established in 2006, in response to complaints from the EP that the comitology process excluded Parliament from procedures that, in fact, came down to adopting legislative acts. Accordingly, a Council Decision established *Regulatory Committees with Scrutiny*, a format that, for the first time, gave the EP a means of monitoring the Commission (Council Decision 1999/468/EC of 28 June 1999, amended by Council Decision 2006/512/EC of 17 July 2006). In these cases, Commission proposals, either accepted or rejected by the Committee, had to be forwarded to the EP and the Council for approval or rejection. If either the Council or the Parliament subsequently adopted the Commission proposal, the measure could be enacted (Alfé *et al.* 2008; Nugent 2010: 128–30).

While an Advisory Committee was usually chosen for more or less consensual issues, Management Committees were generally established in the area of agricultural policy and policies 'with substantial budgetary implications' (Council Decision 1999/468/EC of 28 June 1999, amended by Council Decision 2006/512/EC of 17 July 2006, preamble). Finally, Regulatory Committees applied to a broad range of policy areas with a legislative impact and, in general, to policies where major controversies between member states persist. According to Commission statistics, of 266 committees working in 2009, 22 were Advisory Committees; 38 were Management Committees; 51 were Regulatory Committees, and 11 were Regulatory Committees with Scrutiny. The bulk of the remaining committees, a total of 143, worked under several procedures (European Commission 2010: 5).

The Lisbon Treaty fundamentally changed the system for supervising the Commission in secondary legislation. The Treaty introduced a two-track system that distinguishes between delegated and implementing acts (Christiansen and Dobbels 2013: 43). *Delegated acts* imply that the power to adopt 'non-legislative delegated acts' can be delegated to the Commission. The precise regulations for this are laid down in each legislative act (Art. 290 TFEU). In these cases, both the Council and the EP hold supervisory powers, as they may revoke the delegation of powers to the Commission. They also have the right to veto the adoption of a delegated act (Christiansen and Dobbels 2013: 43). In the case of *implementing acts*, the powers to adopt secondary legislation or other rules for implementation are conferred to the member states (Art. 291(1) TFEU). Only where uniform rules are required does this right fall to the Commission (Art. 291(2) TFEU; Christiansen and Dobbels 2013: 44). In both cases, the Council or the EP may not exercise any additional control. Yet, the Lisbon Treaty stipulates that the Council and the EP must set out the principles and rules under which member states may check the Commission's exercise of its powers of implementation (Art. 291(3) TFEU). To this end, in 2011, a new regulation was adopted that defines these principles and rules. According to this regulation, two procedures apply: the *advisory procedure* and the *examination procedure* (Christiansen and Dobbels 2013: 45). These procedures envisage two types of committees that roughly correspond to the three variants of the former comitology system. While the advisory procedure will involve advisory committees, the examination procedure will involve two forms of committee that correspond to the previous management and regulatory committees. The examination procedure applies to measures that are quite broad in scope, or to cases with significant budgetary implications. In other words, it applies to sensitive issue areas (Christiansen and Dobbels 2013: 45). In case of dissent between the Commission and the member states about an implementing act, the case will be referred to an appeal committee consisting of high level representatives of the member states. Compared with the old system where disagreements were generally referred to the Council, this is quite an innovation (Christiansen and Dobbels 2013: 45).

Scholars assess the Lisbon Treaty's new regulations surrounding comitology as a mixed bag. According to Christiansen and Dobbels (2013: 47), the Lisbon Treaty constitutes a milestone in the evolutionary process of comitology. However, the authors also note that the distinction between regulatory and implementing acts is not clear-cut and might 'engender political conflict, legislative deadlock and judicial review in the future' (Christiansen and Dobbels 2013: 55). Brandsma and Blom-Hansen (2012: 952) point to additional problems, as they state: 'it is evident ... that the new system is a Byzantine arrangement'. Furthermore, they conclude that 'although the legal base of the comitology system has changed fundamentally, the new system in a material sense resembles the old comitology system to a great degree' (Brandsma and Blom-Hansen 2012: 955). In fact, the new reform, with its two-track system, gives Parliament and the Council direct, although ex-post, control over the Commission when it adopts delegated acts. In case of the implementing acts, the comitology procedures continue to apply, albeit in a slightly modified form. In terms of the overall aim to control the Commission in the process of issuing secondary legislation, we are again faced with a mixed bag. On the one hand, control functions are now more diluted among different actors, with the Parliament holding important rights in the sphere of delegated acts. In a few cases, the Commission can actually act autonomously. On the other hand, it is the Council that continues to exercise real control, either directly or indirectly. In the case of delegated acts, the Council has the same rights as the Parliament. In the framework of implementing acts, the Council continues to hold supervisory powers, even though they are now devolved to the member states and an appeal committee, which will likely continue to represent member states interests.

However, one can question whether the supervisory systems, both former and current, exerted on the Commission and its role in secondary legislation, really fulfil the expectations of the Council (Alfé *et al.* 2008). Empirical evidence has shown that Commission proposals are rarely rejected by the committees and resubmitted to the Council. According to many authors, this happens in less than 1 per cent of cases (see e.g. Alfé *et al.* 2008: 211). This extremely low rate of rejection might be caused by the fact that the Commission anticipates the interests and preferences of the member states and adjusts its proposals according to their wishes and expectations (Pollack 2003: 129, Alfé *et al.* 2008: 211). It might also result from a lack of unity within the committees, meaning that their ability to take decisions in opposition to Commission proposals is actually quite limited (Guéguen 2011). Furthermore, individual delegates of the member states are constrained in their freedom of action. If they openly attempt to maximize returns for their own country, they may be isolated in decision-making (Schäfer and Türk 2007: 192). Finally, the Commission is keen to use the committees as a means for transferring know-how on its policy measures to the member states and for building a transnational consensus on them. In any event, it is hard to hold the committees accountable for their decisions, either at the European or the national levels (Brandsma 2010). The new regulations of the Lisbon Treaty will not fundamentally change these observations. In the case of implementing acts, a committee system continues to exist and will face the same restrictions in exercising outright control on the Commission. In case of delegated acts, the powers of the EP and the Council to revoke rights delegated to the Commission are rather blunt weapons. In particular, the EP must overcome high hurdles to implement such a step.

Yet, it is also probable that the Commission, under this 'shadow of hierarchy', will, to the best of its ability, adapt delegated acts to the preferences and expectation of the member states and the EP.

The Commission is further constrained in its executive functions by other means of supervision and control. The Parliament, in particular, increasingly exercises a monitoring and supervisory role with regard to the Commission (Lord 2004: 144–55; Westlake 2006). Each year, the Commission is required to submit reports on its work to the Parliament as a whole. In addition, the Commission must submit more detailed reports on single policy or issue areas to the responsible Parliamentary committee. Commission officials often present their reports personally to the European legislature. In turn, the Parliament or the *rapporteurs* of the committees elaborate a critical report, highlighting the weaknesses or failures of the Commission policy. For highly-contested policy or issue areas, the Parliament may organize public hearings, where Commission officials are required to defend their case in plenary (Judge and Earnshaw 2003: 240–1). In case of severe negligence or failures of the Commission, the Parliament may turn to the Court of Justice. In extreme cases, if there is evidence of serious mismanagement or misbehaviour by the Commission, the Parliament may even cast a vote of censure against the College of Commissioners as a whole. Unsurprisingly, such a hard sanction has never been used, even though it nearly came about in 1999. During that year, the Santer Commission was accused of severe mismanagement (Schön-Quinlivan 2011: 57–63). In this case, the threat of a vote of censure was sufficient for the Commission to resign. Similarly, the Parliament rarely makes use of its right to invoke the Court. In general, the Parliament relies on the sanctioning impact of 'naming and shaming'. By making any misconduct public, the Commission is threatened with losing face and reputation. Such a strategy is clearly effective, as the Commission's poorly-defined executive role and its overall legitimacy deficit make it highly dependent on public perception and a positive image. However, the papers, reports, and resolutions produced or issued by the Parliament are only blunt weapons. The MEPs, as generalists, vested only with limited 'technical' resources and expertise, are hardly able to make skilful scrutiny of the labyrinthine routes of policy implementation, let alone to determine in detail the manifold factors contributing to policy failures. Moreover, in case of policy failure, it is hardly possible to separate the blame of the member states from that of the Commission.

## Conclusion

This chapter considered the interaction among the main institutions of the EU in the process of decision-making. It highlighted their position, their powers, and their ability to shape European policies and politics. Three categories of decision were of particular importance: legislation and rule-making; fundamental decisions regarding enlargements of the Union and Treaty revisions; and executive decisions around policy implementation. We saw that EU institutions are involved in these processes of decision-making to varying degrees, with varying competences, and with varying skills in shaping decisions beyond their formal competences.

Thus, the Commission is powerful in the realm of initiating legislation and, to a lesser extent, policy implementation. It uses its formal powers to a maximum by shaping the procedures of decision-making, setting the agenda, defining substantive issues, and launching consensual proposals. However, the Commission is constrained in its power by the supervisory activities of both the Council and the Parliament. Through the comitology system and the new procedures regarding the adoption of secondary legislative acts, the Council attempts to supervise the Commission even after legislation is made. The Parliament monitors the work of the Commission mainly through indirect means, such as requesting information on projected activities, future plans, and past achievements (or failures). Furthermore, the EP has gained some oversight on the Commission in secondary legislation. Only in exceptional situations does the Parliament threaten to exercise its right of censure. Nevertheless, in the day-to-day practice of legislation and decision-making, the Commission and the Parliament often form an alliance in order to increase their collective position regarding the Council.

The Council is a powerful actor in all three forms of decision-making that we considered in this chapter. In European legislation, the Council is the decisive actor. Since the Lisbon Treaty has come into force, it has to share these powers with the Parliament. Accordingly, it must often seek compromise with the Parliament. Regarding fundamental decisions, the Council is involved in preparing decisions, discussing details, and also in taking a final vote. In matters of policy implementation, the Council acts in a supervisory role with regard to the Commission. However, in practice, this task is largely delegated to high-level national representatives, or civil servants.

The Parliament, again jointly with the Council, also plays a decisive role in the ordinary procedure of legislation. However, the extensive powers can only effectively be used if the EP is willing to compromise with the Council. Only in extreme cases can the Parliament make use of its powers of veto. By forging alliances with the Commission, the Parliament can improve its position in relation to the Council. In policy implementation, the EP plays only an indirect role by requesting information and commenting on Commission reports. Fundamental decisions lie beyond the realm of the EP – except in the case of enlargement, where it has the right of consent.

The European Council, as the most powerful institution of the EU, takes all decisions on enlargements, institutional reform and, more generally, the overall course of integration. Even though it is supported in these decisions by the other institutions and their substructures to varying degrees, it is clear that these fundamental decisions clearly fall within the purview of the European Council. However, with the introduction of the Convention procedure for Treaty revisions, a specific support structure for such fundamental reforms has been created. In its first usage, the procedure involved a large number of representatives of the member states and, to a lesser extent, delegates from the EU institutions.

This chapter has also highlighted that the interactions of the core institutions of the EU do not simply reflect the distribution of formal powers among them. On the contrary, the activities of every individual institution clearly mirror their aspirations to shape and dominate integration as much as possible. This applies particularly to the supranational institutions, which seek to compensate their comparatively weaker position with skilful tactics. To this end, the Commission successfully manipulates decision-making procedures, and the Parliament and the Commission often form alliances. However, through their interactions, European institutions also constrain each other. This is most clearly the case with the Council, which often attempts to constrain the Commission – and occasionally even the Parliament. The Parliament, in turn, attempts to constrain the Commission by exerting indirect pressure on it. Ultimately, however, all the institutions, including the European Council, are subject to the pressure to achieve effective policy solutions and promote integration. This is why they engage in complex forms of consensus-building and search for compromise, both centre-stage and behind the scenes. The importance of consensus-building in decision-making does not prevent major conflicts from arising between the institutions. On the contrary, conflicts about competences, powers, and influence remain the order of the day. Since none of the institutions can master decision-making on its own, conflicts between and within the institutions turn out to be a driving force for policy formulation and implementation.

# Chapter 6

# Decision-Making and Consensus-Building within the Core Institutions

The previous chapter analyzed the process of European decision-making and, in particular, the interaction among the institutions of the EU in this endeavour. In this chapter, we explore the process of decision-making *within* each individual institution, and consider how this process evolves within the context of, and alongside, the previously discussed inter-institutional relationships. In order to elaborate fully on the specifics of each institution, I also examine the respective internal organization, procedures, and performances. This will highlight how every institution attempts to maximize its real power and influence in the European concert, by making as much use as possible of its formal powers and institutional resources, and also by improving its overall capabilities. Improving its performance involves developing sophisticated means of internal consensus-building, as well as devising specific tactical skills to exercise influence over the other institutions. In this way, we will learn how the institutions use different strategies in their individual struggles for dominance, even as they maintain an overarching consensual spirit that characterizes also the internal relations of the EU institutions.

## In search of collegiality: the European Commission

As we have seen already, the Commission's role, structure, and modes of operation, like much of the EU, are characterized by contradictions. On the one hand, the Commission assumes a collective responsibility, as expressed in its commitment to take all decisions jointly. On the other hand, each Commissioner is responsible for a distinctive portfolio, an arrangement that has been reinforced through the successive expansion of European policy-making. Moreover, the Commission, as the 'motor of integration', has a genuinely political task. At the same time, it performs significant administrative functions within the framework of the legislative initiatives, as well as the implementation of Council decisions (Nugent 2001).

These contradictions are reflected in the organizational structure of the Commission. Each Commissioner is assigned a specific portfolio (see Table 4.1). The allocation of portfolios is the responsibility of the Commission president, although member states nominate the Commissioners and typically exercise pressure to obtain a prestigious portfolio for 'their' office-holder (Spence 2006a: 34–6, 44–5). The large member states can be particularly forceful in their exertion of pressure and, as a result, the president is by no means free in his choice. Consequently, portfolios are not only allocated based on the qualifications of the respective Commissioner, but also take politics and representativeness into consideration (Nugent 2010: 113). Each Directorate-General is presided over by a Director-General, who is responsible for the individual portfolio and acts as head of the service (Spence 2006b: 128–35). Specialized intermediary institutions, known as the cabinets of Commissioners, operate between the Commissioners and the Directorates-General. The cabinets were established to support the Commissioners in their political work. Increasingly, however, they have taken on a role that places them as intermediaries between the political and the 'technical' levels (Spence 2006a: 60–72). The cabinets currently consist of seven to eight members. This is a marked growth over the two to three members that formed the cabinets in the early years of integration. As the tasks of the Commission have grown so, too, have the cabinets. As a rule, the cabinets were staffed with experienced politicians or experts from the Commissioner's home country, with at least one cabinet member holding a different nationality. Following the reform of the Commission under President Prodi, the cabinets have become more multi-national in order to prevent them from either actually or supposedly pursuing national interests over European interests. (Nugent 2010: 113). At present, cabinets usually have two or three members originating in countries other than the Commissioner's home country.

The cabinets of the Commissioners have evolved into a substructure that acts fairly independently under the College of Commissioners. Nugent even observes that 'they do, in fact, virtually constitute a separate policy and decision-making layer in their own right' (Nugent 2001: 4). As with COREPER, the '*chefs de cabinet*' meet weekly to debate Commission proposals and even take preliminary decisions on these proposals. Permanent or *ad hoc* committees consisting of cabinet members of different Commissioners may be established to consider specific issues that cross-cut the Commission portfolios. Each cabinet is responsible for giving advice to its Commissioner (Spence 2006a: 63–5, 69; for a detailed description of the cabinet of Delors, see Ross 1995).

Initially, cabinets were only expected to perform a political task, but their role has gradually evolved into an important place for dealing with substantive issues. Thus, the cabinets can be viewed as bridging the gap between the politically acting Commission and the 'technically' oriented administrative services. In practice, however, the cabinet's pivotal role has created additional problems by provoking conflicts about competences and by exacerbating friction between cabinet members and Directors-General (Spence 2006a: 69–70; Nugent 2010: 120).

The portfolios and tasks of the DGs vary in quality, magnitude and importance. Some DGs – for example, Economic and Financial Affairs (ECFIN), or Employment, Social Affairs and Inclusion (EMPL) – encompass a very broad policy domain. Foreign Affairs used to be an important DG with a large portfolio of its own. However, it has recently merged with departments of the Council Secretariat to constitute the European External Action Service (EEAS) under the guidance of the HR. Other DGs are concerned with more narrowly defined areas, such as Regional Policy (REGIO), Maritime Affairs and Fisheries (MARE), or Enlargement (ELARG). In addition, some DGs are not responsible for a policy area at all but, rather, deal with administrative tasks (e.g. DG Budget) (see Table 4.1). The size of the DGs also varies, depending on their tasks. The number of civil servants of the DGs may range from a maximum of roughly 3000 employees down to a minimum of approximately 200. Both the size and the portfolio help to determine the actual political weight of the DGs. Thus, Competition (COMP), ECFIN and the EEAS, as well as Trade (TRADE), Agriculture and Rural Development (AGRI), and Internal Market and Services (MARKT), play a prominent role, whereas the Directorates Employment or Environment are generally perceived as being less important (Spence 2006a: 44).

Besides the DGs, the Commission has a Secretariat General (SG) and other services from which it draws administrative support. The official task of the SG is to improve the coordination between the DGs and their portfolios, and to provide support to the President of the Commission. As with all institutions of the EU, over time the Secretariat has evolved far beyond its initial functions. In particular, it has assumed the role of a mediator to manage a broad range of organizational and coordination problems, as well as some controversial substantive issues. During the last few years, the SG has been transformed into a service for the Commission President (Kassim and Peterson 2013). Furthermore, it even took on specific high-priority or highly controversial dossiers (Kurpas *et al.* 2008: 42–3). Beginning in 1999 under the direction of President Santer, and later implemented during the Prodi Commission, the Secretariat General was also responsible for elaborating proposals for the reform of the Commission's civil service.

Closer examination of the decision-making system within the Commission highlights a complex and highly-differentiated mediation process

(Spence 2006b: 144–55). This process encompasses a wide spectrum of actors internal to the Commission, as well numerous external advisors and stakeholders. Generally, after a decision to act in a specific policy area has been taken at a higher level, a unit in the responsible DG will draft an initial proposal. Prior decisions may also act as a catalyst to prompt action. For example, EU-regulations and directives often include a date by which a legislative act must be revised. First, the proposal is considered, adjusted, and amended vertically; that is to say, within the hierarchy of a given DG. This may include the responsible Commissioner. In the second step, the proposal is horizontally adjusted, at which time the draft is forwarded to the Directorates-General in related policy areas for review (for details, see Hartlapp *et al.* 2013). Depending on the subject matter in question, meetings may be convened and task forces or working groups established, to bring together delegates of several DGs to allow for joint action (Spence 2006b: 147–50). This can lead to tensions, as the DGs are torn between their expressed intention to cooperate, and the competitive behaviour that frequently characterizes the relationships between them. However, by cooperating in the early stages of elaborating policy proposals, it is possible to forge winning coalitions for decision-making in the College of Commissioners.

Following the circulation and discussion of the draft among the DGs, it is then forwarded to a variety of internal and external actors. Internally, the College of Commissioners, the *chefs de cabinet*, and specific committees of cabinet members are involved in scrutinizing the proposal for broader political, strategic, and integration-oriented concerns, and eventually amending or even rejecting the proposal (Spence 2006b: 150–2). Along the way, the proposal will also be adjusted to better reflect the preferences and positions of different categories of external actors. The list of those to be consulted may include such diverse actors as members of national governments and administrations, independent experts and advisors, as well as representatives of interest associations and lobby groups.

The representatives of the member states are generally brought into the policy formulation process through the establishment of special advisory committees or groups (Spence 2006b: 146–7; Larsson and Murk 2007; Nugent 2010: 124–5). Besides high ranking officials in the relevant ministries, lower-level civil servants and experts of other public institutions are increasingly included in these committees or groups. Wessels (2008: 235) estimates that, in 2004, advice was provided to the Commission by 1702 groups of experts. This approach allows the Commission to gain, at an early stage, valuable information on the preferences of the member states, the varying impacts of its proposals on national regulatory systems, and also an understanding of any potential resistance that may emerge against a European policy initiative (Larsson and Murk 2007: 80–9). Accordingly, the Commission may adjust its proposal to the expectations and preferences of national governments and stakeholders long before formal decisions are taken.

Experts and other advisors are incorporated into the process of policy formulation in order to support the Commission as it formulates and drafts proposals. These experts may act directly as policy advisors in the committees. Additionally, they may be commissioned to carry out studies or research that serve to elaborate or justify the policy concepts. In both cases, experts augment the expertise within the Commission and, thus, help to develop considered and well-founded proposals (Larsson and Murk 2007). Experts also play a role in shifting the process of decision-making to a more 'technical' level and, in this way, may contribute to de-politicize the issue at stake. Whereas the assignment of studies or research to external experts was initially handled in an *ad hoc* manner, it is now subject to formalized procedures. These tendering procedures, supervised by the member states through administrative committees (see Chapter 5), have to navigate contradicting demands and, therefore, require skilful management by the Commission. On the one hand, the Commission must select the best and cheapest offer; on the other hand, a certain degree of proportionality among the member states must also be respected. It is obvious that under such circumstances, the boundary between efficiency requirements and national interests is difficult to draw.

Including interest associations and lobby groups in decision-making has shown itself to be a further complicated balancing act (Mazey and Richardson 2006; Greenwood 2011). Difficulties arise because interest groups and associations frequently have divergent, and even contradictory, concerns and preferences. In general, the Commission prioritizes European umbrella associations during consultations for its policy proposals. These associations usually work to express a position that represents a compromise among the national member organizations (Mazey and Richardson 2006). However, this strategy is not without problems. Most of the interest associations, because of highly divergent preferences of their member associations and their constituencies, have difficulties organizing themselves under a European roof and finding a common denominator (see also Chapter 10). While lobby groups primarily seek to influence Commission officials behind the scenes, interest associations are systematically included in the decision-making of the Commission through their participation in advisory committees (Mazey and Richardson 2006).

After a proposal finally reflects the preferences and positions of internal and external actors, it enters into the last stage of Commission decision-making. Here, the *chefs de cabinet*, acting as a quasi-College of Commissioners, decide on the proposal and, if necessary, strike compromises among the DGs (Spence 2006b: 150–2). If they are successful, the College of Commissioners does not need to discuss the proposal any further and instead proceeds to take a formal decision. If there continues to be disagreement and dissension among the *chefs de cabinet*, the College of Commissioners or – if some minor issues arise – a group of Commissioners will discuss the issue. A final decision is then taken by the College as a whole.

Decisions in the College require only a simple majority to pass; at present, this is 15 of 28 votes. In other words, in principle, 13 Commissioners – and, thus, essentially 13 member states – can be out-voted. Usually, however, a consensus is sought between all members of the Commission. Only in difficult and highly controversial cases is a vote cast. According to Kurpas *et al.* (2008: 23), no vote was cast during the first years of the Barroso Commission while, under Prodi, there were approximately 20 votes cast over the duration of his tenure. The authors also report that interviewees have commented that 'voting was not a political option anymore'. Kurpas and his collaborators assume that this is 'an inevitable consequence of the new composition of the Commission', where the 5 large member states are represented only with 5 (out of the then 27) Commissioners. In this new constellation, out-voting them would not be a viable political option.

When a clear consensus exists among the Commissioners or for routine decisions, it is also possible to apply a written decision-making procedure (Spence 2006b: 152–3; Kurpas *et al.* 2008: 38). In these cases, the proposal is sent to the Commissioners in writing. If objections are not made within a certain time limit, the proposal is considered to be automatically adopted. Finally, the Commission may also take a decision through delegated decision-making. This procedure allows one or several members of the Commission to take decisions in the name of the College as a whole. The procedure is 'usually used in areas of a managerial or administrative nature' (Spence 2006b: 152), that is, in non-controversial cases.

At this point, one might get the impression that the College of Commissioners plays a prominent role only in the initial and final phases of decision-making. This is, however, misleading. The College, meeting weekly, accompanies and structures the process in all its phases. In addition, each Commissioner significantly influences and structures the process of decision-making in his or her DG until a draft proposal is elaborated. He or she also advocates for the final proposal in the College of Commissioners. In this way, the College of Commissioners is involved in all phases of the elaboration of legislative proposals and, thus, exercises a far-reaching influence on proposals in both substantive and political terms.

The requirement of collective decision-making in the College of Commissioners – initially intended to prevent national interests from playing a decisive role – has repercussions for policy proposals. Because it is necessary to reach consensus in the College, policy proposals have to be modified and adapted in multiple ways and highly controversial initiatives are often excluded from the outset or, else, can succeed only with the strong backing of the President (Kurpas *et al.* 2008: 23). Besides his or her own opinions and preferences, every Commissioner must also take advantage of opportunities to build coalitions. This often results in trade-offs or package deals between Commissioners, addressing a number of proposals at once. However, the necessarily consensus-oriented attitude of the Commissioners ensures that national interests, as well as explicit political positions, barely come into play. Instead, the collective decision-making procedure actually favours the emergence of a European corporate identity among the Commissioners (Ross 1995).

The Commission's decision-making procedures as outlined above refer primarily to legislation and rule-making in regard to European policies. The Commission can, however, also launch more encompassing political proposals or far-reaching concepts for integration as a whole. In these cases, it can present its own political ideas and proposals during the Council debates (Nugent 2001: 7). The Commission President can play a particularly important role in these debates. Especially, Jacqes Delors was able to generate creative ideas and to skilfully advocate for them in the European Council (Ross 1995; Tömmel 2013). The Commission can also set up procedures for generating creative policy ideas and proposals. For example, in addition to the ordinary advisory committees, President Delors established a special think-tank within the Secretariat General that was charged with the exclusive task of providing creative ideas and project proposals (Nugent 2001: 152). This mode of procedure was continued under Delors' successors, who have set up a permanent advisory board: the Bureau of European Policy Advisers (BEPA). The task of the BEPA is to give advice to the Commission President and the individual Commissioners, and to elaborate policy proposals. Meanwhile, other procedures for generating policy concepts have also evolved into routine measures. Perhaps the best example of this is the European Round Table of Industrialists, which plays an important role in designing and debating new policies. In addition, events organized by the Commission, such as conferences and meetings, may serve as a forum for exchanging ideas and best practice experiences, and launching policy proposals (Tömmel 2011b).

The Commission usually launches new policy concepts and proposals by publishing reports and White or Green Papers, to which European institutions, national governments, and other stakeholders then respond. Important White Papers that have resulted in expansive policy reforms have included the White Paper on the Completion of the Internal Market (1985); the White Paper on Growth, Competitiveness and Employment (1993); as well as Governance in the European Union: A White Paper (2001). Most recently, the Commission has also undertaken online consultations (Quittkat 2011). In this way, the Commission tries to organize a Europe-wide process of policy formulation. Although this does not involve the wider public, it nevertheless draws a wide variety of interest groups and stakeholders into the debate. Through this process, the Commission can form transnational coalitions in support of certain policy proposals and integration steps, long before the Council has officially entered into the debate (Tömmel 2011b).

## Bargaining or problem-solving: the Council and the European Council

Unlike the Commission, the Council of Ministers and the European Council are not rigidly organized institutions with a clearly articulated administrative structure. Rather, as they represent the governments of the member states, they are heterogeneous bodies. The members of the Councils are, first and foremost, office-holders in their respective national governments. Their tasks in the EU are secondary and only possible because they hold a specific office at home. The primary role of the Council of Ministers is to decide on legislative proposals, put forth by the Commission, and, through its decisions, to transform them into legally binding acts. The Council is also responsible for taking policy decisions in foreign and security policy, and justice and home affairs (for details, see Chapter 7). The European Council, by contrast, does not have a legislative function. However, as the highest authority in the EU, it gives direction to the overall project of integration, and also steers policy in areas that are predominantly a responsibility of the inter-governmental institutions.

### The Council

The Council is sub-divided into a number of different formations, giving it a very heterogeneous nature. In addition, the Council draws on a highly diversified substructure that prepares, supports, and sometimes even performs a portion of the Council's work. The Council formations include the General Affairs Council and the Foreign Affairs Council, which both consist of the foreign ministers of the member states and, in some cases, also the ministers responsible for European affairs. In addition, there are the 'technical' Councils (see Chapter 4); these, in turn, are subdivided into the important Councils that meet regularly (i.e. ECOFIN and Agriculture), and those that meet only occasionally. Whereas the General Affairs Council and other important Council formations meet at least once a month, the others hold between two and six meetings each year (Hayes-Renshaw and Wallace 2006: 38–9). The frequency of meetings depends on whether the specific Councils act on established EU policies, or whether they deal with convergence or coordination of national policies (Hayes-Renshaw and Wallace 2006: 38–9). Besides the ministers, secretaries of state and high-ranking officials of the respective ministries also participate in the meetings. In general, a national delegation consists of 10 to 15 members. The heterogeneous structure of the Council was codified for the first time in the Treaty of Lisbon. Article 16(6) TEU-L states: 'The Council shall meet in different configurations'. In addition, the Treaty acknowledges the General Affairs Council and the External Affairs Council as different institutions with different functions (Article 16(6) TEU-L).

Two components – COREPER and its institutions, and the Secretariat General of the Council – make up the Council's support structure (Hayes-Renshaw and Wallace 2006: 68–132). For its part, COREPER is further subdivided into two sections: COREPER II, responsible for 'high politics' – that is, foreign policy and major integration initiatives; and COREPER I, dealing with the remaining policy areas, and what amounts to the domestic politics of the EU(Lewis 2012: 319). The two formations of COREPER meet weekly and are responsible for preparing the substantive and political Council decisions. Naturally, there are some exceptions, and these exceptions have increased over time. Thus, the important Council formations are not supported by COREPER, but by Special Committees that are usually composed of senior officials from national ministries (Hayes-Renshaw and Wallace 2006: 82–95). Accordingly, we find a Special Committee on Agriculture, an Economic and Financial Committee (Art. 134 TFEU), and an Article 207 Committee (TFEU, for external trade issues; formerly known as Article 133 Committee). In addition, Special Committees also aid the Councils responsible for foreign and security policy, and for justice and home affairs (the Political and Security Committee (Art. 38 TEU-L) and the Article 71 Committee (TFEU; formerly known as Article 36 Committee). Even though COREPER is internally fragmented, it is regarded as one of the most powerful institutions in the EU. For example, Hix and Høyland (2010: 63) consider COREPER 'as the real engine for much of the work of the Council'. However, COREPER's power has been weakened as the Union increasingly devolves important tasks to Special Committees. COREPER is supported by a number of working groups (213 in 2013, see Chapter 4), which are established either permanently or on an *ad hoc* basis. The groups are composed mainly of staff of the Permanent Representations in Brussels, and are responsible for scrutinizing Commission proposals and considering their impact on national regulatory systems, in order to elaborate an initial common position. Despite the fact that COREPER officially acts in the name of the member states, often the body deliberately pursues a common European interest, even above those of the member states. This has led some scholars to refer to COREPER's 'Janus face' (Lewis 2012: 333–5).

Compared to this diversified conglomerate of committees and working groups, the Secretariat General of the Council is a clearly organized permanent structure (Hayes-Renshaw and Wallace 2006: 101–32). Its tasks consist primarily of preparing and attending the meetings of the Council in technical and logistical terms. In addition to these managerial tasks, the Secretariat General has also, to a certain degree, taken on a political role. As early as the 1990s, Kirchner noted a gradual increase in this political role (Kirchner 1992: 27). This role is a logical consequence of the Secretariat's longstanding experience with intergovernmental negotiations. Thus, the Secretariat functions as an important resource to provide advice to the presidency on how to best conduct negotiations and broker compromises (Beach 2008). The Treaty of Amsterdam introduced a High Representative for Foreign Affairs, to act as Secretary General of the Council. This meant to assign a substantive policy role to the Secretariat General for the first time. This type of role would, in general, fall within the exclusive competences of the Commission. With the Lisbon Treaty and the formation of the EEAS under the HR, this substantive task is partly reintegrated into the Commission machinery.

The presidency of the Council is a further institution that facilitates decision-making and consensus-building. Tallberg even considers it 'the most important institutional mechanism through which EU governments reach efficient bargains' (Tallberg 2008: 201). The presidency of the Council rotates among the member states for a six-month term. Depending on the power, capacities, and resources of the member state holding the presidency, this institution can have significant, though varying, political weight (Tallberg 2006, 2008; Westlake and Galloway 2006). Since a successful presidency has become a matter of prestige, the government holding the position will try to conclude as many Council decisions as possible. As a result, when setting the agenda, presidencies tend to prioritize less controversial issues, or issues with which the member state in question is particularly qualified to deal (Tallberg 2006, 2008; Westlake 2007). However, the presidency does not have an exclusive right to set the agenda. It must select its issues through close cooperation with the Commission and from within the framework of the troika. The troika refers to a cooperative formation among the current, previous, and subsequent presidencies. This procedure of joint agenda-setting helps to ensure continuity and a timely completion of various dossiers (Hayes-Renshaw 2007). According to Warntjen (2008), the advantage of the presidency over other Council members lies in its 'proposal power'.

As has been noted, the quality of the presidency depends on the capacities and resources of the state in question (Quaglia and Moxon-Browne 2006). In general, large and 'old' member states are regarded as more successful than smaller and new member states. This is, however, not always the case. Large member states may have difficulties because of internal disagreements that can be exacerbated during their presidency (Quaglia and Moxon-Browne 2006; Schout and Vanhoonacker

2006). Furthermore, the presidency may be strongly influenced by internal and external circumstances, and the impact of these on the state in charge (Elgström 2003a). Upcoming elections, a change in government, or major problems in domestic politics can all form a heavy burden to a successful presidency. External pressures, such as extreme policy constellations or unexpected political developments and events, can also have a negative impact.

It is the responsibility of the member state holding the presidency to preside over all the meetings of the Council's substructure. In other words, the presidency is responsible for chairing the meetings of COREPER, the Specific Committees and the working groups; until the Lisbon Treaty came into force, it was also responsible for the European Council. As a result, these bodies perform their tasks under rotating leadership. As an institution, the Council presidency works to coordinate all bodies involved in intergovernmental decision-making and facilitates the vertical communication among them. Nonetheless, its short-term rotation hinders the continuity and coherence in managing the Council's agenda (Elgström 2003a). Often, just as a state is getting a handle on its role and the opportunities for action, its term as presidency is over.

This again highlights that the Council is not, and neither can it be, a coherent institution. Because it is premised on the principle of proportionality among the member states, it is necessarily guided by the national governments jointly. With different governments taking turns in the driver's seat, the quantity and quality of decision-making can widely vary. A weak or even Eurosceptic presidency can become a major obstacle to the Union taking steps towards further integration. The consequences of this were particularly visible when the negotiations of the Constitutional Treaty failed under Italian Prime Minister Silvio Berlusconi (Leconte 2012). A strongly self-interested presidency may suffer a similar fate and be unable to broker compromise among the members. However, in general, the presidencies, are expected to act as an 'honest broker' and put their national interests aside in favour of the collective good (Elgström 2003b).

Generally, decision-making in the Council is organized in a 'hierarchical' manner. Preliminary decisions are taken by the lower level institutions, while the ministers, at the top of the hierarchy, have the final say. In practice, however, the procedure is much more complex. Legislative proposals may be revised several times, or transferred up and down between different levels of decision-making. Revisions are only possible if the Commission is willing to incorporate them into its proposals. Generally, the Commission displays a willingness to do so, as its refusal would possibly jeopardize any decision. After a proposal has been formally submitted to the Council by the Commission, it is then forwarded to a working group of COREPER. The responsible group examines the impact of the proposal on the member states. In case of routine issues or non-controversial 'technical' questions, the proposal will quickly be forwarded via COREPER to the Council. In fact, such cases are definitively decided by COREPER, which negotiates an appropriate compromise. The Council then adopts these proposals, referred to as A-issues on the agenda, *en bloc*, without prior debate. It is estimated that about 90 per cent of the issues are adopted in this way. However, one has to bear in mind that the remaining 10 per cent are the complex – and, therefore, laborious – cases. When more complex and controversial issues are tabled, COREPER will strive to reach a preliminary decision. The remaining conflicts, however, can probably be resolved only through tough negotiations in the Council itself. These more controversial proposals appear as B-issues on the agenda. If no agreement can be reached, the proposal may be returned to the Commission for amendment, or the Commission itself may withdraw it.

Empowering the EP in legislation has further complicated decision-making. Conflicting issues are no longer resolved by the Council alone, but have to be reconciled with the positions of the EP. In order for this to succeed, sophisticated procedures have been put in place. The Council must first formulate a Common Position and, thus, needs to find a compromise, albeit a preliminary one, quite early on (first reading, see Figure 5.1, p. 122). After this decision is taken, the Commission can no longer amend its proposal. It may only adopt the amendments of the Parliament. If the Parliament proposes amendments, the consensus-building machinery in the Council must start anew (second reading). If there are major disagreements with the Parliament and the conciliation procedure is initiated, then the Council must again reach an internal compromise so that it finally can adopt the proposal (third reading). However, as we have seen in Chapter 5, most of the time the three institutions are engaged in ongoing cooperation in the form of informal trialogues and use this to try to reach a decision during the first or early second reading. In these trialogues, the Council is always represented by COREPER.

However, in spite of these sophisticated procedures, the Council often faces a fundamental problem in decision-making. Reaching viable compromises among the member states in the face of internal dissent can be extremely difficult. The complexity of this process is augmented by the growing number of member states with highly-divergent interests and preferences. As a result, most of the Council's work consists of building consensus among its members. COREPER and the working groups may be successful in reaching this consensus, as these bodies have developed a style of interaction that is marked by transnational cooperation, rather than tough bargains among self-interested national representatives (Clark and Jones 2011). Their primary objective is to promote integration and to make the machinery of decision-making work smoothly (for COREPER, see Lewis 2005, 2012; for the working groups, see Beyers 2005; Clark and Jones 2011). In this way, COREPER plays a particularly important role as a mediator between the specific interests of the member states and their shared interest in building the European Union.

However, when the controversies run especially deep, the ministers themselves must find a compromise, although they often refer back to COREPER even during this phase. In addition, various other actors may also play a key role in the search for a compromise. The presidency often succeeds in striking a final bargain by elaborating consensual proposals, building winning coalitions, persuading hesitant member states, isolating opponents, or offering them side-payments in exchange for their consent (Hayes-Renshaw 2007). The Council Secretariat with its longstanding experience in intergovernmental bargains may provide support to the presidency by proposing compromise formulae or certain tactical moves. The Commission can also play a pivotal role in the final search for consensus. By reformulating its proposals, the Commission often defines the common position within the member states' diverging preferences. In addition, the Commission may initiate issue linkages or package deals so that the benefits and burdens of proposals are more evenly distributed among the member states. Furthermore, in order to reach a breakthrough in decision-making, there may be bilateral and also multilateral consultations and negotiations going on behind the scenes (Clark and Jones 2011). The German–French tandem is an important player in these cases, as it often represents the most important conflicting parties and, at the same time, can identify a compromise acceptable to all.

In practice, even with all these sophisticated procedures in place and attempts to build consensus, stalemates can still occur. In the past, when unanimity was the rule, this was even more common. The Treaties generally regulate which procedure applies to which issue or policy area. In practice, however, these rules leave room for different interpretations, and struggles about procedural issues often arise. In these cases, the Commission and the Parliament favour majority voting as much as possible, whereas the Council generally prefers unanimity. In any event, the choice around the form of decision-making has significant repercussions on consensus-building in the Council. In cases where unanimity is required, every single position must to be taken into account. When qualified majority is sufficient, even a coalition of several member states can be out-voted. This threat of being ignored can influence the behaviour of national delegations, so that they often do not strictly oppose a decision but, rather, attempt to achieve minor concessions in exchange for their compromising attitude. However, even in cases where unanimity is required, a single member state blocking the proposed legislation in the name of national interests is not always seen as legitimate. On the contrary, it is often seen as an attack against the presumed cooperative spirit of the Council. In any event, explicit voting in the Council rarely occurs; instead, ministers adopt the vast majority of decisions by consensus, even when majority voting officially applies (Heisenberg 2005; Hayes-Renshaw *et al.* 2006).

In conclusion, we see that the expansion of qualified majority voting in the Council has had some paradoxical effects. On the one hand, it significantly facilitates decision-making and, thus, improves efficiency in the European Union. On the other hand, it increases the complexity of consensus-building because of the increased influence of the Commission and the Parliament in the process. With the enactment of the new rules of the Lisbon Treaty for qualified majority voting in 2014, the situation will change even more. The lowering of the threshold to reach a majority in the Council will further weaken the positions of individual states and even larger groups of member states (Art. 16(4) TEU-L; see also Tömmel 2010). Building blocking coalitions will be more difficult, and the Parliament will have more leverage to influence the decisions of the Council.

The expansion of majority voting in the Council, however, does not imply that its intergovernmental character might change in favour of a more supranational orientation. The procedural changes described above only apply to the less controversial issues and to decisions that are merely following up on more fundamental matters. In other words, they apply to those cases where a basic consensus between the member states already exists. In contrast, sensitive policy issues will continue to be decided by unanimity, and these issues are increasingly withdrawn from the interference of the Commission and the Parliament. This is clearly the case in foreign and security policy, as well as in sensitive issues of justice and home affairs, where the Council holds almost exclusive competences. It also applies to monetary policy, where the Council is still an important player, while supranational competences are delegated to the ECB (for details, see Chapter 7). Thus, we can conclude that the intergovernmental character of Council decision-making will hardly change.

### The European Council

When we consider the European Council and its decision-making principles, procedures, and practices, we can begin from the observation that those described above for the Council generally also apply to this body. However, there are also significant differences. First, the type of decisions is different. According to the Lisbon Treaty, the European Council 'shall not have any legislative function', but 'shall define the general political directions and priorities' of the Union (Art. 15(1) TEU-L). Second, since its members are heads of state or government and represent the highest political authorities in their respective countries, they bear responsibility for a much broader set of issues. Hence, decision-making in the European Council is marked by more deep-rooted conflicts. At the same time, though, the European Council is also constrained to forge compromises on fundamental questions and principles of European integration. Third, in general the European Council decides 'by consensus' (Art. 15(4) TEU-L). In practice, this means that formal votes are not taken. However, it also means that unanimity is always required. There are, however, some exceptions to this rule. For example, nominating a Commission president or electing the president of the European Council requires only a qualified majority. In these cases, the voting rules of the Council of Ministers apply. Yet, in practice, the 'culture of consensus' tends to prevail in these decisions, too (Heisenberg 2005).

In the process of decision-making, the European Council makes use of the same support structures as the Council. Thus, the Council Secretariat as well as COREPER (particularly COREPER II, the 'political' branch) prepare or accompany its work. A difference, however, lies in the fact that, to a certain extent, the Council of Ministers acts as a support structure for the European Council. For example, in foreign policy and justice and home affairs, both institutions work hand-in-hand. Whereas the European Council takes the fundamental decisions, the Council of Ministers acts with more of an executive function. However, the division between these functions is not always clear-cut and, as a consequence, there is a great deal of overlap in the activities of the two institutions (Hayes-Renshaw and Wallace 2006: 165). The European Council can, to a certain extent, also draw on the resources of the Commission in preparing its work. The Commission provides reports, analyses, and, in certain cases, even policy proposals. As a regular member of the European Council, the Commission President can advocate such proposals during meetings and propose compromise formula in cases of dissent. Delors is reported to have been very active and successful in this regard (Tömmel 2013).

Until the enactment of the Lisbon Treaty, the European Council, as all Council formations, worked under the principle of the rotating presidency. These alternating presidencies with six-month terms meant that the quality of the work of a presidency significantly varied and, with it, the capacity of the European Council to achieve consensus. Since the European Council, as has been noted, is faced with deep-rooted conflicts among national governments, the role of the presidency as broker or mediator is especially important. A look at a range of outstanding summit meetings of the past confirms this. Thus, for example, the Nice Summit in 2000 failed to adopt more extensive proposals for Treaty reform because the French Presidency primarily defended its domestic interests during negotiations. The Italian Presidency in December 2003 failed to broker the adoption of the Draft Constitutional Treaty, an event that was mainly attributed to the notoriously Eurosceptic attitude of Prime Minister Berlusconi. By contrast, the UK government, in December 2005, successfully concluded the negotiations on the Multi-annual Financial Framework for the period 2007–2013, even though the reduction of the British rebate figured high on the agenda. The German Presidency in June 2007 successfully managed the adoption of a mandate for the IGC on the Lisbon Treaty, in spite of strong resistance, particularly from Poland.

It was these unpredictable successes and failures of the rotating presidencies that finally led to the establishment of a permanent presidency for the European Council. When the Lisbon Treaty came into force in 2009, the heads of state or government nominated former Belgian Prime Minister Herman van Rompuy for this position. At this point, we cannot yet accurately assess the achievements of the office-holder. Even though he was re-elected in March 2013 for a second term, and also elected as President of the Euro-Summit (see Chapter 7), it seems that van Rompuy has not been able to shape the agenda to any great extent; neither has he been able to influence the outcomes of European Council decisions. His major achievements to date consist in improving the efficiency of meetings and fostering conciliation among the members of the European Council (Howorth 2011; Gostynska 2012). Thus, we can assume that major conflicts continue to jeopardize, or even paralyze, decision-making in the European Council. The outcomes of recent summit meetings seem to confirm this assumption. For example, it was not possible to integrate the rules of the Fiscal Compact into the Treaties; instead, in 2012, 25 member states concluded a specific treaty that has the status of an international agreement. Similarly, an agreement on the Multiannual Financial Framework for the period 2014–2020 was reached only after almost one year of difficult bargains. Overall, we can conclude that the European Council has made significant progress in improving its internal proceedings, but this progress does not pay off in speedy consensus-building. However, the difficulties of the European Council in rapidly building consensus also stem from the fact that it must resolve increasingly complex and controversial issues and, sometimes, as the financial and sovereign debt crisis proves, it must react to and cope with unforeseen events.

## Transcending party politics: the European Parliament

The Parliament is the representative of the citizens of Europe. As such, it holds a special role in European decision-making. In order to exercise influence on European legislative decisions, it often has to reach an absolute majority of the votes (see Chapter 5). Since none of the party groups in the EP holds such a huge majority, the groups have had to develop unique mechanisms that allow them to reach consensus. As a result, Parliament's preferences and positions emerge from a complicated process of mediation among and between political parties and party groups. The parties and groups represent a wide variety of political and ideological positions and, as a result, it can be quite difficult to find common ground among the members of the European Parliament. In addition, the external pressures resulting from the need to cooperate with the other institutions can also pose problems for internal consensus-building. However, the Parliament can only be in a position to exercise an influential role in European decision-making if it is willing and able to compromise with the other institutions of the EU (Farrell and Héritier 2004; Reh *et al.* 2010; Héritier and Reh 2012).

## Political parties

Members of the Parliament are elected from each member state according to that state's electoral and party system (Duff 2010: 58–63). The elections take place separately in each of the member states. Consequently, the MEPs represent an extremely diverse spectrum of political orientations. In fact, the Parliament is an aggregate of a huge number of national political parties. McElroy and Benoit (2010: 3), reported that in the 2004–2009 legislature, elected shortly after the Eastern enlargement, there was a total of 182 parties represented. This number has slightly declined to a total of 161 in the legislature 2009–2014, in all probability the result of the consolidation of the party systems in the new member states (Rose and Borz 2013: 476). Nonetheless, the number of parties is quite large. A small country such as the Netherlands, with 25 seats in the EP, is represented by 9 political parties. Since the introduction of a representative electoral system for European elections in 1999, the two dominant parties of the UK – Labour and the Conservatives – have had to share the British seats in Parliament with 9 smaller, often regionally-based parties. Italy participates with not less than 6 parties in just one parliamentary group: the European Peoples Party (EPP). Taken all together, the MEPs form a heterogeneous conglomerate of a few larger parties and a wide variety of smaller, highly-fragmented parties. This fragmentation results, in part, from the fact that voters in European elections tend to give their vote to parties that they would not elect at the national level (Hix and Høyland 2010: 147–8). The fragmentation of the party spectrum in the EP has been further exacerbated by Eastern enlargement. The accession states are, to an even greater extent, characterized by extremely fragmented and highly volatile party systems (Lord and Harris 2006). In European elections, opposition parties that may not survive until the end of the legislature often win the majority of the seats. The extremely low voter turnout in these countries also favours fragile, non-consolidated parties.

Two large political groups dominate the Parliament and its work (see Table 6.1). The largest group, the EPP, brings together a broad alliance of mostly Christian democratic and conservative parties. With the elections in 2014, it won 221 seats in Parliament. The second largest group, the Progressive Alliance of Socialists and Democrats (S&D), consists mainly of social-democratic parties which together hold 191 mandates. In a distant third place follows a recently formed right-wing and Euro-sceptic group, the European Conservatives and Reformists (ECR), with 68 seats. This group was founded by the British Conservatives and has quickly overtaken the other smaller party groups. Thus the Alliance of the Liberals and Democrats for Europe (ALDE) with currently only 67 seats was ousted from its traditionally third place in the EP. The fifth position is held by the European United Left–Nordic Green Left (GUE-NGL), which, after a drop in 2009, could increase its mandates to 52 in 2014 and thus overtake the Greens–European Free Alliance (Greens–EFA) with currently only 50 seats. Finally, the smallest group, an alliance of minor, extreme right-wing and, at the same time, Euro-sceptic parties, referring to themselves as the Europe of Freedom and Democracy (EFD), consists of 31 MEPs. The Italian Lega Nord and the United Kingdom's Independence Party (UKIP) are members of this group. EFD was formed with the merger of two right-wing party groups, IND/DEM (Independence/Democracy) and UEN (Union for Europe of the Nations). Both of these party groups lost so many votes in the 2009 elections that they were unable to form independent groups. Since the political groups enjoy certain privileges, even the members of highly diverse mini-parties strive to come together in such a group in order to benefit from these privileges. However, these highly diverse groups are usually very unstable and often collapse before the end of the legislature. An example of this is the ITS group (Identity, Tradition, Sovereignty). This right-wing formation of different political colours could only be formed in 2007 after the accession of Bulgaria and Romania to the EU. When the five MEPs from Romania left the group later in 2007, it was dissolved. Actually, 43 members of the Parliament figure under the label '*non-inscrit*' (NI). This means that they do not belong to any political group. They only have a secretariat at their disposal to support their work. This group includes extreme right-wing parties like the French National Front (Front National), the Flemish Interest (Vlaams Belang) of Belgium, and the Freedom Party of Austria (Freiheitliche Partei Österreichs). Eleven MEPS have not yet joined a party group or the NI-group, but aspire to do so; thus the size of the groups might further change.

As Table 6.1 shows, the size of the party groups in the EP did not significantly change between the 6th and the 7th legislature, while the elections of 2014 brought about major changes. These changes mainly affect the smaller groups and, in particular, the right-wing parties, which are, at the same time, 'hard' Euro-sceptics. They were particularly successful in increasing the number of their seats and will certainly impact the future work of the EP.

Table 6.1   *Members of the European Parliament, by party group, 6th–8th parliamentary term (2004–19)*

| Party group | Parliamentary term 2004–09 | Parliamentary term 2009–14 | Parliamentary term 2014–19 |
| --- | --- | --- | --- |
| EPP (until 2009: EPP-ED) | 268 | 265 | 221 |
| S&D | 200 | 184 | 191 |
| ALDE | 88 | 84 | 67 |
| Greens-EFA | 42 | 55 | 50 |
| GUE-NGL | 41 | 35 | 52 |
| ECR | – | 54 | 68 |
| IND/DEM | 37 | – | – |
| UEN | 27 | – | – |
| EFD (merger of IND/DEM and UEN) | – | 32 | 48 |
| NI | 29 | 27 | 43 |
| Other | – | – | 11 |
| Total | 732 | 736 | 751 |

EPP: Group of the European People's Party; ED-European Democrats, S&D: Group of the Progressive Alliance of Socialists and Democrats in the EP; ALDE: Group of the Alliance of Liberals and Democrats for Europe; Greens–EFA: Group of the Greens/European Free Alliance; GUE/NGL: Confederal Group of the European United Left–Nordic Green Left; ECR: European Conservatives and Reformists Group; IND/DEM: Independence/Democracy Group; UEN: Union for Europe of the Nations Group; EFD: Europe of Freedom and Democracy Group; NI: Non-attached/Independent Candidates.

*Sources:* 6th and 7th terms European Parliament 2013b – all numbers for the incoming Parliament; 8th term: European Parliament 2014d – incoming Parliament, provisional results.

Since the 1970s, 13 transnational parties have been founded, spanning the corresponding parliamentary groups, as well as smaller, non-aligned parties (see Table 6.2). These federations of national parties are legally recognized by the EU (Raunio 2012: 352). The traditional parties clustered around the centre-right and the centre-left each united early on in the process of integration to form European federations. In contrast, the smaller transnational parties, particularly those on the far right of the political spectrum, were only recently formed. The party federations elaborate common political positions, especially about European affairs. In public, however, these party groups rarely play a role (Duff 2013: 150). As with the umbrella organizations of interest associations, their primary objective is to mediate between national positions, rather than to elaborate genuinely European ones. In addition, it is the MEPs who provide major input into the work of the federations, rather than the federations providing input into Parliamentary work.

For the most part, the two large Parliamentary groups determine the face of the EP and, to an even larger extent, the process of decision-making. However, it is important to note that the groups are internally much more heterogeneous than political parties in national legislatures (McElroy and Benoit 2010; Nugent 2010: 193–5). Depending on the MEPs' parties of origin, there may be significant differences in their political and ideological positions. For example, there are fundamental differences among a British Labour deputy, a Spanish Socialist and a German Social Democrat. These differences are further exacerbated by diverging national political cultures and traditions. The party group of the EPP is made up of no less than 41 parties (Rose and Borz 2013: 478) and is characterized by the most pronounced political and ideological divergences. This group has deliberately attempted to become, and to remain, the largest in Parliament. In order to achieve this, the membership of the EPP spans from right-wing parties – for example, from the Italian People of Freedom to the Portuguese Social Democrats. Moreover, again depending on the MEPs' country of origin, their preferences and positions on European integration may widely vary. For example, German Social Democrats and Greek Socialists, or German Christian Democrats and British Conservatives, hold very different positions. The Euro-sceptic attitude of the British Conservatives in the EP was reason enough for 11 French Centrists to leave the EPP group and, instead, to join the Liberals (Hrbek 2004: 216). Meanwhile, however, the Conservatives themselves left the EPP and formed their own group, the ECR, drawing on support from MEPs from Eastern European countries (see Table 6.1). Furthermore, the party groups in the EP are not linked to a government or a formal opposition, as they usually would be at the national level. As a consequence, the MEPs are not bound to strict party discipline, but are comparatively free to express their individual preferences and positions.

Table 6.2　*European political parties legally recognized by the European Union, 2014*

| Political party | Acronym | Political alignment |
| --- | --- | --- |
| European Peoples Party | EPP | Christian democrats and conservatives |
| Party of European Socialists | PES | Social democrats and socialists |
| Alliance of Liberals and Democrats for Europe | ALDE | Liberals and centrists |
| European Green Party | EGP | Greens |
| Alliance of European Conservatives and Reformists | AECR | Euro-sceptics, conservatives |
| Party of the European Left | PEL | Socialists and communists |
| Movement for a Europe of Liberties and Democracy | MELD | Euro-sceptics, nationalists |
| European Democratic Party | EDP | Centrists, pro-Europeans |
| European Free Alliance | EFA | Regional parties |
| European Alliance for Freedom | EAF | Euro-sceptics, right-wing populists |
| Alliance of European National Movements | AENM | Extreme right, nationalists |
| EU-Democrats | EUD | Euro-sceptics |
| European Christian Political Movement | ECPM | Christians |

*Source:* European Parliament (2014c).

The high degree of political fragmentation in the Parliament is partially offset by other factors that can help to bridge party differences. One important factor in this respect is nationality. Depending on the issue at stake, nationality may act as a common denominator across party groups. Lord refers to this as 'a second party system behind the dominant organizing framework of the EP' (Lord 2004: 101). In addition, convergent positions may arise where MEPs from various parties simply share basic views and attitudes about European integration, or about specific political issues. Such attitudes may result in the creation of inter-groups that cut across party alignments (Judge and Earnshaw 2003: 198–9; Nugent 2010: 195). The most well-known inter-groups were the Crocodile club and the Kangaroo group. In the 1980s, these groups both advocated for further integration. The Crocodiles sought a federal Europe, while the Kangaroos advocated for the creation of the single market. In 1986, the Crocodiles were renamed the 'Federalist Intergroup for European Union'. Also using the name Spinelli group, at present, its members work to promote federalism and combat Euro-scepticism in the EP (Duff 2013: 148). The number of inter-groups is estimated to be around 100 (Nugent 2010: 195). Gender has also been shown to play an important role in bridging some of the differences across the political spectrum. It is not uncommon, particularly when equal opportunity issues are at stake, to see women of all political colours jointly push for progressive legislation (Kantola 2010; Mazey 2012). Success in this is facilitated by a comparatively high percentage of female members in the EP (35.5 per cent in the 2009 election) (Kantola 2010: 60). In Europe, only the Scandinavian and a few other countries can claim higher female representation.

Overall, it is perhaps best to characterize the European Parliament as having multiple internal dividing lines, many of which cross-cut party and group alignments. At the same time, numerous ties exist between party groups to facilitate the emergence of common ground. This again exemplifies the relative freedom of MEPs to act according to their own conscience and convictions. In addition, it highlights how Parliament can often achieve a broad consensus among its members in spite of multiple dividing lines.

## Internal organization and decision-making

The EP has 20 standing committees tasked with preparing decisions and improving the overall efficiency of Parliament's work (Neuhold and Settembri 2007; Raunio 2012: 348–50; Maurer 2012: 70–1). The committees deal with all major policy and issue areas, including the respective legislative acts, as well as with institutional questions (see Table 6.3). Depending on the policy or issue area at stake, the workload of the committees may vary widely (Maurer 2012: 148–50). Committees primarily involved in European legislation, such as Environment, may face a particularly high workload (Whitaker 2011: 30–3). Committees with an especially broad mandate may also form subcommittees. In practice, only the Committee of Foreign Affairs has formed two subcommittees, one to deal with human rights, the other with security and defence. In general, every MEP participates in two committees, but only one of these forms the core area of his or her work.

In order to facilitate cooperation between Commission and Parliament, the portfolio of the committees is largely congruent with that of the Commission DGs (compare Tables 4.1 and 6.3). For specific questions, the EP may establish temporary or specific committees (Maurer 2012: 71). At present, no specific committee exists. In 2013, a specific committee was mandated to consider criminal matters. Other recent

Table 6.3    *Committees of the European Parliament, 7th parliamentary term, 2009–2014*

| | Standing committees |
|---|---|
| *Acronym* | *Committee* |
| AFET | Foreign Affairs |
| DROI | Human Rights |
| SEDE | Security and Defence |
| DEVE | Development |
| INTA | International Trade |
| BUDG | Budgets |
| CONT | Budgetary Control |
| ECON | Economic and Monetary Affairs |
| EMPL | Employment and Social Affairs |
| ENVI | Environment, Public Health and Food Safety |
| ITRE | Industry, Research and Energy |
| IMCO | Internal Market and Consumer Protection |
| TRAN | Transport and Tourism |
| REGI | Regional Development |
| AGRI | Agriculture and Rural Development |
| PECH | Fisheries |
| CULT | Culture and Education |
| JURI | Legal Affairs |
| LIBE | Civil Liberties, Justice and Home Affairs |
| AFCO | Constitutional Affairs |
| FEMM | Women's Rights and Gender Equality |
| PETI | Petitions |

*Source:* European Parliament (2014b).

committees have been dedicated to matters of policy challenges and the financial, economic, and social crisis. The Treaty of Maastricht, in addition, gave Parliament the right to establish committees of inquiry that may investigate into cases of serious misbehaviour or mismanagement (Art. 193 TEC-M).

In general, Parliamentary positions or reports on legislative proposals and other decisions are first addressed in the responsible committee (Maurer 2012: 70). The chairs of the committees play an important role, in that they are responsible for structuring the committees' work. Furthermore, along with the *rapporteur* on a certain dossier, the committee chairs negotiate compromises with the other institutions, particularly when the ordinary procedure of legislation applies. Finally, they perform an important role in mediating political struggles within the Parliament (Neuhold and Settembri 2007: 157–9).

Decision-making and policy formulation in the Parliament is organized as a step-by-step process and involves successive stages of consensus-building. A Commission proposal is first discussed in the relevant committee (Neuhold and Settembri 2007: 157–9; Maurer 2012: 104–5). A position or a series of amendment proposals is then elaborated in a report drawn up by a *rapporteur*. If necessary, consultation and coordination with other relevant committees will take place. After a decision at the committee level, the proposal is forwarded to the plenary. During this phase of the procedure, the rather 'technical' issue undergoes a political process of mediation between the political groups. If there are no major controversies, the plenary follows the vote of the committee (Raunio 2012: 349). Particularly in those cases where early agreements are concluded with the Council through the informal trialogues, the plenary has to accept the compromise as it stands (Héritier and Reh 2012). If it is necessary to go to conciliation, the two large political groups generally dominate the process, while the smaller ones play, at best, a subsidiary role (Judge and Earnshaw 2003: 151–4). However, none of the large groups alone commands the absolute majority that is often needed; neither can they form a majority coalition with only the smaller political groups. As a result, it has become common practice for the EPP and S&D groups to negotiate a compromise. This 'grand coalition' or 'duopoly' (Raunio 2012: 343) of the two large groups is often criticized. However, one has to bear in mind that it is not a coalition in the strictest sense, since compromises are negotiated on a case-by-case basis. The smaller groups can choose either to support the compromise or to be sidelined. In the best case scenario, the smaller groups may even be able to bring in some minor amendments. Their only other option is to take a minority position, which has no actual bearing on the decision. In most cases, the smaller groups prefer to support the proposal, even though they often delay doing so until the last possible moment. On the whole, parties consider it advantageous to participate in a broad coalition, since this can help them to gain a more influential position in the long run. This applies not only to the smaller groups, but also to the large ones. Indeed, with the support of one or more small groups, a single large group may achieve a compromise that better reflects its own preferences. A broad consensus, supported by both the large groups and a number of small ones, is most advantageous, since it increases the political weight of parliamentary proposals in relation to its counterparts and also enhances their overall legitimacy.

The stable 'grand coalition' in the Parliament, supported by smaller consensual groups, has implications for the whole process of policy formulation, and even for the MEPs themselves. First, less controversial issues tend to attract the most attention, whereas those issues likely to generate more conflict are often eliminated from the agenda or circumvented. Second, several commentators have noted that representatives of different political parties are increasingly converging in their political positions, attitudes, and expectations (Ovey 2002; for an opposing view, see Scully 2005). This is especially true when 'new' issues are at stake, or when issues that do not correspond to the classical spectrum of party politics at national level are on the agenda. Unsurprisingly, the Parliament has been able to achieve broad consensus and major successes in issues such as human rights, environmental protection, and immigration, as well as equal opportunities for men and women. In contrast, in the area of social policy, a highly controversial issue among national political parties, there has been very little progress. Third, a consensual style of interaction is emerging even around procedural questions. Though the MEPs express diverging political positions in plenary and in committee sessions, they do not usually engage in hostile debates, or competitive races between political parties, as is often the case in national legislatures. The consensual style of interaction may actually be supported by the considerable distance that MEPs are from their electorate. European parliamentarians are not compelled to sharpen their own political profile by over-accentuating their merits, or by blaming members of competing parties for set-backs.

The emerging broad consensus among the MEPs also influences other aspects of Parliamentary work. Leading positions and offices are proportionally distributed among the Parliamentary groups. The two large groups occupy the top positions, but the smaller parties also receive an appropriate share. As a rule, the position of the president of the Parliament is divided into two parts during the five-year legislative period. Until 1999, the Socialists – at the time, the largest group – held the presidency in the first phase of the legislature, followed by the EPP in the second phase (Raunio 2012: 344). With the elections of 1999, the EPP became the largest group in Parliament. At this time, it abolished the former rule and took the presidency in the first phase, while nominating a member of the liberal group for the second phase. However, this attempt to forge a smaller, centre-right coalition was only short-lived. When the post-enlargement elections of 2004 were held, the EPP again won the largest number of seats, but its relative share in the enlarged assembly was much smaller. It therefore returned to the former model of sharing the presidency with the Socialists and, in so doing, supported the 'grand coalition'. The model is also being followed in the 2009–2014 legislature, with an EPP member acting as president during the first term (Jerzy Buzek from Poland) and a S&D member presiding in the second term (Martin Schulz from Germany). Vice-presidents, committee presidents and the *rapporteurs* in the committees are nominated in a similar cooperative manner, based on the principle of proportionality among the party groups (Hix and Høyland 2010: 59). In all these cases, however, it is also important to aim for a certain degree of proportionality among national delegations.

These methods of operating tend to reduce political polarization or party competition in the Parliament. Although there are occasional struggles for power and influence, these are generally conducted behind the scenes. Nevertheless, open and tolerant attitudes have increasingly emerged between members of different political orientations and nationalities. This helps to foster a cosmopolitan spirit in Parliament.

With the introduction of the cooperation and co-decision procedures, and the transformation of the latter into the ordinary legislative procedure, decision-making in the Parliament has become more complicated. Besides considering substantive issues, the Parliament must now also consider strategic and tactical questions. Simply championing its most favoured position may not lead to the best possible outcome overall. Parliament has to consider whether the Commission is likely to support its proposals. Moreover, it needs to explore whether there is a degree of strife within the Council that it will subsequently be able to exploit to its own advantage. Over the years, Parliament established a strong cooperation with the Commission, in spite of numerous differences of opinion. This cooperation is a strategic asset for both sides. With the support of the Commission, the Parliament may expand its limited resources and access substantive expertise. In addition, Parliament benefits when the Commission adopts its proposals. Empirical studies have shown that parliamentary proposals adopted by the Commission have a much greater chance of passing in Council (Hix and Høyland 2010: 72).

The Parliament has also developed close relationships with the Council, largely through the ordinary legislative procedure – and, particularly, the provisions for early agreements. Thus, if the majority of the members of the Council are determined to take a decision on a legislative proposal, then there is some pressure to reach a compromise with the Parliament. In the informal trialogues, the Council does not act on its own behalf but it is represented by COREPER. Parliament has been able to establish stable relationships with the Brussels-based COREPER, thus contributing to increased confidence and cooperation on both sides. These relationships, however, do not prevent the Parliament from occasionally making use of its power of veto, as it did, for example, in 2010, when it refused to adopt the SWIFT agreement, which envisioned extensive financial data transfers from the EU to the USA (Monar 2010a). In this case, the Parliament saw not only fundamental rights of citizens, but also civil liberties endangered.

## Parliament's political role

Decision-making as has been described refers to the ordinary legislative procedure. However, the Parliament also takes a number of decisions that are not subject to any explicit procedural rules. In these cases, the Parliament not only 'invents' new procedures, but may also transgress its formal competences, or use its powers in ways other than intended. Furthermore, Parliament sometimes also takes initiatives in areas where it has no competences at all. However, with the enormous increase of its workload in the legislative realm, these broader political activities of the Parliament have, to a certain extent, been weakened.

For example, the Parliament successfully 'invented' a new procedure when the Treaty of Maastricht gave it the right of consent to an incoming Commission (Lord 2004: 139–43; Spence 2006a: 36–8). Although this right refers only to the College of Commissioners as a whole, the Parliament did not hesitate to thoroughly examine whether individual Commissioners were qualified for their portfolios. After intensive interrogation of the candidates in the respective committees, the Parliament signalled that five designated Commissioners lacked the necessary qualifications. Only intense negotiations behind the scenes and significant concessions by the incoming Commission President, Jacques Santer, secured a vote of consent in plenary. When the Prodi Commission was nominated in 1999, the incoming Commissioners were aware of the procedure of interrogation and were, as a result, better prepared. In this case, the vote of consent was cast without major problems. With the nomination of the Barroso Commission in 2004, the Parliament clearly went a step further. It vehemently rejected the nomination of two Commissioners who did not, in the view of a majority of the MEPs, fulfil the criteria for the position. The designated Commission president, Barroso, as well as the respective national governments, had no choice but to nominate new candidates for the office of Commissioner (Spence 2006a: 37; Westlake 2006: 267–8). In 2009, the next logical step was to question the qualification of José Manuel Barroso, who was nominated as Commission president for a second term. As the consent of the Parliament was not guaranteed, it could, again, negotiate on concessions in exchange for its favourable vote. The procedure of interrogating single Commissioners and assessing their qualification was, in fact, a transgression of competences. In this case, Parliament's success was twofold. It was able to increase its influence over the composition of the Commission, but also, and perhaps more so, it was able to expand its competences in the long run: therefore, the Lisbon Treaty specifies that the Parliament may elect the Commission President (Art. 17(7) TEU-L). However, it is the European Council that proposes a candidate to the Parliament. In practice, then, the Parliament has only a power of veto regarding the Council's candidate. However, at present, we observe that the EP attempts to reverse the procedure, by launching its own proposals for possible candidates.

We can also observe a systematic transgression of its powers in the day-to-day practices of the Parliament. For example, long before the Maastricht Treaty was implemented, Parliament practised an informal right of prompting the Commission to take initiative in a certain policy or issue area. In a similar vein, the EP practised a sort of conciliation procedure before the introduction of co-decision, by negotiating with the Council on amendments to a legislative proposal. These examples highlight that the transgression of competences not only serves to solve the problem at hand, but can, in the long run, often lead to an expansion of the EP's formal competences.

In terms of its budgetary powers, Parliament has also been particularly active in using its competences for purposes other than originally intended. More than once, Parliament has threatened to reject the adoption of the EU budget, if the financial resources were not rebalanced among policy areas. In this way, Parliament successively achieved reductions of the expenditure for agriculture and increases in financial resources for the Structural Funds. Furthermore, the Parliament managed regularly to increase the financial assistance to the transformation states of Central and Eastern Europe. Because such redistribution often led to additional reforms in the relevant policy areas, the Parliament could exercise extensive influence on these policies in both substantive and procedural terms (Pollack 2003: 215–6; Westlake 2006: 266).

The Parliament may also take initiatives without having explicit competences at its disposal. A favourite method is to adopt resolutions around minor, but also more significant political events. Such resolutions do not directly impact on the other institutions of the EU, but they may influence public opinion, or at least raise public awareness for certain issues. For example, the Parliament has often accused certain states of violating human rights. Occasionally, this has resulted in the postponement of trade negotiations, or the freezing of development aid for these states.

However, the most important initiatives in this context are those taken to further promote European integration and improve the institutional structure of the EC/EU (Maurer 2012: 124–38). With such initiatives, the Parliament has always also aimed to expand its own realm of competences. Thus, the Parliament was the first to open the reform debate in the beginning of the 1980s by launching a complete 'Draft Treaty for the establishment of a European Union'. Although this draft was not accepted as a whole – nor was even a single part of it adopted – it nevertheless influenced the reform debates. In the long run, though, many of the EP's proposals have been included, in some form, in successive revisions of the Treaties. Similarly, the Parliament achieved major successes in terms of the expansion of its own powers. First, the cooperation procedure; then, co-decision; and, finally, its expansion to an ever-growing range of policy areas have brought Parliament much closer to the goal of equality with the Council. The last step in this direction was made with the ordinary legislative procedure as introduced in the Lisbon Treaty. This, however, does not imply that the Parliament holds a position equal to that of the Council. In policy areas not regulated by legislation, the Parliament, even under the Lisbon Treaty, plays only a minor role. This applies not only to foreign policy, but also to policies governed by the Open Method of Coordination (OMC) (for details, see Chapters 7 and 8).

In summary, we can conclude that the European Parliament has been able to acquire a significant position in European decision-making and policy formulation, in spite of its initial weaknesses and lack of power. This grew largely out of Parliament's own activism through, first, the skilful use of existing procedures and competences; second, the full exploitation, or even transgression, of the realm of formal competences; and, third, the steady advocacy of major integration steps, as well as the improvement of its own position in the institutional architecture of the EU. However, the EP has had to pay a price for its growing successes in relation to the other institutions. Internally, it must increasingly adopt and maintain a consensual style of interaction and, thus, downplay political polarization. This, in turn, implies paying an additional price – a growing alienation from the electorate. The citizens of Europe are hardly able to perceive, let alone to understand the preferences, positions, and tactics of the Parliament and its political groups. They are even less able to understand the rationale of power struggles and consensus-building with the other institutions of the EU, which often take place behind the scenes. The enormous distance between the EP and its electorate has resulted in an extremely low and continuously decreasing voter turnout in European elections, which has contributed to a weakened legitimacy of the EP (see Chapter 12). Some scholars therefore claim that the Parliament needs a clear political polarization along a left–right divide (Hix 2005b; Hix *et al.* 2007). However, given Parliament's position within the overall structure of the EU, a left–right polarization is neither a realistic nor a desirable option (Bartolini 2005b).

## Conclusion

This chapter has focused on the internal organization of the core European institutions, their modes of decision-making and consensus-building, and their performance, as it is structured by the interaction among the institutions. In conclusion, we can state that all four institutions – the Commission, the Council, the European Council, and the Parliament – have developed sophisticated mechanisms for preparing and adopting decisions. Furthermore, they have created additional institutions and procedural arrangements designed to facilitate internal consensus. For the supranational institutions, achieving consensus is important, as this improves their power position with regard to their counterparts. For the intergovernmental Councils, consensus is a must, as it secures their capacity to promote integration and, in the case of the European Council, to provide leadership to the Union as a whole.

However, the four institutions differ in their methods, procedures and practices of decision-making and consensus-building. The Commission uses its large administrative machinery in order to prepare policy proposals, and to implement Council decisions and other policy measures. This implies a complex process of internal adaptations and fine-tuning, which involves all levels of the organization. In this process, the Commission needs to strike a balance between the technical and the political aspects of its proposals and activities. Even though the Commission can decide with a simple majority, it always seeks consensus among the Commissioners. In the process of elaborating policy proposals, the Commission also draws on a multitude of external actors to serve as advisors. It thus adapts its proposals at an early stage to the preferences and expectations of the member states and of the various stakeholders.

The Council, as an intergovernmental body, is confronted with considerable internal diversity. Since consensus-building is not simply a matter of goodwill, it has created an additional, comprehensive, and highly-differentiated substructure for preparing its work. In addition, it can rely on the agency of the Council presidency. Furthermore, the Council, through amending the Treaties, has steadily expanded and facilitated qualified majority voting with the aim of containing the veto-players in its own ranks. Even though the Council continues to strive for consensual decisions, the shadow of a vote and the necessity to compromise with Parliament puts pressure on its members to accept decisions that may not fully correspond to their preferences.

The European Council, as the top-level intergovernmental body, has developed into a supra-structure above the Council and the Union as a whole. However, since it decides on fundamental and highly sensitive issues, consensus-building among its members is particularly difficult. The European Council partly makes use of COREPER, the Commission, and also certain Council formations when preparing and adopting its decisions. In order to provide stability and continuity to its work and to facilitate consensus-building, the European Council has created the position of a permanent president. Nevertheless, dissent among the heads of state or government continues to dominate summit meetings – not least, because the European Council is increasingly confronted with more complex and controversial policy problems.

The Parliament, for its part, achieves broad majorities in decision-making by transcending party politics and bringing as wide an array of party groups as possible into its decisions. This gives Parliamentary decisions more weight in the eyes of the other institutions and can help the EP increase its influence regarding its counterparts. This strategy, however, has a price. It blurs the dividing lines between political groups, eliminates party competition to a considerable extent, and ultimately de-politicizes the European legislature. Consequently, the EP fails to mobilize the voters in support of its proposals and activities. Parliament also increases its political weight by using its competences to a maximum, or even acting beyond its reach. It 'invents' new procedures for enlarging its scope of action and raises public awareness on contested issues. It thus exercises pressure over the other institutions to take its positions into account.

In summary, we can conclude that the Union's core institutions operate in a way that improves their capacities of decision-making, by establishing elaborate procedures and creating additional institutional arrangements that enable or facilitate consensus-building. These processes of internal consensus-building are, for a large part, structured by the inter-institutional relations, which themselves are characterized by conflicts and seeking consensus. The three institutions involved in the legislative process can improve their influence on the outcome and their power position in relation to their counterparts only by relying on strong internal agreement. The European Council needs unity among its members in order to fulfil the aspired leadership role for the Union as a whole. Thus, we may assume that the consensus-building machinery that characterizes all decision-making in the EU, among its institutions as well as within them, is a core characteristic of the European polity.

# Chapter 7

## Expanding and Diversifying the Core Institutional Structure

Chapter 4 provided an outline of the EU's core institutional structure; in reality, however, this structure is even more complex and diverse than is apparent from an analysis of only the main institutions, and their roles and power in the system. A wide variety of additional institutions have gradually been created in order to make the European Union work more efficiently and effectively. However, the desire to improve efficiency and effectiveness has not been the only factor behind the EU's institutional expansion and diversification. Rather, this expansion and diversification is also encouraged by the power struggles among the European institutions and, more broadly, the omnipresent conflict between the inter-governmental and supranational forces. This arrangement has led to a sequence of actions, reactions, and counteractions among the European institutions. Along the way, each institution has attempted to optimize its own competences and procedures for decision-making, in order to gain greater influence on the entire process, or to contain the expansion of power and influence of their counterparts. This jostling for power and influence has resulted in a sophistication of the procedures of European decision-making, in the establishment and consolidation of a number of additional institutions, and in relatively flexible and informal institutional arrangements.

In order to strengthen the supranational dynamics of the Union, the Commission created additional institutions in support of its activities. For example, the Commission has called a host of advisory groups into existence in order to assist in drawing up legislative proposals. However, these groups were not formally established. Rather, they are set up as flexible institutional arrangements. Furthermore, the Commission has often proposed to the Council that it would be useful to establish new institutions; for example, in the form of independent agencies. The Commission has hoped that these institutions would assume a supranational bias over the long term. The European Court and the Parliament do not have competences in this area and, as such, they have not played a role in this form of institution-building.

On the intergovernmental side of the system, the Council – and, in particular, the European Council – have made extensive use of the power to build additional institutions. In fact, these are the bodies that command the powers formally to establish or alter the institutional setting of the EU, either by Treaty amendments or by secondary legislation. The Councils' motives to push forward institution-building have been twofold. First, the Councils have repeatedly recognized the need to expand integration to new areas, or to react to newly emerging external challenges by establishing common policies. However, they have been unwilling to expand the Commission's role and reach in these areas, as this might increase the body's relative power. The solution has therefore been to establish and formalize new institutions that allow for common action at the European level, but which are largely withdrawn from the Commission's sphere of influence. As a result, the EU typically expanded its institutional structures either by creating various forms of transnational cooperation under tight intergovernmental control, or through independent agencies with a Council-defined mandate. When there has been major dissent among national governments preventing further integration, the Councils turned to forms of differentiated integration; that is, projects and institutional arrangements that include only a smaller number of member states. In any event, all these institutional innovations promoted by the Councils reflect the will of the member states to act together at European level, and also their reluctance to expand the powers of the supranational institutions. These strategies have led to a strengthening of the intergovernmental dimension of the EU and a weakening of the power of the supranational forces.

This is not to say, however, that the European Union is being transformed into a political system predominantly governed by intergovernmental forces. Rather, we can see a continuous fluctuation between these two competing forces that constitute the EU. The institutions that are primarily governed by the Council or the European Council often do not function as efficiently and effectively as expected. In these cases, the Councils may choose to empower the supranational institutions selectively, particularly the Commission and the Parliament, in the relevant policy areas. Furthermore, after a certain period of intergovernmental cooperation in a given policy area, the number of consensual issues increases; so specific powers and functions in these areas can be transferred to the supranational institutions. Thus, the cases of institution-building described in this chapter exemplify the tendency to expand and diversify the intergovernmental institutional setting of the EU, as well as the selective empowerment of the supranational institutions in the respective policy areas.

The following sections outline the evolution and nature of this broader institutional architecture by analyzing the most salient examples of institution-building. I consider, in particular, the creation and reorganization of specific intergovernmental arrangements for sensitive policy areas, the so-called 'pillars' and their institutional follow-ups after the Lisbon Treaty. Moreover, I examine a wide variety of independent agencies that fulfil specific purposes in European politics and policies. Finally, I present selected forms of differentiated integration; that is, integration steps that do not include all member states. To explain these developments, I draw on the arguments of historical and rational choice institutionalism, as these are better placed than the traditional integration theories to highlight the motives underlying specific institutional choices and the resulting tendency towards diversifying the EU's institutional structure.

## Building intergovernmental annexes: the second and third pillars and their follow-up institutional arrangements

As noted, as an emergent political order, the European Union is constantly expanding and diversifying its institutional structure. One of the most important examples of this expansion is found in the creation of a distinct institutional arrangement to transfer two highly sensitive policy areas to the European level. Both the common foreign and security policy (CFSP) and justice and home affairs (JHA) were considered issues of importance to national sovereignty and were marked by major dissent among the member states. Nonetheless, with this shift, national governments aimed at fostering integration in these policy areas, but in such a way as to ensure that they remained under tight intergovernmental control.

The Treaty of Maastricht, which formally established the European Union, introduced these new intergovernmental arrangements. In the language accompanying the negotiations on the Maastricht Treaty, the Union was conceived as a classical temple, supported by three pillars under a common roof. The existing Community was defined as the first pillar. The second and third pillars were added to represent the new European policy areas: the CFSP and JHA. The first pillar encompassed all policies that dealt with market integration, as well as a number of policies, including EMU, that were later added to the Union's competences. The symmetry of classical architecture to which the temple metaphor referred could not, however, hide the imbalance that characterized the European edifice. The first pillar represented the entire *acquis communautaire*; that is, the whole body of European legislation, which constitutes the central building of the EU. The second and third pillars, by contrast, encompassed only specific initiatives towards integration in limited policy areas. Rather than forming strong pillars that sustain the whole structure, these only constituted smaller annexes to the European house, built in addition with far less sturdy materials. Nonetheless, the pillar metaphor correctly highlighted that the newly integrated policy areas were governed by the EU's intergovernmental institutions and, therefore, distinctive from the set-up of the Community – and, indeed, barely connected to it.

The Lisbon Treaty conferred the European Union with legal personality. Previously, this had been granted only to the Community (Art. 47 TEU-L). As a consequence, the term 'Community' disappeared from the new Treaties, Accordingly, the pillars were said to be abolished, although this term was not formally used in any Treaty. In fact, the intergovernmental forms of governance in the CFSP and JHA with their distinctive procedures of decision-making and specific allocations of competences continue to exist, although with some modifications (Laursen 2010: 6, 10). In the following, I use the term 'pillars' to refer to the intergovernmental forms of governance during the period from the Maastricht Treaty to the Lisbon Treaty. When referring to the whole period of integrating policies in the framework of intergovernmental institutions or to the post-Lisbon era, I speak of the respective policy areas; that is, the CFSP and JHA, or of specific institutional arrangements.

## Variegated intergovernmentalism in foreign and security policy: building and dismantling the second pillar

The roots of establishing a common foreign and security policy date back to the early years of integration. However, the history of integration in this sensitive policy area is marked by failures or, at best, moderate successes (Smith 2004; Bretherton and Vogler 2006; Ginsberg 2007: 283–328; Giegerich and Wallace 2010). As early as the 1950s, there was an attempt to undertake a common project in this area: the European Defence Community; yet, this failed to be adopted (Gilbert 2003: 56–62; see also Chapter 2). During the 1960s, expansive policy proposals were launched, but none was ever implemented. Although the 1970s and the early 1980s were marked by modest attempts towards the coordination of national policies under the label of European Political Cooperation (EPC), it was not until the adoption of the SEA in 1986 that there was a renewed effort at integration in foreign affairs (Bretherton and Vogler 2006: 165–7). The SEA offered a blueprint of well-defined procedures in intergovernmental decision-making. In addition, it foresaw procedures for coordinating the policies of the member states and modest tools for joint action. Thereafter, special meetings of the ministers for foreign affairs began to be convened, thus underlining that foreign policy was to have its own role next to 'regular' European policy-making.

The Treaty of Maastricht (in force since 1993), then introduced the pillar structure. This implied that foreign and security policy was now firmly embedded in the portfolio of the Union as an activity of cooperating governments and, thus, separate from the 'regular' policies and procedures (Bretherton and Vogler 2006: 167–8). All decisions in foreign affairs were to be taken either by the European Council, or the Council of Ministers. The European Council took on the task of defining the basic objectives and strategies of the CFSP. The Council of Foreign Affairs was charged with the responsibility for concrete measures and policy implementation. Basic decisions were to be unanimous, while secondary or subsequent decisions could be adopted by a qualified majority. The so-called Political Committee, consisting of high-level civil servants of the member states, prepared the meetings and decisions of the Councils. The Political Committee was established as a specific body, standing in for COREPER in the CFSP (Hayes-Renshaw and Wallace 2006: 82–6). At the same time, the Political Committee was expected to cooperate with COREPER. This often resulted in tensions between the two bodies. The Commission and the Parliament were largely excluded from decision-making in foreign affairs and the Court of Justice was not involved at all in this area.

'Normal' legislative powers were not envisioned for this policy area (Art. J.2(2) and J.3 TEU-M; see also Smith 2001), but within the framework of the CFSP, the European Council and the Council defined legally-binding instruments, such as the Common Position and the Joint Action. The coordination of national policies remained the primary objective of EU foreign policy (Art. J.1(3) TEU-M), thus preserving its intergovernmental character.

The Treaty of Amsterdam (in force since 1999) reaffirmed the intergovernmental nature of the second pillar. However, at the same time, it aimed at further integrating the CFSP into the institutional structure of the EU (Bretherton and Vogler 2006: 168–70; see also Chapter 3). An additional policy instrument, the Common Strategy (Art. 12 TEU-A), to be adopted by the European Council (Art. 13 TEU-A), was introduced. Furthermore, the position of a High Representative for the CFSP was created (Art. 18(3) TEU-A). The officeholder was to act in a dual capacity, both as High Representative for the CFSP and Secretary General of the Council Secretariat. He or she would be assisted by a Policy Planning and Early Warning Unit established at the Council Secretariat (Treaty of Amsterdam, Final Act, Declaration No. 6). This unit served to analyze relevant developments, define the interests of the Union in foreign and security affairs, assess political events, and elaborate policy proposals for the Councils. For the first time, a unit of the Council Secretariat was given a major role in preparing substantive decisions for the EU.

The creation of the office of High Representative for the CFSP highlights the fact that the member states recognized a collective action problem in the second pillar. As a result, they decided to delegate certain responsibilities in foreign and security matters to a third, neutral actor. In so doing, national governments aimed at enhancing the effectiveness of this policy beyond intergovernmental bargains. However, the member states were clearly unwilling to allocate this role to the Commission, in spite of the latter's claims for such a role during the negotiations on the Treaty of Amsterdam. Obviously, member states feared a loss of control in foreign affairs. Nevertheless, the Treaty of Amsterdam opened the door slightly for the supranational institutions, by giving the Commission a non-exclusive right of initiative in the CFSP (Art. 22(1) and 27 TEU-A) and establishing a special troika, comprising the President of the Commission, the High Representative, and the head of state or government of the member state holding the Council presidency, collectively representing the Union externally (Art. 18 TEU-A).

The Treaty of Nice did not mark any significant progress in the CFSP (Bretherton and Vogler 2006: 170–1). It was not until the Constitutional Treaty was drafted that any major attempt cautiously to strengthen the supranational dimension of foreign and security policy was undertaken. This time, the position of a 'Union Minister for Foreign Affairs' was proposed (Art. I-28 DCT). The individual in charge of that position was to act both as President of the Foreign Affairs Council and as Vice-President of the Commission responsible for external relations (Art. I-28(3 and 4) DCT). It was hoped that an individual wearing two hats could bridge the gap between the Commission and the Council or, in other words, the intergovernmental and supranational dimensions of the Union. After the failed referenda on the Draft Constitutional Treaty and the subsequent renegotiation, this ambitious project was slightly reformulated. Among other changes, the term 'foreign minister' was dismissed in favour of the more familiar 'High Representative of the Union for Foreign and Security Policy' (Art 27 TEU-L). Nonetheless, the High Representative, as part of the Commission and the Council, was to wear two hats. This arrangement places contradicting demands on the office-holder (Art. 17(4) TEU-L; see also Müller-Brandeck-Bocquet 2011; Rüger 2011).

Together with building the CFSP, the member states have long been considering improvements to the security dimension of the EU (Howorth 2007: 6–10). After examining different concepts for a defence organization, they initially decided that the Western European Union (WEU) should take on this role. A vaguely formulated article to this end was included in the Treaty of Maastricht (Art. J.4 TEU-M). However, as time passed, it became clear that this would not be a satisfactory arrangement. Although the WEU has been in existence since the 1950s, it has always stood in the shadow of NATO. Besides, many of the neutral or non-aligned member states of the Union have been reluctant to accept any common provisions for defence at all. As a result, the Amsterdam

Treaty, negotiated after the entry of Sweden, Finland, and Austria into the EU, actually weakened the potential role of the WEU. The Amsterdam Treaty made the involvement of the WEU in defence matters dependent on an explicit decision of both the European Council and the individual member states (Art. 17(1) TEU-A). In view of this half-hearted solution and in the face of intense pressures to solve the immediate problem of the Balkan wars and other security threats beyond Europe's borders, a European Security and Defence Policy (ESDP) was proposed (Howorth 2007: 33–60). This concept, adopted at the European Council of Helsinki (December 1999), envisaged that, in times of crisis, Rapid Reaction Forces (RRF) would be available for the rapid deployment of defence forces of the member states. Additional institutional structures were also designed in order to improve decision-making capabilities and provide leadership to the defence forces (Howorth 2007: 61–91). The Political Committee of the CFSP, which was responsible for the preparation of the decisions of both the Council and the European Council, was transformed into the Political and Security Committee (PSC) (Hayes-Renshaw and Wallace 2006: 83; Howorth 2012). In military matters, this Committee is supported by the European Union Military Committee (EUMC). The EUMC, in turn, is assisted by the European Union Military Staff, an essentially technical institution. Together, these institutions represent a new mixture of bodies, staffed by experts, who bear political and technical responsibility for military missions in third countries. The members of both these institutions are selected by national governments, thus further ensuring the intergovernmental nature of European security policy. In 2004, the European Council furthermore decided to establish a European Defence Agency (EDA) to coordinate the national procurement of armaments.

The present institutional structure of the CFSP, as set out in the Lisbon Treaty, contains both elements of the former second pillar, as well as some major changes to the earlier set-up (Laursen 2010). In particular, there were several attempts to give the supranational branch of the EU a stronger role in the CFSP, and to better coordinate policies that were earlier separated by the pillar structure. The Treaty now refers quite generally to the external action of the Union, which allows for coordinated activities in the sphere of foreign trade policy (formerly pertaining to the first pillar) and foreign and security policy (formerly defined as the second pillar) (Art. 21 TEU-L). However, the actual governance of the CFSP remains almost unchanged. For example, the Treaty specifies that, 'The common foreign and security policy is subject to specific rules and procedures. It shall be defined by the European Council and the Council, acting by unanimity, except where the Treaties provide otherwise. The adoption of legislative acts shall be excluded' (Art. 24(1) TEU-L). Consequently, the Councils remain in the driver's seat, while the supranational institutions play only a subordinated role. However, the Lisbon Treaty also introduces major changes aimed at improving common actions in foreign affairs. To this end, the Treaty creates the position of a High Representative of the European Union for Foreign Affairs and Security Policy (HR), who, unlike the former HR, acts as both Vice-President of the Commission and permanent President of the External Affairs Council (Art. 18 TEU-L, Laursen 2010; see also Rüger 2011). The HR 'shall conduct the Union's common foreign and security policy', but 'he shall carry out (that policy) as mandated by the Council' (Art. 18(2) TEU-L). Furthermore, in order to prepare and support the work of the HR – and, more broadly, that of the Councils – a European External Action Service (EEAS), consisting of officials from the European Commission, the Council Secretariat and national foreign ministries, has been established (Cameron 2011). Last, but not least, the existing Commission Delegations in third countries have been transformed into EU Delegations (Laursen 2010: 12–3)

In terms of security matters, the Lisbon Treaty expands 'enhanced cooperation' to the security area and provides for forms of 'permanent structured cooperation' among a smaller group of member states (Art. 42(6) and 46 TEU-L). This clause gives the EU the option to circumvent the resistance of neutral or non-aligned member states towards military commitment (Howorth 2007). Furthermore, the European Defence Agency (EDA), established in 2004, is now formally integrated into the Treaty (Art. 42(3) TEU-L).

In summary, we can conclude that the EU has established a complex institutional framework for undertaking and further developing a CFSP. Key institutions in this realm are the European Council and the Council, whose 'external action' is prepared and conducted by the HR and the EEAS. Furthermore, independent agencies such as the EDA take responsibility for the more technical matters. Thus, besides acting through the intergovernmental bodies, there have been institutional provisions made to help overcome the ever-present dilemmas of collective action. In addition, these dilemmas are countered by preparing and taking decisions in small expert circles, that, in the long run, tend to adopt supranational stances (Howorth 2012). To a certain extent, dilemmas of collective action are also circumvented by allowing for 'enhanced cooperation' in all facets of the CFSP, and for 'permanent structured cooperation' in military matters. The supranational institutions continue to be largely side-lined in this institutional set-up, even though the position of the HR as both Commissioner and president of the foreign affairs Council and the participation of Commission civil servants in the EEAS serve to bridge the gap between the Union's intergovernmental and supranational dimension.

However, in spite of – or, perhaps, *because* of – these institutional arrangements, the achievements of the CFSP remain rather limited. Member states continue to hold widely different opinions and positions in salient issues. The recent dispute on whether to provide arms to Syrian opposition forces is one such example. Since no agreement on this issue could be reached, the Council finally lifted the arms embargo on Syria as of 1 June 2013. In addition, Catherine Ashton, as the first HR under the Lisbon Treaty, has been judged as giving a rather poor performance, despite some achievements, particularly in the diplomatic sphere. Howorth attributes this poor performance to the ill-defined position of the office, but also to the office-holder and the Council's choice for an inexperienced candidate (Howorth 2011). Once more, this choice high-lights the reluctance of national governments to slacken the reins in this sensitive policy area. This remains a persistent problem in the Union's foreign and security policy.

## Variegated intergovernmentalism in justice and home affairs: building and dismantling the third pillar

The area of justice and home affairs consists of a group of policies that are highly sensitive to issues of national sovereignty. Not surprisingly, this policy area has faced even greater obstacles in the process of inte-gration than the CFSP. The institutions governing JHA, termed the 'third pillar', were created by the Maastricht Treaty. The institutional arrange-ments of the third pillar are very similar to those of the CFSP, although the policy area has evolved in a somewhat different way. Moreover, fundamental changes to the policy were adopted as part of the Lisbon Treaty (Monar 2007; Lavenex 2009, 2010; Kaunert 2010).

The first strong impetus to cooperate in the area of JHA was linked to the implementation of the single market programme. Open borders not only facilitate international trade, but can also exacerbate transnational problems, including issues around immigration and asylum, drugs and human trafficking, subsidy fraud, and organized crime. Previously, even though these problems posed serious security threats to the EU, they were not considered serious enough to embark on a common policy. The policy area consequently evolved only slowly and its structure was initially even less integrated than the CFSP.

The impetus for cooperation in JHA arose out of two projects of transnational cooperation: the Trevi group, established in 1975; and the Schengen agreement, first concluded in 1985. The Trevi group initially comprised a network of national officials active in home affairs (Monar 2002; Lavenex 2009). Its responsibilities were directed towards combating international organized crime. Later, its mandate was expanded to include other dimensions of JHA. The Schengen agreement was originally concluded outside the EC institutions and only among five member states (Germany, France, and the Benelux-countries) (Lavenex 2009: 257). It had two main goals: first, abolishing border controls among participating states; second, fostering closer cooperation in the areas of immigration, organized crime, and policing. Between 1990 and 2000, most of the EU's member states adopted the agreement. The UK and Ireland were the exceptions as they chose not to participate fully in the system. The Schengen agreement recently was extended to the new member states, although Cyprus, Bulgaria, Romania, and Croatia still remain outside. Thus, at present, 22 member states of the EU and 3 non-members (Norway, Iceland, and Switzerland) participate fully in the Schengen agreement. Both the Trevi and the Schengen initiatives, with their concerted activities, have constituted important building blocks of what was later termed the 'third pillar' (Lavenex 2009: 256).

The Maastricht Treaty built on these blocks to establish the third pillar, assigning to it the following policy issues: asylum, immigration, external border controls, the prevention and combating of crime, and police and judicial cooperation (Art. 2(29 and 30) TEU-M). As in the CFSP, the aim was not so much to establish a genuinely European policy but, rather, to enhance cooperation among the member states (Lavenex 2010). Accordingly, decision-making was strictly limited to the intergovernmental institutions of the EU. The European Council provided the basic strategic guidelines, while the Council of Ministers decided on common activities. A special committee, the Article 36 Committee, was established to prepare the decisions of the Councils (Hayes-Renshaw and Wallace 2006: 86–8). As in the second pillar, the policy instruments were Common Positions and Joint Actions. The Commission and the Parliament played only a limited role in decision-making and the Court had no role at all.

The Treaty of Amsterdam further enhanced the institutional structure of the third pillar and, at the same time, introduced certain innovations to strengthen the role of the supranational bodies in the policy area. First, the Treaty of Amsterdam renamed the policy area the 'Area of Freedom, Security and Justice' (AFSJ). Some of its former responsibilities, particularly in the area of immigration, were transferred to the first pillar and, thus, placed in the hands of the Community. The Schengen agreement was incorporated into the third pillar. Since the corresponding protocol was signed only by 13 of the then 15 member states, Schengen remained a case of differentiated integration. In juridical terms, this was made possible by the introduction of 'enhanced cooperation' in the Treaty of Amsterdam. This provision enables a smaller group of member states to implement common policies (Art. 43-45 TEU-A). Furthermore, the Treaty of Amsterdam gave the Commission a non-exclusive right of initiative, and expanded the Parliament's role to include consultative powers. However, the roles of the Commission and Parliament remained limited and did not fundamentally restrain intergovernmental decision-making (Lavenex 2009). Measures taken under the framework of the AFSJ usually took the form of 'soft law' or operational cooperation (Lavenex 2009, 2010). Consequently, neither the Commission nor the Parliament was actually able to make use of its limited competences.

In 1993, a Council decision established a European police office, EUROPOL, as part of the third pillar and within the framework of judicial and police cooperation. EUROPOL's scope of responsibility ranged from joint investigations, via coordination of national investigations, to data collection and analysis (Monar 2002: 205–6). The agency, fully operative since 1999, is subject to only marginal control by the Council. Based on the model of EUROPOL, a number of additional independent agencies were subsequently established in the AFSJ (Lavenex 2009: 265–7). The most 'infamous' of these is FRONTEX, established in 2004. This is the agency responsible for protecting the external borders of the EU. Human rights activists accuse FRONTEX of violating European laws and international humanitarian conventions because the agency has the power to turn back refugees and asylum seekers to third countries without a judicial procedure. The proliferation of independent agencies in the AFSJ is indicative of the fact that the member states show a real desire to foster collective action; at the same time, it also reveals their weaknesses in taking and implementing joint decisions (Monar 2002: 205–6; Lavenex 2010: 467–70).

The Lisbon Treaty fundamentally alters the institutional structure of the AFSJ. It expands and improves the supranational dimension of this policy area; at the same time, it also strengthens intergovernmental oversight (Lieb and Maurer 2009: 79–87; Kaunert 2010: 172–3). The Lisbon Treaty establishes the ordinary legislative procedure as the standard even for legislative acts under the framework of the AFSJ. This clearly improves the position of the supranational institutions in decision-making. The Commission gains another area in which it has an exclusive right to propose legislation, although the areas of criminal justice and policing legislation remain an exception to this. In these areas, it shares these powers with the member states. The Parliament, along with the Council, is elevated to the role of co-legislator, and the Court is entitled to exercise judicial review (Kaunert 2010: 172–3). Moreover, the Council's role in legislation is actually weakened slightly, as its decisions are taken by majority voting. However, at the same time, the Lisbon Treaty offers a slight improvement of intergovernmental oversight on the AFSJ. For example, the Treaty entitles the European Council to define the strategic guidelines and operational planning for the policy area (Art. 68 TFEU). This could significantly constrain the Commission's right of initiative in these matters (Lieb and Maurer 2009: 80). For its part, the Council can adopt measures (Art. 70 TFEU), and a standing committee (formerly the Article 36 committee) is set up 'in order to ensure that operational cooperation on internal security is promoted and strengthened within the Union' (Art. 71 TFEU). National governments play an important role in this area as well. They can even 'organise between themselves ... forms of cooperation and coordination' (Art. 73 TFEU). Finally, the principle of mutual recognition is widely applied in the AFSJ, so that deliberate harmonization of national policies is not required (Schmidt 2009: 132–3). Operational cooperation is largely delegated to a host of independent agencies with specific mandates (Lavenex 2009: 265–7; 2010: 467–70). Finally, forms of differentiated integration are also used – as, for example, in the framework of the Prüm Treaty. This Treaty, signed in 2005 by a small number of member states, aims to improve information-sharing as a means of preventing and combating crime (Monar 2010b; Balzacq and Hadfield 2012).

At present, the policies in the framework of the AFSJ display highly diversified patterns of governance. Certain policy areas within this domain are increasingly governed by both the supranational and the intergovernmental institutions, whereas others still rely to a large extent on intergovernmental and transnational cooperation, and extensive networks of lower-level governmental actors and experts. For the resulting 'peculiar mix of governance modes' (Lavenex 2009: 256), Helen Wallace has coined the term 'intensive transgovernmentalism' (Wallace 2010). According to Lavenex (2009: 258), 'intensive transgovernmentalism stresses the role of horizontal network governance that interacts in different ways with more hierarchical governance modes in the EU'. Of course, these governance modes not only characterize the AFSJ, but also a wide spectrum of other policy areas (see Chapter 8). Nonetheless, we can conclude that, in spite of the fundamental changes of the Lisbon Treaty, these governance modes remain an important feature in the domain of justice and home affairs.

Summing up, we can conclude that the institutional structure of what was formerly labelled the 'third pillar' has evolved to a specific state, in which a strong role for both the EU's supranational and intergovernmental institutions combines with transgovernmental and transnational cooperation in order to coordinate national policy-making or achieve a degree of standardization through soft law or mutual recognition. However, in spite of the manifold forms of transgovernmental and transnational cooperation available under the umbrella of Council decisions, substantial joint measures and actions in the ASFJ have rarely emerged. The policy development 'has often been extremely difficult', not least, because parties of the right have 'strived to demonstrate that they are 'tough' on such ... issues' (Buonanno and Nugent 2013: 250). This clearly puts pressure on national governments to be tough as well, and to refrain from soft forms of governance in the context of intergovernmental cooperation.

If we pull together the observations from both the second and third pillars, and their follow-up institutional arrangements under the regulations of the Lisbon Treaty, we can conclude that initially, these specific organizational forms clearly differed from the Union's 'normal' construction scheme. They were not organized as genuine European activities but, rather, as coordinated national endeavours under intergovernmental control. For this purpose, consistent procedures of decision-making, together with corresponding institutional arrangements, were codified and increasingly diversified. However, over time, the intergovernmental pillars have evolved into hybrid institutional arrangements that rely on forms of mixed responsibility. Accordingly, the supranational institutions took over certain functions in these policy areas. In the CFSP, this occurred by establishing institutions (the HR and the EEAS) that helped to bridge the gap between the supranational and intergovernmental dimension of the EU. In the AFSJ, the involvement of the supranational institutions mainly resulted from the application of the ordinary legislative procedure to a broad range of issues in the policy area. Yet, in many cases, where supranational decisions or actions are required, these functions are delegated to specialized, independent agencies or groups of experts. Whether such third-party actors and institutions can improve the efficiency and effectiveness of the two policy areas, or alleviate the collective action dilemma of the Councils, is debatable. In many cases, the powers given to these actors and institutions are quite limited. In any event, the development of the pillars and their follow-up institutional arrangements highlights that national governments are very cautious to transfer powers to the European level in these sensitive policy areas. As a result, they have opted for flexible integration steps that selectively empower the supranational institutions or delegate specific responsibilities to third party actors and institutions.

Overall, we can consider the distinctive intergovernmental or transnational institutions for the governance of CFSP and ASFJ as important building blocks for a more flexible and heterogeneous model of integration under a common European roof, but not in a common house. This form of flexible integration allows member states to act jointly at European level, while retaining stronger control over the respective policy areas. However, such models of integration do not easily lead to effective problem-solving. This is why the Union continuously modifies the governance of these policies and the institutional arrangements that underpin the governance process. It goes without saying that these forms of integration exacerbate the institutional fragmentation of the European polity and the opacity of its institutional structure.

## Establishing a variety of adjacent buildings: independent agencies

As we saw in the previous section, the EU increasingly delegates specific political functions to independent institutions and agencies. This process is not limited to the second and third pillars, and the corresponding policy areas. In fact, it is even more common in the policy domains of what was originally the Community or the first pillar, and in certain political functions that serve the Union as a whole. The creation of a variety of independent agencies, such as the European Central Bank (ECB) or the European Environmental Agency (EEA), moves integration in a new direction. In these cases, the member states seek to further integrate specific policy areas, but they do not want to grant the Commission (i.e. an existing supranational institution) any additional powers. By creating the agencies, they insulate certain decisions and actions from the conflicting interests and power struggles among the member states, as well as those between the supranational and the intergovernmental forces in the EU. Thus, the agencies allow a 'technical' logic to prevail which, in the European context, often comes down to the logic of the market (Majone 1996).

According to Majone (1996, 2005), independent agencies, mostly responsible for 'statutory regulation' (i.e. additional, specific regulation in limited issue areas) were initially established in the United States. European states came to the practice later. They increasingly delegate regulatory functions to specialized agencies, in part because general forms of regulation have often failed to reach their defined goals. However, more than the nation states, the European Union widely practises its own forms of delegation. For Majone, the Commission itself acts as a 'regulatory agency', since the member states have transferred extensive powers to it (Majone 1996). He furthermore believes that a host of other independent agencies exercise important regulatory functions at European level. In the section below, I analyze the nature of some of these institutions and the important role they play in the political system of the EU, even though they are not often vested with regulatory tasks.

## The first generation of independent agencies

First, we consider here the 'traditional' independent agencies that have been an integral part of the European polity for a long time. One such agency is the European Investment Bank (EIB), which was already established in 1958. Its primary objective is to finance large-scale projects that serve the development of the Union (Nugent 2010: 235–8). It provides loans at low interest rates, in particular to the economically less-developed countries and regions of the EU that also receive funding within the framework of the Structural Funds. In addition, the EIB provides financial support to third states, including the transformation states of Eastern Europe, the neighbouring Mediterranean states; and the ACP-states. The ACP-group encompasses 78 African, Caribbean and Pacific states, most of them former colonies of EU-member states. The EIB acts as a development bank and pursues both commercial and public objectives.

Another example of an independent agency is the European Court of Auditors (ECA), which was set up in 1975 by merging two corresponding institutions of the former Communities (Nugent 2010: 240–3; Karakatsanis and Laffan 2012: 243; Stephenson 2012). Its core function is to monitor and control all financial transactions of the Union with regard to their efficiency, effectiveness, and legality. This implies that it exercises control over the Commission and the member states, as well as over all recipients of EU finance. The Court publishes its findings in annual and special reports (Karakatsanis and Laffan 2012: 249; Stephenson 2012: 18). The Commission and other institutions in the EU can reply to the observations of the Court. The reports may also serve the Parliament when it gives discharge to the Commission for the implementation of the budget (Art. 319 TFEU). In addition to its technical functions, the Court has taken on an increasingly political role (Stephenson 2012: 19). By using its reports to criticize the slow or delayed release of financial support, to uncover grievances and abuses, or to point to the negative impacts of certain policies – such as agricultural, regional, and social policy; or the assistance programmes for Central and Eastern Europe – the Court exercises an indirect, but broad, influence on the implementation of European policies (see the Annual Reports of the Court of Auditors; Karakatsanis and Laffan 2012). For example, the Court has repeatedly criticized the negative impact that the implementation of the Structural Funds has on the environment. The Parliament subsequently used this criticism against the Commission and was able to insist on a change of policy. Broadly speaking, the Commission is highly sensitive to negative comments of the Court (Karakatsanis and Laffan 2012: 251–4). Insofar as possible, the Commission tries to adapt its policies in order to avoid tarnishing its image. Not surprisingly, it was information provided by the Court of Auditors that played a decisive role in the resignation of the Santer Commission in 1999 (Karakatsanis and Laffan 2012: 253–4). In 1999, yet another independent agency emerged: OLAF (Office Européen de Lutte Anti-Fraude) (Karakatsanis and Laffan 2012: 248, 254). With the establishment of this agency, the Prodi Commission took an important step to combat fraud and corruption in the EU. As a response to transnational pressures, 'legal Europe is attempting to catch up with criminal Europe' (Karakatsanis and Laffan 2012: 254).

In addition to its 'regular' functions, the Court of Auditors may issue statements on certain matters, either on its own initiative or on request. Several times the Council or the European Council has requested that the Court elaborate on a study concerning specific policy initiatives of the Commission. In those cases, the Councils have used the independent position of the Court to rein in the activism of the Commission, in other words, to limit the 'creeping' expansion of competences in certain spheres of influence at the European level (Pollack 1994). The Parliament can also make use of the Court to control the Commission's financial management.

In nation states, cartel authorities are one common form of independent agency. Interestingly, however, the European Union does not have a cartel authority, although issues concerning cartels (i. e. competition policies) have held a prominent role since the foundation of the Communities. Instead, the European Commission is vested with broad competences in this area. In the late 1970s and early 1980s, the Commission launched detailed proposals to establish such an agency. However, the Council did not take any decision on the Commission proposal. Clearly, member states did not want to delegate the corresponding competences to an agency. At that time, the Commission seemed to be a relatively weak actor, so the member states actually preferred to let it do this task. However, this situation has fundamentally changed. The Commission increasingly used its competences in competition matters to a maximum and pursued a highly proactive policy (Cini and McGowan 2008). Thus, it has taken on an authoritative position in cartel issues with regard both to the member states and private firms. In certain cases, it has even succeeded in using its far-reaching competences for purposes other than those originally intended. For example, under the guise of safeguarding fair competition, it forced the liberalization of public utilities in the member states, partly against the declared will of national governments (Schmidt 2004). Nevertheless, the Commission is constrained in exercising the function of a cartel authority, because of the enormous number of cases with which it has to deal. Hence, it is often compelled to monitor the implementation of competition rules in a highly selective manner.

The enormous workload of the Commission led to the decentralization of a significant part of competition policy from the European to the national level in 2004. This reform obliged member states to establish their own cartel authorities. This, in turn, prompted the establishment of a transnational network of these authorities, acting under the auspices of the Commission, in order to ensure the uniform application of competition law (Cini and McGowan 2008; Lehmkuhl 2009; Wilks 2010). Thus, instead of establishing one strong and independent agency at European level, a choice was made for a two-level institutional structure. The major reform of competition policy might appear to be an empowerment of national authorities at the expense of the Commission. However, in this institutional configuration, the Commission is clearly in the driver's seat. For the most part, it defines the rules to be applied in the member states, it gives advice to national agencies on how to deal with concrete cases, and it exercises indirect control on the activities of these agencies. It thus propels the harmonization of anti-cartel policies throughout the European Union to a hitherto unknown extent.

## The second generation of independent agencies

Whereas the first generation of independent agencies was based on the models of corresponding national institutions, the second generation agencies are different and display characteristics that reveal new trends in European integration (Majone 2002). Although most of these new agencies do not have 'rule-making' powers (Majone 2002), they are becoming increasingly independent, primarily because the Union lacks the institutional structure and the authority to exercise tight political control.

The European Environmental Agency is a good example of a typical second-generation independent agency (Kelemen and Majone 2012). Its primary scope of activity consists of collecting and analyzing data on the state of the environment in Europe. It draws up research reports, exercises monitoring functions and raises public awareness of environmental problems (Majone 2002; Zito 2010). Yet, these seemingly 'soft' policy functions can have strong impacts. They can lead to the introduction or enhancement of new policy concepts. The mostly regulatory environmental policy of the Union has had little impact, in general, because member states have not been willing to implement it. As a result, there has been a shift towards new instruments, based on market mechanisms, self-regulation, voluntary agreements, as well as communicative activities (Knill 2003; Holzinger *et al.* 2009; Lenschow 2010). The EEA is expected to play a major role in launching and supporting the implementation of this new strategy. In addition to its 'regular' functions, the agency also acts as a lobbyist for the environmental cause. Its expertise and independent status provide it with a high level of legitimacy and credibility. In short, the EEA, as an advocate of environmental concerns, makes up for the limited competences of the Commission and the limited authority of the Union as a whole.

Although less visible than the EEA, several other independent agencies have been created over the past years (Kelemen and Majone 2012). They fulfil important roles in the formulation and implementation of various policies. The European Agency for the Evaluation of Medicinal Products (or the European Medicines Agency: EMA), established in 1993), and the European Food Safety Authority (EFSA) (set up in 2002) are two examples of many (for a detailed analysis, see Groenleer 2009). The EMA acts in a supervisory function evaluating the quality, safety, and efficacy of medicines for the European market; the EFSA performs an advisory role on questions of food safety.

However, the most outstanding case of an independent agency of the second generation is the European Central Bank (McNamara 2002; Dyson and Quaglia 2010: 677–87; Nugent 2010: 238–40; Hodson 2012b). Established in 1999 at the start of the third stage of monetary union, the Bank holds extensive autonomous powers (Art. 105 TEC-M, now Art. 282 TFEU). These include issuing the Euro, setting the interest

rates for the Euro-zone, and the exchange rates relative to other currencies. The primary objective of the ECB is to maintain price stability (Art.
105(1) TEC-M, now Art. 282(2) TFEU). Furthermore, the Bank is entitled to enact European regulations that are legally binding on the
member states, even though the legislative institutions of the Union are
not actually involved in decision-making (Art. 108a TEC-M, now Art.
132 TFEU). The independence of the Bank is guaranteed by the Treaty
(Art. 107 TEC-M, now Art. 130 and 282(3) TFEU), which states that
members of the Bank may not 'seek or take instructions from Union
institutions, bodies, offices or agencies, from any government of a
Member State or from any other body' (Art. 130 TFEU). The only influence member states have over the ECB is indirect, insofar as they are
able to nominate the president and members of the Executive Board.
The Board consists of the president of the Bank, the vice-president, and
four additional members. The European Council nominates these
members by qualified majority (Art. 283(2) TFEU). The officeholders
are expected to be of 'recognized standing and professional experience
in monetary and banking matters' (Art. 283(2) TFEU). It is clear that
there is little room in this job description to allow states to pursue
specific interests through the nomination procedure.

With the creation of the ECB, the member states of the Euro-zone
were required to create their own independent central bank regime,
based on the German model. However, the establishment of the ECB
meant that the national banks were deprived of their core functions.
They play a major role only within the framework of transnational
cooperation. Under the auspices of the ECB, they constitute the European System of Central Banks (ESCB) (Dyson and Quaglia 2010: 685–7,
Hodson 2012b). Together with the members of the Executive Board of
the ECB, the presidents of the national central banks form the Governing
Council of the ECB (Art. 283 TFEU). In addition, an enlarged Council
also includes the presidents of the central banks of those member states
that have not adopted the Euro. Thus, the architects of monetary institutions have chosen a two-level structure, even though the definitive
authority over monetary policy pertains to the European level. The ECB
takes extensive decisions in monetary affairs without any interference of
national governments or European institutions. Hence, the European
Central Bank is even more independent than the German Bundesbank
has ever been (Elgie 1998).

The economic and financial crisis of the past years has shown what
this independence may imply in practice (Hodson 2012b: 211–13).
While national governments were strongly divided over the issue of
introducing Euro-bonds as a tool to bring down the interest rates for
the highly-indebted states, ECB president Mario Draghi announced that
the Bank would purchase an unlimited number of government bonds
from the indebted states (see Chapter 3). Such purchases almost have

the same effect as the introduction of Euro-bonds. Furthermore, Draghi decided to provide cheap loans to troubled banks, so that the ECB can act as a lender of last resort. This step essentially leads to a significant increase in money supply, which might counteract the most prominent objective of the Bank: to maintain price stability and to combat inflation. With these two steps, the ECB took swift and forceful actions to tackle the crisis, while national governments were unable to achieve consensus, even on minor issues (Beck 2012). Thus, the ECB was highly effective in tempering financial speculation in the Euro-zone. However, these actions clearly surpass the Bank's mandate, or even violate the regulations of the existing Treaties. It is not surprising that legal scholars are concerned that the ECB's activities might undermine the rule of law in the European Union (e.g. Joerges 2012). In contrast, economists and political scientists argue that the Treaties do not prohibit such steps (De Grauwe 2010) and that the 'unorthodox' response of the ECB to the sovereign debt crisis was inevitable (Schelkle 2013). In any event, it seems that national governments actually welcomed the ECB's unorthodox policy, since it not only contained the turbulences of the financial markets, but also relieved national governments from justifying such costly and risky decisions to their electorates.

Despite the extensive powers of the ECB, the Councils also play a major role in European monetary policy, particularly in those areas that continue to fall under the responsibility of the member states. For example, ECOFIN, the Council for Economic and Financial Affairs, supervises the economic performance of the member states and, more specifically, oversees their adherence to a strict budgetary policy, as required by the Treaty of Maastricht and the Stability and Growth Pact of 1997 (which will be discussed in the next section). The ECOFIN Council is supported in its tasks by a specialized committee that carries out the duties that would normally fall to COREPER (Hayes-Renshaw and Wallace 2006: 88–90; Dyson and Quaglia 2010: 685–7). This Economic and Financial Committee (EFC) is composed of delegates from the Commission, the ECB and the member states (top-level civil servants, as well as the vice-governors of national central banks) (Art. 134 TFEU). The Commission plays only a limited role in monetary affairs. It is entitled to draw up reports on the economic performance of the member states – in particular, when there are excessive deficits or when there is a strong likelihood of such deficits (Art. 126(2) TFEU). These reports serve as the basis for Council decisions (Art. 126(6) TFEU). In addition, the Commission can present proposals for monetary policy and serve in a consultative capacity as well. In most cases, the Parliament needs only to be informed about decisions taken by the Council. Hence, we can conclude that as far as independent institutions such as the ECB and the ECBS are constrained in their autonomy, decision-making remains the exclusive domain of the Councils and, thus, subject to the intergovernmental dimension of the Union (Verdun 2003). Nicoll therefore coined the term 'fourth pillar' some 20 years ago, as a means of describing the largely independent and intergovernmental institutional structure of the EU's monetary policy (Nicoll 1994: 195–6).

The recent economic and financial crisis urged European leaders to make further institutional and procedural choices that reaffirm and rein-force this concept of the fourth pillar, governed by the Councils, the ECB, and additional independent agencies. The threatening destabiliza-tion of private banks will lead to a significant expansion of the ECB's scope of action. Possibly beginning in 2014, the ECB will have supervi-sory powers over private banks, especially over large, systemic banks. Even though the detailed regulations are still under review by the EU institutions, this so-called 'Banking Union' is clearly being established. The concept of a Banking Union implies not only an expansion of the ECB's competences; but also involves the establishment of additional independent agencies for specific supervisory functions. In fact, three such agencies were already established in 2010: the European Banking Authority (EBA), the European Securities and Markets Authority (ESMA), and the European Insurance and Occupational Pensions Authority (EIOPA). The redefinition and expansion of the powers of the three agencies is envisaged (European Commission 2012). One critical observer has concluded that 'a new set of European agencies was thus created, set aside from earlier agencies by the broader range of powers that they are *formally* granted' (Busuioc 2013: 112, emphasis in the original). Besides further empowering independent agencies, the super-visory functions of the Councils with regard to the member states were also expanded. Hence, in 2011, the EU institutions adopted six new legislative acts: the Six-Pack (see Chapter 3).

In conclusion, we can say that national governments, confronted with the Euro-crisis, viewed further transfers of powers to the European level as inevitable. However, in most cases, they opted to increase the role of independent agencies, as well as their own role, to carry out the cor-responding regulatory and supervisory functions.

## The rationale underlying independent agencies

In order to consider the rationale underlying the creation of independent agencies, I turn here to Majone, who is the most prominent scholarly advocate of these institutional arrangements (Majone 1996, 2002, 2005, 2009; Kelemen and Majone 2012). Majone considers independent agen-cies to be particularly advantageous to the Union for several reasons. In his view, the agencies perform their tasks with 'technical rationality' and specific expertise, insulated from political conflicts. This, in turn, enables them to provide credibility to European governance. Policies are implemented with higher continuity, output, and efficiency, and they are more flexibly tailored to real-world situations and problems. Other scholars, however, emphasize the problems associated with independent agencies. They suggest that such agencies may pursue objectives and policies that differ from the preferences of their principals. In addition, independent agencies can easily be 'captured' by specific interest groups or by stake-holders in various policy areas.

Whether their effects are positive or negative, the choice to establish independent agencies arises out of the institutional structure of the EU and the related problems of collective action. Conflicting interests of the member states may allow some broad decisions to be made, but these conflicts hinder a more detailed expression of strategies for policy implementation and regulatory intervention (Scharpf 1999). Furthermore, conflicting interests can prevent the swift action that is clearly needed in crisis situations. As a result, certain policy functions are delegated to independent agencies in order to evade or circumvent major conflicts and to prevent non-decision. Furthermore, the establishment of independent agencies and institutions may be fuelled by the structural conflict between the Council and the Commission (see Chapters 1 and 13; Groenleer 2009: 103–8). As the Commission acquires and consolidates ever more power, the Council prefers to delegate additional competences in policy-making to specialized agencies. This allows it to exercise supervision and control more easily (Groenleer 2009: 105–7). Remarkably, it is not only the Council that prefers to establish independent agencies. The Commission often does so as well, although for quite different reasons. Its primary goal is the expansion of the reach and the scope of European policies and, with it, the reach and scope of its own role (Groenleer 2009: 104–5).

Thus, we can conclude that conflicts between member states on the one hand, and the structural conflict between the Commission and the Council on the other, have fostered the emergence and proliferation of independent agencies. The enormous growth and increasing complexity of regulatory functions at European level are at the heart of this development, while the political means and institutional structures to tackle policy problems are poorly-developed. As Majone has observed, there is a 'mismatch between the increasingly specialized functions of the Community and the administrative instruments at its disposal' (Majone 2002: 306). Thus, independent agencies are established to alleviate this mismatch and, sometimes, they are able to achieve the expected successes in problem-solving, as the most recent activities of the ECB prove. However, independent agencies can also exacerbate the institutional fragmentation of the EU and they may raise questions about the democratic legitimacy of their activities.

# Differentiating integration: the Euro-group

## Varieties of differentiated integration

With the successive enlargements of the European Union and the expansion of policy-making to an even larger number of issue areas, it has become increasingly difficult to integrate all the member states to the same extent and at the same pace. Furthermore, it has proven increasingly difficult to transfer entire policy areas to the European level. Whereas, in the early years of integration, dissent among the member states about what to integrate and to what extent usually resulted in non-integration, the Union later responded to such dissent in a completely different way. It simply 'invented' the method of differentiated integration.

Differentiated integration can take the form of either vertical or horizontal differentiation (Leuffen *et al.* 2012: 12). Vertical differentiation refers to policy areas where competences are partially transferred to the European level and remain, partially, a national responsibility. Horizontal differentiation refers to those cases where a policy is transferred to the European level, but not all member states participate in this European policy. In the previous chapters, we already considered several forms of differentiated integration – including, for example, the Schengen agreement aimed at abolishing controls at the internal borders of the EU. The agreement was concluded in 1985 by a small group of member states, but its membership has since increased to 24 EU states and four non-members. The Schengen agreement is a case of both horizontal and vertical differentiation. It does not include all member states of the EU and two states – the UK and Ireland – do not take part in all regulations of the agreement. Other forms of differentiated integration can be seen in the many opt-outs that the EU has granted to certain states – often, but not only, in reaction to negative referenda. Furthermore, various forms of differentiated integration characterize those policies that are organized under intergovernmental control (i.e. foreign and security policy, and justice and home affairs). With the adoption of the Treaty of Amsterdam, the concept of differentiated integration was first formally codified in the Treaties as a specific institutional arrangement. The Amsterdam Treaty defined this arrangement as 'closer cooperation' between a group of member states (Art. 11 TEU-A). The Lisbon Treaty speaks of 'enhanced cooperation' (Title IV TEU-L). These Treaty regulations were introduced in the wake of Eastern enlargement. Following enlargement, the 'old' member states were afraid of deadlocks, as the accession states might be less inclined to support further integration.

More generally, the rationale for embarking on differentiated integration lies primarily in the serious divergences among the member states regarding the course of integration. Thus, horizontal differentiation is a preferred option when a group of member states is highly interested in taking joint action at European level, but others strongly oppose it. In these cases, a small group of integration-minded states hopes that it can act as an *avant garde*, which will encourage others to follow sooner or later. The Lisbon Treaty therefore stipulates that enhanced cooperation among others 'shall ... reinforce its [the Union's] integration process' (Art. 20(1) TEU-L). Vertical differentiation, in contrast, is preferable when there is a clear need to integrate, but member states are highly reluctant to transfer far-reaching powers to the European level. In these cases, a halfway solution may prove to be the appropriate compromise formula.

It is not the place here to deal with the whole spectrum of differentiated integration that has emerged in the context of the EU (for more details, see Kölliker 2006: Dyson and Sepos 2010: Leuffen *et al.* 2012). Consequently, this section will focus specifically on EU monetary policy as the most prominent case of both horizontal and vertical differentiation. EU monetary policy is an example of horizontal differentiation, as not all member states are willing, or permitted, to participate in it. Those willing to participate must first qualify for membership by fulfilling a certain set of criteria, initially laid down in the Maastricht Treaty (Art. 109j(1) TEC-M). These criteria refer to price stability, government finances, exchange rates, and long-term interest rates. More specifically, they are that:

1   the inflation rate may not exceed 1.5 percentage points above the average of the three best-performing states;
2   the annual government deficit may not exceed 3 per cent of the GDP;
3   the gross government debt may not exceed 60 per cent of the GDP;
4   applicant countries may not have devalued their currencies for the last two consecutive years;
5   the long-term interest rate may not be higher than that of the three best-performing states. (Protocol on the Convergence Criteria, TEC-M)

The rationale underlying these criteria is that the states participating in monetary union should reach 'a high achievement of sustainable convergence' (Art. 109j (1) TEC.M). In addition, the Council set these criteria as a means of ensuring that only economically and fiscally stable states would participate in monetary union. In order to safeguard this stability, even after the introduction of the common currency, the Council adopted the Stability and Growth Pact in 1997. The Pact requires member states of the Euro-zone to continue to adhere to those convergence criteria that refer to public finance, that is, the criteria 2 and 3. By contrast, the other criteria are no longer the responsibility of the individual member states but, rather, are incumbent upon the ECB.

However, when the Council decided on membership in monetary union, it also accepted states that did not fulfil all the criteria. Moreover, after monetary union was established, the Council did not take strong action against those members that clearly violated the rules of the SGP. It has often been said that these decisions were taken primarily for political reasons. In other words, motives other than economics played a decisive role. Of the then 15 member states, 11 were initially accepted for monetary union (the 6 founding states of the EC plus Austria, Finland, Ireland, Portugal, and Spain). Greece followed two years later as the twelfth member of the Euro-zone. After Eastern enlargement, another 6 states qualified for monetary union (Cyprus, Estonia, Latvia, Malta, Slovakia, and Slovenia), so, at present, the Euro-zone comprises 18 members. The governments of these 18 states form the Euro-group within the European Council and the ECOFIN-Council.

EU monetary policy is also an example of vertically differentiated integration. Thus, all authority on monetary issues was transferred to the European level (i.e. the ECB and the ESCB – see pp. 188–91), whereas fiscal and other macroeconomic policies were left to the responsibility of the member states. Fiscal and other macroeconomic policies are not merely additional policy areas but, rather, constitute indispensable building blocks for a stable monetary system. As a result, the introduction of monetary Union also allocated specific supervisory and coordinative functions to the European level in order to ensure that national fiscal and other macro-economic policies evolved in accordance with the requirements of monetary union. The Treaty of Maastricht had already established a multilateral surveillance procedure, which allowed the economic developments in the member states to be monitored (Art. 103 TEC-M). For this purpose, the Council adopts broad guidelines for the member states to follow and can then issue recommendations to states whose economic policies are not consistent with these guidelines (Art. 103(3) TEC-M). Similarly, the Council also monitors the compliance of the member states with the fiscal rules of the SGP. Under the framework of the Excessive Deficit Procedure that is also laid down in the Maastricht Treaty, the Council can impose fines on member states in case of non-compliance with the fiscal rules (Art. 104c TEC-M). Interestingly though, these supervisory functions of the European level are also horizontally differentiated. The multilateral surveillance procedure includes all member states of the EU. The fiscal supervision initially only referred to the members of the Euro-group. It has since been expanded to all member states, but sanctions can only be imposed on the members of the Euro-zone.

## The evolution of the Euro-group and the Euro Summit

Obviously, these multifaceted forms of differentiated integration in monetary policy required the establishment of corresponding institutional structures. However, as is so often the case in the process of European integration, the Union went back to a strategy of simply muddling through. As a result, in the wake of the third stage of creating monetary union, in April 1998, the Euro-group held its first, informal meeting. Regular meetings of the group followed, but the informal institutional arrangement remained. Thus, in practice, the finance ministers of the Euro-group meet on the eve of the meetings of the ECOFIN Council, in order to discuss pressing policy problems and measures that need to be implemented. However, formal decisions are to be taken during official Councils meetings. It is important to note that, for issues regarding the common currency, only the ministers of the Euro-group cast a vote (Art. 136(2) TFEU). These confusing procedural arrangements frustrated the other Council members, and they have frequently argued for the right to participate in votes regarding the Euro, as they were also affected by the decisions.

As time passed, the Euro-group, though still an informal institution, has acquired an increasingly important position (Eurozone Portal 2013). In 2004, the group decided to elect a permanent president for a (renewable) two-year term. Up until this point, the Euro-group had acted under the rotating presidencies of the Council, but this process created problems when a government that did not belong to the Euro-zone took the reign. In addition, and more importantly, it seems that the group increasingly felt the need to improve its status, the continuity of its work, and its visibility. Luxembourg's Prime Minister Jean-Claude Juncker was the first to serve as permanent president of the Euro-group and, against all formal and informal norms of the EU, he held this position for nearly nine years. In February 2013, Dutch Minister of Finance Jeroen Dijsselbloem succeeded him in office. The Lisbon Treaty formalized the status of the Euro-group through a protocol annexed to the Treaty. However, the protocol encompasses only two articles. The first confirms that the ministers of the Euro-group 'shall meet informally'; the second stipulates that the group 'shall elect a president for two and a half years' (Protocol No. 14 on the Euro Group, TEU-L). Thus, the group continues to function as an informal body of the EU, even though its status is now defined by formal rules.

Despite its informal status, the Euro-group has become an ever-more important structure within the institutional architecture of the EU. This is not so much the result of its supervisory functions regarding the member states in the framework of the excessive deficit procedure, but mainly a consequence of the international financial crisis and the ensuing sovereign debt crisis. In this situation, the Union has had to search for new solutions to the debt problems of individual states, and has had to respond to the destabilizing impacts of these problems on the whole Euro-zone. The authority on these matters was clearly the Euro-group. At the same time, authority also partly shifted to a higher level, from the ministers of finance to the heads of state or government. Accordingly, heads of state or government initiated their own Euro-group: the Euro Summit. The first meeting took place in 2008, followed by a second in 2010. Since 2011, Euro Summits have become regular events, taking place at the end of European Council meetings. The Euro Summit is even more of an informal body than the Euro-group. Nevertheless, its utmost importance 'as a forum for concerted action on Euro area issues' is unquestionable (Eurozone Portal 2013). In addition to the creation of a supra-structure for the Euro-group, part of the workload was also devolved to a sub-structure, by establishing a permanent working group for preparing the meetings of the ministers.

In summary, as a result of the economic and financial crisis, the Euro-group has been transformed from its initial moderately important formation within the ECOFIN Council to an institution of utmost importance. Furthermore, the Euro Summit has been formed as the supreme authority for the Euro-area. However, despite their extensive decisions, the Euro-group and, particularly, the Euro Summit remain informal or under-formalized institutional arrangements. Even though the extensive decisions taken by these bodies affect primarily the countries of the Euro-zone, they nevertheless also impact the other member states that do not play an active role in the decision-making.

A first momentous decision was reached in 2010, when the member states of the Euro-group established a temporary instrument, the European Financial Stability Facility (EFSF), to provide financial assistance to highly-indebted member states of the Euro-zone, In 2012, they signed a treaty that established the European Stability Mechanism (ESM) as a permanent means of providing financial assistance to Euro-zone members; this is expected to replace the EFSF. The Treaty defines the purpose of this instrument as follows: 'to mobilise funding and provide stability support under strict conditionality ... to the benefit of ESM Members which are experiencing, or are threatened by, severe financing problems' (Art. 3, ESM Treaty). Furthermore, in 2011 the Euro Summit initiated the adoption of a 'Treaty on Stability, Coordination and Governance in the Economic and Monetary Union': the Fiscal Compact. This Treaty is another case of differentiated integration. It is meant to redress the weaknesses of the rules and procedures for supervising member states' economic and fiscal performance. Among its many provisions, it envisages automatic sanctions against a member state that is found to be in violation of the fiscal rules of the SGP. It also formalized, to a degree, the status of the Euro Summit. The Treaty was signed in 2012 by 25 member states – the UK and the Czech Republic remained outside the agreement. Interestingly, the Treaty envisages different rules for the members of the Euro-group than for the other contracting parties. The Treaty entered into force in January 2013, after it had been ratified by 12 member states. Besides acting in the framework of these new institutions and treaties, the Euro-group takes also significant decisions in regard to individual, highly-indebted member states. It does not hesitate to apply the 'strict conditionality' announced in Article 3 of the ESM Treaty. Particularly, the small debtor states are forced to implement far-reaching reforms – such as privatizations of public enterprises and services, fundamental reorganizations of the banking sector, painful cutbacks of wages and pensions, and extensive reductions of government personnel – in order to receive financial assistance. Unsurprisingly, in view of these decisions, public support for European integration has dramatically decreased. Whereas citizens of those states who finance the ESM fear a bottomless pit of money transfers and overall instability in the EU, those of the recipient states are upset about the rapid deterioration of their economic position and the ensuing social decline. Furthermore, in the face of the obvious powerlessness of their governments, the citizens of these states are turning in large numbers to populist, or even undemocratic, parties that propagate the exit from the Euro-zone and even the EU.

In summary, we can conclude that the various forms of differentiated integration are institutional solutions to the ever-present problem of diversity in the EU. They may be temporary arrangements where those member states that initially remain outside the agreement will soon enter, or those issues not yet integrated will sooner or later be integrated. Differentiated integration can also constitute institutional arrangements that are fairly stable over time, based on more persistent differences among the member states. However, differentiated integration could also evolve into a threat to one of the Union's basic principles: the formal equality among the member states. If a smaller group of member states is entitled to take decisions that may greatly influence other individual states and the Union as a whole, then these arrangements become questionable. It is therefore not surprising that critical observers of the activities of the Euro-group are highly concerned about both the substantive dimension of these decisions and their democratic legitimacy.

## Conclusion

This chapter has examined how the European polity, along with the process of ever-closer integration, expands and diversifies its institutional structure. In particular, the chapter has explored those institutional innovations that tend to enhance the intergovernmental dimension of the European polity. As we have seen, the Union has established new policy areas (CFSP and JHA or ASFJ) that were subject to an intergovernmental institutional setting and corresponding procedures of decision-making. Furthermore, it has created a host of specialized independent agencies, with the ECB as the most outstanding case. Finally, it has embarked on forms of differentiated integration and created corresponding institutional arrangements to ensure that these function. The chapter has also shown that these three variations in institution-building are not strictly separated in practice, as each of them also draws partially on the other institutional forms. Thus, within the framework of the CFSP and JHA or AFSJ, independent agencies support their work, and differentiated integration plays a major role. At the same time, independent agencies, particularly the ECB, are accompanied by intergovernmental decision-making and, again, often rest on differentiated integration. Finally, differentiated integration is usually governed under intergovernmental control and accompanied by independent specialized agencies. Therefore, we can conclude that the three forms of institution-building presented in this chapter constitute basic patterns for promoting integration under conditions of pressing external challenges and persistent diversity among the member states. It is highly probable that the future will see a proliferation of these institutional patterns.

However, we must also further consider the idea that these three forms of institutional diversification enhance, primarily, the intergovernmental dimension of the European polity. In the case of the CFSP and JHA or AFSJ, it is obvious that the pillars and their institutional follow-ups serve this objective, in that they are directly governed by the Council and the European Council, even though the supranational institutions are selectively included in decision-making. The independent agencies are a different case. Independent agencies do not clearly fit into either the intergovernmental or the supranational side of the European polity. Rather, they often serve both sides. However, when they are vested with extensive regulatory powers, especially as is the ECB, then they clearly have a supranational mandate. Yet, in these cases, the supranational dimension of the European polity is not only strengthened, but also at the same time is further institutionally fragmented. We can therefore conclude that the creation of such agencies results in the dilution of supranational powers and, thus, indirectly strengthens the intergovernmental forces within the EU. Other independent agencies, which do not have a broad mandate, serve primarily to insulate certain functions of European policy-making from both the persistent conflicts among the member states in the Council and the Commission's aspirations to expand its scope of action and, ultimately, its autonomy. As such, they may also dilute the power of the supranational side and, at the same time, indirectly strengthen the aggregated power of the intergovernmental forces. Forms of differentiated integration are yet another case. In the case of vertical differentiation, where competences are only partially transferred to the European level – as, for example, in EMU – it is not even the intergovernmental forces that strive to retain control but, rather, the individual member states. In the case of horizontal differentiation, where only a smaller number of member states participate in a policy project – as, again, in EMU – then the advancement of integration may be secured by excluding the reluctant states and those that do not fulfil the required criteria. In any event, both forms of differentiated integration facilitate progress in integration and, thus, indirectly strengthen the aggregated power of the intergovernmental forces.

At this point, however, it has to be stressed that the ongoing process of the EU's institutional expansion and diversification is not a zero-sum-game, where intergovernmental power successively increases, while supranational power diminishes. It only shows that institution-building in favour of the intergovernmental side of the European polity evolves in a formalized manner, and is often firmly anchored in Treaty regulations. In contrast, the supranational institutions use means other than the Treaties to expand their power. Thus, in spite of the asymmetries between the intergovernmental and the supranational institutions, a certain balance of power continues to characterize the relationship between them. We may therefore assume that the continuous expansion and diversification of the EU's institutional structure in formal terms is a reaction by the intergovernmental forces to the supranational institutions' expansive use of their powers (see also Chapter 13).

The institutional choices described in this chapter are best explained with neo-institutionalist theories and approaches. Historical institutionalism, with its concept of path dependency, sheds light on the fact that the Union rarely sets up completely new institutions; rather, in most cases, the Union continues along the path of earlier institutional choices, which eventually, through a step-wise process, adapt to new challenges. The formation of the Euro-group within the Council and the election of its president is a case in point. Rational choice institutionalism, with its emphasis on the incomplete control of the principals (the Council and the European Council) with regard to their agents (mainly the Commission), highlights why national governments increasingly chose to build primarily intergovernmental institutions to promote integration or, why they chose to further dilute the power of the supranational element.

# Chapter 8

# Promoting Integration: Policies, Policy-Making and Governance

The previous chapters have analyzed the EU's institutional structure and its processes of decision-making. This chapter now takes a different direction and focuses on EU policy-making, its evolution, its specific forms, and its modes of governance, as they are shaped to a large extent by the EU's institutions and their interactions. Thus, this chapter picks up on the themes of the earlier chapters, but integrates them in a different way.

As a political system, the EU is largely defined through policy-making. In fact, one could make the argument that it was the functional need, as well as the explicit will of national governments, to establish common policies at European level that triggered and further promoted European integration and shaped the European polity into its current form. Thus, as much as EU institutions and their interactions shape policy-making and governance, the inverse is also true. European policy-making and governance also shape the EU's institutions and the procedures of decision-making to a large degree. National governments were often reluctant to transfer policies to the European level and to grant the EU powers that were necessary to implement their collective decisions. This resulted in a piecemeal process of policy transfers and an incomplete and asymmetric policy portfolio of the EU, compared with a nation state. Furthermore, since the states often only agreed partly to transfer competences, they created complex policy processes that can include numerous institutions at the European, national, and sometimes even the regional levels, resulting in a wide variety of actors sharing competences and responsibilities. Together with these complex policy processes, European governance also took on specific forms. Depending on the distribution of powers in the Union's multi-level system, governance modes vary widely along a spectrum that ranges from hierarchical steering carried out at the European level, to various forms of policy coordination among the member states, with the Union only formulating policy objectives and targets, and playing a monitoring role.

The first section of this chapter analyzes the evolution and characteristics of the EU's policy portfolio. Chapters 2 and 3 have already provided an overview of the step-wise transfers of policies and powers to the European level during the course of integration. Now, in this chapter, we look more specifically at these processes and their outcomes, in order to understand why and how the EU's policy portfolio differs from that of member states.

The second section then focuses on the policy processes and governance modes that characterize European policy-making. As has been noted, the European polity is not independent of the member states, but relies to a large extent on their support. This support, especially if it includes transfers of powers to the European level, is given only reluctantly by national governments. As a result, the extent and pattern of sharing competences among the levels of government and the use of governance modes vary widely across policy areas. Thus, the second part of the chapter analyzes variations in policy processes according to the distribution of competences among the government levels, and how this relates to different governance modes.

The third section offers examples of how European policy-making and governance evolve and work in practice. For this purpose, I have selected three policy areas that are representative of the differences in the distribution of competences among the government levels, the resulting variations in policy processes and, accordingly, the variations in governance modes. This includes competition policy, cohesion policy and the European Employment Strategy. Competition policy is hierarchically governed by the European level, with the Union holding extensive powers. Cohesion policy is marked by a policy process that involves all three government levels of the EU and primarily makes use of governance through negotiation.

Finally, the European Employment Strategy is a case exemplifying the EU's innovative governance modes, characterized by complex processes of policy coordination among all government levels, with formal competences remaining the purview of the member states. We will learn how these policy areas are structured by the EU's institutional setting, as well as its procedural rules. In addition, we will look at how policy-making in these areas contributes to further building and diversifying the institutional architecture of the European polity.

## The policy portfolio: evolution and characteristics

Much like the overall evolution of European integration, we can also identify four phases in the process of establishing the policy portfolio of the EU (see Chapters 2 and 3). The *first phase* started in 1950 and, characterized by building the European Communities, set up a limited policy package for establishing a customs union and roughly outlining a common market. The *second phase*, beginning in the mid-1960s, was marked by major conflicts among the member states. This stage established new policies on a small scale and in a somewhat experimental form. In general, these policies specifically took the differences among the member states into account, or even attempted to level them out. The *third phase*, beginning in 1985 and characterized by an enormous leap forward in integration, saw the most rapid and comprehensive expansion of the European policy portfolio. The newly established policies pursued all the objectives of the preceding phases. They either aimed at completing and consolidating the single market, or dealt explicitly with the omnipresent divergences among the member states. The *fourth phase*, starting in the mid-1990s, was no longer marked by significant expansions of European policies but, rather, by exploring new methods of policy-making and governance without major power transfers to the European level. Furthermore, during this phase, policy transfers from the EU to non-member states played an important role. Overall, we can distinguish between two types of phases. The first and the third were marked by significant expansions of the European policy portfolio, and corresponding transfers of powers. The second and the fourth phases were characterized by experiments in the design of policies and governance modes, but with fewer power transfers to the EU. Unsurprisingly, the phases of rapid expansion of the policy portfolio correspond to the dominance of supranational forces in the integration process, and those of a rather cautious, experimental nature correspond to tighter control of the intergovernmental institutions. Let us first take a closer look at these four phases, in order to understand the characteristics of the European policy portfolio.

*Phase 1* (1950–1965) of establishing policies at European level started as a limited endeavour for supranational cooperation in two sectors: coal and steel (Milward 1984: 380–420; Dinan 2004a: 37–41). However, this endeavour was not as modest as it seems from our present perspective. In the 1950s, coal and steel were highly important primary industries that provided raw materials to a wide variety of manufacturing industries. Moreover, in many of the six original member states, these sectors were state-owned or run under extensive state control. Putting them under a European umbrella was the first step in regulating these sectors based on the objectives of a transnational, common market. After this initial step, the six member states of the ECSC quickly proceeded with founding the EEC and EURATOM in 1957 (Dinan 2004a: 64–79). With the EEC, they established a customs union and a common market, including tough rules for safeguarding undistorted competition. EURATOM focused on nuclear energy, another primary sector that was expected to constitute the future key technology in the energy sector. At the same time, national governments anticipated that there could be problems for the agricultural sector under a liberalized market system. Consequently, they agreed to regulate this sector at the European level – in particular, through the control of market prizes and specific compensatory measures in case of market failure (Milward 2000: 224–317). Thus, during this initial phase, the transfer of competences to the European level was driven primarily by the objective of creating a common market. This included a very small step towards establishing market-correcting measures.

*Phase 2* (1965–1985) began when the first conflicts about the precise nature of agricultural policy arose. However, it was not specifically this policy that determined the future pace of expanding the European policy portfolio but, rather, the pressure to mediate between the diverging interests of the member states. After ambitious integration plans had failed to materialize – in particular, a plan for a monetary union – the Community embarked on more realistic and modest steps towards expanding the realm of European policy-making. Hence, the 1970s were marked by the establishment of a regional policy (later subsumed under cohesion policy), specific directives for gender equality, first steps towards environmental protection, and a technology policy. Furthermore, the creation of the European Monetary System (EMS) marked an initial experimental step towards monetary convergence (Gilbert 2003: 138–45) and last, but not least, national governments embarked on the coordination of their foreign policies (Bretherton and Vogler 2006). These policy approaches either attempted to lessen the economic disparities among the member states, or proactively to manage them so that their impact was less harmful. A few policy experiments during this phase aimed at enhancing the role of the Community as a whole. However, all new policy initiatives were merely based on Council decisions, a fact that confirmed their experimental status. Only with the adoption of the SEA – that is, at the beginning of the third phase – were these initiatives anchored firmly in the Treaties.

*Phase 3* (1985–1995) started with the project of completing the single market (Gilbert 2003: 169–74; Dinan 2004a: 206–23). In fact, this was not just a matter of completion but, rather, of building an EU-wide integrated market. Not less than 300 regulations and directives were to be issued to make the single market work. Furthermore, competences and powers that had already been transferred to the European level, particularly those dealing with questions of competition, were now being used more proactively. These proactive measures even included sanctions imposed by the Commission (Cini and McGowan 2008). As in the first phase, the initial successes in building the single market triggered much more ambitious steps towards further facilitating market integration. The most spectacular among these was the establishment of EMU and the design of an institutional path towards achieving this end. Furthermore, in the wake of these far-reaching integration steps, a number of other policy initiatives evolved that were only indirectly linked to market issues. Consequently, the Maastricht Treaty (1993) mentions a series of policies, including trans-European networks, education, culture, public health, and consumer protection, as European endeavours. However, the role of the Community in these areas was strictly defined as limited to supporting or supplementing national policies, or contributing to their development. Finally, a common foreign policy was also established, as well as cooperation in justice and home affairs (see Chapter 7). These policies were organized as purely intergovernmental activities. In summary, the third phase was marked by the most spectacular expansion of the European policy portfolio to new areas and domains, but this phase also included setting up different institutional patterns and procedures for policy-making, which allowed member states more control over the whole process.

*Phase 4* (from 1995 onwards) is not characterized by significantly expanding policy-making at European level but, rather, by intensifying the EU's influence on national policies and by designing new governance approaches for this purpose. Only one new policy area, the European Employment Strategy (EES), was added by the Amsterdam Treaty (1999) (Mosher and Trubek 2003). The EES sparked the introduction of a new governance mode: the Open Method of Coordination (OMC). This method clearly reflects the reluctance of the member states to transfer major competences to the European level and, at the same time, the need to embark on some form of joint action in a number of policy areas and domains. In 2000, and together with the launch of the Lisbon Strategy, the European Council formally adopted the provisions of the OMC. The declared objective was to coordinate all those national policies that, according to this agenda, required thorough reform. These included labour market policies and pension schemes, as well as a broader set of environmental regulations and, more generally, all policies aimed at stimulating economic growth, competitiveness, and employment. In 2010, the Lisbon Strategy was replaced by the Europe 2020 Strategy, which essentially pursues the same objectives. Another notable characteristic of phase 4 is the increased transfer of EU policies to non-member states. This includes the transfers to accession states, accompanied by soft or hard mechanisms of conditionality, as applied in the framework of Eastern enlargement (Schimmelfennig 2003; Schimmelfennig and Sedelmeier 2005), as well as transfers to the neighbouring states of the EU (Del Sarto and Schumacher 2005; Kelley 2006; Tömmel 2013b). Furthermore, during this phase, the Union also attempted to export its model of market integration, competition policy, and regional integration more generally, both to individual states and to other regional organizations throughout the world (Lenz 2012). In summary, the fourth phase of establishing the European policy portfolio is mainly characterized by the coordination of national policies that make power transfers to the European level obsolete, and by transfers of the European policy-model to other parts of the world. Table 8.1 provides a summary of the four phases, showing when important policies were transferred to, or coordinated by, the European level; where competences were allocated; and what objectives guided these steps. However, we have to bear in mind that this table does not account for later changes – including, for example, the decentralization of certain powers in agriculture and competition policy back to the national level.

If we consider all four phases together, it becomes clear that the policy portfolio of the EU has evolved through a continuous expansion of the spectrum of policy areas. In this process, phases of accelerated expansion of European policy-making (phases 1 and 3) alternated with phases marked by experimenting with setting up new policies (phase 2), or new governance approaches (phase 4). Furthermore in this process, competences were initially allocated to the European level, while later there was often a choice made to share competences between the government levels, to allocate competences only to the Councils, or to merely coordinating national policies. As the next section will show, these variations in allocating powers resulted in diverging policy processes and governance modes. Finally, the objectives underlying European policies also shifted. The first and the third phases were dominated by objectives around market creation and even a few steps towards market correction. In contrast, during the second and the fourth phase, tackling diversity among the member states figured high on the agenda. If we consider the whole period, we can see that the Communities started with a policy model inspired by national-level policy-making whereas, later, the Union developed a variety of specialized policy models that were much better adapted and fine-tuned to its power resources and institutional setting.

As a result of these processes, the present policy portfolio of the EU covers nearly the whole spectrum of policy areas known from national level, 'suggesting that no policy area is now beyond the EU's reach' (Buonanno and Nugent 2013: 5). Yet, despite this, we have to bear in mind that 'policies concerned with the internal market are still very much at the heart of the Union's policy portfolio' (Buonanno and Nugent 2013: 8). The asymmetry between market-making policies – or, more broadly, economic policies – and market-correcting policies, focusing on social or common-good issues, is clearly expressed in the distribution of responsibilities among the Commission DGs and the Commissioners (see Chapter 4; see also Table 4.1). This asymmetry is further accentuated because the involvement at European level differs between market-making and market-correcting policies. Whereas in the first case, the

**Table 8.1** *The evolution of the EU's policy portfolio*

| Phase | Policy transfer | Allocation of competences | Main objective |
|---|---|---|---|
| **1**<br>(1950–1965) | Coal and steel<br>Common market<br>Competition policy<br>Agricultural policy | European level<br>European level<br>European level<br>European level | Market creation<br>Market creation<br>Market creation<br>Market correction |
| **2**<br>(1965–1985) | Regional policy<br>Social policy (sel. issues)<br>Technology policy<br>Monetary coordination<br>Foreign policy coordination | Europ./national level<br>Europ./national level<br>Europ./national level<br>Intergov. coordination<br>Intergov. coordination | Alleviating diversity<br>Alleviating diversity<br>Alleviating diversity<br>Enhancing role EC<br>Enhancing role EC |
| **3**<br>(1985–1995) | Completion common market<br>Monetary union<br>Environmental policy<br>Non-market-related policies<br>Foreign and security policy<br>Justice and home affairs | European level<br>European level<br>Europ./national level<br>National level<br>Intergov. decision<br>Intergov. decision | Market creation<br>Market creation<br>Market correction<br>Reducing diversity<br>Enhancing role EU<br>Reducing diversity |
| **4**<br>(from 1995) | European employment strategy<br>Lisbon/Europe 2020 strategy<br>Policy transfers to non EU-states | National level<br>National level<br>National level (non-EU) | Coordination national policies<br>Coordination national policies<br>Approximation to EU |

Union generally holds extensive – and, to a degree, even exclusive – competences, market-correcting policies for the most part are defined by shared competences. More often, they even fall under the exclusive competence of the member states, with the Union exercising only coordinative functions. The reasons for this asymmetry are obvious. Market integration benefits more or less all member states, so that it is easier to find consensus in this domain and to accept the necessary power transfers to the European level. In contrast, social and, more broadly, common-good policies touch on sensitive issues of national sovereignty and may have highly diverging distributive impacts on the member states. As a result, attempts to transfer these powers to the EU often meet strong resistance (Scharpf 1999; Majone 2005, 2009). Nevertheless, as the next section shows, the EU has also acquired a certain role in the area of market correction. However, this development has only been possible by the development and implementation of unconventional modes of governance that do not depend on major power transfers to the European level.

## Policy processes and governance modes

When analyzing European policy processes and governance modes, we must first ask why the Union has evolved to include so many different forms of policy-making. A simple answer to this suggests that it was necessary in order to make European policies work. A more detailed answer to this question, however, would have to consider why European policies did not operate as smoothly as initially expected. The problem lies with the nature and institutional structure of the European polity. Since the EU is not a sovereign state, but an emerging political order superimposed on sovereign states, the EU cannot determine its own competences, but is always dependent on transfers of powers from the member states. This means that, in many cases, it cannot rely on governance through legislation, because national governments do not transfer the corresponding powers. Furthermore, the Union does not have the formal authority to command or control the lower levels. As a result, the EU is severely constrained in its ability to implement policies through hierarchical rule. Another explanation is that the voluntary cooperation between the European and national levels that is necessary to achieve common goals is very much dependent on the goodwill of the member states. As a result, EU policy processes and governance modes vary widely across policy areas and according to the distribution of competences among the relevant institutions and government levels.

## Variations in policy processes

As noted, EU policy processes vary according to the distribution of competences among the institutions and government levels of the EU. In turn, these differences in the distribution of competences imply variation in the patterns of interaction among the relevant institutions and government levels. This leads to a variety of policy processes. In order to conceptualize these variations, I refer to Scharpf's system of 'modes of Europeanization' (2001). In his seminal article, Scharpf distinguishes between four different modes, based on the type of vertical interaction in the multi-level system of the EU. Hence, his typology is primarily based on the varying institutional configurations that structure EU policy processes and the distribution of competences among the institutions and government levels.

Scharpf defines the four modes of Europeanization as mutual adaptation, intergovernmental negotiation, joint decision-making, and hierarchical direction. Whereas the first category is the 'outcome of strategic actions among governments that are aware of their mutual interdependence', the other three categories are 'modes of institutionalized interaction' (Scharpf 2001: 6).

Thus, *mutual adaptation* does not actively involve the European level. Rather, national governments 'continue to adopt their own policies nationally, but they do so in response to, or anticipation of, the policy choices of other governments' (Scharpf 2001: 7) In this case, the European level has no competences at all, and does not even intervene by actively coordinating national policies.

*Intergovernmental negotiation* is a mode where 'national policies are coordinated or standardized by agreements at the European level, but national governments remain in full control of the decision process' (Scharpf 2001: 8). In this case, competences are not transferred to the European level; nevertheless, decisions taken by the Councils at the European level are binding on the member states.

*Joint decision-making* 'combines aspects of intergovernmental negotiations and supranational centralization' (Scharpf 2001: 12). This refers specifically to the EU's ordinary legislative procedure – the Community method – where all three legislative institutions of the EU are involved (see Chapter 5). The Commission launches legislative proposals, while the Council and the EP take the decisions on them. This process may include negotiations, particularly among the members of the Council, and also between the Council and the EP. However, the final outcome is a legislative act that constitutes a form of supranational centralization, as it is binding on the member states.

The mode of *hierarchical direction* implies that 'competencies are completely centralized at the European level and exercised by supranational actors without the participation of member-state governments'

(Scharpf 2001: 9). These competences are incumbent on the Commission (e.g. in competition policy), or the ECB (in monetary policy).

Of course, these four forms of European governance are ideal types. In practice, they rarely exist in a pure form but deviate from the abstract model, or constitute mixtures of various types. Scharpf discusses one such mixture, the OMC, a mode that he places between intergovernmental negotiation and mutual adaptation (Scharpf 2001: 18). Deviations from the ideal type or combinations of the different modes occur in many forms and variations and, thus, constitute variations in the policy process. Let us now consider the most important of these.

For the purpose of our analysis of European policy-making, mutual adaptation in its pure form is relatively uninteresting, because it refers exclusively to national policies and strategies. However, this mode is not as independent from the European level as it might seem at first glance. It is the dynamics that result from European integration – and, especially, from market integration – that foster competition among the member states and, thus, spur the processes of mutual adaptation. When mutual adaptation is combined with intergovernmental negotiation, as in the case of the OMC, it is accompanied by deliberate efforts by the Union's institutions to coordinate the policies of the member states. In this case, the Commission also plays a role, even though formal decisions rest exclusively with the Council and the European Council.

Looking at the other extreme, to the hierarchical direction, we find that this mode also rarely exists in pure form; that is, without any interference of the member states. It is true that decisions taken by the European Central Bank in monetary matters – or by the Commission, in competition matters – are formally taken exclusively by these institutions. However, as the history of competition policy proves, tough decisions are only taken when a tacit consensus on such steps has emerged among the member states (Cini and Mc Gowan 2008). Furthermore, Commission decisions in competition matters are often preceded by negotiations between the European level and national authorities, or the private addressees of these decisions (Van Miert 2000; Lehmkuhl 2009). Similarly, when the ECB recently announced to buy government bonds in order to alleviate the impact of the financial crisis, it acted on its own account, but did so because a majority of national governments were clearly in favour of these actions. Furthermore, the Executive Board and Governing Council of the ECB is staffed with governors from national central banks and high-ranking government officials and, thus, remains closely linked to member state institutions, their views and policy preferences. Thus supranational centralization, although based on exclusive competences of certain European institutions, is indirectly also determined by a tacit consent of the member states.

Similar arguments can be made about intergovernmental negotiation, which mainly refers to foreign and security policy, some aspects of justice and home affairs, and parts of EMU. Although the formal authority of decision-making rests exclusively with national governments acting through the Councils, the extent and substance of joint activities result from a negotiation process. These negotiations may take the form of hard bargains, or problem-solving (Elgström and Jönsson 2000). However, when decisions are achieved, they are European decisions, and are binding on the member states. Nevertheless, even in these cases there is a certain degree of Commission involvement in the decision-making process, as the Commission holds a non-exclusive right of initiative and may act in an advisory or mediating function. The Parliament, for its part, may at least express its opinions. In addition, independent agencies play a major role in these domains. Thus, in practice, policy processes of this type of interaction may be quite complex, involving not only the intergovernmental institutions of the EU, but a wider set of institutions.

Finally, joint decision-making – the most widespread mode of Europeanization, as it applies to the largest number of EU policies – is, in itself, a hybrid. It displays aspects of intergovernmental negotiations when it seeks and achieves consensus on a legal act, and shows elements of supranational centralization once the law is adopted (Scharpf 2001: 12). This type of interaction involves all three legislative institutions of the EU, and all of them have substantial competences to shape legislation (see Chapter 5). However, there are also variations in the policy process visible in this case, depending on whether the legal acts under consideration are regulations or directives. For regulations, the legal act is directly binding on all addressees and the policy process is therefore restricted to the European level. In contrast, directives and especially framework directives must be transposed into national law. In this way, directives give the individual states a role in the policy process and provide national governments with a degree of discretion to adopt legislation according to their policy objectives within the EU's legislative framework. Furthermore, joint decision-making can also imply decisions other than simply legislation. For example, in cohesion policy, decisions involving the European, national, and even the regional government levels play an important role in allocating EU subsidies to projects and programmes implemented by the member states (see pp. 221–4). These processes of decision-making often take the form of negotiations among the parties involved.

In summary, we can distinguish between four modes of Europeanization that correspond to four basic patterns of policy processes. These four modes clearly differ in terms of the competences of the individual institutions and government levels, and their involvement in decision-making. They constitute ideal types, with the exclusive involvement of only national governments or only the EU's supranational institutions at the opposite extremes. In practice, however, all four modes tend to also include the other levels and institutions, although these often play a minor and informal role. We can therefore conclude that the four modes converge, in so far as they all involve complex horizontal interactions among the supranational and intergovernmental institutions of the European level, and vertical interactions among the government levels of the EU. In practice, although the European policy processes can be reduced to specific basic patterns, they display a wide variety of forms and it is not inconceivable that this variation will increase in the future. In turn, these differences in policy processes imply differences in the EU's governance modes.

## Variations in governance modes

The issue of EU governance has attracted much scholarly attention over the last decade (e.g. Kohler-Koch and Rittberger 2006; Sabel and Zeitlin 2008, 2010; Tömmel and Verdun 2009, 2013; Börzel 2010; Héritier and Rhodes 2011). Many scholars have attempted to conceptualize the characteristics of European governance by comparing it with governance on the national level. Whereas some observers assume that the differences are minimal, others emphasize larger and more fundamental differences, which they attribute to the possibilities and constraints inherent in the EU's political system. However, the issue that has attracted most scholarly attention is the 'new modes of governance' (e.g. Héritier and Rhodes 2011). New modes of governance are roughly defined as non-hierarchical modes of political steering. In other words, it encompasses all forms of directing policy-making through 'soft' means, including coordination, cooperation, and persuasion. A lively debate has emerged around the questions of whether these non-hierarchical modes of governance really constitute a new phenomenon, whether they are effective in directing the behaviour of the addressees, and whether they are unique to the EU. Whatever the answer to these questions, we can state that these innovative or experimentalist forms of governance, as they are labelled in some of the literature (Sabel and Zeitlin 2008, 2010; Tömmel and Verdun 2009), constitute an important means through which the Union may direct policy-making in the member states.

The literature on the concept of governance usually distinguishes between the structural and the process dimensions of governance. The structural dimension refers to the institutional structure that underlies governance processes. Since this text deals extensively with the EU's institutional structure, the focus here is primarily on the process dimension of European governance. This means that we need to take a closer look at the mechanisms that allow the EU to give direction to policy-making. To this end, I distinguish four basic modes of governance that differ in the mechanisms that serve to direct the behaviour of the addressees: hierarchy, negotiation, competition, and cooperation (Tömmel 2009; for similar definitions, see Benz 2009; Börzel 2010). These governance modes are not specific to the EU, but are also characteristic of governance at national level. However, in the institutional context of the EU, they can take a special form. It goes without saying that these four modes of governance are ideal types. In practice, they are used in different combinations and in hybrid forms.

As a mode of governance, *hierarchy* is exercised primarily through legislation and rule-making. It involves binding decisions that are accompanied by powers and actions to enforce compliance. In the European context, hierarchy is primarily exercised by the supranational institutions, as far as they are vested with the necessary powers. Hierarchy may also be exercised by the European Council; for example, when it takes binding decisions in monetary affairs. Furthermore, hierarchy is exercised through joint decision-making that results in binding legislation. However, in EU legislation hierarchy can be softened to a degree when directives are adopted, and legislation is thus organized as a two-level process.

*Negotiation* is a mode of governance that involves various types of actors who have a say in decision-making, or are even in the position to act as veto players. Negotiation is the preferred mode of governance for accommodating highly diverse interests among actors. It is therefore particularly well-suited to the EU and, in fact, plays an important role in all decisions of the Council and the European Council. However, negotiations also occur in other institutional contexts and configurations; for example, in the interactions between the various levels of government of the EU (see the case of cohesion policy, pp. 221–4). Negotiations can result in binding decisions or even formal contracts, but these are not usually accompanied by hard sanctions that enable a body to force compliance. Negotiation can also be used as an additional instrument to bring about compliance with rules or decisions.

Whereas both hierarchy and negotiation refer to processes of decision-making and/or rule-setting, *competition* as a mode of governance constitutes a mechanism affecting the decisions and actions of individual or institutional actors and, thus, coordinates their behaviour. However, competition does not emerge by itself but, rather, is established and sustained by defined rules that are, for the most part, set by governments or public authorities. At the same time, competition relies on individual and institutional actors accepting the rules and complying with the ensuing mechanisms. This implies that compliance, in contrast to hierarchy, is not being enforced but, rather, is triggered by stronger or weaker incentives and disincentives. Competition is particularly important in the European context, since it underlies the system and functioning of the common market. It often also structures policies that are not market-related. In certain policy-areas, competitive mechanisms may be deliberately established as a means of directing the behaviour of actors with an apparently 'invisible hand'.

*Cooperation*, for its part, encompasses a plurality of highly diverging actors and a wide variety of measures aimed at guiding or coordinating their behaviour. It does not at all rely on coercion, but is based on voluntary participation in a more or less organized process. This implies that compliance with jointly taken decisions or common agreements is also voluntary. Thus, compliance is not guaranteed. Cooperation, therefore, is a mode of governance with unpredictable outcomes. Its effectiveness can vary according to the actors involved, the extent of their commitment, external circumstances, and specific favouring conditions. In the EU, cooperation is the preferred governance mode where the European level lacks extensive powers, but it may also complement other, more binding governance modes. Cooperation is the mode of governance that underlies the OMC procedure, even though in most cases it is complemented by competition. Generally, this mode fits very well with the consensual style that characterizes the interactions among European institutions and actors.

### EU governance in practice

Having defined various modes of European governance, we can now turn to the analysis of their role and importance in EU policy-making. In this context, it is of particular interest to question whether the EU prefers some governance modes over others, whether certain governance modes dominate at any given time, whether we can detect a distinctive sequence in the evolution of governance modes and, last but not least, whether the oft-cited new modes of governance really are new.

During the *first phase* of EU policy-making (1950–1965), when some initial steps towards building a common market were put into place, hierarchical direction – or, simply, hierarchy – was the preferred mode of governance. In fact, during these early years, the governance modes that dominated national policy-making were simply transferred to the European level. However, these governance modes, even though they were based on clearly defined powers, were not particularly effective. This was, in part, because the European Communities lacked the necessary detailed rules and the institutional infrastructure for implementation. It was also partly because national governments resisted, or even blocked, any interference from above by delaying or preventing the adoption of additional rules and other necessary policy measures. France's politics of the 'empty chair' show this tactic most clearly. The Commission reacted to this stalemate by launching policy experiments to improve market regulation that were based on voluntary cooperation – such as, for example, in the area of standard setting (Egan 2001). These approaches, however, did not result in major successes.

The *second phase* (1965–1985) then saw the creation of new policy areas that took into account the economic divergences among the member states and the sensitivity of national governments regarding their sovereignty. In these policies, the framework for action was set by hierarchy; that is, through legislation adopted with the Community method. However, the details of implementation were defined by negotiations among the European and the national government levels. The tendency of national governments to resist European interventions was softened by providing subsidies for policy implementation; for example, in regional, social, and technology policies. In those policy areas that necessitated only legal rules at European level, the Commission launched numerous legislative proposals that resulted in non-decision, because intergovernmental negotiations on these proposals did not achieve consensus. Finally, during this phase certain policies, including the creation of the EMS, drew extensively on both competition and cooperation as governance modes within a framework of some basic rules set at European level (Verdun 2009).

The *third phase* (1985–1995) was marked by an enormous expansion of EU policy-making surrounding the completion of the single market, as well as new areas such as foreign and security policy, justice and home affairs, and monetary policy. These are only the most important innovations. These, however, did not mean that there was a corresponding expansion of governance through hierarchy. On the contrary, the governance approaches were now clearly following two diverging paths. One approach, relating primarily to issues of market regulation, was subject mainly to legislation and, thus, to hierarchical rule. The other followed the route of intergovernmental negotiations, with the supranational institutions playing only a minor role. To an extent, a third path, promoting policy coordination through more or less organized forms of voluntary cooperation, also opened up. We find this mode in parts of justice and home affairs (Lavenex 2009, 2010), as well as in a number of new policies that the Maastricht Treaty defined as being 'of common concern' – such as the trans-European networks, health, consumer protection, and education.

The *fourth phase* (from 1995 onwards) has been marked by new experiments in EU governance, even though the realm of policy areas has hardly been expanded. These new approaches refer primarily to the OMC, which, in the wake of failed attempts to coordinate through open forms of cooperation, then established an organized process of cooperation. The OMC procedure draws a wide array of institutional actors at European, national and regional level into a cooperative process of policy coordination. At the same time, this governance strategy is embedded into, and accompanied by, strong competitive mechanisms that are reinforced by peer reviews and the exchange of best practices (Benz 2009). Another governance approach of this phase involves the policy transfer to non-EU countries, including accession states, other neighbouring states, and regional organizations worldwide. In these cases, the Union uses a mixture of negotiation and cooperation as governance modes, with competition also playing a role. The Union applies strong conditionality in order to achieve policy transfers; in the case of the accession states, it also provides financial incentives to achieve its goals (Schimmelfennig 2003). For other neighbouring states and regional organizations, the promise of access to the single market forms an attractive incentive to follow the policy models propagated by the EU (Bauer 2011; Lenz 2012).

This brief overview of the evolution of European governance modes, together with the expansion and diversification of EU policy-making, could only sketch the most important developments and changes. In practice, the governance modes and the combinations among them, as well as the corresponding institutional arrangements, are much more diverse and sophisticated. Nevertheless, this brief overview allows the drawing of some conclusions (Tömmel and Verdun 2013).

First, it is obvious that EU governance modes and the corresponding institutional configurations have evolved over time, as EU policy-making has also evolved and expanded. Second, this evolution is marked by an enormous diversification in the use and combination of different governance modes, as well as the underlying institutional arrangements. Third, non-hierarchical, experimental, or innovative governance modes are not an invention of the most recent phase, but have accompanied European policy-making from its beginnings. Yet, over time, these modes of governance have evolved into much more sophisticated forms. The most important catalyst spurring on the quest for alternate routes to direct the behaviour of the member states and other addressees of EU policies has been the resistance of national governments to interference from above. This has particularly been the case during the fourth phase, where these governance modes have developed into firmly organized procedures. These are designed to have a stronger coercive impact on the addressees than former variations of non-hierarchical governance. Fourth, there does not appear to be a clear pattern in the use of governance modes; for example, beginning with hierarchy and moving to softer forms of governance, or vice versa. The only pattern that we can clearly detect is a move from simple to more complex governance modes. In addition, there are more complex and flexible combinations of governance modes, and more clearly organized institutional underpinnings. This increasing complexity is a response to the incomplete power transfers to the European level. Thus, during the course of integration, the Union has developed the skill of effectively exercising governance in spite of its limited competences.

The next section, analysing three selected policy areas, will examine how, in practice, European policy processes and governance have evolved in relation to the distribution of formal competences in these areas.

## Selected policy areas: competition policy, cohesion policy, and the European Employment Strategy

In this section, together with the most significant governance approaches, I will present three selected policy areas that are representative of the EU's dominant patterns of policy processes: *competition policy*, *cohesion policy*, and the *European Employment Strategy*.

### Competition policy

Competition policy is a domain that corresponds most explicitly to Scharpf's type of hierarchical centralization, or to the governance mode of hierarchy. However, the governance of this policy is not an exclusive domain of the Commission, as Scharpf claimed. Other actors and government levels are also involved in decision-making. Nevertheless, this mode is mainly based on binding decisions – in other words, hierarchy – even though negotiations and, sometimes, even forms of cooperation usually come before these decisions.

The ECSC Treaty already included the basic rules for a European competition policy. The founding of the two other Communities in 1957 confirmed the commitment to strong interventions in this domain. The Treaties provided for a set of rules aimed at ensuring undistorted competition for the foreseen common market (originally Art. 85-94 TEC; now 101-109 TFEU). These rules regulated three core aspects of competition policy: restrictive practices (prohibition of cartels), the abuse of a dominant position, and state aid. Furthermore, the Treaties vested the Commission with extensive and, at the same time, exclusive competences to ensure compliance with these rules. Where necessary, the Commission could also impose sanctions. However, in contrast to these far-reaching powers, the Commission faced great obstacles in using them accordingly. As Akman and Kassim (2010: 112) put it: '[t]he Treaty had granted the Community extraordinary powers, but in a context where the regulation of anti-competitive practices was a novelty'. After the competition rules had been laid down in the Treaties, an effective policy still needed to be built. This took place through a gradual process of defining and adopting additional rules, setting the stage for strong decisions, and introducing innovations in policy design (Cini and Mc Gowan 2008: 11–40; Wilks 2010). Thus, EU competition policy evolved through a process that covers all four phases. The Commission played a decisive role in this process. However, it was national governments that, through their reluctance, pressure, non-decision, and also partly their commitment, eventually directly and indirectly shaped the policy to a degree. In addition, the European Court contributed to the evolution of the policy through its rulings, which defined what anti-competitive practices meant in more detail.

The *first phase* (1950–1965) of building a European competition policy was characterized by setting up the basic parameters and practices for implementation. The Council, acting on proposals of the Commission, adopted several regulations; these specified the criteria for interventions in competition cases, as well as the exemptions of the rules. Furthermore, during this phase the Commission laid the groundwork for dealing with and making decisions on competition cases. However, the common market was not very well-developed yet, and the member states were very concerned about any invasion of their sovereignty. The Commission therefore acted in a very selective way, and focused its activities on prohibiting cartels. The Court, through its rulings on contested cases, reinforced the Commission's position and so supported the overall strategy.

The *second phase* (1965–1985) was characterized by only limited progress in competition policy. During this phase, the Commission and the Court achieved some progress, but the member states frustrated any further evolution of the policy. During this phase, the Commission broadened its scope, as it now also considered the abuse of a dominant position. The Commission took a series of strong decisions in this domain that helped to establish legal precedent. For its part, the European Court not only confirmed these decisions but, in practice, also acted as a legislator. In most cases, its rulings interpreted the law quite restrictively and, thus, served to define what was really meant by the abuse of a dominant position. In addition, by launching a proposal for a regulation in the area of merger control, the Commission tried to expand European competition policy into a new issue area. However, the member states were not ready to adopt such a regulation and, as was so often the case during this phase, the Commission proposal ended in non-decision.

In contrast, the *third phase* (1985–1995) led to both a significant consolidation and forceful expansion of European competition policy. Since a European-wide liberalized market necessitated the control of unfair practices in competition, the single market project spilled over into competition policy. Moreover, the member states had by now come to realize the necessity and benefits of a strong European competition policy. In light of this, the Commission proactively enforced the competition rules and did not hesitate to impose sanctions. Furthermore, it expanded its activities from industrial enterprises to those of the service sector. As a result, banks, insurance companies, and other big players in services came under the scrutiny of the Commission. Through most of its rulings, the Court supported the Commission in its activities and strategies. The prospect of completing the single market also caused a wave of mergers and acquisitions among European enterprises, leading the Commission to place the issue on the agenda once more. The issue had been neglected in initial Treaty regulations and even in later Council deliberations. This time, however, national governments were willing to adopt a regulation on merger control. Finally, during this phase, the Commission dared for the first time to make bold use of its competences in the third issue area of competition policy – the control of state aid (Blauberger 2009). The preceding phase had been marked by economic downturns and restructuring, and national governments had significantly expanded both direct and indirect forms of state aid to private and public enterprises. Under the condition of a single market, these strategies to improve the competitive position of individual states at the expense of others would no longer be acceptable. The Commission consequently took firm decisions, aimed at containing all forms of state aid and preventing a subsidy 'race to the bottom' among the member states.

The most spectacular step forward during this phase was the application of the EU's competition rules to the public utilities of the member states, intended to liberalize what were mostly state-owned sectors (Schmidt 2004). In this case, the Commission used its right to issue binding decisions without any interference from the Council. Needless to say, the Commission met strong resistance from the member states against this strategy. However, the Court ruled that the Commission was acting within its rights when it autonomously issued decisions. The national governments had no choice but to give in. Some governments even welcomed the Commission's activities in this domain, as they themselves had since embarked on a policy of liberalization. In any event, the Commission's strategy resulted in a gradual process of liberalizing public utilities, moving from telecommunications, to energy provision, then postal services and, finally, public banking. The strategy continued during the fourth phase. However, it faced increased resistance from the member states, so the Commission could not simply apply the rules in a straightforward manner but, instead, needed to reach compromises with the national governments.

The *fourth phase* (from 1995 onwards) moved beyond building and expanding EU competition policy. Instead, the agenda in this phase was dominated by new approaches to the implementation of the policy. The most important policy change of this phase was enacted by a regulation in 2003 and requires a partial decentralization to the national level of the extraordinarily centralized policy (McGowan 2005; Lehmkuhl 2009; Wilks 2010). On the one hand, administrative bottlenecks triggered this reform. In the wake of Eastern enlargement, the Commission's services threatened to be more burdened by an overload of cases than ever before. On the other hand, the reform is representative of the period, which has been marked by shifting the balance towards an increased involvement of the national level in European affairs. It is important to note here that competition policy was not the only highly centralized policy area that faced increased involvement of the national level. The CAP, too, was decentralized at the same time. The decentralization of competition policy involved two steps. First, the member states had to set-up their own competition authorities in the form of an independent agency.

Many of them had never had such an institution before. These authorities were granted power to decide in minor competition cases that were largely nationally significant, rather than European-wide. Second, transnational competition networks were established, staffed with delegates from each national competition authority and acting under the auspices of the Commission. For each of the three sectors of competition policy – cartels and monopolies, mergers, and state aid – a separate network was set up. The networks discuss competition cases, allocate them to the appropriate level, and elaborate proposals for further European policy initiatives or common standards at the national level (Lehmkuhl 2009). In sum, they coordinate national policies horizontally, as well as vertically, with the (still comprehensive and path-setting) policy initiatives and strategies of the Commission. Even though the reform might appear to represent a weakening of the European level in competition policy, in fact it strengthens the authority of the EU with regard to both national governments and private actors (Tömmel 2011b).

In conclusion, we can say that, although EU competition policy was clearly set down in the Treaties, it still had to be further developed by defining its procedural rules and substance. This occurred through an incremental process of Commission decisions aimed at fighting cartels, abusive practices, and state aid, and at controlling mergers. The Commission also used competition policy to liberalize public utilities. It thus expanded the policy beyond its initial scope and beyond the intentions of the member states. The policy of the Commission was often supported by the Court – which, for its part, served to define and substantiate the rules. In this way, it actually performed as a co-legislator. Member states tended to contain Commission activism but, in the long run, had to accept this for the sake of a functioning single market. Even though competition policy is predominantly governed by hierarchy exercised by the European level, other governance modes – and, consequently, other actors and institutions – also play a role. The most recent decentralization of the policy, as well as a number of related steps that were not outlined here, show that it is not exclusively the Commission and the Court that govern this policy. National governments, courts, private actors and particularly the competition authorities are all also involved. Consequently, in practice, the competition policy has increasingly become a multi-level business, even though the Commission remains in the driver's seat. Many of the softer forms of cooperation, negotiation and even competitive mechanisms that shape the governance of the policy are clearly exercised in the shadow of hierarchy (Lehmkuhl 2009).

## Cohesion policy

At first glance, cohesion policy is mainly characterized by joint decision-making that ends in hierarchical rule. However, this only applies to decisions at European level that revolve around the procedural rules of the policy and which are laid down in binding regulations. In contrast, the process of policy implementation is best described as driven by intensive interactions among the various levels of government. These interactions mainly take the form of negotiations, but are also complemented by cooperation and, sometimes, even competitive mechanisms.

The EU's cohesion policy generally grew out of the second phase of policy-making, although its roots reach back into the first phase. The policy was formally established in 1975 after the first enlargement of the Community (Hooghe and Marks 2001; Allen 2010; Begg 2010). At this time, a severe economic crisis – which affected the member states and increased the disparities among them – prompted the establishment of this policy. Initially, cohesion policy was envisioned as a support to national-level regional policies. However, the Commission aimed to influence, rather than support, the activities of the member states and, through its proactive leadership, the policy soon developed a life of its own. As has been noted, the basic parameters of the policy evolved through joint decision-making among the European institutions and were laid down in binding regulations. However, these hierarchical rules concerned themselves almost exclusively with the basic procedures governing the policy. Successful implementation required more sophisticated and nuanced procedures that allowed the European level to determine the substance of the policy. Consequently, negotiations on policy objectives and implementation strategies became increasingly important, and involved all actors and government levels responsible for policy-making in this area. The most recent reform introduced an OMC procedure into cohesion policy that aims to define common, European guidelines and to make them more binding on the member states (Tömmel and Verdun 2013). Thus, as with competition policy, cohesion policy has evolved as a result of an ongoing process of reforms and governance innovations, accompanied by a reorganization of its institutional setting. Since cohesion policy ended up offering powerful tools to influence the policies of the member states, it has provided a procedural template for a series of other EU policies, and for policy transfers to third countries. Overall, the policy area displays a strong, expansive logic.

When cohesion policy was set up during the *second phase* (1965–1985) of EU policy-making by a Council regulation (1975), it envisioned a simple policy model. A Regional Fund was established that provided subsidies to foster economic growth in peripheral or less developed regions of the member states, focusing particularly on industrial investment and infrastructure projects. The financial aid of the

European level was contingent upon national efforts in this domain. In other words, it was intended to augment member states' policies in this area. Since the Council fixed every member state's share in the Regional Fund *a priori*, in practice, the policy did not involve much more than a financial transfer between rich and poor states. However, from the outset, the Commission sought to transform this policy model and give it an explicit European imprint (Hooghe and Marks 2001; Wozniak Boyle 2006). Through two reforms (1979 and 1985), the Commission introduced procedural innovations that allowed the European level to define policy objectives and procedures for implementation to a certain degree. Furthermore, it used the opportunity provided by Mediterranean enlargement to propose specific innovative programmes to improve the economic position of the Mediterranean members of the Community. The Council, however, attempted to contain the Commission proposals as much as possible, by lowering the share of these activities in the overall policy, and reducing the financial resources allocated to them, so that in the end they did not resemble much more than limited experiments.

However, during the *third phase* (1985–1995), which was dominated by the goal of completing the single market, the Council was no longer able to exercise its strategy to contain Commission activism. The poorer member states of the Community forcefully advocated for compensation for their increased exposure to the harsh winds of unleashed competition. The Commission used this opportunity to give cohesion policy an enormous boost. It proposed to subsume all Structural Funds under cohesion objectives (the Regional Fund, the Social Fund, and the Guidance Section of the Agricultural Fund), and to double the financial resources allocated to these. In exchange for these enormous side-payments to the poorer member states, the Commission proposed to redesign the policy approach, so that the European level could expand its influence on national policy-making. The Council adopted all these proposals without major amendments. Furthermore, the Commission introduced the partnership procedure, as a way to institutionalize what were so far only informal negotiations among the three government levels involved in cohesion policy. The objective of these negotiations among the Commission, national governments, and regional governments and authorities was jointly to specify policy objectives and strategies for implementation. According to the wording of the regulation, the three government levels had to cooperate in order to achieve common goals. In practice, however, these three levels were involved in difficult negotiations and even bargaining over development programmes, the allocation of funds, and the practices of implementation.

With the adoption of the Maastricht Treaty and its core concept of monetary union, cohesion policy again offered means to compensate economically weaker member states for the possible repercussions and losses incurred under the framework of a single currency. Those states that feared such losses – in particular, Spain – claimed additional financial resources of the Funds for compensation. The Commission used this opportunity to propose another set of expansive reforms. Again, the financial resources of the Funds were nearly doubled, an additional fund was created, called the Cohesion Fund, and the system of partnership was expanded to include the economic and social partners. Thus non-state actors were now involved in the policy, in particular to increase pressure on national and regional governments to implement the envisioned programmes.

The *fourth phase* (from 1995 onwards), is generally characterized by member states' attempts to reduce the Commission's influence in policy-making – something that, after the extraordinary expansion that took place in the previous phase, would severely threaten the position of the cohesion policy. However, in face of this threat the envisioned Eastern enlargement provided a way out. The accession states had to adapt their economic performance and political systems to European standards. The best way to trigger such adaptations, without dictating them, was to make use of the procedures and the financial incentives of cohesion policy. To this end, the Commission launched Agenda 2000, a concept for preparing the accession states for EU membership (European Commission 1997). Thus, cohesion policy acted as a template for the accession strategy and, after enlargement, as an instrument for further improving the economic competitiveness of the new member states, as well as their administrative performance. Furthermore, cohesion policy also formed an important instrument of European foreign policy, as it facilitated policy transfers to and transnational cooperation with the EU's new neighbourhood in the post-enlargement era. Finally, cohesion policy was defined as an important instrument to achieve the objectives of the Lisbon strategy (see p. 226). This was another strategic step on the part of the Commission to prevent the dismantling of the policy (Begg 2010: 83).

The fourth phase also further reformed cohesion policy, once in 2000 and again in 2007. These reforms apparently shifted more competences to the member states; yet, in fact, the reforms decentralized only certain tasks to the lower levels, while the Commission took a firm hold of the supervisory powers in the policy area (Bachtler and Mendez 2007). Furthermore, these reforms expanded the system of partnership to more non-state actors (2000) and, finally, to organized civil society in general (2007). The 2007 reform of the Structural Funds introduced an OMC procedure into the policy area (Tömmel and Verdun 2013). This is, quite striking at first glance, as procedures under the OMC generally apply to policy areas where the European level lacks competences. However, in this case the OMC procedure serves to further increase the influence of the European level on member states' policies. On a proposal of the Commission, the Council adopts guidelines for policy implementation.

The Commission, the Council, and additional actors and institutions inside the member states monitor compliance with these guidelines. The Council can also give recommendations to individual states. Thus, the procedure, even though it uses only non-binding governance modes such as cooperation and competition, clearly strengthens the influence of the European level on national policies, particularly by making use of the Council's authority with regard to the member states.

In summary, the evolution of EU cohesion policy highlights both similarities and differences to competition policy. Obviously, the differences lie in the use of various governance modes. While competition policy rests primarily on hierarchy, cohesion policy is mainly characterized by negotiation under the shadow of hierarchy, with cooperation also playing a specific role. The similarities are visible in the development of the two policies. As with competition policy, cohesion policy is characterized by a strong expansive logic that spilled over into other policy areas. Furthermore, cohesion policy evolved from a simple concept, derived from existing policies in the member states, to a complex and differentiated set of procedural rules and practices that matched with the institutional structure of the EU. During this process, obstacles to due implementation were regularly tackled through extensive reforms, which resulted in diversifying the governance approach, and in transforming the actor structure and the institutional context of the policy. The interactions between the Commission and the Council gave the policy its basic outline, but its further refinement increasingly included all government levels of the EU and even non-state actors. It is the commitment of these institutions and actors that makes the policy work. In Chapter 9, we will learn more about the consequences of these multi-level interactions for the evolution of the EU's political system.

## The European Employment Strategy

The European Employment Strategy is the best example of governance through the OMC procedure, where cooperation is the dominant governance mode in this area. In addition, competition provides an additional trigger to direct or influence the behaviour of institutions and actors responsible for policy implementation.

The European Employment Strategy only emerged during the fourth phase of EU policy-making, although even here we can see that the roots of the policy reach far back to earlier phases. The EES is important, as it was through this strategy that the OMC procedure was developed and further refined. Consequently, the EES acts as an exemplary case to highlight the evolution of European governance.

For a long time, the Commission had been attempting to create a European employment policy, and it had used a number of straightforward and more subtle strategies to reach this goal (Rhodes 2010:

287–93). However, the member states successfully resisted all these attempts. Finally, they accepted a limited European dimension in this area, under the condition that the European level only acts to coordinate policy. Since its inception in 1997, the OMC procedure that governs the EES has undergone several reforms and, in 2005, the Strategy was merged with the coordination of the Broad Economic Policy Guidelines of the Stability and Growth Pact. The outcome of this reform can be interpreted in one of two ways. Either the reform served to weaken the whole policy area, or the intention of the reform was to save it from dissolution. Since the policy is still a recent phenomenon, and not yet consolidated, it is too soon to make a final judgement on its role and importance in EU policy-making.

The origins of the EES can be found in the year 1993, when the Delors-Commission published a White Paper on Growth, Competitiveness and Employment (European Commission 1993) that laid the groundwork for a European Employment Strategy. However, initially, the White Paper was all but ignored in Council or the European Council, save for the formulation of some policy guidelines for national employment policies. It was only in the *fourth phase* (from 1995 onwards) of policy-making that the decisive break-through for a European employment policy was achieved (Mosher and Trubek 2003; Rhodes 2010). The Amsterdam Treaty, adopted in 1997, included a new Title on employment policy. However, it established this policy as an exercise in policy coordination. The Treaty stipulated: 'Member States and the Community shall ... work towards developing a coordinated strategy for employment' (Art. 125 TEC-A) and 'Member States ... shall regard promoting employment as a matter of common concern and shall coordinate their action in this respect within the Council' (Art. 126(2) TEC-A). The Treaty also already set out the procedure for achieving this coordination (Art. 128 TEC-A). It envisaged that, each year, the European Council would consider the employment situation in the Union, and would adopt conclusions on the issue. The Council, on a proposal of the Commission, had to draw up guidelines 'which the Member States shall take into account in their employment policies' (Art. 128(2) TEC-A). Under the guidelines, the member states were obliged to report on their policy measures annually. The Council then had to examine these measures 'in the light of the guidelines' (Art. 128(4) TEC-A) and make recommendations to individual states. Finally, the Commission and the Council were to draw up a report on the employment situation in the EU, which would serve as the basis for the conclusions of the European Council. At this point, the yearly cycle would begin afresh. In this way, the Amsterdam Treaty already defined the OMC procedure and its individual steps, even though it not phrased in these words. It even included an article that envisaged the use of benchmarking, peer reviews, and the exchange of best practice experiences (Art. 129 TEC-A), a toolbox for exercising influence on national policies that the Commission had earlier used in some limited experiments. Interestingly, the Treaty also stipulated that the Employment Strategy should be consistent with the Broad Economic Policy Guidelines of the Stability and Growth Pact (Art. 126(1) TEC-A), thus linking the EES closely to the requirements of economic growth and competitiveness in the member states.

In 1997, once the Amsterdam Treaty had been adopted but had not yet come into force, the Commission took the first steps to coordinate the member states' policies. It formulated the policy guidelines for the Employment Strategy, adopted them with major amendments by the Council, and urged the member states to elaborate National Action Plans (NAPs) that substantiate the measures envisioned in the framework of the guidelines (Mosher and Trubek 2003). With these activities, the whole cycle of the coordination procedure was set up. During the first years of its working, the guidelines were regularly reviewed and expanded, and horizontal objectives were added. According to Armstrong and Kilpatrick (2007: 664), this initial phase of the EES was characterized by the 'most demanding' guidelines, 'on paper at least'. Furthermore, during these years the Commission sought to flank the new policy with a whole range of supportive measures. It made extensive use of benchmarking and peer reviews, and formulated clear targets for policy implementation in the member states. In addition, it initiated the adoption of Council directives in the area of employment (Armstrong and Kilpatrick 2007: 664). Finally, it used the instrument of the Social Fund to foster and subsidize innovative employment initiatives in the member states that could serve as models for broader policy concepts (Regalia 2002: 5). The coordination procedure was significantly upgraded by the decision of the Lisbon European Council in 2000 to apply this procedure to the implementation of the Lisbon Strategy, aimed at improving the competitiveness of the EU in a broad spectrum of sectors. Since then, the procedure operates under the label 'Open Method of Coordination'.

In 2003, the first revision of the EES was undertaken (Armstrong and Kilpatrick 2007). It reduced the number of guidelines, but set more clearly quantifiable targets. The guidelines partly converged with objectives of the Structural Funds, so that the financial incentives of the Funds could easily be used for employment initiatives. In formal terms, the Council adhered to the yearly revision of the guidelines but, in fact, it only reformulated the guidelines every second year. The social partners were invited to participate actively in the policy. They were expected to take a role in the design and implementation of policies within the member states and also to act as whistle-blowers, if national authorities did not comply with European guidelines.

In 2005, the EES was subject to a fundamental reform (Armstrong and Kilpatrick 2007). The policy was now more closely integrated into the Lisbon strategy, which was itself the subject of a major overhaul during the same year (Weishaupt and Lack 2011). The most significant step in the reform was the merging of the employment guidelines with the Broad Economic Policy Guidelines of the Stability and Growth Pact to create a set of integrated guidelines. Of a total of 24 guidelines 8 referred to employment issues. The guidelines were formulated for a period of three years. National Action Plans were replaced by National Reform Programmes (NRPs) that included both economic growth and employment issues, and were also valid for three years. The Commission and the Council had to elaborate an integrated report on the economic and employment situation in the member states that served the European Council to formulate its conclusions.

In 2010, the Lisbon strategy expired and Europe 2020 was launched as a new strategy for economic growth. The strategy propagates a smart, sustainable and inclusive economy, to be reached through five objectives. One of the five objectives is employment; two others, education and social inclusion, are indirectly linked to employment issues. Within the framework of these objectives, the EU has set Headline Targets, while the member states may set their own targets in the framework of their National Reform Programmes (Weishaupt and Lack 2011). Furthermore, 10 Integrated Guidelines were adopted. Of these, 4 refer to the 3 Headline Targets on employment. Finally, 7 Flagship Initiatives accompany these guidelines and targets, with 3 of these referring to employment issues.

Thus, at present, the EES constitutes a policy that is closely linked to the EU's strategy to direct the economic policies of the member states through the framework of the Stability and Growth Pact. The procedures for supervising national activities in this domain were recently tightened. A complex process of policy coordination, involving all levels of government and, to a lesser degree, non-state actors, is used to exercise influence by the European level on national employment policies. The EES is embedded in the Europe 2020 Strategy, which acts as a broader concept to spur on reforms at national level in various policies that are expected to impact on economic growth and innovation.

Clearly, the present policy approach deviates from the phrasing of the OMC procedure as laid down in the Amsterdam Treaty. However, even though the coordination procedure no longer corresponds to the precise wording of the Treaty, the reforms have not triggered any revisions. Both the Nice and the Lisbon Treaties contain an almost unaltered Employment Title. The deviation of the actual OMC from the Treaty provisions lies particularly in the extension of the coordination cycle from one to three years. This extension can be interpreted as a simplification of the original OMC design, since yearly coordination cycles require an enormous workload for all institutions and actors involved in the procedure (Heidenreich and Bischoff 2008).

In contrast, the most significant policy change – the integration of the EES into economic policy coordination – was envisioned under the Amsterdam Treaty (see Art. 126(1) TEC-A). Some scholars assume that this policy change comes down to a silent dismantling of the ambitious project of a European Employment Strategy, or at least a subordination of employment objectives to those of economic growth and competitiveness. A critical observer even claimed that the revised EES 'amount(s) to an attack on the European social model' (Raveaud 2007: 430). Another scholar observed that, after the reform, the effect of the EES on member states' policies has diminished, rather than increased (Mailand 2008) – an observation that indicates a weakening of the policy.

However, the integration of the EES into the Europe 2020 Strategy appears to put employment issues back at the top of the agenda. Particularly in times of economic and financial crisis and enormously high levels of unemployment in many of the EU's member states, employment issues, and the accompanying measures of education and skills training, is increasing in importance. Therefore, the most recent shift in the EU's policy seems to reinstate the EES as a strong concern for the European level. Yet, the EES continues to be subject to priorities of economic growth and, thus, to neo-liberal strategies of economic recovery, as Weishaupt and Lack (2011) suspect. Nevertheless, these scholars credit the EES with a series of positive impacts: it 'has triggered critical reflections of policy, shaped national policy agendas, introduced common focal points such as flexicurity and the New Skills agenda, and – arguably – convergence of policy instruments in the long run can be expected' (Weishaupt and Lack, 2011: 33; see also Heidenreich and Bischoff 2008).

We can conclude that, although the EES relies primarily on cooperation as a mode of governance, from the outset, a whole set of rules and procedures that give guidance to the employment policies of the member states have evolved, but without any formal prescriptions. The policy is characterized by intense interactions among the institutions of the European level, as well as between the European level and member states' authorities. To a certain extent, non-state actors are also involved in the policy. During the short period of its existence, the policy has undergone several reforms that simplified its procedures and subsumed it under the broader objectives of economic growth and competitiveness. At the same time, the policy was embedded into the larger framework of, first, the Lisbon Strategy and, most recently, the Europe 2020 Strategy. The reforms have also partially shifted the balance between the European and the national levels, apparently favouring the latter. However, we should not interpret this as a weakening of the European level. In other policy domains, we have seen that these shifts can actually work to improve the commitment of the lower levels to fulfil European demands. Consequently, we can assume that the EES also tries to profit from increasing 'ownership' of national and sub-national authorities and other actors (Weishaupt and Lack, 2011: 26). Finally, the OMC procedure, once developed in the framework of the EU's employment policy and also the macro-economic policy surveillance (Hodson and Maher 2001), has served as a model for coordinating many other policy or issue areas. It has thus contributed to the expansion of the realm of European policy-making, and has worked to improve the effectiveness of long-established policies, including, as we saw in the previous section, cohesion policy.

## Conclusion

This chapter has analyzed various aspects of European policies, policy-making, and governance, ranging from the evolution and expansion of the policy portfolio, through the emergence and differentiation of the corresponding policy processes and governance modes, to the development and successive reforms of selected policy areas that are representative of distinct governance approaches. This analysis has shown how European policy-making, initially only acting in but a few areas and domains, has expanded to a broad spectrum that encompasses nearly all policy areas that we recognize from national political systems. However, it has also highlighted that European policies are formulated and implemented through governance modes that clearly differ from those used at national level.

Initially, the Communities relied largely on hierarchy as the dominant mode of governance. However, this mode often did not work as expected, as it gives the member states no discretion in policy implementation. Therefore, with progress in integration and the expansion of the policy portfolio, European governance evolved in the spirit of the multi-level and multi-actor structure of the European polity. In many cases, this has implied respecting, as much as possible, the sovereignty of the member states, while at the same time trying to shape the policies of the national and, in part, also the regional levels as much as possible. Thus, EU governance made use of hierarchy, where member states' positions and preferences converged and resulted in a consensus on the advantages of strong European interventions and the corresponding transfers of powers. This has been most obvious in single market issues and competition policy. Where such converging positions or a fundamental consensus did not exist, or did so only to a small degree – as for, example, in cohesion or employment policy – other governance modes were applied. These included procedures for consensus-building – in particular, through negotiation – or sought to accommodate the divergences among the member states by relying on voluntary cooperation. In addition, competition was used as a governance mode that steers with an 'invisible hand'.

The extensive use of non-hierarchical governance modes in the EU does not automatically mean that these modes have had little impact.

On the contrary, EU governance modes may sometimes result in stronger impacts than one might expect at first glance. Their impact, however, is conditional on various factors, particularly the capacity of EU institutions to choose governance modes that provide sufficient scope for member states to pursue their specific policy objectives within a framework set at European level. At the same time, it is dependent on the will and commitment of member states' authorities to comply with, or adapt their policies to, European rules, guidelines, or targets. In other words, European governance is often more effective if it involves all relevant institutions and actors in policy-making, and if it succeeds in triggering their commitment to forceful action.

This chapter has pointed out that European policy-making and governance is characterized by intense interactions among the EU's institutions, the government levels, and a variety of other institutions and actors involved – and, hence, a variety of policy processes. Yet, these interactions and policy processes vary with the governance modes in use. In the case of hierarchy, they mainly involve the European level, even though we do see that there is also some vertical cooperation between the government levels, and horizontal cooperation among the member states, as for example in competition policy. Where negotiation is the dominant governance mode, both the EU's institutions and all three government levels are involved in interactions, as we saw in the discussion of cohesion policy. In cooperation, which characterizes the governance of the EES, the same institutions and levels are involved, but the interactions and the procedures of decision-making are even more complex and intense. However, at the same time, the institutions and actors involved are formally independent of each other.

The analysis of the three selected policy areas highlighted that each area has displayed an explicit expansive logic; that is, their governance mechanisms have been used in ways other than originally intended (competition policy), or for launching new initiatives in other policy areas (cohesion policy and Employment Strategy). This expansive logic indicates the Commission's activism in transferring effective governance modes to other domains, thus putting pressure on the Council to accept a further expansion of the realm and scope of European policies.

As we have seen, European policy-making and governance evolves in adaptation to the possibilities and constraints set by the institutional structure of the EU. However, the opposite is also true. To a certain degree, EU policy-making and governance shapes the institutional structure of the European polity. The continuous processes of transferring tasks and competences to the European level, as well as re-decentralizing them from the European to the national and even to the regional levels or to non-state actors, re-shapes the institutional architecture of the EU, as Chapters 9 and 10 will show.

# Chapter 9

# Building a Multi-Level System

As an emergent political order, the European Union is constantly expanding and altering its institutional structure. This process leads to the creation of additional institutions at the European level that complement the basic structure of the system (see Chapter 7). Within the member states, European decision-making and policy implementation transforms existing institutions and affects the actors involved. These processes primarily incorporate national governments and administrations but, over the long term, they also affect lower level governments, semi-public institutions and agencies, and private actors and their organizations (see Chapter 10). None of these institutional changes is the direct consequence of a concise and coherent strategy to build and expand the European polity. Instead, they are the responses to the contradictions and imperfections of the system itself. Since the member states are not willing to build strong European institutions, even when the pressure to put forth common solutions is intense, they respond to emerging problems by expanding the Union's institutions in a piecemeal fashion and a decentralized manner. One way to do so consists of involving existing state-level institutions in European affairs. In the long run, these processes inevitably lead to a gradual transformation of national political systems. Furthermore, the EU itself has morphed into a system that spans the member states with a web of loosely coupled policy networks. These networks have reached such a degree of complexity and differentiation that they are themselves regarded as a core characteristic of the European polity (Kohler-Koch 1999).

At the national and, at times, the regional levels, the European polity expands and evolves by selectively incorporating public institutions into processes of policy formulation and implementation. These procedures act to create a vertical nexus between levels of government, and thus compensate for the absence of clearly-defined hierarchical relationships between them (Beck and Grande 2007). Furthermore, by creating transnational networks of member state institutions under a European umbrella, the Union establishes a horizontal nexus that fosters convergence among the diverse national political systems (Tömmel 2011b).

231

In this chapter, I examine how the European Union expands by incorporating institutions and actors already existing at the member state level into its own procedures of decision-making and policy implementation. The multiple interactions in the European polity draw, most particularly, on national governments and administrations. But, increasingly, they have come to include the regional level as well. This occurs regardless of the constitutional order of the member states, and includes regions in fully-fledged federations, as well as purely unitary systems.

Since the 1990s, the increasing importance of the regions in European affairs has brought about new interpretations of the EU's institutional structure and modes of operation. Thus, the concept of 'multi-level governance' was put forth to better conceptualize the increasingly closer ties and the multiple interactions between the European and the 'lower' government levels (see e.g. Hooghe and Marks 2001). Eventually, the Union as a whole has come to be conceptualized as a multi-level system. Hence, in this chapter I analyze the incorporation of the member states into European decision- and policy-making as a process of building a multi-level system. However, it is important to note that the member states are only partially and selectively incorporated into the functioning of the EU, with the result that they are not absorbed into it, but continue to exist as fairly autonomous units (Beck and Grande 2007). Nonetheless, the Union can trigger certain processes of transformation and modernization or, more precisely, Europeanization in the member states. This may, in the future, have far-reaching consequences for the individual political systems (see e.g. Featherstone and Radaelli 2003; Ladrech 2010; Bretherton and Mannin 2013). The following sections will deal in greater detail with selected aspects of these developments.

## Incorporating the national government level

Jacques Delors once said that, after the completion of the single market, up to 80 per cent of national legislation in economic affairs would be determined by European law. This implies that national legislative institutions are significantly constrained in their autonomy and that they are compelled to adapt their own regulations to a framework set elsewhere. Thus, European legislation creates a strong, though *indirect*, systemic nexus between the European and the national government levels that allows the EU to direct the member state with an 'invisible hand'. Yet, the degree of steering 'from above' is not equal in all policy domains. In the economic sphere, European direction may be as high as approximately 80 per cent, while in areas such as cultural and educational policy it is substantially lower. Indeed, in these policies, EU legislation barely plays a role. In these areas we see, at most, the establishment of a system of coordinating national policies to foster voluntary adaptation to a framework set at European level (see Chapter 8). In the long run, this might result in increased convergence among national policies.

The degree to which steering from above occurs is also dependent upon the type of regulation; for example, whether it pertains to 'negative' or 'positive integration' (Scharpf 1999). In the case of 'negative integration', the EU adopts laws and measures to remove barriers to the creation of the single market (e.g. customs or non-tariff trade barriers). Even though these measures have an indirect impact, they imply that there is some form of effective steering by the forces of the market. In contrast, policies pertaining to the realm of 'positive integration' require proactive design and decision-making. Since an overall consensus among the member states is often hard to achieve in these domains, the corresponding legal acts or policy concepts, if adopted at all, are usually formulated in an ambiguous way and leave member states much discretion. Accordingly, political steering in these cases is much weaker, or of a more indirect nature. In more general terms, we can say that the steering capacity of the Union depends on the degree of integration of a policy area, which may widely vary (see Chapter 8). Furthermore, steering mechanisms originating at the European level rarely provide strict guidance but, instead, leave broad leeway for the 'lower' levels of governance to shape policies according to their own objectives and preferences (for a theoretical underpinning, see Chapter 1). Thus, when European institutions are engaged in elaborating directives, they are fully aware of the need to anticipate differences in implementation at the national level. Therefore, prudent European legislation focuses on the creation of a flexible framework to provide ample room for regulatory and administrative differences among the member states.

Furthermore, it is important to note that European legislation is not simply imposed on the member states. In fact, it is the result of decisions made by the Councils. Input from member states' administrations, together with a variety of interests at the national level, is essential to the process, so that the creation of an indirect nexus between levels through legislation is always preceded by complex forms of direct interaction (see Chapter 5).

With regard to *direct* forms of interaction, it is important to distinguish between the formulation of policy and its implementation. In the *formulation* of policy, which in the European context essentially implies legislation, multiple inter-relations among the levels evolve. Even at the earliest stages of policy development, the Commission relies on the advice of large numbers of top level civil servants and experts (see Chapters 6 and 10). Even though civil servants participate in these groups '*a titre personnel*' (i.e. representing their own personal positions), their preferences rarely differ significantly from that which is ultimately adopted. The explanation for this is quite simple. Individuals who advise the Commission often also participate in the working groups of the

Council (Wessels 2008: 235). This dual role that national civil servants can play at the European level is advantageous to both the Commission and the Council. Even in the formative stages of policy development, legislative proposals from the Commission can be adapted to the positions and preferences of the member states and this, in turn, allows broader consensus to emerge on policy proposals. There are also other, long-term advantages to this informal system of cooperation. Since expert groups from various disciplines tend to share preferences and expectations, they will frequently assume a common, European perspective on policy matters. Their points of view are subsequently conveyed to national administrations and make it more possible for a variety of actors to cooperate effectively. The result is the formation of stable policy networks that cut across the various levels of government, and facilitate even closer integration (Peterson 2004).

According to policy network theories, loosely institutionalized structures are formed and maintained through the exchange of a variety of resources among the actors involved (Börzel and Heard-Lauréote 2009: 137). In the European context, representatives of member states offer their knowledge and their expertise in policy issues in exchange for policy concepts that correspond as much as possible to their own preferences. In addition, both sides benefit from the cooperation – the Commission can improve its poorly institutionalized position and its legitimacy, while national experts can improve their position with regard to other actors at home who may hold different points of view.

It is not only the Commission, but also the Council that seeks to establish and maintain close ties with representatives of national governments and administrations. Of course, the Council itself and its whole substructure consist of members or delegates of national governments. But, occasionally, the Council also needs to pull other national actors into European decision-making. As we have seen, a highly-differentiated range of permanent and *ad hoc* working groups prepare the decisions of COREPER and the specific committees (see Chapters 4 and 6). It is the task of the experts in these working groups to assess whether or not Commission proposals are compatible with national interests. However, since their ultimate goal is to reach consensus, their views often tend to converge and they assume common 'European' perspectives. This is particularly true for those issues that do not provoke distributive conflicts. The presence of the Commission in the working groups favours the emergence of common perspectives. For their part, members of the working groups convey European perspectives to the national arena.

Direct interactions between the European and the national levels also occur in *policy implementation*. The administrative committees, better known under the label 'comitology', are set up in nearly every policy area and form the institutional framework for the evolution of these relationships (see Chapter 5). The committees, consisting of national civil servants, work under the auspices of the Commission. Their function is to accompany and supervise the Commission in the implementation of European policies. Despite conflicts between the Commission and the Council concerning the number and competences of such committees, their members are primarily concerned with efficient and effective problem-solving. Accordingly, they are highly consensus-oriented and seem to focus their efforts towards consensus building, rather than exercising the monitoring functions ascribed to them (Guéguen 2011).

The examples presented above all consider the incorporation of national actors into European affairs. Yet, in the implementation of policy, the opposite is also true, and the European level is increasingly influential in national policies and decision-making procedures. This applies to policies of a pure regulatory nature, as well as to those found along the distributive spectrum. For example, as we have seen in competition policy, the Commission has extensive powers in the areas of cartels, mergers, and state aid, so that it can take decisions without interference from other institutions and actors. In practice, however, it tries to solve many problems through negotiations with the parties concerned, whether they are national governments or private firms. Over time, this strategy has resulted in a more stable relationship between the European and the national levels. Most recently, certain matters in competition policy were decentralized and committed to the national level. At the same time, though, an institutionalized network of national competition authorities has been established under the auspices of the Commission (see Chapter 8; McGowan 2005; Wilks 2010).

In the realm of distributive policies, the Commission plays an active role in national policy-making by allocating European subsidies. The result of this has been an intensive interaction among all levels of government, including the European, the national, and the regional levels. Within the framework of cohesion policy, such interactions were initially *ad hoc*, but with the fundamental reform of the Structural Funds in 1989 they were institutionalized through the system of 'partnership' (see Chapter 8; see also p. 237). This system includes representatives from all three levels of government. Together, they negotiate on the substance of programmes for developing less-favoured regions, on the modes of policy implementation, and on the allocation of funds for these programmes. The supervision of the implementation of policy is also organized as a joint endeavour among all three levels of government. Increasingly, non-state actors have become involved in these deliberations and in the implementation of policy. Thus, altogether, intensive interactions between the European Union, national and regional governments and, partly, private actors characterize the implementation of distributive policies in the EU. Ultimately, such interactions result in adaptations of decision-making procedures, policy-styles, and performances in the member states to the governance modes of the EU (Tömmel and Verdun 2009).

When policies are coordinated through the OMC, even more frequent, intense, and direct interactions are required between both the institutions of the EU and the various levels of government (see Chapter 8). The OMC primarily makes use of communication and coordination, or mutual learning as a 'soft' means of political steering (Eberlein and Kerwer 2004; Heidenreich and Bischoff 2008; Benz 2009; Sabel and Zeitlin 2010).

Consequently, we can conclude that the incorporation of national governments and administrations into European policy-making has led to complex interactions between the levels. On the one hand, a broad spectrum of national actors and organizations has been effectively incorporated into European decision-making. On the other hand, the European level becomes increasingly involved in the implementation of its policies in the member states through both direct and indirect interventions. These complex relationships, based to a large extent on direct communication and interaction, have resulted in the formation of more stable policy networks (Börzel and Heard-Lauréote 2009). Contrary to what one might assume, this has not led to a tendency towards the dismantling of the nation state. Instead, it marks the diffusion of specific, often innovative policy styles across the EU, and the adaptation of national actors and institutions to these styles (Tömmel and Verdun 2009, 2013; Sabel and Zeitlin 2010). This process of Europeanization of the national political arena, in turn, results in changing perceptions and performances of the actors involved (Featherstone and Radaelli 2003; Ladrech 2010). The inclusion of the national level into European decision- and policy-making may ultimately lead to the modernization of national political systems, as well as to their transformation into compatible, but relatively autonomous, elements of the European polity.

## Incorporating the regional government level

Since building the EU has always been a project of national politics, the increasing involvement of national governments in European decision-making may seem self-evident. The incorporation of the regional level into the political system of the EU, however, is more surprising. During the early years of integration, direct connections between the European and the regional levels did not exist. In fact, such connections were explicitly prohibited, since national governments regarded EU politics as foreign policy matters and, thus, their exclusive domain (Jeffery 2000). National governments therefore tended to monitor the evolution of any direct relationships between the Commission and regional authorities very carefully, viewing them with suspicion and, in some countries, even forbidding them outright.

Just as remarkable as the existence of direct relationships between the EU and the regions is the fact that these relationships have evolved independently of the constitutional order and administrative division of the member states. Contrary to common belief, it was not only fully fledged sub-national governments, such as the German '*Länder*', that were able to gain access to the institutions of the EU. In fact, virtually all regional authorities succeeded in establishing direct relationships with the European level of governance (Jeffery 2000; Rowe 2011). This, it would seem, indicates that it was the Commission that actively pursued a policy of establishing linkages with regional government levels.

## Incorporating the regions into policy-making

Indeed, as early as in 1977, the Commission initiated a strategy for mobilizing the various regions as actors in European cohesion policy (Hooghe 1996). In spite of enormous difficulties – particularly, the fact that the regions were by no means prepared to carry out such a role – the Commission succeeded in expanding and improving its strategy incrementally through a series of reforms (enacted in 1979, 1985 and 1989). In particular, the 'grand' reform of cohesion policy (1989) in the wake of the single market project allocated a major role in European policy-making to the regions. As noted, a system of 'partnership' was established as an institutional arrangement for cooperation in cohesion policy between the various levels of government of the Union. The system was primarily meant to provide a framework for structured negotiations between the Commission and the national governments on the elaboration, adoption, implementation, and evaluation of development programmes. By explicitly including the regions in the system, the informal contacts that already existed between the European and the 'third' government level were embedded in a formalized framework and thereby legalized. The closer relationships which consequently developed between the Commission as policy initiator and the regions as authorities responsible for implementation of these policies, served to fine-tune both procedural and substantive issues in this area.

In the longer term, the interaction between the Commission and the regions resulted in the formation of more stable network structures, also including representatives of national governments. In these networks, all parties pursue their own specific interests and thus engage in tough negotiations on policy objectives, projects, and programmes, as well as procedures of implementation. This multi-level structure also opens up new opportunities for building alliances. In some cases, the national and the regional levels jointly assume a common position in relation to the Commission. In other cases, the Commission's position coincides with that of the central governments. Yet, in most cases, an alliance emerges between regional authorities and the Commission (Hooghe and Marks 2001). This is remarkable because, in most member states, the regional level is formally subordinate to the national one. Such alliances therefore tend to soften the hierarchical relationships between the government levels within the member states. At the same time, they create a systemic nexus between the European and the regional level and, thus, tend to transform the EU into a multi-level system (Hooghe and Marks 2001).

Encouraged by these successes, the Commission launched additional concepts for mobilizing sub-national units in European politics and policies. In the framework of the Structural Funds, it designed Specific Initiatives that called upon the regions to cooperate across borders in order to implement transnational policy projects (Tömmel and Verdun 2013: 393). In particular, the INTERREG programme, which delibe-rately fostered cross-border cooperation, proved to be a major success. After three experimental periods, the 2007 reform of the Structural Funds incorporated the approach into the mainstream of cohesion policy. The Commission's Specific Initiatives, aimed at mobilizing the regions, had a significant impact on them. They helped to increase the capacity of the regions to design and implement development policies and programmes. Furthermore, they tended to increase the relative autonomy of regional authorities in their relationships with their national governments. They also intensified vertical relationships with the Commission as well as horizontal cooperation in transnational settings (Tömmel 2011b). These relationships, in turn, fostered the formation of transnational interest associations, which advocated the policy positions and preferences of regional and local authorities in the European arena (Keating and Hooghe 2006: 277).

## Representing the regions at European level

As a consequence of the increasing interactions with the Commission, the regions no longer acted as passive objects of European policy-making. Increasingly, they themselves have sought access to the Euro-pean arena. The most remarkable step in this regard has been the establishment of regional 'representations' in Brussels, a strategy first initiated by the German 'Länder' (Rowe 2011). In fact, the German 'Länder' are represented by 15 different offices in Brussels; two Länder, Hamburg and Schleswig Holstein, share one representation. Soon, other regions followed their example, beginning with the larger member states (i.e. France, the UK, Italy, and Spain). They were followed by the smaller states, with the exception of Luxembourg. Most recently, the emerging regional authorities of the accession states of Central and Eastern Europe have established representations in Brussels as well

(Moore 2008). In 2007, the overall number of regional representations amounted to 182 (Studinger 2012: 104). In addition to the regions, local authorities have also established offices in Brussels. Large cities run their own representation; smaller cities operate through their associations (e.g. the municipalities of Bavaria). Research into the motivations of the regions to establish a representation in Brussels reveals that it was clearly rational calculations of the costs and benefits that caused these steps (Studinger 2012).

Representations of regional and local authorities in Brussels do not, however, enjoy a status comparable to that of the Permanent Representations of the member states. Whereas the national representations assume an eminent position in European decision-making – in fact, they represent the members of the Council in Brussels – those from the regional and the local levels function, at best, as lobbyists for their respective territories. Furthermore, regional representations may vary widely in their organizational form and position (Keating and Hooghe 2006: 275–6). For example, those of the German '*Länder*' are, in fact, branches of their home governments. British regional offices, on the other hand, are based on a public–private partnership between regional and local authorities and private consortia, such as development agencies (Moore 2008). Between these extremes there exists a wide variety of mixed forms. In view of such highly divergent institutional patterns, it is rather unlikely that the regional representations can acquire a formal role in European decision-making.

In spite of their differences, regional representations in Brussels share a common trait. They all engage in actively advocating the interests of their home region in European affairs (Rowe 2011: 83–125). Their activities may range from attempts to influence European decision-making to the transfer of know-how on the EU to their home base. They may include the search for European funding opportunities or promotional activities in favour of local and regional businesses, as well as public institutions. Although the weight and the mix of these activities may vary widely, the advocacy role of the representations remains largely the same. The medium used for performing this role – direct communication – is also essentially the same.

The Commission is the most important interlocutor for direct communication. Regional offices aim at networking with Commission officials in order to gain important information at an early stage. The quest for such information may address legislation or funding opportunities. However, if the regions wish to exercise effective influence on European decisions, they have to rely on the intervention of their national governments. A large part of direct communication also focuses on the regional government at home. The offices in Brussels provide first-hand information on upcoming decisions, events, and trends in the Union, as well as advice for strategic choices and actions to be taken. Generally speaking, the offices in Brussels are much better informed on European affairs than their home bases and they also possess more sophisticated strategic knowledge and insight. Often these offices assume a didactic function, in that they 'teach' regional and local civil servants how to understand the EU and how to deal with the 'Brussels bureaucracy'. Non-state actors based in the regions are also included into intense communications, in order to inform them of important decisions or funding opportunities at the European level. At the same time, the representations advocate the business interests of their regions within the EU. Finally, offices in Brussels are involved in dense communication networks with one another in order to exchange information, pursue common interests, or even to cooperate in joint projects. Such forms of cooperation refer mostly to offices of the same member state, but they are also practised across borders – in particular, between neighbouring regions. In sum, 'regional representations today operate as Euro-savvy entrepreneurs' (Rowe 2011: 3).

In conclusion, we can state that the representations of the regions in Brussels constitute an important link between the European and the regional governmental levels. Through intensive contacts and communication, they launch ideas and advocate proposals for policy-making at the European level, while at the same time transferring valuable information, strategic insights, and know-how on European affairs to their home governments and administrations, and even to non-state actors.

### Creating an arena at European level: the Committee of the Regions

The Committee of the Regions (CoR) (or the EU's Assembly of Regional and Local Representatives), was established in 1994 after the Maastricht Treaty came into force. It constitutes another important link between the European and the regional levels (Jeffery and Rowe 2012). This body, modelled after the Economic and Social Committee (EESC, see Chapter 10), serves as an advisor to the Commission, the Council, and the Parliament in all matters regarding the regions (Art. 13(4) TEU-L). This encompasses a broad range of European policies – in particular, those that pertain to the spectrum of 'positive integration' (Scharpf 1999). Thus, Transport (Chapter VI TFEU), Employment, Social Policy and Social Fund (Chapters IX-XI), Education, Vocational Training, Youth and Sports (Chapter XII), Culture (XIII), Environment (XX), Energy (XXI), and, most importantly, Cohesion (XVIII) are all explicitly mentioned in the Treaty as requiring the consultation of the CoR in case of legislation, or other decision-making. In addition, the Committee 'may issue an opinion on its own initiative' (Art. 307 TFEU). In fact, the Committee enjoys rather broad powers to deliberate on and advise in most aspects of European affairs. It thus constitutes an integral part of the basic institutional architecture of the EU. However, because in practice the Committee also serves as a platform for advocating regional and local interests at the European level, it constitutes an important building-block in shaping the multi-level structure of the Union.

The role of the Committee as an advocate of particular interests of the regions was not envisaged when it was first established. Its final institutional configuration resulted from compromises among the institutions involved in decision-making. At the time, the German '*Länder*' sought maximum involvement of the regions by claiming the establishment of a 'third chamber' alongside the Council and the Parliament. In contrast, the Commission favoured a more 'technical' advisory body that would serve its own demand for information and support from the 'third level'. For its part, the European Council was divided between those who advocated a limited advisory role for the regions and those who were strictly opposed to any involvement at all. In the end, the institutional form of the CoR represents a compromise between these positions, as it is set up as a comparatively 'weak' advisory body (Jeffery and Rowe 2012). However, in spite of its formally weak position, in practice the CoR assumes a stronger role.

When the CoR was established, there were no clear regulations concerning its membership. The Maastricht Treaty defined only the overall number of seats, the size of national delegations, and the procedure for the nomination of delegates. Through successive enlargements of the Union, the size of the Committee has increased from its original 189 seats to the present 353 seats. The size of national delegations for large states varies from 21 to 24 members and, for small states, from 5 to 15 (TFEU, Protocol No. 36, Art. 8). The delegates are nominated by the Council on the basis of proposals from each state. Because of the ill-defined rules, conflicts arose among the European institutions as to whether the delegates should be elected officials, or whether they might also be civil servants (Nugent 2010: 231). In the end, it was determined that only elected politicians would serve, a rule that is now included in the Treaty (Art. 300(3) TFEU). The choice of how to distribute the seats between the regional and the local level is left to the member states. This leads to an acceptable proportion of an approximately two-thirds representation for the regional and one-third for the local level.

The choice for nominating elected office-holders had far-reaching consequences. Unexpectedly, in the first round of nominations in 1993, high-ranking politicians at the regional and local levels struggled to win a seat on the Committee. Prime ministers of the German '*Länder*', presidents of provincial or regional administrations, as well as mayors of large cities, all competed for nomination. Although the level of the delegates' rank has declined in recent years, it is still relatively high. Holding a seat in the Committee provides politicians with certain incentives. First, they may be able to make contact more easily with colleagues from other regional or local authorities. This is important, since many EU-funded programmes require transnational cooperation among regional or local actors. Second, a role on the European stage may improve one's political profile at home. Third, and most important, the European stage may be used to put pressure on the national government of the home country to fulfil certain demands of the regions. The presence of high ranking politicians provides the Committee with a political weight that it would otherwise not command. Furthermore, it provides democratic legitimacy to the Committee, a rare, though important asset in the EU.

Another factor influencing the political weight of the Committee is the level of support received from the Commission. Commissioners, especially those responsible for regional policy, maintain close relationships with the Committee (Christiansen and Lintner 2005). The Commission is always eager to consider the views of the Committee, not just in the case of regular legislative procedures, but even at a much earlier stage, when proposals are first elaborated (Jeffery and Rowe 2012). This provides the Commission with valuable information and the Committee with privileged access to decision-making within the Commission. Finally, the Commission provides feed-back by regularly reporting on its implementation of the Committee's recommendations (Christiansen and Lintner 2005). Close relationships with the CoR are also advantageous for the Commission, as it is always in need of allies.

In its operation, the CoR is torn between a political and a more 'technical' function. The first implies acting as an advocate of the 'third' government level in the EU; the second means accepting the role of a technical advisory body, primarily serving the Commission. The Commission tends to draw the Committee into technical matters in order to improve its leverage with the Council and to assure proper implementation of its policies at the regional level (Christiansen and Lintner 2005). However, if the CoR follows the Commission's route, it might well lose its capacity to act as a powerful voice of regional and local interests at the European level (Cole 2005: 66–8).

Acting as this voice is precisely what appeals to the Committee. For the first time in the history of European integration, the regions, through the Committee, are in a position to jointly express their interests at the European level, and thus to rejoin the political power of regional and local authorities. Consequently, the institutions of the EU can no longer ignore the voice of the regions (Jeffery and Rowe 2012: 373). Although the Council as a whole tends to pay little attention to the Committee's recommendations, individual governments do take them into account, lest they face strong opposition at home. The Parliament assumes a more ambiguous stance, as it considers the Committee to be a potential rival in European decision-making (Christiansen and Lintner 2005). Yet, the Parliament is also in constant search for allies in its dealings with the Council. The Treaty provides that 'the Committee of the Regions may be consulted by the European Parliament' (Art. 307 TFEU). Generally speaking, the CoR is anxious to safeguard its independence and to entertain good relationships with all the institutions of the EU (Cole 2005). Furthermore, it seeks to address the European public; for example, by organizing large conferences or discussion forums on salient political issues (Christiansen and Lintner 2005). Activities such as these serve to underscore demands for democratizing the Union by giving the 'third' government level a stronger voice in decision-making.

The daily operation of the CoR reveals the conflict between its political and technical functions. In general, its members tend to prefer a more political stance at the European level. There are several reasons for this. First, members who perform high-ranking executive tasks at home are not accustomed to dealing with technical details. Second, consideration of more detailed issues might evoke controversy in the Committee and diminish its influence in the eyes of the other European institutions. Third, the Committee lacks internal coherence, not least, because it rarely meets in plenary (five times per year) and its members are primarily committed to their tasks and duties at home. In contrast, the substructure of the CoR, a secretariat with approximately 540 civil servants that forms part of the European Commission, tends to privilege the technical function of the Committee.

In addition to this, the Committee has difficulties in forging the diverging opinions of its members into a single, common position (Jeffery and Rowe 2012). This is to some extent the result of its weakness in forming political alliances. Although party groups increasingly play a role in the Committee – the five largest groups of the EP are also organized in the CoR – they do not provide the cohesion necessary to balance other alliances (Christiansen and Lintner 2005). Alternative alignments arise in a variety of ways (Brunazzo and Domorenok 2008). They may form along national lines, between regional and local authorities, and on a north–south axis. More recently, an east–west division has begun to emerge. Even these basic alignments are further fragmented by additional fault lines, such as those between economically prosperous and less developed regions, or between politically more autonomous and well-resourced regions and those which find themselves in a more dependent and comparatively disadvantaged position. As a consequence of this multifaceted fragmentation, it is often difficult for the CoR to reach common decisions (Cole 2005; Christiansen and Lintner 2005).

In view of this situation, the party groups have recently increased in importance. As in the Parliament, a 'grand coalition' has emerged between the European Peoples' Party (EPP) and the Party of European Socialists (PES). Both of these groups seek to strike compromises ahead of plenary debates and decisions. They try to conciliate their political positions internally and to distribute influential positions among themselves. Unsurprisingly, this strategy is met with opposition from the smaller party groups which feel excluded. Furthermore, party groups often do not really represent the political preferences of regional and local leaders. Although they are members of political parties, as heads of the executive at regional or local levels, they often face specific problems that are not reflected in party positions and programmes. Therefore, even though the party groups may play a role in the Committee, they are generally only tolerated for pragmatic reasons. Empirical studies have shown that decisions taken in the Committee do not reflect party alignments. Rather, for the most part, they reflect a consensus of the views of all groups of the Committee (Hönnige and Kaiser 2003; Brunazzo and Domorenok 2008).

In summary, we can conclude that the CoR has evolved into a representation of the 'third' government level in the EU, although this was not the original intention of those who created it. The Committee has gained respectability among European institutions, primarily as a result of the political weight of its members. This, in turn, is a consequence of the increasing political influence of regional and local authorities in both national political systems and the EU. The Committee is also viewed in a favourable light, since its members have the ability to communicate directly with their home base and to inform their constituency what the Union is all about. This however does not result in its transformation into a consistent part of the institutional structure of the EU, as would be the case with a third chamber. Instead, the Committee acts as the representative of regional and local interests at the European level. In addition, it acts as a medium for transferring European ideas, discourses and policy approaches to the regional and local levels.

Overall, we can state that the inclusion of a 'third' government and administrative level in the EU's institutional structure has evolved through different channels. First, within the framework of the implementation of European policies – in particular, the EU's cohesion policy – direct relationships have evolved between the European and the regional levels. Second, through their presence in Brussels, regional and local authorities may represent their individual interests in the EU. Third, the CoR, as an advisory body to the European institutions, advocates the aggregated interests and preferences of the 'third' level in European decision-making. In all of these cases, the relationships between the EU and the regions are not codified in formal rules and rights. Rather, they are embedded in an institutional framework that allows for consultation, negotiation, and direct forms of communication and interaction. Since the inclusion of the 'third' level of government in the EU was not the preference of national governments, it has had to evolve on the basis of a partial convergence of interests – though not free from contradictions – between the European level and the regions.

## Conclusion

This chapter has highlighted the interactions between the EU and the national as well as regional government levels. Particularly, it has examined the selective inclusion of institutions and actors from the national and also, in part, from the regional government levels in European decision-making and policy implementation. This analysis has pointed out that the relationships between the EU and the member states are characterized by multiple interactions, both direct and indirect. On the one hand, delegates of national governments participate extensively in decision-making at European level. They do so partly, through the Council and its substructure and, partly, through advisory as well as supervisory committees at the service of the Commission. At the same time, European actors increasingly seek to influence policy-making at national level and, consequently, interact directly with the responsible office holders. Furthermore, the European and the national level are linked by an indirect nexus, resulting from European legislation.

Increasingly, the regional government or administrative level is also involved in European affairs. The process began when the European Commission mobilized sub-central authorities to participate in the implementation of European policies, particularly in the framework of cohesion policy. Consequently, the regions themselves aspired to get a voice in the European arena. They successively set up their own representations in Brussels, in order to lobby for the interests of their territories, but also to transfer first-hand information from the EU to their home base. With the creation of the Committee of the Regions, the 'third' level was empowered to collectively express its voice in the European concert, although only in an advisory function. The dense interactions between the three government levels – the EU, the member states and the regions – created a vertical nexus among them, which compensates for the fact that hierarchical relationships, as we know them from nation states, do not really exist in the EU. In conclusion, therefore, we may state that these intense interactions shaped the Union as a multi-level system.

Building a multi-level system was certainly not a conscious intention of European leaders, let alone of national governments. Rather, such a system emerged from piecemeal steps towards tackling intractable policy problems through expanding the realm of actors involved, decentralizing decision-making, and improving procedures of implementation. Nevertheless, a clear rationale underlies this process. Thus, the Union itself barely has the capacity to tackle the manifold policy problems it is faced with. In view of this, the Union turns to the actors and institutions most directly concerned with the problems at hand and attempts to include them into processes of decision-making and policy implementation. Thus, initially, it included the national level in European affairs and, later, the regional government and administrative levels. Furthermore, the Union is often faced with stalemates. There are stalemates in decision-making in the Council, in the implementation of European policies at the national and the regional levels, and in the acceptance of and political support for its policies. In these situations, power sharing with actors and institutions of national political systems provides opportunities to overcome these stalemates. Finally, the European level is not directly linked to the national and regional levels through a clearly defined hierarchical relationship. European decisions cannot be simply imposed upon the 'lower' government levels, since national governments continue to be formally sovereign. Thus, multiple interactions with 'lower' government levels help to persuade them voluntarily to comply with European norms and activities, and to mediate conflicts as they arise. In addition, decentralizing and delegating responsibilities as much as possible to the 'lower' levels minimizes their resistance against European endeavours or, conversely, increases their 'ownership' of the policies or activities in question.

The incorporation of the member states into European decision-making and policy implementation results in a further diversification of the EU's political system and its institutional structure. Thus, functional specializations emerge within the system, as well as cooperative arrangements between the actors and institutions involved. As a consequence, the system increasingly builds on loosely coupled policy networks and more complex institutional arrangements (Börzel and Heard-Lauréote 2009). In addition, the system relies on various actors who perform as intermediaries, to manage the interfaces between the European and the national or regional levels of governance.

On the whole, this chapter has shown that the EU does not necessarily move to further concentrate political power at the European level. It actually tends to compensate for the lack of centralization by empowering the actors and institutions of the 'lower' levels in European affairs. Accordingly, the EU has not evolved into a system that is hierarchically superimposed to the member states. Instead, it evolves to a multi-level system that incorporates, permeates, and finally transforms the 'lower' levels. It goes without saying that this indirect method of expanding and consolidating the European polity has the effect of exacerbating the system's complexity and, consequently, its opaqueness for the citizens of the EU.

# Chapter 10

# Building a Multi-Actor System

The previous chapter highlighted the role of public actors and institutions at the national and regional levels in the political system of the EU and the subsequent evolution of a multi-level system. This chapter will explore the role of non-state actors in European decision-making and policy implementation. The role of these actors and their associations ranges from 'classical' forms of interest representation and lobbying to advisory functions and direct participation in decision-making, including legislation in certain cases (Falkner *et al.* 2005; Coen and Richardson 2009; Greenwood 2011). Furthermore, non-state actors and organizations also perform various functions in the implementation of European policies at different government levels.

In general, the Commission is the most important target for the representation of specific interests and lobbying activities (Bouwen 2009). However, the growing powers of the Parliament have increasingly forced interest groups and lobbyists to address its members as well (Lehmann 2009). For its part, the Commission aims to establish closer relationships with interest groups and associations (Bouwen 2009; Greenwood 2011). It encourages these groups to organize themselves at the European level, and invites them to participate in advisory bodies. The result of this is an intense interaction between institutions of the EU and organized interests. This, in turn, has the effect of transforming interest groups into European actors and organizations.

In the area of social policy, in specific cases, non-state actors are allowed to draw up European laws (Falkner *et al.* 2005). In the area of technical standardization, private associations are granted broad competences to define detailed technical standards within a general legislative framework set by the EU and to monitor compliance with these standards (Egan 2001). The role of non-state actors in the implementation of policy is even more complex. The Commission tries to involve these actors in the implementation of projects or the administration of grants, particularly within the framework of cohesion policy (see Chapter 8). Yet, it also expects them to play a role in other policy areas; for example, in technology policy, environmental matters, and the EES. The delegation of all these functions to non-state actors implies a certain extent of self-regulation, even though these functions are performed in the shadow of hierarchy set by the EU.

Overall, non-state actors play an important role in the political system of the EU (for an opposite view, see Börzel 2010). They provide substantive input in European legislation; they improve the EU's output by their commitment to the implementation of policy and by monitoring compliance with European norms. Non-state actors and organizations therefore increasingly constitute an integral part of the expanding European polity.

## Interest representation in European decision-making

As in national political systems, interest representation plays an important role in the European polity. Interest representation was even acknowledged in the Lisbon Treaty as part of the democratic culture of the EU. Thus, the Treaty stipulates: 'The institutions shall ... give ... representative associations the opportunity to make known and publicly exchange their views in all areas of Union action' (Art. 11(1) TEU-L), and 'The institutions shall maintain an open, transparent and regular dialogue with representative associations and civil society' (Art. 11(2) TEU-L). However, in the context of the EU, interest representation assumes specific organizational forms and modes of operation. First, it is the fragmented structure of European institutions that makes interest representation a complex process with uncertain outcomes. Furthermore, the fact that, by now, the Union consists of 28 member states with highly-diverging economic structures, political cultures, and regulatory systems – and, consequently, diverging interest constellations – further exacerbates this complexity. Thus, not only the specific interests of national groups or associations, but also their aggregated European interests need to be represented in European legislation and other policy decisions. Hence, interest representation in the EU assumes, to a certain extent, a multi-level structure.

### The evolution of interest representation

Even in the early years of integration, there was already a clear presence of interest associations at the European level. As early as the 1950s, the agricultural sector in particular had succeeded in forming two European peak associations called  the Committee of Professional Agricultural Organizations, representing the farmers (COPA) and  the General Committee for Agricultural Cooperation in the European Union, representing agricultural cooperatives (COGECA). In 1962, the two organizations merged to create a joint secretariat under the name

COPA-COGECA. In fact, both are umbrella organizations that represent more than 60 (COPA) and 40 (COGECA) national organizations from the EU member states and from 36 partner organizations, including representatives of non-member countries such as Iceland, Norway, Switzerland, and Turkey. The organization has more than 50 staff members; it is one of the best resourced European associations and has a highly-differentiated internal structure (Nugent 2010: 356–7). COPA-COGECA was so successful in exercising influence over the Common Agricultural Policy (CAP) that it was regarded as the model of excessive associational power in European affairs.

However, industry and private business in general have been no less successful in using various channels to exercise influence on European decisions. They operate either as individual firms, or through their own particular branch, sector, or national representations. In addition to these efforts, they voice their interests through BUSINESSEUROPE (until 2008: UNICE, Union of Industries of the European Community), a general employers' association founded in 1958 as the representative of corresponding national organizations. BUSINESSEUROPE represents 41 business associations from 35 states. Its membership thus also covers a wider area than merely the EU. By changing its name in 2008, the association highlighted its growing independence from its member associations, as well as its aspirations to speak for the European business community as a whole. Besides BUSINESSEUROPE, there are other peak organizations that represent private business interests – including, for example, UEAMPE (European Association of Craft, Small and Medium-Sized Enterprises).

Many scholars view the domineering presence of private business at the European level as distortion of pluralist interest representation and, consequently, as a major problem for European governance (e.g. see Coen 2007 and the references there). However, we must recognize that this situation is partly a result of the asymmetry in the competences of the Union. For a long time, European legislation referred mainly to market regulation, the setting of product standards, and the liberalization of capital transfers. Accordingly, private business interests have always been most directly affected. Furthermore, within the framework of the ECSC and EURATOM, the Commission was given broad sectoral competences that fostered close cooperation with the businesses in these domains. Cooperation with the business community is important in general for the Commission, since it does not have the necessary expertise at its disposal within its own ranks (Bouwen 2009; Greenwood 2011). Hence, the Commission is often dependent on the 'advisory' role of interest associations and lobbyists. The self-perception of the Commission as a primarily 'technical' body has also contributed to closer relationships with the business community than is normally the case in national political systems.

In spite of the clear dominance of employers' associations in the EC, and later in the EU, trade unions have also been able to organize themselves at the European level (Greenwood 2011: 121–5). A peak association, the European Trade Union Confederation (ETUC), uniting a group of umbrella organizations already in existence, was formed in Brussels in 1973. ETUC encompasses 95 member organizations; 85 of these are national associations of 36 states, whereas 10 are Europe-wide sector federations. That means ETUC has a hybrid structure; furthermore, as with EUROBUSINESS and COPA-COGECA, it is not congruent with EU-Europe, but its membership covers a much larger area. In postwar Europe, ideological differences among the national trade unions hampered the creation of a Europe-wide organization. Whereas in some countries – for example, France and Italy – the unions are organized along political lines, in others (Germany, the Netherlands, the United Kingdom, and the Scandinavian countries), the unions are traditionally organized according to sectors and branches. It was only after ideological divides had lost their salience that ETUC was able to expand its membership and acquire more political influence. However, the scope for a stronger commitment of the trade unions in European decision-making has remained limited, not least because the social issues with which they concern themselves were rarely at stake in the early years of integration. When the Commission nevertheless submitted legislative proposals aimed at improving working conditions, the Council refused even to discuss them, let alone to adopt them. In those years, the national governments dealt primarily with improving labour legislation and social welfare within the member states, so that the unions focused their activities and resources on the national arena. Nevertheless, transnational associations of sector unions increasingly organized themselves at the European level in order to monitor decision-making that might affect their constituencies. Finally, even national trade unions have sought a presence in Brussels, as they are differently affected by European legislation or decisions. Thus, both labour and capital clearly represent the interests of their constituencies at the European level.

From the earliest days, employers' associations and trade unions have constituted the backbone of European interest-representation, although they have always been present to widely differing degrees. They have had access to an advisory body in the form of the European Economic and Social Committee, which gave them an official voice in European decisions (see pp. 251–2). In addition, the Commission has consulted them on a number of specific issues.

This situation changed with the launch of the single market project and the adoption of the Single European Act (1986). Due to the expansion of European competences, not only in economic affairs, but also in a broad range of other policy areas, lobbying groups and activities proliferated at the European level (Coen and Richardson 2009; Greenwood 2011). Individual enterprises as well as interest associations increased their presence in Brussels, or sought representation through professional lobbyists. Private or societal groups and even public institutions embarked on plans to improve the representation of their interests in the EC (Greenwood 2011: 184–96). Lobbying groups representing new social movements emerged for the first time as actors in the European arena (Freise 2008; Della Porta and Caiani 2009; Kohler-Koch and Quittkat 2011a; Liebert and Trenz 2011). The European Environmental Bureau (EEB) and the European Women's Lobby (EWL) are examples of this. Yet, in spite of these developments, associations representing the interests of employers remain dominant, although to a decreasing degree. According to Mazey and Richardson (1993: 7), at the beginning of the 1990s, 95 per cent of the Euro-groups represented business, whereas the trade unions, and environmental and consumer groups together constituted the remaining 5 per cent. Greenwood, by contrast, estimates that in 2011 'business interest associations constitute a little more than half of the entire constituency of EU associations, compared to two thirds in 2000' (Greenwood 2011: 13; see also Wonka *et al.* 2010).

With the founding of the first Community, interest representation was also institutionalized at European level. Thus, the 1951 ECSC-Treaty already set up the European Economic and Social Committee (EESC). The task of the EESC has always been to act as a permanent advisory board to the European institutions (Dinan 2010b: 282–5; Nugent 2010: 227–30). It is to be consulted in legislative matters and numerous other issues. Furthermore, it may issue opinions on its own initiative (Art. 300-304 TFEU). The Committee currently consists of 353 members, with the large member states holding 21 to 24 seats and the smaller states 5 to 15 seats. The members of the EESC represent three categories of social groups: the social partners – i.e. employers and employees – and other interest groups or professional associations (Eisele 2008; Westlake 2009). Hence, 'society' – or, at least, specific groupings of society – has been formally represented in European decision-making since the inception of the EC. However, the definition of who is representative of European society has significantly changed over time. Thus, the ECSC-Treaty of 1951 stipulated that the members of the Committee 'shall comprise equal numbers of producers, of workers, and of consumers or dealers' (Art. 18 TECSC). Later, the Treaty defined the members of the EESC in much broader terms as 'representatives of the various categories of economic and social activity, in particular, representatives of producers, farmers, carriers, workers, dealers, craftsmen, professional occupations and representatives of the general public' (Art. 257 TEC-A). The Lisbon Treaty finally gave civil society a prominent place by stipulating 'the Economic and Social Committee shall consist of representatives of organizations of employers, of the employed, and of other parties representative of civil society, notably in socio-economic, civic, professional and cultural areas' (Art. 300(2) TFEU).

Not only its membership, but also the position of the Committee has changed over time. Thus, in the early years, the Committee was exclusively 'attached to the High Authority' (Art. 18). From 1957 onwards, both the Commission and the Council were its addressees (Art. 262 TEC-A). At present, it serves as a consultative body to the Commission, the Council and the Parliament (Art. 300 TFEU). In spite of these changes, the basic consultative function of the Committee has remained unaltered (Eisele 2008; Westlake 2009).

### Organizational forms of interest representation

A common characteristic shared by all interest groups operating in the European context is their small-scale organizational form. Instead of relying on unwieldy bureaucratic organizations, they operate through flexible offices, often run by just one person. In a report released in 1993, the Commission counted about 3000 lobby groups with 10,000 employees (Greenwood 1997: 3). Their numbers have since increased. Wonka *et al.* (2010: 466) have counted about 3700 groups, but estimate the number to be even higher. Yet, the small-scale organizational structure has persisted. For example, national trade unions are often represented by only a few staff members. Peak associations that direct their activities towards sectoral issues usually have 5 to 10 employees, and even ETUC's personnel does not exceed 35 members. Large enterprises often have only one representative in Brussels.

At first glance, these numbers may seem extremely low in view of the multitude of tasks the associations and lobbyists have to perform. Often, however, the peak or umbrella associations located in Brussels can call upon the resources of their member associations with their expertise, and even their human resources. Thus, staff members of national organizations might also take a seat on the advisory committees of the Commission. For this reason, even the employers' associations can manage their tasks with a limited number of staff. Powerful associations such as the European Chemical Industry Council (CEFIC), take the lead with 80 employees, while BUSINESSEUROPE has 40 (Hix and Høyland 2010: 166). Many enterprises do not have a representative in Brussels at all. If salient issues emerge, they rely upon the services of professional lobbyists or law firms.

The small-scale structure of organized interests in the EU has its advantages, but there are also disadvantages. On the one hand, this structure is highly dispersed and fragmented, so that the Commission often has difficulties finding suitable partners for consultation. Furthermore, it is difficult to identify serious lobbyists, and to offer open and well-balanced access to the decision-making process for all business and societal interests. On the other hand, the small-scale structure allows for extensive specialization and flexibility in dealing with the Commission. Furthermore, this structure allows for the creation of networks of interested parties based on the issues at stake (Della Porta and Caiani 2009; Long and Lörinczi 2009). Trade unions and employers' associations, for example, can create networks within their respective areas of interest and, thus, acquire more political influence at the European level. They may also consult each other or even collaborate within the same branch, sector, or nationality, and conclude agreements before Commission decisions are taken. In some cases, they can even successfully insert themselves into the policy networks of the Commission or the Parliament. In short, the small-scale structure provides the flexibility to combine interest representation according to the issue at stake and, thus, to fine-tune reactions to proposals and projects of the Commission.

Interest associations active in Brussels are also fragmented according to nationality. In its 1993 report, the Commission indicates that 535 of the 3000 lobby groups are European umbrella organizations or associations. Since then, this number has significantly increased to 941 (Eising and Kohler-Koch 2005: 15). Wonka and his co-authors count an astonishing 1674 peak organizations at EU-level (Wonka *et al.* 2010: 469). The increase has been the result of pressure, but it also reflects the level of support offered by the Commission. Nevertheless, the majority of interest groups remain bound to their national origin, with the large and also the 'old' member states dominating the European scene (Wonka *et al.* 2010: 468–9). In one way, this situation is regrettable, since it clearly indicates that the dividing lines between the member states have not disappeared. On the other hand, it does reflect the present state of the European Union. As long as the member states constitute relatively unified regulatory systems, business as well as labour and other interest groups alike will be affected primarily by European regulations according to their national affiliation. Against this background, it appears logical that the representation of interests at the European level still follows national divides (Grossmann 2004), while transnational economic, sectoral, or societal groups and organizations will emerge only slowly (Debardeleben and Hurrelmann 2011). The fragmentation of interest groups along national lines facilitates the deliberate mediation of the divergent national interests and the creation of acceptable 'European' solutions. The fragmented 'world' of European interest groups can be regarded as an appropriate expression of the complexity of these interests. It is likely that the presence of more powerful and centralized European interest associations would neglect the many divergences that characterize the EU.

The fragmentation of interest groups in the EU results not only from the complexity of European decisions; some scholars also attribute it to the fragmented and, at the same time, open institutional structure of the Union itself (Grossmann 2004; Mazey and Richardson 2006: 251; Coen and Richardson 2009). Indeed, European institutions are often more open and accessible to external influences than national institutions (Beyers *et al.* 2008: 1114). In particular, the Commission tends to consult non-state actors widely; this, in turn, encourages their presence in Brussels (Bouwen 2009; Princen and Kerremans 2010). Furthermore, the fragmented structure of the Union offers numerous access points for organized interests. Consequently, not only the Commission but also the Parliament, with its increased powers in legislation, forms a prominent target for lobbyists (Bouwen 2009; Lehmann 2009). Even the Council or the Permanent Representations of the member states in Brussels may be addressed by lobbyists or interest associations (Hayes-Renshaw 2009). Yet, with the introduction of majority voting in the Council, single member states no longer enjoy a veto position. It follows, therefore, that lobbyists must direct their activity at a group of member states, if they wish to exercise influence on European decisions. Clearly, the complex institutional structure of the Union and the many points of access to its decisions foster both flexible and differentiated lobbying activities and corresponding organizational structures of interest representation.

### The practice of lobbying

As we examine how interest representation works in practice, we find that the lobbyists primarily seek access to the European Commission. Early on, they collect information on the Commission's proposals and the officials who are responsible for defining them. Although the Commission publishes its working programme at an early stage, it may change its priorities and, as such, the information is rarely complete. Consequently, in the early stages of drawing up a policy proposal, there could be discrepancies between the information held by well-informed lobbyists and that available to others who lack access to detailed information. But even armed with the correct information, lobbyists are not guaranteed success. The Commission clearly prefers lobbyists who are able to provide substantive input in its own work. As a result, it aims to establish closer relationships with those select individuals who are able to consider the policy problems at hand. In other words, it prefers 'technically' skilled experts over representatives who advocate narrow interests or ideologically based positions (Coen 2007). It also leans more heavily on input that represents a compromise of diverging interests. Consequently, groups that are able to perform such preparatory work are more successful in exercising influence than individual lobbyists.

In spite of its preference for 'technical' experts – mostly business representatives – the Commission also includes political or societal groups in its advisory circles (Greenwood 2007, 2011; Kohler-Koch

2007). Thus, trade unions, which demand a 'social dimension' in the EU, are particularly welcome as allies of the Commission in its dealings with the Council. The trade unions are also welcome since they represent a wide spectrum of member organizations and are, thus, in the position to convince their constituencies that certain European decisions or compromises are in their best interest. The same logic applies to the increasing inclusion of representatives of diffuse interests in consultation procedures, such as environmental or consumer groups (Greenwood 2007; Long and Lörinczi 2009; Della Porta and Caiani 2009; Kohler-Koch and Quittkat 2011a; Quittkat 2011). Such groups are also welcome because they often help to identify specific gaps in the regulatory system of the EU, or implementation deficits in the member states. Furthermore, they might also act as allies when the Commission seeks to expand European regulation. Finally, if these groups support certain legislative proposals, they lend legitimacy to the actions of the Commission (Mazey and Richardson 2006: 249; Greenwood 2011: 200–25; for a critical assessment, see Kohler-Koch 2011).

The Commission attempts to structure interest representation and, where possible, to adapt it to its own needs. An initial attempt to accomplish this dates back to the year 1993. Under strong pressure from the Parliament, the Commission issued a 'code of conduct' and established a register for lobby groups. The Commission also proposed creating a professional association of lobbyists, which could act as a self-regulating institution. These efforts, however, did not result in any major success and the Commission subsequently launched a transparency initiative in 2005. According to this initiative, lobbyists were required to register and to observe a code of conduct (Commission of the European Union 2006). A voluntary register containing information on various lobbying and interest groups, as well as their clients, was opened in 2008 (Obradovic 2009). By July 2010, 2836 organizations had registered. The register serves as a guide to European institutions interested in consulting lobbying groups, but it also focuses on increasing the transparency of the European lobbying community.

The Commission also attempts to structure the lobby scene by encouraging the formation of Europe-wide umbrella groups. Such groups are offered preferential access to advisory bodies. In certain cases, the Commission even finances European groups, particularly those representing diffuse interests and social movements (Bouwen 2009; Della Porta and Caiani 2009). Usually, the financial incentives provided to these groups take the form of grants for research projects or studies.

Over time, and through the interplay between the two sides, lobby groups may adapt to the needs and requirements of the Commission (Kohler-Koch 2007 Bouwen 2009). The invitation to participate in advisory bodies is, in itself, a strong incentive for interest groups to adapt to the expectations of the Commission. As indicated above, such expectations refer primarily to technical proposals and less to general political statements. In exchange for their cooperation, the Commission offers the groups an opportunity to participate in the formulation of legislative proposals. Obviously, it is primarily the representatives of the business community who are directly affected by European legislation and who are able to deliver well-defined legislative proposals. Groups that are indirectly affected, such as those who represent new social movements or diffuse interests, may tend to bring in more general political arguments, which is less of interest to the Commission. Nevertheless, even these groups have slowly adapted to the expectations of the Commission as they increasingly try to act as technical experts in European affairs (Ruzza 2004; Kohler-Koch 2011).

Whenever the Commission invites interest groups to participate in its advisory committees, it must carefully consider the diverse viewpoints of the potential candidates. Of course, the Commission might prefer to invite only those groups that tend to support its own proposals, but it must also try to maintain a pluralist equilibrium by inviting those who hold opposing political views, too. In this way, the Commission may be better prepared to face the conflicts that might later arise in the Council. Obviously, it is to the Commission's advantage to invite associations that might be able to mobilize support for European decisions, and to convince their constituencies that the final compromise is in their best interest. Thus, it is evident that the selection of participants for the advisory committees involves a difficult balancing act that takes into account the provision of both technical expertise and political support. In addition, for reasons of democratic legitimacy, it must ensure that all stakeholders have balanced and democratic access to European decision-making (Obradovic 2009).

Whereas the Commission attracts and often rewards technically-skilled lobbyists and specific interest groups, the Parliament also provides a forum for civil society groups and social movements (Beyers 2004; Lehmann 2009). This is not surprising, since it is the Parliament that deals with political choices, rather than with technical details. Accordingly, trade unions, environmental groups, consumer advocacies, and women's lobbies often find support for their demands in this arena. Yet, MEPs are also frequently faced with vigorous lobbying activities from business groups. Business lobbyists in particular target MEPs of their own nationality in order to access the decision-making process. *Vice versa*, MEPs also welcome representatives of interest groups to expand their expertise in certain areas. In particular, the *rapporteurs* responsible for assessing legislative proposals make extensive use of these groups. However, since lobbyists often do not play a fair and transparent game, the Parliament has repeatedly pleaded for defined limits and tighter control on their activities, and asked the Commission to take action in this regard.

Organized interests may also attempt to exert influence on Council decisions. Such endeavours, however, are directed either to individual national governments or to the Permanent Representations of the member states, as well as the working groups who act as the Council's substructure in Brussels (Hayes-Renshaw 2009). Lobbyists choosing this venue generally tend to pursue narrow national interests, and are less concerned with broader strategies that would foster Europe-wide solutions.

In summary, we can conclude that interest representation at the European level has become an extremely complex process. A wide variety of interest groups, together with individual lobbyists, continuously attempt to augment their influence on the decision-making process by gaining access to EU institutions through various channels. Although the departments of the Commission – including the Commissioners, cabinets, and civil services – are the primary targets of lobbyists, the Parliament and even the Councils come under attack, too. As far as the Commission and, to some extent, the Parliament are concerned, interest groups and lobbyists are welcomed as a source of information, expertise, political support, and, at times, legitimacy. Thus, an almost symbiotic relationship has evolved between the institutions of the EU and the representatives of interest groups. The patterns and structures of interest representation, however, remain fluid, in accordance with the 'open' and fragmented structure of the European polity. Consequently, concepts such as pluralism or neo-corporatism, which have come down from the national political arena, are hardly applicable to the European situation. Rather than the systematic and politically-motivated processes of interest mediation under the auspices of an arbiter (the state), found nationally in both pluralist and corporatist political arenas, interest representation at the European level tends to create loosely-knitted network relations between public and private as well as societal actors (Mazey and Richardson 2006; Greenwood 2011). We therefore can conclude that, in the political system of the EU, new forms of interest representation evolve together with new ways of accommodating non-state actors in the decision-making process.

## Delegating responsibility to non-state actors

In the preceding section, we saw how private and societal actors, interest associations, and social movements all play a role in influencing European decision-making. These actors, however, also perform a broad range of functions in policy-making. For example, the social dialogue between employers' associations and trade unions can result in agreements on legislative acts of the EU. Furthermore, important regulatory functions may be delegated to private associations, and non-state actors can also perform various tasks in implementing policy. In such instances, private or societal actors assume functions that normally are incumbent on the state or the public domain. Thus, the European Union, by increasingly incorporating non-state actors into its legislative and executive functions, expands the reach and effect of its policies, and builds a multi-actor system. By presenting a few specific examples, I will highlight these trends in the following sections.

### The role of social partners in legislation

The social dialogue between employers' associations and the trade unions was first formalized in the Treaty of Maastricht. Previous attempts to establish such a dialogue on a voluntary basis – and, specifically, the efforts to this end made by the Delors Commission – failed because of obstruction on the employers' part (Streeck and Schmitter 1991; Falkner *et al.* 2005). During the negotiations on the Maastricht Treaty, a British veto prevented the inclusion of a social chapter in the Treaty. However, 11 of the then 12 member states wanted progress in this area. Consequently, they signed a 'social protocol', appended to the Treaty of Maastricht that enacted a specific procedure for European legislation in social affairs. According to the protocol, the new procedure would be that the Commission first informs the social partners that it intends to initiate legislation in a certain issue area. If the social partners agree, they are mandated to negotiate an appropriate legislative proposal by themselves. If the partners are able to reach a consensus on a legislative proposal, that proposal may be transposed directly into European legislation. The Council still has to take a decision on the proposal, but it may not amend its substance (Protocol on social policy, TEC-M).

Commission President Delors pushed this procedure through the Maastricht Summit after Britain's veto against any European commitment in social affairs (Ross 1995: 151–6). Since the procedure was only defined in a protocol and signed by only 11 of the 12 member states, its expansive implications were not really recognized at the time. However, the situation changed when the Labour Party in the UK came into power in 1997. The newly-elected government under Tony Blair gave its consent to the social protocol so that it could be included in the Treaty of Amsterdam. This Treaty provided for two modes of implementation for agreements concluded by the social partners at the European level (Art. 139(2) TEC-A, now Art. 155(2) TFEU). First, agreements could be implemented 'in accordance with the procedures and practices specific to management and labour and the Member States', or, second, they could be implemented 'at the joint request of the signatory parties, by a Council decision on a proposal from the Commission'.

Independent of these Treaty regulations, the social partners were first mandated to negotiate a legislative proposal in 1995 on European works councils, some four years before the Amsterdam Treaty came into force

(1999). However, the negotiating parties did not reach an agreement. There were several reasons for this failure. First, the positions of the social partners on the matter were so widely divergent that it was almost impossible to find common ground among them. Furthermore, the negotiating parties were severely constrained as a result of dissent in their own ranks. For the employers, two peak associations took part in the negotiations, UNICE and the European Centre of Employers and Enterprises providing Public Services (CEEP), respectively representing private and public enterprises. In particular, UNICE experienced strong resistance from its member associations. It comes as no surprise that the British industrialists acted as the most outspoken opponents against any social regulation at the European level. The trade unions, represented by ETUC, were also internally divided. Finally, both sides had to learn their new roles in drawing up legislative proposals. In the end, the negotiating parties had to inform the Commission that they had failed to reach an agreement, so that the latter could pave the way for a regular legislative procedure. The European institutions then promptly adopted a corresponding directive.

Not long thereafter, the first successes were achieved with a directive on parental leave and another to address the problem of atypical work (Falkner *et al.* 2005: 140–58). These issues were handled more easily. Parental leave in itself is a clearly contained issue; the atypical work issue was given a more narrow focus by limiting the discussion exclusively to part-time work. Even so, negotiations in these two areas still evoked strong adversarial positions among the social partners. Again, these controversies were fuelled by deep dissent within their constituencies. At the time, the parental leave issue was regulated at the national level in a somewhat haphazard fashion, if at all. To complicate matters even further, this issue involved social and cultural norms, such as the perception of the roles of men and women in society. For UNICE, it was particularly difficult to determine the most acceptable compromise between a European regulation preventing unfair competition and the right of the member states to act according to their own discretion. The final agreement envisaged flexible regulations at the European level which left broad leeway for national regulators to set their own rules. After lengthy negotiations, a similar solution was found for the part-time work directive, which was adopted in 1997 (Falkner *et al.* 2005: 159–77). In 1998/99, the social partners concluded a third agreement concerning fixed-time work. In this case, too, the resulting framework directive defines only a few basic principles and employs a language filled with a number of open or 'should' formulations. The adoption of more detailed and precise regulations was left to the legislators at the national level. It is evident, therefore, that when the social partners draw up legislative acts, they tend to exacerbate a problem that already exists with regular legislation in the EU; that is, the vagueness and ambiguity of European legislation. Thus, there is often little more than a flexible regulatory framework defined at the European level. This loose framework may then be interpreted and implemented in a variety of ways at the national level. In the subsequent years, three further directives have been defined by the social partners, but they all refer to narrow, sector-specific issues. These directives include an agreement on the organization of working time of seafarers (1998), on the organization of working time of mobile workers in civil aviation (2000), as well as on certain aspects of the working conditions of mobile workers engaged in interoperable cross-border services in the railway sector (2004). Since 2004, the procedure has not been used. Between 2002 and 2004, the social partners concluded only a few agreements at the European level in accordance with the procedure of Art. 139(2) TEC-A (now Art. 155(2) TFEU) that assigns all legislative powers to the national level.

The adoption of somewhat open and flexible directives by the social partners seems to have suited all parties. UNICE, in particular, has pursued an explicit strategy to prevent stricter regulation at the European level, while ETUC accepted weak compromises that gave a great deal of discretion to the member states, in view of the many and divergent positions of its member associations. Even the Commission appears to have anticipated this outcome, since it has designed the second procedure (Art. 139(2) TEC-A, now Art. 155(2) TFEU) that decentralizes regulation to the member states, once the social partners have reached a framework agreement at the European level. This procedure has the additional advantage of fostering closer cooperation at all levels of social dialogue.

The procedure of defining European legislation by the social partners, although practised rarely and only for a limited period of time, had a number of repercussions on the European polity. It enhanced the position of UNICE and ETUC in relation to their member organizations. Moreover, it put severe constraints on the legislative powers of the European institutions in social policy. In those cases where the social partners could reach an agreement on legislation, the Commission's exclusive right to design legislative proposals was clearly undermined; only by defining the mandate of the social partners and by managing the procedure could it exercise some degree of influence. The Parliament was excluded from any role as co-legislator, a role that it had only recently acquired. Above all, the Council was deprived of its powers to amend legislative proposals and, thus, of its right to have the final say. Since it could only adopt or reject a proposal, it was also deprived of its strategy to achieve consensus by offering minor concessions to reluctant member states.

The constraints imposed by the procedure on the European legislative institutions were certainly a major reason for silently abolishing it; but the difficulties of the social partners to reach agreement may have contributed to the ultimate demise of the procedure as well. These diffi-

culties were, above all, the result of the diverging positions of the negotiating parties. Nonetheless, they were exacerbated, as one member of
UNICE put it to the author in interview, by the lack of external pressure.
Such pressure to reach an agreement in pluralist or corporatist systems
is usually exercised by the state. Since an institution commanding
authority in a similar way is lacking at the European level, social
dialogue – a concept derived from national political systems – was
doomed to fail. And yet, in spite of this failure, the procedure had significant long-term impacts on the EU, including a major increase in 'regular'
legislation in the area of social policy, as well as a consolidation of the
position of the peak associations representing the social partners in
European decision-making.

### Self-regulation by non-state actors

Another practice of delegating public responsibilities to non-state actors
consists in the adoption of framework directives at the European level,
while transferring the right to define more detailed standards and to
supervise compliance to professional associations of the corresponding
sectors or branches. This is readily shown in the area of technical standardization of working conditions (Egan 2001). As was the case with
social policy, attempts to create a Europe-wide system of harmonized
standards were long doomed to fail because of the complexity of the
issues and the regulatory divergences among the member states. These
divergences refer to the substance of regulation and the procedures for
implementation, as well as the basic 'philosophy' underlying the various
regulatory systems. The complexity of the issue is primarily the result of
the enormous proliferation of new technologies. Unsurprisingly, public
regulation lags far behind this development. The problem is exacerbated
in the EU with its unwieldy procedures for decision-making and
consensus-building. In some cases, the adoption of European directives
that set technical standards has taken up to 10 years. In view of these
time frames, it seemed unlikely that regulation could ever catch up to
technological innovations.

With the launch of the single market project, the issue of technical
standards became extremely important. Persisting regulatory divergences
among the member states in the area of technical standards posed major
non-tariff barriers to free trade. Consequently, a completely new approach
for tackling the problem was introduced (Egan 2001). Analogous to the
German model, the European level adopts only a set of framework directives to define certain basic principles. The definition of standards is then
delegated to specialized bodies such as the Comité Européen de Normalisation [European Committee for Standardization] (CEN) and the Comité
Européen de Normalisation Electrotechnique [European Committee for
Electrotechnical Standardization] (CENELEC). These organizations

comprise European industrial associations, as well as the bodies responsible for standardization within the member states. Their mandate to define standards within the framework of the European directives is then assigned to special committees.

Although these standards are not legally binding, products and production processes conforming to them have unrestricted access to the single market. Otherwise, the enterprises themselves have to prove the conformity of their products and production processes with European standards. This could be costly and imply major risks to market access.

This new approach has been effective, as it does not require the complex procedures of consensus-building in the Council, where each member state strives to transfer as much of its own regulatory approach as possible to the European level. Since the decision-making process in the Council deals only with basic principles, it can be significantly accelerated, while the process of setting standards is enhanced and the density of regulation is increased. Ultimately, although technical standards are now defined in more open and flexible ways, their effectiveness has in no way been diminished. Furthermore, the new approach to standardization has led to a number of more comprehensive objectives, including, for example, major innovations concerning working conditions. The new European standards take into account both the human and the technical aspect of working conditions. Included here are physical and mental health issues, a dynamic assessment of risks, and the participation of those concerned in shaping their own working environment. Surprisingly, European standards are not defined at the level of the lowest common denominator. In fact, they often rise above the level of even the most advanced member states. Nevertheless, this approach does not negatively impinge on national standard-setting. On the contrary, it provides an impetus for innovative action of both public authorities and private associations within the member states. They increasingly proceed according to the European model, that is, by separating the definition of basic rules from the specification of detailed standards.

In summary, including non-state actors in the domain of technical standardization has, for the first time, made it possible to regulate this sector at the European level. Limiting the scope of European regulations to the act of defining only the basic principles, and leaving the details to specialists, has helped the EU to succeed in raising the level of workers' protection. The delegation of regulatory functions in this area to non-state actors has enabled the EU to accelerate regulation and, thus, to improve its efforts to keep pace with technological innovation. However, implementation is left to the actors concerned and compliance is only achieved by 'soft' or indirect means (i.e., by voluntary acceptance, or an appeal to competitive advantage). This approach could lead to divergences among the member states in their compliance with technical standards and, thus, undermine European-wide harmonization.

At this point, one might argue that the development described above refers to a very limited area. While this is the case, the approach, once 'invented', has spread to other policies, too. Thus, at present, it is widely applied over a broad range of policies, with non-state actors involved to differing degrees (see the case studies in Tömmel and Verdun 2009; Sabel and Zeitlin 2010). From these examples, it is clear that a new mix of public regulation and private self-regulation is evolving in the European Union. In view of the widespread failure of traditional intervention, the new approach is proving to be very effective.

## Non-state actors in policy implementation

Non-state actors are also active in the implementation of European policies. An example of this is European cohesion policy, where non-state actors are involved in decision-making, mostly at the regional and the local levels. Furthermore, they may assume specific responsibilities in policy implementation, by administering and distributing European subsidies. Both these roles were formally introduced with the 'grand' reform of the Structural Funds in 1989; since then, they have been further expanded. Non-state actors, and particularly the social partners, are involved in cohesion policy through the system of partnership (see Chapter 8). This system, introduced in 1989, initially included only the regional government levels in European decision-making and policy implementation in formal terms, while the social partners were included informally. The reform of 1994 formalized the inclusion of the social partners in the system. Thus, employers' associations and trade unions were expected to participate in all decisions concerning the implementation of cohesion policy. Their participation could range from the elaboration of programmes and the implementation of projects to the final evaluation of the whole policy cycle. The next reform of the Structural Funds in 2000 also included representatives of organized civil society in all phases of policy implementation. The corresponding regulations explicitly mention environmental and women's groups. Finally, the reform enacted in 2007 states that, besides the economic and social partners, 'any other body representing civil society' may be included in the system of partnership (Council Regulation (EC) No 1083/2006, Art. 11; see also Quittkat and Kohler-Koch 2011: 76–7). Non-state actors have also been given seats on the monitoring committees established for each programme within cohesion policy. The committees take decisions relevant to the implementation of projects and programmes. They may assign subsidies to single projects or, if necessary, adapt the programmes in response to changing needs and circumstances. They may also evaluate the implementation process (Council Regulation (EC) No 1083/2006, Art. 65).

The introduction of these procedures has met with strong resistance from member states. Public actors were concerned that they would have to share their responsibilities in cohesion policy with others who are not subject to administrative rules. In addition, they feared that their short-comings in the implementation of this policy would become obvious. However, the social partners were also reluctant to assume these new responsibilities. The trade unions were often not organized at the regional level, particularly not in the less-developed regions and states, which benefit most from the Structural Funds. Neither were employers' associations particularly enthusiastic, even though their participation on monitoring committees could translate directly into economic benefits. The inclusion of participants from civil society in the implementation of the cohesion policy faced even greater obstacles. The actors involved are often even less well-organized to carry out policy functions, and public institutions at both the regional and the local levels are often very reluc-tant to include such actors into their work (Reiter 2010).

The obstacles described continue hamper the participation of non-state actors in the implementation of cohesion policy. The reform of cohesion policy for the period 2014–2020, therefore, has further speci-fied their role in the system of partnership and tightened the rules for their participation. Thus, member states have to conclude a Partnership Agreement with the Commission, and 'each Member State ... shall organize a partnership with the competent regional and local authorities. The partnership shall also include the following partners: ... (b) economic and social partners; and (c) relevant bodies representing civil society, including environmental partners, non-governmental organizations, and bodies responsible for promoting social inclusion, gender equality and non-discrimination' (Regulation (EU) No. 1303/2013, Art. 5(1)). Furthermore, Art. 5(2) of the same regulation stipulates: 'In accordance with the multi-level governance approach, the partners referred to in paragraph 1 shall be involved by Member States in the preparation of Partnership Agreements and progress reports and throughout the prepa-ration and implementation of programmes, including through participa-tion in the monitoring committees for programmes'.

In addition to their participatory role in decisions around the imple-mentation of the cohesion policy, private actors may also take on the responsibility of allocating and managing public funds. Such funds, available under the label 'Global Grant', can be assigned to 'interme-diary bodies'; these, in turn, are entitled to allocate subsidies to the recipients (Regulation (EU) No. 1302/2013, Art. 123). Local business associations, chambers of industry and commerce, innovation centres, development agencies, or consortia of these institutions may act as 'intermediary bodies'. Such institutions, therefore, often comprise a mixture of public and private actors. The beneficiaries of the subsidies may be small and medium-sized enterprises (SMEs), or particularly innovative firms. Any institution wishing to administer a Global Grant must draw up a programme that defines the objectives, scope, criteria, and procedures for allocating subsidies to beneficiaries, and also defines its procedures for evaluation and control. On the basis of this document, the responsible authorities of the member states conclude an agreement with the relevant institution. National and regional public institutions in this context also take on a supervisory function in regard to the management of the Global Grant and due implementation of the envisaged programme. For this purpose, they must submit a report to the Commission and provide all relevant information. Public actors must also perform coordinative tasks and take important basic decisions with regard to the size of the grant and the selection of programmes.

These two cases of including non-state actors in policy implementation illustrate the tendency to redistribute public and private tasks within the European polity. Public institutions, from the European down to the regional levels, are prompted to shift their attention and focus to coordinative, management, and supervisory functions. They are to establish the institutional and procedural framework for the delegation of certain tasks to non-state actors. Within this framework, private and other non-state actors then decide on the elaboration, implementation, and evaluation of programmes, or the allocation of subsidies, according to the defined objectives and the principles of efficiency and effectiveness.

In summary, we can conclude that the inclusion of non-state actors in all stages of policy-making has significantly expanded the capacity of the Union to act effectively. The positive results of this approach have been an expanded scope of action, enhanced efficiency, and a reduction of shortcomings in policy implementation. These changes have further implications for the evolution of the European polity. The transfer of certain legislative and executive tasks to non-state actors has meant that public functions have been redefined or reorganized. Organizational, management, coordinative, and supervisory functions gain in importance. These developments initially affect the European level but, in the course of events, they permeate and, finally, also transform the political systems of the member states, too. Taken as a whole, these developments result in the creation of a systemic nexus between the EU and non-state actors, although this nexus is not as firmly institutionalized as that linking the government levels.

## Conclusion

This chapter has highlighted the various roles that non-state actors play within the political system of the EU. It first explored interest representation and lobbying at European level in its multiple forms. It highlighted the small-scale structure and organizational fragmentation of the corresponding groups and associations, as well as their difficulties in organizing themselves at the European level. Furthermore, it analyzed their intense activities at this level, and the diverse access points they use. Remarkably, the European institutions themselves – in particular, the Commission – deploy a host of activities in order to frame and shape the conduct of lobbyists, and to improve the organizational structure of interest representation.

The chapter then analyzed the role of interest groups in European legislation and rule-making, as well as policy implementation. We saw that interest associations and representatives of civil society play a major role in all these dimensions – even though with diverging success, and sometimes against their preferences. In these cases, too, the Commission turned out to be the actor that most vigorously pushed forward these developments and, thus, tended to innovate not only European decision-making and policy implementation, but also that of the member states. Taken together, these processes tend to blur the distinction between the public and the private or societal sphere, and to reorganize the distribution of tasks between these spheres.

As with the incorporation of the member states into the European polity, the inclusion of non-state actors in European policy-making was not induced by a defined schedule to implement such steps. Rather, the rationale presented in the conclusions of Chapter 9 played a role in this case, too. Thus, the Union's limited resources and capacities to act, the reluctance of the member states to accept European interference in their affairs, and the ever-present challenge to tackle complex and highly-diversified policy problems prompted the Commission to rely on non-state actors in decision-making and policy formulation – and, in the long run, even in some aspects of policy implementation. Using the commitment, expertise, and cooperation of these actors enabled the Commission to put pressure on European and member states' institutions alike to perform more effectively. It pressures the Council to adopt directives in matters of social regulation, and national governments to perform as policy supervisors. Regional authorities are pressurized to better implement European policies.

Taken together, the strategy of delegating certain public responsibilities to non-state actors has resulted in a significant expansion of the reach of European policy-making; a substantial improvement of its market-orientation; and its closer adaptation to private, but also to diffuse, societal interests. It has also contributed to a significant expansion of the implementation activities in the member states. As noted, it tends to create alternative forms of public–private or state–society cooperation, involving not only the European, but also 'lower' levels of government. In summary, it transforms the EU into a multi-actor system. Needless to say, these changes further obfuscate where responsibilities for European decision-making and policy implementation are located and, consequently, which actors and institutions can be held accountable for undesired outcomes.

# Chapter 11

# Assessing the European Union: Efficiency and Effectiveness

The preceding chapters have analyzed various dimensions of the EU including its evolution, its institutional structure, its procedures and processes of decision- and policy-making, and its processes of system-building. However, we did not assess the EU's institutional structure or its performance. This chapter now focuses on an assessment of the emerging European polity, and particularly on two highly-contested aspects of the EU's performance: its efficiency and its effectiveness. Efficiency is generally defined as the relationship between resources and outcomes. Thus, a high degree of efficiency is reached when significant outcomes are achieved with a comparatively low input in resources. Effectiveness refers to the successful achievement of desired results in relation to defined objectives, while the input in resources is not specifically taken into account. Assessing the efficiency and effectiveness of the EU implies assessing its institutional structure, the performance of its institutions in decision- and policy-making, as well as the procedures that shape this performance, and the costs and benefits associated with them. These are very broad themes that could be approached in a number of different ways. For the purposes of the present analysis, they will therefore need to be defined more narrowly.

Under the rubric *efficiency*, I intend to examine the institutional configuration of the Union as well as the organization of its decision-making processes. In this context, a number of questions must be considered. Does the institutional structure of the EU allow it to respond to the manifold challenges facing it, and let it perform its duties within adequate time frames and with appropriate human resources? Or is the Union a gigantic, yet enormously fragmented bureaucratic machine that duplicates the work of national bureaucracies? Are European decisions taken quickly and smoothly, or are they processed through unwieldy negotiations that ultimately result in non-decision, stalemate, and even deeper dissent among the member states?

An assessment of the *effectiveness* of the EU necessarily leads us to question whether European governance allows the Union to achieve its declared objectives and to bring about effective solutions to the political problems at hand. More precisely, one might ask to what extent European decisions and the respective policies match their objectives, or whether they completely fail to do so. European governance is usually brought about as a result of intricate political steering, involving a multitude of actors and institutions (see Chapter 8). Since the Union constitutes an additional political and administrative layer superimposed on the member states, its governance rarely results in direct impacts. Therefore, as we assess the effectiveness of the EU, we must ask more specific questions – such as whether the EU succeeds in motivating institutions and actors from both the public and the private spheres to pursue objectives defined at the European level, so that they finally can be achieved. Or do these actors pursue their own specific interests, which are not in accordance with European objectives, with the result that the effectiveness of European decisions and policies is undermined or even thwarted?

Overall, in this chapter I consider the mechanisms and problems that characterize the operation of the EU and I offer a critical assessment of them. Such an assessment, however, has its limits. First, there is a lack of precise and neutral empirical evidence concerning the efficiency and effectiveness of the EU's modes of operation. Second, the European polity is still evolving and assessments of its functionality are quite preliminary in nature. Third, and most important, the Union is a political system that does not stand by itself but, in achieving its defined objectives, is largely dependent on the cooperation of the member states and non-state actors. It is consequently difficult to determine whether deficits and merits are specific to the European polity, or to the member states and other actors.

## Efficiency: institutional configuration and decision-making

### Institutional configuration

In order to assess the efficiency of the Union, this section focuses on the structural setting of the European institutions, their resources, and their tasks and performance. One might well criticize the dualistic or bicephalous structure of the basic institutional configuration of the EU. The Commission on the one hand, and the Council and the European Council on the other represent two centres of power, without a clear division of competences between them. Both sides exercise executive as well as legislative functions. This gives the impression that each is duplicating the work of the other, and that both are wrapped up in lengthy and complex procedures of decision-making. In fact, however, this dualistic or bicephalous structure is functional, as long as the Union is not transformed into a supranational state. It allows both wider European interests and more narrow national concerns to be represented and articulated, and may encourage mediation between them. By definition, this entails complex negotiations and bargains, and lengthy processes of consensus-building.

The other core institutions of the EU – the Parliament and the Court of Justice – also hold vital roles in the overall system. It is true that the Parliament, as the representative of the citizens of Europe, further complicates decision-making. While having no Parliament might perhaps bring about gains in efficiency, its absence would raise serious problems of legitimacy (see Chapter 12). Without a Court of Justice, the Union would suffer from enormous losses in both efficiency and effectiveness. European decisions – in particular, those resulting in legislative acts – could be ignored or circumvented and, thus, made obsolete.

The function of the two major advisory bodies of the EU – the EESC and the CoR – appears to be less obvious. They are often regarded as insignificant, inefficient, and too unwieldy to have a positive effect on the final decisions. The fact that their role is merely advisory lends weight to this criticism. However, such criticism fails to recognize the complex functions of these bodies. They may suggest recommendations to proposals by the Commission that reflect some of the more specific interests of their constituencies. Since this presupposes an internal process of mediation and consensus-building, they also perform an important function in bringing together and consolidating the voice of both functional or sectoral groups and the 'third' level of government in European politics (see Chapters 9 and 10). Finally, the EESC and the CoR, by providing information on European affairs to their constituencies, create a liaison between the Union and the 'society' or the regions they represent. In summary, these advisory bodies fulfil an important function as the voice of, the arbiter among, and the interlocutor on behalf of the respective societal and territorial groups in the EU. This role cannot be adequately captured by considering only their output in the form of recommendations.

While the EU is often criticized for the configuration of its core institutions, the enormous proliferation of supplementary institutions and substructures may also come under intense scrutiny (see Chapter 7). The ensuing emergence of an institutional jungle – encompassing specific Councils, secretariats, task forces, new or reorganized Directorates-General of the Commission, as well as independent agencies (e.g. the ECB) and transnational bodies (e.g. the ECBS) – has clearly resulted in overlapping functions. Consequently, inter-institutional rivalries and conflicts are frequent. These developments have clouded the transparency of decision-making and led to the accusation of dysfunctional procedures. The far-reaching institutional diversification of the Union can only be explained by considering the specific model of European integration. Since the member states wish to coordinate or harmonize certain policies without transferring major powers to the Commission, this inevitably results in additional arenas of interest mediation and consensus-building and, consequently, in the creation of a specific, highly-differentiated set of institutions. Inefficiencies that arise out of this institutional structure may only be mitigated if the member states can achieve a persistent consensus on specific integration steps and the transfer of corresponding powers to the European level.

An examination of individual institutions of the EU reveals further inefficiencies. The European Commission is often criticized as having an enormously oversized bureaucracy, an unwieldy and sometimes even corrupt machine, as well as outdated administrative practices (Schön-Quinlivan 2011). In terms of personnel, the Commission is the largest institution at the European level with 24,944 civil servants (permanent and temporary posts, specific offices included; *Official Journal of the European Union* 2013). This may seem to be a huge bureaucracy, but we have to bear in mind that one third of the Commission staff is engaged in translation services, a necessary burden for all European institutions. The size of the Commission's administrative service does not exceed that of a larger ministry at the national level, or the administration of a large city. Therefore, some of the criticism on the huge Brussels bureaucracy misses the point. The Commission is severely understaffed to face the complex tasks before it (Dinan 2012: 38). Moreover, the comparatively small civil service of the Commission – and other European institutions – corresponds to the decentralized structure of the EU. Most European decisions are taken by institutions and bodies consisting of national delegates, who come together in a variety of combinations in different places. The implementation of European decisions is even more decentralized. Against this background, the lean administrative machinery at the European level might seem most effective. However, the reverse might also be true. It is precisely *because* European institutions are so severely understaffed, that they are forced to delegate parts of their responsibilities to other bodies, mostly in the member states. Although such a situation is clearly welcomed by the member states, it leads to inefficiencies; for example, more coordination and control of decentralized agents, and the risk of ineffectiveness, or at least delays in policy implementation.

Most of the other European institutions, the Council and the European Council and their extensive substructure are staffed with delegates of national governments, or administrative services. With the exception of the Permanent Representatives and their staff in Brussels, they all primarily perform functions in their national political systems. Their European role is an additional task. However, they are supported in these functions by a permanent administration located in Brussels. Thus, the Council has a Secretariat General with 3153 civil servants (*Official*

*Journal of the European Union* 2013: 121). This still seems a large number. However, only about 400 of them perform policy functions, such as preparing and attending meetings. The others work in the translation service, which is much more extensive here since legislative acts have to be translated into all languages of the EU.

Although their staffing has significantly increased in recent years, the Permanent Representations in Brussels are not large 'embassies'. This increase has accompanied the continuous expansion of policy-making at the European level and a corresponding increase in the number of meetings. The permanent advisory bodies, EESC and CoR, have secretariats with 727 and 537 employees, respectively (*Official Journal of the European Union* 2013: 121).

The European Parliament, with currently 766 deputies, clearly exceeds the size of the legislative chambers of even the large member states. After the election of 2014, the number will be reduced to 751, as stipulated in the Lisbon Treaty, but this number is still high. The enormous expansion of the Parliament's size, however, has come about only since Eastern enlargement. Before this enlargement, the size of the EP roughly corresponded to that of the large member states. In the face of the need to represent all nations and their political parties adequately, the EP does not appear to be oversized. Its permanent staffing of 6713 members (*Official Journal of the European Union* 2013: 121) is not excessive, if we take into account the complex issues and legal acts with which the EP must concern itself, particularly, since it is a co-legislator in conjunction with the Council.

The European Court of Justice, with currently 28 judges and 1995 staff members (*Official Journal of the European Union* 2013: 121), is also not an oversized institution. On the contrary, its capacities repeatedly proved to be insufficient, so that the General Court was established to cope with the increasing workload. Furthermore, parts of the tasks of the European Court are decentralized to the courts of the member states (see Chapter 4).

Does the fact that the EU is able to manage a huge number of complex tasks with a limited number of personnel mean that it is an efficiently organized political system? Such a statement would be misplaced. European institutions are overloaded with work and severely understaffed. This situation is not so much a test of the efficiency of the system but, rather, the cause of manifold problems. Since adequately staffing EU institutions would imply a power shift to the European level, a change in this situation is not very probable. Member states would hardly welcome such a development.

The limited number of personnel assigned to the European institutions implies that a large part of their work has to be performed by others. First, the burden of decision-making and the implementation of European policies are largely borne by the member states. Although this division of labour was already evident, even in the early years of integration, the enormous expansion in European policy-making has exacerbated the problem. Yet, the member states have been unwilling to transfer adequate powers to the EU. The increase in policy functions at the European level therefore goes hand-in-hand with an even more extensive increase in political responsibilities of the member states (see Chapters 8 and 9). Second, part of the workload of European institutions is delegated to independent agencies that perform specific executive tasks, but they also assume a role in generating policies (see Chapter 7). Yet, most of these agencies operate on a small scale and are normally obliged to cooperate closely with corresponding institutions in the member states (Tömmel 2011b). Third, included in policy-making are several non-state actors and organizations that also perform legislative and executive tasks (see Chapter 10). Finally, a substantial amount of the Commission's work is outsourced to private firms. The nature of this work can range from editing European documents and reports, through to the elaboration of draft policy proposals, or the implementation and evaluation of programmes. However, this method of reducing the Commission's workload often comes up against a fair amount of criticism. Most recently, there were allegations of mismanagement and fraud. The Commission was alleged to have been unable to exercise adequate control over sub-contractors and private firms. Therefore, with the most recent reform of the Commission service, non-core tasks are to be delegated to independent agencies that are supposed to act under the tight control of the responsible DG (Schön-Quinlivan 2011: 117).

From the arguments outlined, it is clear that the institutional structure of the European level appears, on the surface, to be efficient; however, it raises a multitude of related issues that are downloaded to the member states and other actors and organizations. Any assessment of the efficiency of the Union should, therefore, take into account this multi-layered and multi-faceted institutional architecture and its associated costs. However, the complexity of the European polity and the intertwining of the government levels make it hard to make an accurate determination of the costs of its operation and its overall efficiency.

## Decision-making

Decision-making is the main activity of the European Union. This is not to say that the processes of decision-making are organized in a particularly efficient manner. On the contrary, we can observe many cases of preliminary decisions, non-decision, deadlocked negotiations, repeated negotiations on one and the same issue, and even the revision of decisions already taken. When a decision is reached, it often remains unclear whether that decision will lead to an effective solution to a pressing political problem, or will only serve to remove the issue from the table.

Either way, agreements are reached only after an enormous investment of time and effort, not to mention related financial costs for a multitude of actors. In addition, we must also consider the added expenses for meetings at alternating places, translation services, and other logistic inputs. The whole process produces a high amount of externalities, which fall to the public institutions of the member states, and also non-state actors and organizations (Majone 2005).

We might also question the efficiency of European decision-making on a more qualitative basis. Except for detailed market regulations, which are directly binding, most European laws are adopted in the form of directives. Such directives only define the objectives to be achieved and some very basic parameters, minimum standards or 'corridors', and procedural norms (see Chapter 5). Directives are, in some ways, only the bare bones of the legislation. It is left to national governments and their interpretation of the legal framework set at the European level to add flesh to the bones. In practice, member states often fail to transpose European directives into national legislation expeditiously and in accordance with the spirit of the legal frame (Falkner *et al.* 2005; Falkner and Treib 2008; Hartlapp 2009; König and Mäder 2013).

The trend to define only basic parameters in European legislation is further reinforced by the increased tendency to adopt 'framework directives', which replace a number of older, more detailed legal acts (e.g. in environmental policy; see Lenschow 2010). This trend reflects the persistence of divergent views among member states and underscores the difficulties in building consensus. It also reflects the fact that creating a European regulatory system as dense as those of the member states is neither reasonable nor possible. Over the course of the 1980s, the earlier idea of creating a supranational state or a fully-fledged federation was definitively abandoned in favour of a model of integration that sets a regulatory framework for directing national legislation into more narrow channels. Such a model implies that large parts of the legislative effort are offloaded primarily to national legislative institutions, but to a certain extent also to non-state actors participating in the process (see Chapter 10). This has consequently led to the emergence of a two-tiered European legal order that is characterized by a high degree of variation among the member states. Moreover, even though proposals are carefully elaborated by the Commission, the efficiency of the legislative process is frequently diminished by a significant degree of non-decision. The late 1970s and early 1980s marked the peak of the inability of the Council to take definitive decisions. However, even today, a number of the Commission's proposals are mired in deadlock; for example, the proposals for tighter surveillance of the economic policies of the member states. The ensuing non-decisions result from the complex process of consensus-building in the Council. These difficulties in reaching consensus, in turn, originate from the highly complex and contradictory interest constellations, the divergent expectations surrounding the impacts of European regulations on national political systems, and nearly incalculable political junctures.

The problem of building consensus in the Council is not restricted to legislative matters. It has an even greater impact on fundamental decisions, such as Treaty revisions. Thus, successful decisions concerning the institutional architecture of the EU and deepening integration are usually achieved only after lengthy negotiations within the framework of Intergovernmental Conferences (IGCs) (see Chapter 5). These conferences have the effect of multiplying the usual marathon negotiations, since they require a series of summit meetings of the heads of state or government. Furthermore, before the IGC, a multitude of advisory bodies, institutions, organizations, and actors may present their particular point of view on upcoming integration steps. In spite of such elaborated preparations, negotiations on Treaty revisions are generally defined by major delays in achieving consensus, unsatisfactory compromises, and a significant degree of non-decision, labelled as 'left-overs'.

The Lisbon Treaty is an excellent case in point. It took almost a decade to achieve the successful completion of its adoption and final ratification. Although some of the delays were the result of failed referenda in the member states, the European-level negotiations were particularly cumbersome. The Convention was initially established as a means of introducing new actors into the process of Treaty revision, thus reducing intergovernmental bargains and accelerating decision-making. Yet, once the Convention had completed its work and submitted a Draft Constitutional Treaty (DCT), it took almost a year (and two presidencies) to reach an agreement on the DCT in the European Council. In 2007, when the process was re-launched after the negative referenda in France and the Netherlands, it again took two presidencies to reach a final compromise. Ratification by the member states was no less problematic. By the end of 2009, the Lisbon Treaty finally came into force, eight years after the Laeken declaration initiated the process of fundamental Treaty revision (see Chapter 3). Thus, progress in European integration and in building the European polity was only achieved after lengthy processes of consensus-building.

There is, however, also a positive note in Council decision-making. The increasing use of majority voting has significantly reduced the number of non-decisions or compromises around the level of the lowest common denominator. With the introduction of majority voting for issues of market integration, and the subsequent expansion to a variety of other policy areas, the number of decisions and the speed with which they are taken has increased significantly (König 2007). However, these gains in efficiency have been somewhat compromised by other factors connected to the ongoing process of integration. First, decisions taken by majority voting tend to be in issues where a basic consensus among the member states has already been given (e.g. in common market matters). Other issues (e.g. foreign policy or overseeing member states' economic policy) are much more contested and are, therefore, subject to unanimity. Second, the Parliament first acquired rights of co-decision, and then later the role of co-legislator, and with it a veto-power. While the threat of a veto may not necessarily block decision-making, it invariably results in a time-consuming conciliation procedure (König 2007). The 2010 SWIFT agreement with the United States illustrates the problem. In this case, the Parliament cast a veto against the initial agreement concluded by the Council. The Council then had to renegotiate the issue and to take into account the Parliament's objections. It took a year before a final compromise could be reached. Third, even when majority voting is the rule, the Council will attempt to reach a consensus that includes all member states. Needless to say, this is a time-consuming endeavour. Overall, however, the use of majority voting has changed the practice of decision-making in the Council. Those member states that frequently resort to the veto are considered uncooperative and are often side-lined as a result of their actions. Even in those cases where unanimous voting is the rule, the threat by a member state to use a veto is no longer considered to be appropriate behaviour. As co-legislator, the EP is often willing to compromise with the Council at an early stage in the legislative procedure, so that decisions are frequently taken more quickly (Héritier and Reh 2012).

In summary, we can conclude that the efficiency of European decision-making is a somewhat mixed bag in both quantitative and qualitative terms. In terms of quantity, the cumbersome procedures, the involvement of a multitude of actors, and the enormous amount of time and resources invested in meetings and negotiations certainly combine to have a negative impact on efficiency. In terms of quality, the low degree of regulation in certain issue areas, the limitation often to adopt only regulatory frameworks, as well as the frequent failure to take decisions all lessen the prospect of efficient decision-making. It is not so much the management of the processes that causes these problems. Rather, it is the difficulties encountered in building consensus among the member states. Although, in principle, increased majority voting fosters smooth decision-making, any progress in efficiency associated with the increased majority voting rules is, at least temporarily, undermined by the simultaneous expansion of Parliament's co-legislative powers and by expanding the scope of European decisions to ever-more contested policy areas. This, in turn, leads to contradictory results. On the one hand, consideration of sensitive policy issues relating to national responsibilities often exacerbates conflicts between the member states. On the other hand, such conflicts can be mitigated by involving an increasing number of government officials and other national experts and actors in the decision-making process. In this way, consensus is often achieved even before the formal decisions are taken in the Council. When facilitated majority voting in the Council becomes the norm, as it is envisioned by the Lisbon Treaty for the year 2014, the situation might further improve.

We thus observe that gains in efficiency achieved by institutional innovations in procedures of decision-making are often offset by the expansion of the rights of other institutions, or the expansion of policy-making at European level (see also Hayes-Renshaw and Wallace 2006). In other words, gains in efficiency may be offset by progress in European integration. But we also see a competing trend, whereby the expansion of majority voting in the Council tends to increase procedural efficiency.

Inefficiencies may particularly occur in recently or weakly integrated policy areas. In contrast, they hardly play a role in consolidated policies, sustained by a basic consensus between the member states. Inefficiencies therefore must be assessed in relation to the degree of integration. Clearly, such an assessment provides a more positive and also a more realistic picture. We also might value inefficiencies as indicators of a progressively advancing process of integration, where problems tend to arise when new ground is broken.

A final assessment should not overestimate the obvious inefficiencies in EU decision-making. In light of the dimension and the complexity of the policy problems at hand, the uniqueness of the European project that seeks to unite independent states on a voluntary basis, and given the regulatory output to date in a vast array of policy areas, we may conclude that the Union is able to act in a cooperative and consensual manner (Dinan 2012). The Union, as a highly-differentiated negotiated order (see Chapter 13), has achieved a considerable degree of overall efficiency, in spite of a variety of inefficiencies in detail. By taking into account the interests of member states, as well as those of a variety of external groups, it has minimized conflict and established an impressive quantum of common regulations and procedural norms.

## Effectiveness: governance and steering capacity

To make a complete assessment of the Union's success as a political system, we must consider whether European governance and policy-making have effectively shaped developments in the member states, or in the Union as a whole. More precisely, we need to consider whether the EU has achieved its objectives and been successful in solving the political problems that it faces. I attempt to answer these questions by focusing on a few select examples. These examples might help to highlight some basic principles of success – or failure – in European governance.

The analysis of the effectiveness of European governance must consider some specific features that are closely linked to the institutional structure of the Union (Knill 2006: 353–63; Tömmel 2009):

- First, in most cases, European governance involves several levels of government and a multitude of actors. Accordingly, political steering is organized as a series of impulses that activate and give guidance to policy-makers in the member states. Thus, European governance implies long chains of political steering, with often indirect impacts and unpredictable outcomes. During these extensive and often complex chains of political steering, a variety of frictions can arise that can dramatically reduce the effectiveness of European governance.
- Second, because additional actors involved in the process of political steering – in particular, national governments – are fairly autonomous, their input may significantly reduce, distort, or even reverse the objectives and intentions underlying European governance.
- Third, the lack of sovereignty and the inability to determine its own powers limits the EU's ability to exercise authoritative power in the process of governance. Therefore, a great deal of energy is expended by the European institutions to find and carry out alternative strategies to compensate for the lack of formal powers. As a result, the Union and, in particular, the Commission tend to 'invent' innovative modes of governance that make formal powers obsolete (Sabel and Zeitlin 2008, 2010; Tömmel and Verdun 2009).

The literature on European governance and policy-making distinguishes between regulatory and distributive policies (Wallace 1983; Majone 2005), as well as between negative and positive integration (Scharpf 1999). Regulatory policies mainly steer through the law and legal channels, whereas distributive policies typically use financial incentives and/or have major distributive impacts (Lowi 1964). However, these two categories do not cover those policies where the European level only works to coordinate the member state policies, and where the member states only voluntarily comply with the European level. I therefore refer to these policies as 'cooperative', based on their defining mode of governance (see Chapter 8). The distinction between negative and positive integration goes back to Tindemans, who coined these terms in the 1960s. Negative integration refers to policies that remove barriers, mostly those for free markets, whereas positive integration encompasses policies that are deliberately designed to shape certain developments, or to result in defined outcomes. In particular, Scharpf (1999) has used these categories as an analytic tool for elaborating some basic features of European governance and policy-making. In the following analysis, I mainly use the categories 'regulatory', 'distributive', and 'coordinative', but I also refer to 'negative' and 'positive' integration, and draw on the governance modes defined in Chapter 8.

It is generally agreed that the EU's regulatory policies, particularly those that take the form of negative integration, are well-developed and highly effective. Within the realm of these policies, those with a strong deregulating impact are seen as particularly effective. Conversely, policies of the positive integration spectrum, mostly distributive policies, but also some types of regulatory policies, such as environmental regulation, are considered to be less effective. Because these policies require a deliberate consensus in the Council, it is much more difficult to establish and sustain them at the European level (Scharpf 1999; Majone 2005). Cooperative policies, broadly defined by the OMC, are generally regarded as less effective. Scholars ascribe this ineffectiveness to the lack of binding rules, the voluntary character of cooperation, and to the fact that member states often pursue their own objectives instead of those defined at European level (see e.g. Schäfer 2006; Heidenreich and Bischoff 2008; Mailand 2008).

In the following sections, I assess the effectiveness of the EU in three areas of policy: the regulatory, the distributive, and the cooperative spectrum. In each case, I consider as factors determining the effectiveness of a given policy area: the length of the chain in political steering, the degree of autonomy of the institutions and actors involved in the governance process, and the extent of the formal powers held by the European level.

## Effectiveness of regulatory policies

EU regulatory policies are highly effective in common market issues and in the deregulation of national regulatory systems. In short, they are effective in the realm of negative integration (Scharpf 1999; Young 2010). Success in this area is relatively straightforward, as measures establishing the free movement of goods, capital, labour, and services 'only' require member states to remove market barriers. As a result, it is comparatively easy to build consensus among the member states. Projects such as the completion of the single market have been fairly successful in the EU. However, this project also required a considerable amount of re-regulation, or positive integration – which was, in general, also implemented in an effective manner, mainly because the member states expected significant gains for themselves (Scharpf 1999; Blauberger 2009; Young 2010). However, other forms of positive integration in the framework of regulatory policies – for example, the liberalization of public utilities – are not always welcomed by member states (Schmidt 2004).

While the effectiveness of the single market project depends on regulatory measures, it remains the role of the European Commission to oversee the implementation of these measures in the member states and to supervise their compliance therewith (Knill 2006: 353–5). Commission oversight has been particularly effective in the area of competition policy, where the responsible Commissioners have performed their tasks with increasing authority and success, and often with the support of the

ECJ (see Chapter 8; Van Miert 2000; Cini and McGowan 2008; Wilks 2010). It is interesting to note that individual member states and private enterprises alike often invoke the Commission, if they suspect their competitors are violating the rules. This, of course, lends credibility to the Commission and its decisions.

Scharpf (1999) considers the EU's competition policy so effective that, in his view, it far exceeds anything national governments ever intended to achieve. National monopolies, as well as regulated markets, have been successively dismantled by this policy. The deregulation of these sectors has served to expand markets and to establish competitive mechanisms for regulating them. However, as Scharpf argues, this has also deeply affected the welfare systems of the member states. It has had a detrimental effect, for example, on public utilities, which also perform functions of social welfare. The same can be said for state monopolies, which often cross-subsidized sub-sectors or branches. The application of European competition rules to these sectors that were previously run by the state has led to a need to dismantle the corresponding redistributive policies of the member states.

The high degree of effectiveness of the single market programme and European competition policy is largely a result of the fact that the particular features of EU governance that have been mentioned hardly play a role. Thus, in this realm we do not find long chains of political steering, since most rules regarding the single market are directly binding on the member states. Furthermore, member states rarely infringe or obstruct these rules – in part because they deliberately endorse them, in part, because they fear disadvantages if other states violate them, and, finally, because private firms might act as 'whistle-blowers' against them. Finally, the EU and, in particular, the Commission hold extensive legislative, supervisory, and control powers in these areas (Scharpf 1999; Schmidt 2004).

By contrast, other regulatory policies that imply positive integration are less effective (Knill and Tosun 2012). This is true, for example, of the EU's environmental policy. Environmental policy was not initially mentioned in the Treaties, but it has since become an important part of European regulation (Knill 2006: 358–70; Lenschow 2010; Jordan *et al.* 2012). Formal competences in this area were established with the SEA (Art. 130 r-t, now Art. 191-193 TFEU). As Dehousse (1992: 395) argues, this transfer of competences occurred only because highly regulated member states feared that, without common regulations, the single market would encourage environmental dumping by states with low standards. Once competences had been established at the European level, highly-regulated states pressed for their own regulatory models to be transferred to the EU as a whole. Yet, finally, new models of governance that combined various approaches evolved (Knill 2006; Jordan *et al.* 2012). A flexible regulatory framework left significant scope to the discretion of national governments. At the same time, innovative policy experiments were launched. These were based on cooperative modes of governance and the voluntary commitment of institutions and actors in the member states (Holzinger *et al.* 2009; Lenschow 2010). These voluntary forms of cooperation are partly complemented by competitive mechanisms, such as eco-auditing or eco-labelling. Private firms that participate in these procedures may enjoy an advantage over their competitors as a result of their improved image.

Innovative modes of governance in environmental policy did not emerge only in response to the reluctance of member states to set strict, uniform standards at the European level, or to transfer significant competences to the EU. They were also an attempt to tackle ubiquitous policy problems, including the sluggish transposition of European laws into national legislation and the huge implementation deficits in the member states (Knill and Tosun 2012). However, the discretion offered to both public and private actors to date has not resulted in greater effectiveness of EU environmental policy (Jordan *et al.* 2012). In addition, it preserves the diversity of environmental regulation and policy among the member states (Knill 2006).

In summary, we can conclude that regulatory policy around environmental issues is, in general, less effective than those regulations that focus on market liberalization and competition. Although a high level of protection might be achieved in some cases, the member states' resistance to strict European regulation and the difficulty in the implementation of policies at home continue to pose major problems. This is the case not only for states with low environmental standards, but also for those that have embraced a high standard of regulation. These states fear problems of compatibility with European standards. They are also reluctant to give up their own regulatory models. European environmental policy thus faces major obstacles that generally characterize the process of governance in the EU. The European institutions hold only limited formal competences, the member states remain largely autonomous, and the policy area requires fairly long chains of political steering. In order to find a solution to these problems, the Commission often resorts to linking environmental regulation to market regulation, by using the 'distortion of competition' argument for setting uniform standards. If this strategy fails, states may take comfort in open and flexible standards, and in policies that appeal to the voluntary commitment of both public and private actors. It is almost impossible to calculate effectiveness in these cases, as it is contingent on so many variables.

### Effectiveness of distributive policies

The effectiveness of European governance can vary widely in the realm of distributive policies. The common agricultural policy (CAP) is one policy that has been widely criticized by academia and the public alike (Rieger 2005; Nugent 2010; Roederer-Rynning 2010; Conceição-Heldt 2012). Within that policy, the system of agricultural price support that was in place until recently was plagued by unintended consequences and perverse impacts. Initially, in the 1960s, the CAP was designed to create an integrated market for agricultural products, when protectionism was widespread in most member states (Daugbjerg 2012: 90). However, whenever the prices for the producer threatened to fall below a certain level as a result of Europe-wide competition, the Community would intervene with direct price support (Daugbjerg 2012: 92). Such interventions in the market were originally intended to be used in only exceptional cases, but they soon became the norm (Rieger 2005). This resulted in an enormous expansion of production and several other unintended consequences, including tremendous storage costs and additional subsidies for dumping these products on world markets (Nugent 2010: 359–64; Conceição-Heldt 2012: 162–5).

It was not until the 1990s, when two key factors came together – Eastern enlargement, and the international pressure from negotiations at the World Trade Organization (WTO), that reversal of the Union's agricultural policy became necessary and possible (Rieger 2005: 180; Daugbjerg and Swinbank 2007; Daugbjerg 2012). As a result, subsidies were significantly reduced by lowering the level required for intervention and, in some cases, subsidies were abolished altogether. In 2003, a major reform led to the revision of the entire policy. As in environmental policy, disparities between the member states were now acknowledged. Accordingly, there were only basic policy objectives and parameters defined at the European level, and most of the implementation measures were left to the discretion of the member states (Daugbjerg and Swinbank 2007; Roederer-Rynning 2010; Daugbjerg 2012: 100–2). Thus, after more than 40 years of adherence to a largely dysfunctional policy, the objective of creating a common agricultural market was silently abandoned in favour of a policy patchwork, primarily managed by the member states.

Why was the common agricultural policy such a failure? The explanations do not lie with a lack of competences at the European level, or in excessively long chains of political steering but, rather, in the fact that certain member states – France, in particular – used their veto power to prevent policy change. Furthermore, agricultural associations succeeded in capturing the EC/EU for their own particular interests (Nugent 2010: 356–8). Unfortunately, this did not benefit the majority of farmers, who were extremely discontented with the European policy. However, as we assess the CAP, we have to bear in mind that, for a long time, this policy area was an exception in the European context. The willingness to intervene in the market was a leftover from the early days of integration when this type of practices was common, particularly in the coal, steel, and atomic energy sectors. Yet, the EC/EU silently dismantled interventionism in these sectors after it had lost its effectiveness. Attempts to dismantle the CAP, however, met strong resistance from the member states and agricultural interest associations, so that reforms could only materialize under intense external pressure (Nugent 2010: 355–6; Daugbjerg 2012).

In contrast, cohesion policy represents the more usual approach to distributive policies within the context of European governance. Here, specific procedures were designed to circumvent obstacles that are inherent in the institutional structure of the EU. These procedures, which were then transferred to other policy areas, allowed for a substantial widening of the realm of distributive policies (see Chapter 8).

European cohesion policy was shaped primarily by the Commission, even though the member states had their own concept of what this policy should be. The member states preferred a simple financial transfer between rich and poor states, whereas the Commission pursued a model that deliberately fostered economic development in peripheral or other disadvantaged regions. It successfully established this model by means of a series of reforms. At the heart of the Commission's governance approach is the 'system of partnership' (see Chapters 8 and 9), which enables the European level to interact directly with national and regional authorities and non-state actors throughout the whole policy cycle.

The effectiveness of the European cohesion policy lies primarily in this innovative mode of governance. Unsurprisingly, it was soon transferred to other distributive policies. It successfully overcomes the difficulties that arise from the limited competences of the European level, from extremely long chains of political steering, and from the relative autonomy of the actors involved in policy-making. However, when we examine the implementation of cohesion policy, we see a somewhat less positive picture. Projects and programmes are often implemented very slowly and incompletely (Charron *et al.* 2012). Furthermore, many frictions arise between the government levels. It appears that the glue of the 'system of partnership' is effective in motivating the actors towards devising common policy objectives, but its influence does not extend to all facets of the implementation stage.

### Effectiveness of cooperative policies

New approaches to governance have emerged in the realm of cooperative policies that do not rely on either regulatory or distributive steering mechanisms. This has often occurred in policy areas where member states were not willing to transfer the necessary competences or financial means to the European level, even though there was intense pressure to act. The Commission, backed by the consent of the Council, has succeeded in establishing policies that rely on organized forms of *cooperation*, supported to some extent by competitive mechanisms (Benz 2009; Tömmel 2009). The EES is a case in point.

As we saw in Chapter 8, the procedure of coordinating national policies within the EES consists of four stages (Armstrong and Kilpatrick 2007). The governance process involves the Commission, the Council, the European Council, national governments and, to a degree, even non-state actors. Benchmarking, peer reviews of national policies, and the exchange of experiences and 'best practice' examples among public and, to a lesser extent, non-state actors then complement the process.

Participation in the coordination procedure is binding, but member states are formally free to conceptualize and implement their policies according to their own objectives. However, it is obvious that national policies are greatly influenced by the competitive pressures that result from the process of comparing policies with other member states within the framework of common guidelines. They similarly are influenced by the experiences of others, and by participating in peer reviews (Benz 2009). The OMC procedure spread surprisingly quickly from the EES to a number of other policy areas. These policy areas range from weakly integrated and highly contested policies – such as the fight against poverty and social exclusion, to well-established policy areas – such as cohesion policy, where the procedure complements other modes of governance (see Chapter 8).

It is difficult to assess the effectiveness of governance through cooperation, because these innovative modes of governance have only recently been applied to entire policy areas. In many other cases, they are used in conjunction with other modes of political steering. Furthermore, the question remains whether we can attribute the impact of OMC procedures at the implementation stage to the mode of governance, or whether other facts are responsible. As a result, some scholars assume a high degree of effectiveness of these policies, whereas others take a more critical position (see e.g. Schäfer 2006; Heidenreich and Bischoff 2008; Mailand 2008). In my view, the major impact of this approach to governance lies in its ability to mobilize autonomous actors to pursue European policy objectives. Whether the actors actually do this depends upon their convictions and commitment. These are hard to influence, since strong incentives – such as subsidies – are not available. Only competitive mechanisms might improve the effectiveness of cooperation as a mode of governance.

The examples I have chosen lead us to conclude that the effectiveness of European governance is not uniform. *Regulatory policies* are most effective when the Union has direct competences at its disposal, so that a long chain of political steering is obsolete and the autonomy of the member states limited. However, this applies only to those policies that form part of negative integration; that is, policies that are designed to remove barriers to a free market and which are based on a sound consensus among the member states. In contrast, regulatory policies in the realm of positive integration – for example, environmental policy – are less effective, even in those cases where strict European standards are adopted under the guise of single market regulation. In these cases, a policy seems to be more effective when it succeeds in stimulating the commitment of both public and private actors in the member states, either by adopting framework directives at the European level that leave much discretion to national governments, or by making use of indirect steering instruments, such as voluntary agreements or competitive mechanisms.

In the realm of *distributive policies*, we can recognize an inverse correlation. Agricultural policy was an utter failure, in spite of the fact that the European level possessed widespread powers in this area. A robust interventionist policy, based on generous subsidies, led to mainly unintended consequences. Instead of achieving the goal that the Union had set, which was a European-wide agricultural market, the policy resulted in overproduction, market distortion, and increasing protectionism, followed by further interventionism. The only way this policy could be turned around was to dismantle the extensive system of subsidies and partly to decentralize the competences in this area back to the member states. Cohesion policy, on the other hand, proved to be more effective in spite of limited competences at the European level. Relying on negotiations to structure a process of political steering, the policy brought decentralized, public as well as private actors on board in the pursuit of European policy objectives. Recurrent negotiations on policy formulation and implementation facilitated cooperation among the actors. Steadily increasing subsidies has provided strong incentives for member states to comply with European objectives.

Cooperative policies, such as the EES, aim to mobilize decentralized actors, too. However, here, there are neither strong policy competences at the European level nor strong incentives in the form of subsidies. Instead, decentralized actors work through the indirect means of political steering and specific competitive mechanisms to achieve policy coordination. This may ultimately result in a degree of compliance.

In conclusion, we can state that the effectiveness of positive integration policies is dependent on an active role of the member states, as well as participation by other actors at all levels. They may be mobilized in a variety of ways: in regulatory policies, they are mobilized through an open and flexible framework of regulations; in distributive policies, through extensive negotiations on the allocation of subsidies; and in cooperative policies, through complex procedures of policy coordination. In all these cases, voluntary agreements and competitive mechanisms can reinforce the impact of these forms of mobilization. Consequently, all these policies, although they are characterized by very different levels of competences at the European level, increasingly rely on modes of governance that do not encroach on national autonomy.

Indeed, they take advantage of national autonomy. However, these forms of governance cannot definitively determine the outcomes of a given policy.

In general, we can conclude that European governance tends to evolve in an open and flexible manner. Strong intervention, or the use of hierarchy as a mode of governance is only suited to the European polity in specific cases, such as single market matters. In other cases, it evokes the opposition of the member states and, thus, thwarts policy effectiveness. Therefore, European governance and policy-making increasingly attempt to shape and structure the context under which national and sub-national governments and administrations, as well as non-state actors, are able to adapt their policies and activities to the common objectives of the European level. This can occur through negotiation, competition, or cooperation, or by combining these governance modes in various ways. However, such forms of contextual governance cannot determine the final outcome of policy-making, as the final outcome is contingent on a number of variables. As a result, European policy-making often appears to be ineffective (Knill 2006). Moreover, its effectiveness in steadily building the context for European governance to be exercised is rarely perceived as an achievement.

## Conclusion

In this chapter, we have assessed, first, the efficiency of the EU's institutional configuration and processes of decision-making and, second, the effectiveness of European governance. In both cases, the conclusions were ambiguous. Indeed, the efficiency and effectiveness of the EU cannot be evaluated definitively, since positive and negative aspects of these dimensions are closely interwoven. Any evaluation is therefore highly dependent on the criteria applied. It also depends on whether we are considering the EU through the lens of national political systems, or within the context of an emerging political order beyond the nation state.

With regard to *efficiency*, we can conclude that, if we consider the EU as similar to a state, then it does not appear to be a particularly efficient system. There are several reasons for this. The dualistic or bicephalous nature of its institutional structure; the multifaceted overlapping and intertwining among its institutions, as well as among the European and the 'lower' levels of government and administration; the elaborate, yet wasteful procedures of decision-making; and the deferral of a large part of externalities to the member states, all come into play. However, our conclusion is different when we consider the EU from the perspective of building a political community that integrates a number of substantially different nation states, without significantly encroaching on their sovereignty. Seen this way, the highly-diversified institutional structure of the

EU and its complex processes of decision-making appear to be fairly efficient and well-suited to achieve the goals of the project of European integration. Indeed, they may be assessed as remarkable and, in view of other international or regional organizations, as unique.

The *effectiveness* of the EU, defined in terms of its capacity in governance and political steering, also appears to lag behind, if we compare it to the effectiveness of nation states. In most cases, European governance only has an indirect impact on the developments in the member states. It is defined by complex sequences of political steering involving a multitude of institutions and actors, and its final impact depends to a large degree on the commitment and voluntary cooperation of national and regional authorities and stakeholders. The EU only achieves a high level of effectiveness in the area of market regulation, where it holds substantial competences, so that it can address economic actors without much interference from national governments. In addition, this effectiveness is based on an explicit consensus among the member states about a common policy of market liberalization. In fact, it was the objective of liberalizing markets that gave a strong impetus to found the European Community and later transform it into the European Union.

When viewed as an emerging political order beyond the nation state, the EU's effectiveness appears remarkable. The EU has established specific forms of governance – forms that cannot directly determine the final outcome in a policy area, but which are effective in mobilizing public institutions and non-state actors at all levels of government to pursue European objectives and effectively to implement EU policies. By focusing on structuring the *context* for effective governance in the member states, European governance can be quite successful. It is this form of 'contextual guidance' (Willke 2007) that constitutes the EU as an effective system of policy-making, even though it is not able definitively to determine the final outcomes of its policies.

In summary, the EU constitutes an emergent political order beyond the nation state. In order to assess its efficiency and effectiveness, we must consider the EU in this light. At the same time, we must bear in mind that the political system of the EU is still evolving. Consequently any assessment – both in terms of successes and failures – can only be viewed as preliminary.

# Chapter 12

# The Democratic Legitimacy of the EU

One of the most widely discussed problems in the EU centres around the issue of legitimacy, often referred to as the 'democratic deficit'. This issue, which has accompanied the EC/EU since its inception, became particularly acute with the passage of the Treaty of Maastricht. At that time, it became clear that citizens were no longer willing passively to support the European project. On the contrary, as the referenda on the Maastricht Treaty in Denmark and France proved, citizens were deeply concerned about the incalculable consequences of European integration and wanted to see the process slowed down (Dinan 2004: 258–61; Down and Wilson 2008). From that point on, it became necessary for European elites to take public opinion into account when making decisions on the speed, direction, and model of integration. As a consequence, the European elites put the issue of improving the democratic accountability of the EU on the agenda. However, improving the EU's democratic constitution based on a model of national democratic systems would necessarily strengthen the supranational dimension of the European polity (e.g. Majone 2005). It is obvious that neither national governments nor the citizens of the EU want this. Thus, correcting the democratic deficit of the EU becomes a project of squaring the circle.

The academic discussion around the EU's democratic state usually asserts that the legitimacy is either lacking or has not evolved sufficiently at the European level. The ensuing 'democratic deficit' is ascribed to the institutional structure of the EU and, in particular, to the limited powers of the Parliament. In addition, the insufficient separation of powers between the European institutions and the non-transparent decision-making mechanisms are defined as root causes of this deficit (Huget 2007). In his writings, Scharpf distinguishes between two dimensions of legitimacy: input and output legitimacy (1999: 6–42). The former refers to 'government by the people'; that is, political choices are legitimate 'if and because they reflect the "will of the people"' (Scharpf 1999: 6). The latter refers to 'government for the people'. 'Here, political choices are legitimate if and because they effectively promote the common welfare of the constituency in question' (Scharpf 1999: 6). Scharpf assumes that the EU is primarily marked by a deficit in input legitimacy, while the output legitimacy of the system is, in his view, less problematic. However, other scholars also question the output legitimacy of the EU. In this chapter, I will only consider the input dimension of democratic legitimacy, as it is this dimension that is directly related to the EU's institutional structure. In contrast, the EU's output legitimacy reflects whether its achievements in policy-making correspond to the preferences and wishes of the citizens. This is a complex issue that cannot be fully addressed here.

In the following sections, I examine what constitutes the democratic deficit of the EU and to what degree this deficit affects the legitimacy of the Union. Furthermore, I offer an overview of the scholarly literature around correcting the democratic deficit of the European polity. Finally, I consider the democratic 'potential' of the Union's institutional structure and its procedural norms, which clearly deviate from what we know of national political systems. I argue that it is precisely the democratic deficits of the European polity that could form a starting point for the evolution of new forms of democratic representation and participation and, thus, provide legitimacy to the EU.

## Democratic deficit

### The characteristics of the EU's democratic deficit

The scholarly literature on the democratic deficit of The EU identifies the following, highly interdependent characteristics:

- The anomalous distribution and insufficient separation of powers between the European institutions;
- An absent or insufficient democratic legitimacy of the European institutions;
- The extensive transfer of decisions from the legislature to the executive, and the ensuing difficulties for democratically legitimized institutions to monitor and control decision-making.
  (Lord 2004; Follesdal and Hix 2006; Hix 2008; Majone 2009; Rittberger 2010; for an opposing view, see Moravscik 2002, 2008)

Some scholars additionally point to the democratic deficits that result from the successive transfers of competences from the national level to the European level. According to these scholars, this shifts the rights of decision-making away from democratically legitimized institutions in the member states without establishing similarly legitimized procedures in the EU (Greven 2000). This perspective reconfirms that the EU lacks democratic legitimacy, but does not really contribute to the discussion beyond the points listed above.

A closer look at these points reveals, first, that the principle of *the separation of powers* is insufficiently respected in the institutional set-up of the EU. As we have seen in Chapter 4, both the Council and the Commission are vested with legislative *as well as* executive powers, though to differing degrees. The Council and the Parliament share powers in ordinary legislation, but the Council holds additional powers in specific forms of legislation and in policy areas that are not primarily based on legislation (see Chapters 5 and 7). Both the Parliament and the Council are constrained in exercising their legislative powers, as they do not have the right of initiative, which remains with the Commission (Bartolini 2005a: 153–60; Follesdal and Hix 2006).

Second, the *absent or insufficient democratic legitimacy* applies to those institutions that hold extensive power in the EU: the Commission, the Council and the European Council. The Commission, with its extensive legislative and executive powers, is not at all democratically legitimized. The Council and the European Council possess only indirect democratic legitimacy, as their members are elected office-holders at national level. However, these bodies cannot be held collectively accountable for their decisions (Lord 2008). Moreover, the Parliament, as the only democratically elected institution of the EU, continues to lack certain powers that national legislatures typically have (see pp. 290–2). None of these institutions has significant monitoring powers over the others. Only the Parliament may, to a degree, supervise the performance of the Commission (see Chapter 4). However, the Commission is designed to act as a largely independent institution. The Council and the European Council are not accountable to any other European institution. Only individual members of the Councils may be held accountable by their national legislatures, but this does not necessarily 'add up to control of the Council' (Lord 2008: 318; see also Bartolini 2005a: 154). In addition, the lack of transparency in European decision-making precludes effective control of the Council members. To date, the introduction of new supervisory powers for national parliaments, as enacted in the Lisbon Treaty, have not resulted in a strong democratic control (Cooper 2012).

The third issue, the *transfer of decisions from the legislature to the executive*, is closely connected with the problem of indistinct and anomalous separation of powers. However, since it has certain specific characteristics, it is worth considering it independently here. Although they share power with the EP, the Commission, Council, and European Council are primarily responsible for taking the core decisions in the EU. By and large, these institutions are all executives, or represent executives. The same applies to the institutional substructures of the Commission and the Councils, whose members are responsible for the more detailed decisions in the EU. Advisory bodies of the Commission, COREPER and the working groups of the Council, and the comitology committees assigned to the Commission are staffed with members of national executives. Even the CoR, which is assumed to improve the input legitimacy of the EU, consists mainly of representatives of regional and local executives (see Chapter 9). As executives grow to dominate in European affairs, legislatures at the national and regional level are increasingly stripped of their powers and rights. National parliaments are hardly in a position to hold their governments accountable for decisions and activities taken at the European level, even though the Lisbon Treaty explicitly entitles them to do so (Auel 2007; Auel and Benz 2007; Cooper 2012). They are even less able to give them a clear mandate. Regional legislatures are often not even informed when competences from this level are transferred to the EU. In addition, the decrease of the rights of national legislatures also leads to a decrease in the influence of economic and social partners, as well as other organized interests at national level.

The extensive list of democratic deficits may even grow, if we examine the individual issues in more detail. Yet, in the following I focus on the ways in which the European Parliament suffers from a legitimacy deficit. At first glance, it may be surprising to think that these deficits exist in the EP, since it is a directly elected body. However, when we look more closely, it becomes obvious elections alone are insufficient to provide democratic legitimacy. The democratic deficiencies of the EP are the subject of much scholarly debate and they serve to support the EPs claims that it needs to expand its powers within the Union.

## The legitimacy deficiencies of the EP

The Parliament clearly lacks substantial legislative powers. In particular, it lacks the right to propose legislation and to decide in specific legislative matters. But its legitimacy is further undermined by a number of other factors that actually originate in the EP's institutional foundations and procedural norms. First, there are clearly imbalances in representation, given that MEPs from large member states must represent a much larger number of citizens than those of the small states. Furthermore, the electoral procedures, which are organized separately in the member states and are based on their own practices, can lead to an inequality of representation (Duff 2010: 58–63). It was not until 1999 that the UK adopted a system of proportional representation for European elections. Before then, the UK relied on its national system of majority voting in European elections. This regularly led to a disproportionately large number of either Conservative or Labour deputies in the EP, which then had a disproportionate weight in the respective party group (see Chapter 4). Since 1999, proportional electoral systems have been the norm throughout the EU, but there are still differences in representation. Some of these differences depend on whether the national electoral system uses thresholds to access the EP. Thus, 11 member states use such thresholds, usually ranging from 3 to 5 per cent. This means that smaller parties often fail to win seats. In contrast, in other member states in which there is no such threshold members of extremely small parties may be elected to the EP.

More importantly though, there is no Europe-wide electoral contest in the EU (Hix 2008). Since European elections revolve around national parties, campaigns are centred on national issues and European elections are seen as second-order elections (Reif and Schmitt 1980; Marsh and Mikhailov 2010). Consequently, citizens cannot make a choice based on the positions and performances of the parties in the EP (Follesdal and Hix 2006). Moreover, by relying on national party configurations, citizens are not able to express their opinions about whether and how European integration should proceed, since, with the exception of those parties on the extreme left and right, national parties are rarely polarized on these issues. This clearly reduces citizens' interest in the elections and, as a result, voter turnout in European elections is extremely low (43 per cent in the 2014 elections).

Following the EP elections, the delegates of national parties organize themselves in the Parliament according to political groups. However, the coherence of these groups is quite different from parliamentary party groups in the member states (see Chapter 6). For example, the socialists and democrats (S&D) group in the EP is far from homogenous, and there are major ideological differences among the various national parties. Similarly, the Christian democrats and conservatives (EPP) group lacks coherence, at least partially a consequence of its strategy of admitting a wide variety of parties in order to become the largest group in the EP. Minor party groups in the EP have no real choice other than to enter into marriages of convenience. Consequently, the party groups of the EP face difficulties in developing clear political profiles. It is even more difficult for them to form a polarized party system. Accordingly, they do not represent the preferences of the voters (see, e.g., Rose and Borz 2013), although Hix and his collaborators actually claim that the EP is already quite polarized (Hix *et al.* 2005; Hix 2008).

The emergence of a polarized party system in the EU is also constrained by other factors that are inherent in the institutional structure of the EU. Since the Parliament does not have the role of electing a government or an executive of the EU, there is no clear-cut delineation between government and opposition groups. In turn, this prevents the parties from presenting strongly-differentiated party positions to the electorate. Procedural norms also hamper attempts to create clear distinctions of the positions of the various parties. When the ordinary procedure of legislation applies, the Parliament often needs to take decisions with an absolute majority. This type of majority can be achieved only if the two largest party groups form a 'grand coalition'. It is important to note, though, that this is not a true coalition, as the groups only cooperate on the particular issue at stake. If the voters take any notice of this coalition at all, a 'grand coalition' of conservatives and socialists does not really entice them to the polls. Thus, the consensual style of decision-making that dominates in the EP ultimately leads to a low voter turnout in European elections. Consequently, the democratic legitimacy of the EP, as well as its power in relation to the other European institutions, is considerably weakened. The link between Parliament and the electorate is tenuous at best. The EP does not enjoy strong political support from the voters (Bartolini 2005a: 343–6).

Weak representation and limited formal powers are two manifestations of the democratic deficit that characterizes the European Parliament. But the problems run even deeper than this, and contribute to a vicious circle. The electoral system, insufficient competences, and the Parliament's position in the EU's institutional structure prevent the emergence of a polarized party system. The absence of a polarized party system results in a low voter turnout and, generally, a weak political support from the electorate – which, in turn, weakens the EP's position in the European arena. This vicious circle can only be broken by transforming the EP into a true legislature in which European political parties compete for representation in European elections. But such a solution is not feasible as long as the Union, as a political system, is divided along national lines.

However, the democratic deficits of the European Parliament appear to be so grave because we explicitly or implicitly use national political systems as a yardstick. Comparing the EP with national legislatures can help to elaborate the basic features of the EP's democratic constitution and legitimacy problems, but it tends to ignore the fact that a democratic legislature beyond the nation state may take on a completely different form (Lord 2004). More precisely, these comparisons overlook specific aspects of the EU's institutional structure and its potential to frame new, transnational forms of democracy (Lord 2004; Lord and Harris 2006). In the following section, I discuss various concepts and proposals for building post-national or transnational forms of democracy.

## Post-national forms of democracy: possibilities and constraints

Recognizing the democratic deficit of the EU and aware of a growing demand for legitimacy in Parliament, scholars increasingly focus on concepts that might offer solutions to these problems. On the one hand, they theorize the conditions and the possibilities of post-national or transnational forms of democracy, and consider solutions that emanate from these concepts (Abromeit 1998; Zürn 2000; Lord 2004, Erikson and Fossum 2007; for an overview, see Rittberger 2010). On the other hand, they empirically explore the potential for enhancing the democratic condition of the EU (Lord 2004, 2008; Hix *et al.* 2005, 2007; Lord and Harris 2006; Hix 2008). Jürgen Neyer adopts a third position when he claims that, as a multi-level polity, the EU cannot be a democratic system at all. In his view, the EU's decisions can, at best, be justified (Neyer 2010, 2012).

In this section, I do not consider the multitude of theoretical approaches and empirical studies on this subject. Rather, I have opted to offer a more narrow analysis of the concrete proposals for democratizing the EU. There are two ways to approach this problem: first, scholars may draw on concepts that are derived from national forms and patterns of democracy; second, they attempt to design post-national or transnational forms of democratic governance. Scholars who adhere to the first approach envisage an incremental improvement in the democratic practices of the EU. Scholars focusing on transnational forms of democratic governance hope for more radical innovations in institutional settings, procedural norms, and forms of representation.

### Democratizing the EU according to national models

It is noteworthy that the first group of scholars does not generally suggest a simple expansion of the EP's powers in order to resolve its democratic deficit. They recognize that those conditions that frame democratic will at the national level are, at the European level, neither a given nor easy to create. They allude to the fragmentation of the Union along national lines, which implies that it is impossible to make extensive use of the majority rule (see e.g. Abromeit 1998). As a result, these scholars suggest several small improvements that could help to overcome certain aspects of the EU's democratic deficit:

- The direct election of the Commission President (Hix 2005b, 2008; Decker 2012).
- The use of instruments of direct democracy (Abromeit 1998).
- The improvement of associative forms of democracy (Zürn 2000; Greenwood 2007).
- The improvement of institutional forms of democratic control (checks and balances, Lord 2007; Neyer 2012).

I examine each of these suggestions below.

*The election of the Commission President*: Scholars view the election of the Commission President as an important step towards transforming the EU into a more democratic and more majoritarian system (Hix 2005, 2008; Decker and Sonnicksen 2009, 2011; Decker 2012; for a critique on Hix, see Bartolini 2005b). In their opinion, this step would imply first-order elections and help to mobilize the electorate. In this scenario, several candidates would compete for office so that alternative political options could be presented and discussed. However, this suggestion has drawbacks: while the electoral process would significantly improve the position of the Commission, it would also politicize it. As a result, it would undermine the independent stance of the Commission and its 'technical' orientation, and would thus compromise its capacity to act in the general interest of the member states. This would probably not meet with the approval of the member states. Moreover, the citizens of larger member states would have a disproportionate influence in the elections or, if some form of degressive proportionality were used, the voters of the smaller states might be more influential. This might well upset the delicate balance between large and small states. Finally, it remains unclear whether candidates should have party affiliation. If they did, the Commission would be further politicized and the elections might be influenced by national party preferences. If the candidates were not affiliated with a specific political party, the polls would focus primarily on the personal merits and election promises of the candidates. This hardly seems to be a strong incentive to encourage voters to go to the polls, particularly since they are aware that the Commission President is not the political leader of the EU. Nevertheless, the Lisbon Treaty has endeavoured to take a step into this direction by allowing the EP to elect the Commission President on a proposal of the European Council. This election will be held for the first time after the 2014 elections to the EP. Since none of the major party groups in the EP commands an absolute majority, it is likely that the 'grand' coalition in the EP will search for a compromise on the proposed candidate.

*Instruments of direct democracy*: Many scholars, and even certain political groups and parties, propose holding Europe-wide referenda on important issues. The supporters of this idea argue that treaty revisions, in particular, should be legitimized by mandatory referenda (Abromeit 1998). In addition, Abromeit has presented an elaborate proposal for holding sectoral as well as regional referenda. She assumes that certain regions or functional groups are severely under-represented in European decision-making. Referenda on legislative proposals would give them a voice and, perhaps, even a power of veto (Abromeit 1998). The advantages of referenda are obvious: citizens would have a direct voice on major steps towards integration, as well as in legislative decisions. Direct participation of this sort would increase political support for the European project. Furthermore, minorities, often side-lined in the ordinary procedures of decision-making, would have an opportunity to reject those legislative proposals that may be contrary to their interests. Finally, referenda might intensify public discourse and debates on issues of integration (Zürn 2000).

In spite of these positive aspects of referenda as forms of direct democracy in the EU, there are also some drawbacks. Rather than advance the process of integration, it is more likely that Europe-wide referenda would slow the whole process down. The negative referenda in some of the member states – first, on the DCT and, later, the Lisbon Treaty – seem to confirm this assumption. Another problem is that referenda are expensive and their use would have to be restricted to a few issues of real significance. Furthermore, European issues are often extremely complex and transforming them into straightforward questions for a plebiscite would be difficult. Finally, Europe-wide referenda would face the same problem as Commission presidential elections, in that the large member states would have a disproportionate influence on the outcome because of their size. Until now, national referenda on European issues have reflected the largely negative attitude of the voters on matters of major integration steps (Roberts-Thomson 2001; Taggart 2006). After years of deadlock in the Council, resulting from the use of the veto, the Union has successfully moved forward by introducing majority voting in an increasingly large number of policy and issue areas. These achievements would be undermined by holding mandatory referenda, which would likely reflect a largely negative popular voice.

*Forms of associative democracy*: Improving forms of associative democracy at European level, in particular by including organized civil society in decision-making, is rarely conceptualized as a concrete proposal but, rather, discussed as a demand (e.g. Zürn 2000; Huget 2007). However, empirical studies on the participation of representatives of civil society in European affairs seem to suggest that such forms of democracy are difficult to establish (see e.g. Friedrich 2008; Steffek *et al.* 2008; Kohler-Koch and Quittkat 2011b). The lack of resources, corresponding rules and regulations, intermediary institutions, representative associations, as well as patterns of transnational cooperation all limit the functioning of this form of democratic representation, even though the Commission has been vigorously pushing the matter since the mid-1980s (Greenwood 2011; see also Chapter 10).

*Institutional forms of democratic control*: This proposal involves the improvement of checks and balances in the EU's political system and should also be considered a demand, rather than a feasible proposal. In the past, scholars suggested that transforming the EP into a fully developed second chamber would constitute a step towards achieving this goal (e.g. Grande 1996). Although this step is now nearly achieved, and Parliament clearly acts as an institution that performs checks and balances with regard to the other legislative institutions, the call for institutional control has not diminished. Lord (2007), for example, proposes that the EP should exercise control over the Council in its entirety; yet, he also points to the manifold constraints that the EP would face in carrying out such a role. Other scholars suggest that national parliaments should execute extensive control functions over the European institutions (e.g. Neyer 2012). However, in this case democratic control of the EU's institutions would be fragmented according to national interests and concerns. Even if national parliaments only exercised control on 'their' governments' member in the Council, they would face structural constraints (Lord 2007).

We can see that borrowing even simple principles from the national models to improve the democratic legitimacy of the EU can lead to major difficulties. As a result, most scholars suggest that the way out of this dilemma lies in a system that is a combination of several of these measures (Zürn 2000; Hix 2005b; Lord 2008). Furthermore, they assume, implicitly or explicitly, that the legitimacy of the EU should be built on the legitimacy of the member states (Moravscik 2002, 2008; Neyer 2012). However, it remains doubtful whether such forms of democratic control will work effectively, in practice.

## Creating post-national forms of democracy

The second type of proposal for correcting the democratic deficit of the EU draws on concepts of post- or transnational forms of democracy. Scholars in this group propose deliberative democracy as a new model of democratic will formation. Habermas (2001) is the most prominent advocate of this model (see, further, Cohen and Sabel 2003; Neyer 2006; Huget 2007; Schmalz-Bruns 2007; for an overview, see Rittberger 2010). Alternately, scholars advocate creating a complex combination of institutional settings and procedural norms, some of which already exist at the international level. They also offer some original proposals for building democracy beyond the nation state (Zürn 2000; Lord 2004, 2008).

Certain forms of *deliberative democracy* are occasionally practised at the national level; however, they are probably better suited to the EU and other international organizations (Cohen and Sabel 2003; Huget 2007; Schmalz-Bruns 2007). Deliberative democracy does not rely on majority rule, neither is it based on negotiations. Actors involved in the deliberations are primarily focused on problem-solving and consensus-building. They do not enter the discussions with a binding mandate from their constituencies and they are not obliged to advocate already defined preferences. Consequently, they are free to concentrate on the search for rational and optimal political solutions. Their position allows them to consider the positions of others, and perhaps even be persuaded by other points of view. Thus, deliberative decision-making is characterized by open and reasoned discourse – which ultimately results in consensual decisions. Deliberative forms of decision-making are often found in expert circles and the 'epistemic communities' (Haas 1992) that prepare the decisions of international organizations. Deliberative decision-making also characterizes European institutions and arenas. It ranges from the EU's core institutions through its institutionalized substructure to the multitude of formal and informal networks.

However, the concept of deliberative democracy involves more than just decision-making focused on problem-solving. It qualifies as democratic only if fair access to the respective arenas is guaranteed for all citizens (Cohen and Sabel 2003; Huget 2007; Schmalz-Bruns 2007; Friedrich 2008). Furthermore, the public should be in a position to comprehend these processes, to discuss them (Habermas 2001), and to exercise control over them. Yet, given the complexity of the EU's institutional structure and the lack of transparency inherent in its decision-making, neither of these conditions has been realized.

All other forms of 'complex global governance' (Zürn 1998) that would be applicable to the EU are conceptualized as combinations of institutional configurations and procedural norms analogous to the complexity of international and transnational arenas of decision-making. Thus, scholars put forth the following combinations:

- Deliberative-, majoritarian-, and negotiation-based procedures of decision-making.
- A variety of arenas for negotiations and decision-making (intergovernmental, parliamentarian, and associative).
- Vertical and horizontal arenas of decision-making, loosely coupled with one another.
- Deliberative and associative forms of representation.
  (e.g. Zürn 1998, 2000; Erikson and Fossum 2007; Huget 2007)

Obviously these concepts, which derive from existing democratic practices, tend to multiply the complexity of institutional configurations and procedural norms in the EU. They also envisage even more complex forms of representation. If implemented, these concepts might improve the opportunities for checks and balances in the Union, or in other international organizations. However, transparency – a precondition for democratic control by the citizens, or by national legislatures – would certainly get lost.

On the whole, scholars focusing on transnational or post-national forms of democracy do not provide any definitive solutions for the EU's democratic deficit. However, by searching for potentials for democratic decision-making beyond the national realm, they open new perspectives on the problem and provide counter-arguments against the somewhat pessimistic views of state-centred theorists of democracy (Zürn 2000; Lord 2004).

## Nascent forms of post-national democracy in the EU

Concepts for democratizing the EU can only be implemented if they fit into the existing institutional and procedural configuration of the European polity. More precisely, they have to respect the carefully balanced power relations among the institutions and actors of the Union. Keeping this in mind, I explore the potential of the Union's institutional architecture and procedures of decision-making to foster the emergence of post-national forms of democracy. In this section, my point of departure is the assumption that the most widely-cited deficits of the EU actually form the nucleus for the emergence of new democratic practices. In order to underpin this hypothesis empirically, I examine the following three aspects of the EU's institutional structure and modes of operation:

- The relationship between the Commission and the Council as the core centres of power in the system (when using here the term 'Council', I refer to both the Council of Ministers and the European Council).
- The position of the EP and the rationale underlying its performance.
- The inclusion of societal actors in European decision-making.

### The relationship between the Commission and the Council: checks and balances

Theorists of democracy often criticize the relationship between the Commission and the Council because of the vague and unclear separation of powers between them and the lack of sufficient democratic control over them (e.g. Bartolini 2005a; Majone 2009). Obviously, this criticism is based on the models of democracy found in national political systems. The specific institutional features of the EU are rarely taken into consideration. The relationship between the Commission and the Council is intended to be both complementary and interdependent. In this relationship, the Commission holds the exclusive right of initiative, while the Council commands rights of decision-making. Without the initiative of the Commission, the Council cannot decide. Without the Council's decisions, the Commission has no reason to act. Scholars often ascribe a near universal authority to the Council because of its decision-making powers, whereas the Commission is viewed as subordinate to it (e.g. Moravcsik 1998; Pollack 1998). In reality, however, we can see that the Commission has its own power resources at its disposal (e.g. Sandholtz and Stone Sweet 1998; for a critical opinion on the Commission holding too much power, see Majone 2009). In addition to the powers assigned to it through the Treaties, these powers are derived from the Commission's activities, including its skilful handling of the procedures of decision-making; the submission of reasoned proposals; attention to the views and preferences of interest groups, experts, and stakeholders;

the moulding of multi-dimensional and widely acceptable compromises; and, finally, the mobilization of political support by transnational actors. In summary, the Commission pools *procedural powers* that predetermine and, to some extent, constrain the powers of the Council in *decision-making*. In practice, therefore, the relationship between the Commission and the Council is defined by a balance of power, where neither of the two alone can determine the process of integration (see Chapter 13). Unlike nation states, the Union is not governed by a supreme central authority. Instead, with its two core institutions, it displays a dualistic or bicephalous structure (see also Majone 2005).

This bicephalous, or two-headed, structure works by encouraging the careful mediation of complex interests in the process of European integration. The Commission represents the general interest of the Union as a whole, while the Council primarily represents the specific interests of the member states, as they seek to shape the process according to specific national preferences. This implies that the Council has to mediate internally between diverging national interests. From the perspective of post-national democracy, this dual structure, which also includes the respective substructures of both these institutions, allows for the systematic mediation of both functional and territorial interests. That is not to say that the two institutions negotiate the final outcome. Negotiations between the Commission and the Council are clearly precluded because of the complementary relationship between them and the diverging resources at their disposal. Thus, neither of these institutions has been designed to negotiate with others. The Commission cannot negotiate at all because it does not have the power to take binding decisions on legislation and does not act as a party to the process. Its role is limited to that of an initiator and a moderator. The Council, as the supreme institution in the decision-making process, negotiates only internally in search of common ground. To a certain degree, it may negotiate externally with the EP in order to prevent a parliamentary veto. Thus, mediation between functional and territorial interests is a direct result of the institutional configuration that exists at the heart of the EU. In other words, it results from the *separation of powers between legislative initiative and binding decision-making*.

And so, we may conclude that the constraints on both the Commission and the Council to exercise power unilaterally, and the resulting necessity continuously to balance the diverse interests that they represent, act as a mechanism of institutional control (see also Moravcsik 2002: 609–10, 2004). The EU is therefore comparable to a Madisonian system of checks and balances, rather than a federal or unitary nation state.

At this point, we have to bear in mind that the balance of power characterizing the relationship between the Commission and the Council was by no means intended in the original institutional design of the Communities. The bicephalous structure only evolved under the pressure of forces that foster or hamper integration. The roles of the Commission and the Council must be considered as the expression of these forces.

However, the bicephalous structure alone, representing the most fundamental interest constellations underlying European integration, does not suffice to qualify the EU as a democratic system. A number of other interests must still be considered and mediated. One of these interests involves the representation of the citizens of Europe, as they are not adequately represented in the Commission–Council constellation. We therefore must consider whether the European Parliament can address this issue.

## The position of the EP and the rationale underlying its performance

According to conventional wisdom, the EP lacks a number of features that characterize 'normal' legislatures at the national level. And yet, when we make a careful examination of the performance of the EP, we can see that it is precisely these so-called deficits that allow it to achieve major successes. As the Parliament is not obliged to support a government but, rather, enjoys substantial independence, it is free to develop its own political positions and to push for these positions in confrontations with the other institutions of the EU. At the same time, its relative independence from national political parties, combined with comparatively weak ideological ties among the party groups, allows the EP to form opinions without prejudice (Ovey 2002). Party positions, as far as they play a role, are often set aside in face of the need to compromise and to achieve the necessary absolute majority. The same is true of the dividing lines between national delegations. Whenever disagreement persists, elaborate procedures of mediation lead to common ground.

These features of the EP enabled it to develop a specific stance, especially in new issue areas that have arisen through internationalization and globalization, and which play only a minor role in party competition at national level. Thus, the EP has been particularly successful in dealing with issues such as environmental protection, human rights, minority rights, gender equality, public health, new technologies, and data privacy. Building consensus on these issues is not only fostered by the procedural requirements of the ordinary legislative procedure, but also facilitated by the personal attitudes of the MEPs. There is a tendency among MEPs to embrace what might be termed a 'cosmopolitan' orientation, supported by respect for civil liberties and basic human rights. MEPs partly display this general orientation before taking office, but often they are also socialized to such attitudes through their membership in the EP. Thus, in practice, the Parliament often advocates diffuse interests, which are barely organized and which play a rather subordinate role in national political arenas. In its role as advocate of broad, yet diffuse citizen's interests, the EP has developed a specific stance with regard to the Commission – with its emphasis on functional interests, and the Council – with its representation of territorial interests. Consequently, the Commission and the Council strive for technically sound decisions, while the Parliament frequently introduces ethical and moral viewpoints and, thus, demands justification of European decisions (Neyer 2010). Even in its earliest days the Parliament was perceived as the 'conscience' of the EC.

The function of the EP as the Union's conscience can also be seen in its contribution to further enhance the institutional as well as constitutional development of the European polity. Thus, the Parliament has continuously called for democratic reform of the EU and has argued for making the system more responsive to the citizens of Europe. In fact, it was the Parliament that first identified the idea of a 'democratic deficit' and fostered debate on the issue. Consequently, at every IGC, the EP has submitted extensive proposals for the democratization of the Union. These democratic reforms have been mainly viewed as an expansion of its own legislative powers. Although the Council has never fully adopted these proposals, it has also not been able to ignore them completely. The outcome has been a series of remarkable incremental steps that have systematically strengthened the powers of the Parliament (Rittberger 2005). The Draft Constitutional Treaty, which defined co-decision as the 'ordinary method of legislation' in the EU (Art. I-33(1) DCT), represents the culmination of this development. With the adoption of the Lisbon Treaty, this formulation was slightly amended into 'ordinary legislative procedure' (Art. 46 TEU-L), and co-decision now applies to almost every policy area. In areas that do not involve the legislative powers of the EP – for example, foreign policy, or surveillance of member states' economic policy – the Parliament has been able to acquire at least a voice and has thereby increased transparency for the public. Although success is often not immediate, the EP acts as a strong advocate to democratize the EU. In so doing, it tends to represent the common interest of the European electorate.

In its supervisory functions, the EP also tends to act as the representative of the citizens, rather than as a branch of a governmental system, as national legislatures often do. The Parliament does not hesitate to criticize the Commission when it suspects mismanagement. It can even dismiss the Commission as a whole, as it credibly threatened to do in 1999, when certain Commissioners were suspected of misbehaviour. In this case, not even strong pressure exercised by the larger states could sway Parliament from its position. This affair, as well as the EPs supervisory activities in general, qualifies it as an institution that acts to safeguard politically correct procedures and performances. The Parliament is, in short, a protector of 'good governance'. In national arenas, by contrast, a government is only dismissed if the governing parties lose their majority. Thus, a vote of censure is a matter of party politics, rather than of due control over the government's performance. The EP, precisely because it is only weakly divided along party lines, can pursue such general, widely-accepted objectives and, thus, act in the common interest of the EU's citizenry.

The EP is able to perform its functions successfully because it prefers to practise a deliberative style of decision-making. This applies both to decisions made within the EP and to agreements concluded with other institutions in the EU. In terms of its relationship with the Council, the EP's deliberative style emerged with the introduction of the conciliation procedure (see Chapter 5). Deliberations evolved easily with the Commission, where relationships are not formalized, as both sides have taken advantage of cooperative and consensual attitudes. In both institutions, the deliberative style of interaction further evolved in the framework of formal and informal trialogues. Even within the Parliament itself, it is more appropriate to practise a consensual, deliberative style of decision-making than to stand on principles, or take rigid positions. Unsurprisingly, most decisions taken in the EP are marked by broad majorities, representing far greater consensus than an absolute majority, or even the sum of the votes of the 'grand coalition'. Thus, the claims of Hix (2005b) and Hix *et al.* (2007) to polarize the EP further along party political cleavages ignore the achievements of the Parliament through its consensual style of decision-making (for a critique on Hix, see Bartolini 2005b).

Overall, the EP mainly represents the general interests of the European electorate, rather than politically polarized group or party interests. This is reflected in the fact that the MEP's see themselves as 'trustees', representing the 'common good', rather than as delegates of political parties (Katz 1997; see also Ovey 2002). In particular, the EP gives voice to the citizens in those areas that have recently arisen out of the processes of internationalization and globalization, as well as European integration. These issues often play a secondary role in national party politics. The EP thus assumes a political function that is complementary to both national legislatures and to the core institutions of the EU. Such a function was not assigned to it by deliberate design. Rather, it emerged in the framework of the institutional configuration of the EU. Given that the Commission and the Council, respectively, represent functional and territorial interests, the Parliament has only strengthened its profile by strongly advocating for the general interests of the European electorate. In so doing, it has contributed to enhanced institutional mechanisms of control through checks and balances (see also Neyer 2010).

However, the nature of the EP does not make the EU a full-blown democratic system. Further forms of representation and participation are required to improve the Union's legitimacy. This goal may be achieved by including representatives of civil society in the process of decision-making, in order to strengthen forms of associative democracy in the EU.

## Nascent forms of associative democracy

Scholars often criticize interest representation in the EU because of the obvious asymmetries that exist in the access to European decision-making. These asymmetries are seen as a result of inequalities in financial and informational resources. Furthermore, the EU, represented by the Commission, is often criticized for its bias in the selection of representatives for its advisory bodies. These views, again, assume national patterns of interest representation as the norm, and thus neglect the unique nature of the Union. In the European context, complex policy problems resonate in extremely complex constellations of interest representation (Greenwood 2007, 2011). In addition to a wide variety of sectoral and functional interests, divergent national regulatory systems must also be balanced. Providing equitable access to representatives of all these interests is a huge challenge.

Initially, when European integration was primarily concerned with market issues, the European scene was dominated by trade associations (see Chapter 10). With the expansion of EU policy-making to a broader range of issues, representatives of organized civil society played an increasingly active role in EU decision-making (Ruzza 2004; Greenwood 2007, 2011; Kohler-Koch 2007; Freise 2008; Della Porta and Caiani 2009; Kohler-Koch and Quittkat 2011a, 2011b; Liebert and Trenz 2011). The Commission seeks carefully to appoint a variety of stakeholders to its advisory bodies. Even though the Commission is not guided by explicit political criteria such as equal access, it increasingly selects representatives from across a broad spectrum of interests. This has resulted in a remarkably high degree of participation of actors representing general, but often diffuse and weakly organized interests (Greenwood 2007). Representatives of new social movements, in particular – such as environmental groups, women's lobbies, human rights activists or consumer associations – can increasingly voice their positions. Their function in the Commission's advisory circles is less that of political activists than experts (see Chapter 10).

The Commission not only invites this type of group to participate in its advisory bodies, but it also aims to influence both their organizational form and performance for its own purposes (Greenwood 2007; see also Chapter 10). The Commission provides financial backing to these groups to compensate for their lack of resources, but in exchange expects them to carry out studies and provide expertise. Furthermore, it asks representatives of civil society to present positions that have already undergone a phase of mediation among the different groups. This motivates the groups to cooperate more closely with one another without, however, merging to larger associations (Ruzza 2004; Della Porta and Caiani 2009).

Furthermore, the Commission mobilizes a broad spectrum of stakeholders and even individual citizens to voice their views and interests. By launching Green Papers, organizing large scale symposia, citizens' conferences or more narrowly-focused fora, and opening up internet consultations on salient policy issues, the Commission fosters broader public debates with the goal of elaborating creative and innovative solutions for pressing policy problems (Quittkat 2011; Quittkat and Kohler-Koch 2011). The participants range from individual citizens and representatives of organized civil society to classical interest groups, sub-national governments and administrations, as well as other public and private institutions that have a stake in any given issue. Stakeholders are increasingly involved in both the formulation *and* implementation of policy, not only at European level, but also within the member states. In summary, it is clear that the number and variety of non-state actors involved in European deliberations and policy-making has increased exponentially in recent years (Greenwood 2007; Kohler-Koch 2007).

This increase of the role of non-state actors in European deliberations is often interpreted as serving the Commission's interest by mobilizing political support for its policy proposals and lending legitimacy to these proposals (see e.g. Smismans 2003; Ruzza 2004; Mazey and Richardson 2006: 249). However, the significance of this development is even broader than it first seems. According to Andersen and Burns (1996), this indicates a more fundamental transformation of interest representation. These scholars argue that the traditional large associations who represent broad interests can no longer effectively act as legitimate representatives of their membership. Instead, they suggest, smaller groups of stakeholders who directly advocate issue-specific interests and participate in the corresponding networks are much more effective (Andersen and Burns 1996). In short, self-representation of individual interests has increasingly become the norm.

These new forms of interest representation have recently evolved at both the national and the European level. However, the EU is set up in a manner that offers much better conditions than national political systems for these activities to evolve. This is because the large and powerful associations that might act as gatekeepers at European level are either absent or unable to perform such a role. Even aggregated interest associations such as BUSINESSEUROPE and ETUC are small organizations, rather than powerful actors. The business community has also increasingly embarked on forms of self-representation. Thus, many large firms have their own offices in Brussels for lobbying the Commission. Furthermore, this type of development is fostered by the apolitical stance of the Commission, which is more concerned with problem-solving than encouraging political debate and mediating controversial positions (Turner 2008). Finally, the legitimacy deficit of the EU (and not just of the Commission) favours the evolution of these forms of interest representation (Kohler-Koch 2007).

Hence, in the case of civil society representation as well, the democratic deficits of the EU actually work to create space for the emergence of alternative practices. While classical forms of associative democracy, based on a strong and polarized representation of labour and capital, barely evolve at the European level (Streeck and Schmitter 1991), diffuse and weakly organized interests, often taking the form of self-representation, have a greater chance to express their voice (Greenwood 2007).

Since networks of experts and stakeholders, working under the auspices of the Commission, collaborate in preparing decisions, the policy proposals of the Commission ultimately reflect both broad, general interests and more specific, particular interests. When the Commission proposals are submitted to the Parliament and the Council, they are examined by these bodies in view of territorial (Council) as well as public goods aspects (Parliament) and are modified accordingly.

Decision-making in the EU is therefore a two-step procedure. The first step, under the direction of the Commission, focuses on problem-solving. In this phase, a broad spectrum of experts and stakeholders plays a role in elaborating policy proposals, and the Commission often includes some of these claims when it advances its proposals (Friedrich 2008). The second step consists of taking formally binding decisions by the Council and the EP. In this phase, inter-institutional forms of mediation among functional, sectoral, and territorial interests take place. However, at this stage, interest groups and other stakeholders are rarely admitted as interlocutors, and their claims often do not appear in the final Council decision (Friedrich 2008). In view of extremely complex interest constellations in the EU, the two-stage procedure makes it possible to fine-tune solutions for pending policy problems and to scrutinize these under explicit political criteria. This procedure also takes the burden of detailed decisions away from the political level of the EU (Council and Parliament), if a consensus can be achieved at the 'technical' level (Commission) (see for a similar argument, Gehring and Kerler 2008). Finally, the procedure brings a broad spectrum of civil society actors into the decision-making process, and in this way contributes to the increase in the democratic legitimacy of the Union.

However, the procedures for the inclusion of civil society representatives in European decision-making do not fully correspond with democratic norms. Unequal representation remains a major problem, although it may be less of an issue at present than it has been in the past (Kohler-Koch 2007). Furthermore, there is a danger that networks of experts and stakeholders could develop into a sort of 'sub-government' that is not subject to democratic control or public scrutiny (Anderson and Burns 1996; Turner 2008). Because deliberations and decision-making in these circles is anything but transparent, the public is not in a position to understand them, let alone to participate in them.

In summary, we can conclude that nascent, post-national forms of democracy increasingly appear in the EU and help to provide legitimacy to the polity. In particular, they evolve through the framework of those institutional settings and practices of decision-making that reflect the so-called democratic deficits. The institutions of the EU are defined by a particular type of separation of powers, which divides the legislative initiative from legally binding decision-making. This allows for systematic mediation between territorial and functional interests. The powers of binding decision-making are increasingly shared by the Council and the Parliament. The relative independence of the Parliament allows it to function in the *general* interest of the electorate. As a result, the relationship between the Council and the EP reflects a situation where mediation between territorial interests and certain collective interests of the citizens takes place. Together, the Council, the Commission, and the Parliament constitute a system of checks and balances, analogous to Madison's concept of democracy. Interest representation in the EU, increasingly taking the form of self-representation, allows the European institutions, and particularly the Commission, to consider a broad spectrum of positions during the policy proposal formation phase. However, since interest representatives and stakeholders are, by and large, excluded from final decision-making in the Council and the EP, it is more difficult for both well-organized and weakly-organized interests to exercise any real influence over the process. Hence, the separation of legislative initiative and legally binding decision-making is critical to interest mediation. On the one hand, it allows for the expression of a broad spectrum of particular interests while, on the other, it limits undue influence of a few powerful, mostly business interests.

The nascent forms of post-national democracy in the EU described do not constitute a full-blown democratic system. Yet, they should not be overlooked, as they so often are, when scholars assess the democratic legitimacy of the European polity. Whenever proposals to improve the legitimacy of the EU are on the table, one must consider emergent post-national forms of democracy, since legitimacy can only be improved if it builds on existing democratic practices (Neyer 2010).

## Conclusion

This chapter has examined the democratic legitimacy of the European polity. It began with a discussion of the various aspects of the democratic deficit that currently defines the EU and considered the extensive scholarly debates around this deficit. The chapter then presented an overview of proposals to improve the EU's democratic quality, and highlighted the advantages and disadvantages of each of these proposals. The chapter then examined various aspects of the EU's institutional structure and practices of decision-making in order to consider its potential for developing post-national forms of democratic accountability. This analysis indicated that it is precisely the democratic deficits of the EU that form the nucleus for the emergence of new modes of democratic practice. However, we have to keep in mind that these emerging practices do not constitute a full-blown democratic system.

As we recognized in Chapter 11, any assessment of the EU depends largely on the perspective of the observer. In comparison with national political systems, the democratic condition of the EU is clearly deficient. There is no clear separation of legislative and executive powers among the European institutions. The Parliament is directly legitimized by the European electorate, but it does not hold the powers of a fully-developed legislature. The other institutions hold extensive powers but they are, at best, indirectly legitimized. And, finally, EU institutions barely have powers of control over one another.

However, if we consider the EU to be a nascent political order beyond the nation state, we may recognize that certain aspects of its institutional structure are favourable conditions that can contribute to the emergence of alternative democratic practices. First, the bicephalous structure of the European polity and, in particular, the specific *separation of powers between legislative initiative and binding decision-making* allows it simultaneously to represent both the supranational dynamics of integration, and the intergovernmental demand for controlling and adapting this to national needs and preferences. Moreover, it allows for mediation between these two contradicting dynamics and the interests linked to them. Second, the comparatively independent position of the Parliament allows it to advocate certain collective interests of the European electorate and to pursue the common good, while relegating classical party politics and the competition between party groups to the background. Third, new forms of civil society representation, or associative democracy, have emerged in the European context. These forms of self-representation provide opportunities for smaller groups, representing diffuse interests, to access the EU. However, when definitive decisions are taken, stakeholders are largely excluded from the process, and the influence of these groups is minimized. At the same time, the chance of undue influence of powerful interest associations is also minimized. Moreover, it is the separation of powers between legislative initiative and binding decision-making that allows the EU carefully to take societal interests into consideration and to eliminate, at least to a certain extent, undue influence of the most powerful groups. Finally, all decision-making in the EU is characterized to a large extent by deliberative styles which, in turn, can be interpreted as a nascent alternative form of collective will formation.

In summary, when we assess the EU's democratic quality, we find evidence of an emerging post-national political order at the European level. In Chapter 13, we will apply a more theoretically informed lens so as to examine this order more closely.

# Chapter 13

# Conclusion: The Nature of the European Union

This final chapter seeks to infuse the observations of the book with a more theoretical perspective on the European Union as an emergent political order beyond the nation state. Two questions are central to our investigation:

- How can we characterize the Union as a whole?
- How can we explain the dynamics of integration?

These two questions have dominated theoretical debates on European integration since its inception in the 1950s, but without generating any commonly accepted answers (see Chapter 1). Against the background of these questions and the empirical material presented throughout this book, I consider in this chapter, first, the main characteristics of the EU as a political system; and, second, the forces that have propelled integration and the evolution of a new political order beyond the nation state. I thus proceed from an attempt to classify and understand the nature of the Union as a whole to a theoretically informed explanation of the extraordinary dynamics that underlie and propel its evolution.

## The EU as a political system

For some time, scholarly debate concerning the fundamental characteristics of the EU has centred on two opposing points of view. Is it more fruitful to compare the Union to a (federal) state, or to an international organization? More recently, a third point of view has come into vogue. According to this argument, the EU should be seen as a *sui generis* system (see e. g. Jachtenfuchs 1997). While this label does not actually delineate any specific characteristics of the EU, it does offer the chance to undertake a thorough discussion of these characteristics. In the following sections, I shall consider the EU, first, as a negotiated order; in other words, I will define it according to its basic procedural properties. However, there are also structural features that underpin this negotiated order and which reflect key characteristics of the EU. In particular, the multiple inter-relations between the European and the national levels of governance – and, to a lesser extent, the regional level – are central to the European Union. I therefore also characterize the EU as an intertwined system and, consequently, a multi-level system (see, particularly, Chapter 9). Thus, I do not define the Union by using only one label. Instead, in order to grasp the complexity of its political system, I separately consider the core features of its institutional structure, and its procedural norms and practices.

## The Union as a negotiated order

Negotiated orders are characterized by decision-making on the basis of complex negotiations between different institutional actors. The principle of majority rule plays only a marginal role in this system, if any at all. According to Scharpf (1992), negotiated orders allow decisions to be made in the interest of the collective good, even in those cases where the actors involved strive to maximize their own benefit. There is, however, a problem inherent in this mode of decision-making, which Scharpf defines as the 'negotiation dilemma'. On the one hand, the negotiated order requires the actors involved to focus on problem-solving. On the other hand, the solutions worked out in this way may have highly divergent distributive impacts on the negotiating parties and their constituencies (Scharpf 1992: 21). As a consequence, negotiations are characterized by both cooperation and intense bargaining about distributive issues, and these two forces are difficult to reconcile with each other. This may, in turn, result in stalemates, or in decisions that reflect the lowest common denominator solution. In order to circumvent this problem, Scharpf proposes decoupling cooperative decision-making arenas from those where bargaining is dominant (Scharpf 1992; see also Gehring 2005).

The European Union clearly qualifies as a negotiated order. Since the member states participate voluntarily in their quest for integration and seek to derive maximum benefit for themselves, majority decisions would rarely be appropriate. Instead, decisions are generally agreed through negotiations and almost all European decisions have differential distributive impacts for the member states (Scharpf 1999). This applies to both legislative acts *and* the assignment of subsidies. Depending on their economic performance and regulatory systems, or the 'misfit' between European and national regulations, European decisions can lead to a wide variety of benefits and burdens for the member states (Börzel and Risse 2000). If benefits and burdens are to be balanced fairly so as to prevent the creation of permanent winners and losers, then it is essential to undertake extensive and complex bargaining.

While negotiations are part of all aspects of the European polity, they play a different role within each individual institution. The Council and the European Council, which represent the supreme authority in European decision-making, are particularly defined by intensive bargaining. Nevertheless, their decisions must also reflect the collective good; in other words, they must support integration steps, or legislation that benefits all member states. Therefore, decisions of the Council and the European Council are often taken by unanimous vote. The principle of majority rule generally applies only to those issues where there is already a basic consensus, such as issues related to the single market. However, even where a basic consensus exists, the threshold for the qualified majority remains high and the pursuit of the best interests of all members is always an explicit priority (Moravcsik 2002, 2004).

To a certain degree, negotiations are also an integral part of the supranational institutions of the EU. Although the Commission may decide by simple majority, it usually seeks to take consensual decisions, as we have seen in Chapter 6. Thus, Commissioners sometimes engage in deal-making and bargains amongst themselves in order to secure mutual support for their policy proposals. The Parliament also takes majority decisions. However, in those instances where an absolute majority is required in legislation – for example, when the Parliament casts a veto – the threshold for reaching decisions in that body is even higher than it is in the Commission. It is precisely because of this high threshold, which none of the party groups can achieve on its own, that the groups are forced to bargain among themselves in order to forge broad compromises before taking decisions in the plenary. Moreover, the relationships between the institutions of the EU are also characterized by negotiations. Thus, in the framework of the ordinary legislative procedure, legislation is adopted after intense negotiations in formal and informal trialogues. Furthermore, the EP, in particular, has negotiated a number of inter-institutional agreements with the Commission and the Council in order to acquire certain rights above and beyond those stipulated in the Treaties.

Negotiations also form an important part of the substructures of the EU's core institutions. Indeed, these substructures were specifically designed to optimize the procedures of decision-making, and to encourage carefully negotiated solutions to complex policy problems. COREPER, special committees, and working groups, all engage in these negotiations on behalf of the Council. For the Commission, the advisory bodies sometimes function in this way.

Finally, even the executive functions of the EU are largely carried out through negotiations. This applies, for example, to the EU's cohesion policy, in which partnership provides an institutional framework for negotiations between the Commission and national and regional authorities (see Chapters 8 and 9). It also applies to competition policy, which is usually enforced through negotiations with the parties involved. Finally, in its external relations with partner countries and international organizations around the world, the Union frequently relies on negotiations.

At this point, the question arises as to the degree to which blockades in decision-making occur in the negotiated order of the EU (Scharpf 1988, 1999, 2006). To be sure, they do occur, both in minor as well as in fundamental issues. More than once they have brought the whole process of integration to a standstill, as was the case with De Gaulle's politics of the empty chair. However, what is actually more remarkable than the number of blockades is the extent to which blockades do *not* occur. The fact that the EU is so often able to achieve consensus on complex issues in spite of contradicting preferences of the member states is quite impressive. These achievements have only been possible because the EU has developed a variety of strategies and mechanisms to prevent or overcome stalemates in decision-making.

The nature of the Council and the European Council make them most susceptible to impasses. As intergovernmental bodies representing the member states, they often face difficulties in reaching consensus. Fortunately, from the outset the threat of stalemates has been substantially reduced by having created the Commission as an institutional counterweight with extensive legislative and executive powers. The bicephalous structure of the EU – and, in particular, the separation of legislative initiative from binding decision-making – minimizes the 'negotiation dilemma' by partially separating decisions aimed at achieving the collective good from those marked by distributive conflicts. Since the Commission vigorously promotes integration as a means of pursuing the collective interest of all member states, the Council can concentrate on intergovernmental bargains. However, even the bicephalous structure of the Union's core institutions does not preclude stalemates in decision-making. Since not all member states are interested in fostering the rapid progress of integration to the same degree, proposals made by the Commission do not automatically represent the common good.

In the face of this situation, the advisory substructure of the Commission plays a particularly important role in scrutinizing the distributive impacts of legislative proposals on member states. The comitology committees, which assist the Commission in exercising executive tasks, are also greatly concerned with distributive aspects. At the same time, the substructure of the Council, including COREPER and the working groups, is not exclusively focused on hard bargaining. Rather, it too attempts to reconcile competing perspectives. This is facilitated by the fact that the members of these bodies, as Brussels-based envoys, share knowledge and information – and also often their – attitude on European issues (Hayes-Renshaw and Wallace 2006: 318–19). Even certain Council formations, such as the Council responsible for environmental issues, focus on problem-solving rather than hard bargaining. Finally, the European Council and the Foreign Affairs Council, in which unanimity is the rule and bargains prevail, have, since the Lisbon Treaty has come into force, been placed under the guide of permanent presidents. These presidents are expected to act as honest brokers and to facilitate the formation of the collective will, so that both institutions will be better able to pursue common objectives (Tömmel 2010). In summary, although the core institutions of the EU represent either the common good (Commission) or the divergent preferences and interests of the member states (the Council and the European Council), they all have developed additional institutional arrangements and procedural mechanisms to take the interests and preferences of the opposite side into account. These provisions have largely diminished the 'negotiation dilemma'.

In addition to these institutional arrangements, the Union has also developed other strategies to overcome stalemates in negotiations. Thus, it is famous for its ingenious package deals and systematic side-payments, either provided directly – as financial transfers, or indirectly – as special regulations or exceptions from regulations. However, when decisions on major integration steps are on the agenda, these arrangements do not lead to satisfactory solutions. In these cases, differentiated integration is the ultimate answer to the 'negotiation dilemma' (Kölliker 2006; Dyson and Sepos 2010; Leuffen *et al.* 2012). Differentiated integration can be applied in a 'soft' or temporary form – such as opting-out, or as a 'hard', treaty-based measure – which could take the form of 'enhanced cooperation' (Leuffen *et al.* 2012). Sometimes, as in monetary union, there are very specific criteria for participation. Regardless of how it is executed, differentiated integration has proven its effectiveness, although not in decoupling different arenas of decision-making, but in *decoupling divergent categories of member states*. Those states that are interested in certain steps of integration separate themselves from other, more reluctant states. We can assume that those wishing to pursue further integration are less affected by potential distributive impacts; they may even benefit from them. Obviously, however, this is not the case for the latter group. The model of 'enhanced cooperation' was first included in the Treaties when Eastern enlargement was considered. The question of distributive issues resulting from European integration will be of primary importance to the accession states for some time to come.

Overall, as the central institutions of the EU, the Commission, the Council, and the European Council build a complementary structure that, at least to some degree, allows the partners to separate decision-making aimed at problem-solving from bargains over distributive issues. In addition, by creating corresponding institutional substructures that support both sides, the Commission and the Councils have also encouraged a vertical separation of problem-solving and bargaining. These specific institutional arrangements allow each institution to take the preferences and opinions of the other into consideration before final decisions are adopted. Taken together, these arrangements help the Union to reach more complex decisions that are acceptable to all parties. Furthermore, procedural mechanisms – such as package-deals and side-payments – help to achieve compromises in the final round of bargaining. If all these measures fail, various forms of differentiated integration can help to 'square the circle'. In any event, we can conclude that, even though stagnation or stalemate may temporarily occur, for the most part the Union is capable of overcoming the 'negotiation dilemma'.

Thus, the Union clearly demonstrates the characteristics of a 'negotiated order'. Its institutions rely on extensive negotiations at both the legislative and the executive levels. Moreover, the core institutions of the EU are structured in such a way as to separate problem-solving arenas from bargaining arenas. This allows them to overcome the 'negotiation dilemma'. In certain situations, negotiation dilemmas can also be avoided by separating states that favour rapid integration steps from those that are – for good reasons – reluctant in this respect. It is these institutional arrangements and procedural norms that explain how, in spite of the multitude of contradictory interests of its members, the EU can so often achieve comprehensive decisions and propel the project of integration forward.

### The Union as an intertwined system

Intertwined political systems, mostly federal states, are generally characterized by a significant degree of participation by the lower level of government in decisions of the upper level. Since the two levels frequently have highly divergent preferences, these systems run the risk of impasses, a problem Scharpf refers to as the 'joint decision trap' (Scharpf 1985, 1988, 2006). In other words, the two levels are forced to take joint decisions. Yet, since many veto players are involved in such decisions, a final consensus is difficult to achieve. The result is often non-decision, and, more broadly, the inability of such intertwined systems to implement reforms. Hence, they are 'trapped'. According to Scharpf, this risk is present in the EU, particularly in those cases where decisions are taken with unanimity and every member state can cast a veto. It is interesting to note that Scharpf first published this theory in 1985, at a time when the Union was marked by stagnation and the reliance on unanimous voting. He later revised his theory in light of widespread majority voting in the EU (Scharpf 2006).

Although it is not a classical federation, the Union is an intertwined system insofar as the member states, or lower levels of government, play an important role in decision-making at the European level (Tömmel 2011a). Indeed, they not only play a role; together, they constitute the supreme authority in the EU. Hueglin and Fenna (2006: 207–8) therefore speak of 'council governance' in the EU. In this sense, the EU fulfils the main criterion for an intertwined system. However, whereas in a federal state the upper level of governance enjoys a degree of autonomy, the Union is clearly dependent on the member states in major decisions (Majone 2005: 46). It is for this reason that some scholars consider the EU to be mainly an intergovernmental system (e.g. Moravcsik 1998). Other scholars, however, including myself, choose to emphasize a certain degree of discretion, or even autonomy, of the supranational institutions, particularly the Commission (e.g. Sandholtz and Stone Sweet 1998; Beck and Grande 2007; Curtin and Egeberg 2008; Majone 2009).

Even though the Union does not possess a central authority like a government in a federal state that would generally constitute the upper level of an intertwined system, there are still several reasons why we can characterize it as functioning as an intertwined system. First, taken together, the European institutions constitute a fairly independent governance and administrative level that is separate from the member states. Second, the institutions at the European level are intertwined in such a way that they represent European interests shared by all member states, as well as the specific interests of the individual states (Majone 2005: 59). The most important difference between the EU and clearly defined federal states, however, is the fact that the European level is by no means sovereign or superior to the member states. Rather, it complements them (Tömmel 2011a). This has important implications. The inter-relations between the levels, as well as among the institutions and actors that represent these levels are far more complex and intense than in classical federations. The lack of formalized hierarchical relationships among levels, institutions, and actors contributes to multiple interdependencies.

Both its institutional structure and its means of operating contribute to the formation of the Union as a fairly independent level of governance and administration. The Commission, explicitly conceived in the Treaties as an autonomous institution, performs a wide range of legislative and executive tasks. The Court of Justice passes judgements that are binding on national courts, member states, and individual citizens. The Parliament generally pursues a European rationale in its decisions – for this reason, the member states are reluctant to expand its powers. Even the decisions of the Council are ultimately motivated by European objectives and perspectives, in spite of the tough intergovernmental bargains that precede them.

The inter-relation between the European and the national perspective is also clearly reflected in the structure and the functions of the EU (Majone 2005; Beck and Grande 2007). Most notable in this regard is the complementary and simultaneously interdependent relationship between the Commission, on the one hand, and the Council and the

European Council, on the other. This relationship represents most clearly the intertwining between the European and the national perspectives. Similarly, the substructures of both these institutions complement each other. At the same time, they also complement their respective core institution. In short, the Councils' substructure represents not only national preferences and perspectives, but also takes the European perspective into account. Conversely, the substructure of the Commission does not pursue exclusively European objectives, but also takes the national perspective into account. The Court of Justice cooperates closely with national courts; it is thus able to include the national perspective in its judgements (Alter 2001, 2009). As with the Court of Justice, the EP also reflects national perspectives. This hardly seems unusual, since the MEPs are members of national political parties. However, the national perspective is also reflected through the EPs deliberations and in its cooperation with the parliaments of the member states and, in particular, their European affairs committees, represented by the Conference of the Community and European Affairs Committees (COSAC).

The intertwining of the European and the national perspective is not only expressed in the relationships *among* the institutions of the Union, but also *within* each individual institution. A major reason for this lies in the fact that not only the intergovernmental institutions are made up of delegates of the member states, but the supranational institutions are also staffed by personnel based on nationality, with each government nominating its preferred candidate for the office of Commissioner or Judge in the Court. As can be anticipated, an attempt to reduce the number of Commissioners in the College to a more manageable size proved to be impossible, in spite of strong pressures to streamline this body. In particular, smaller member states were not willing to accept even a temporary exclusion from the College of Commissioners (see Chapter 3). Representation in European institutions is essential to them, even if the institutions in question are obliged by Treaty to act exclusively in the European interest.

Dense intertwining between the European and the national government levels also characterizes the wider institutional structure of the EU. The European Central Bank, for example, is closely linked to national central banks through the ESCB (see Chapter 7). The CFSP and aspects of JHA, though organized as separate intergovernmental institutions, also make use of the services of the Commission and the Parliament (see Chapter 7). Moreover, numerous transnational committees, acting under the auspices of the Commission, provide support to both the European and national institutions in their effort to formulate and implement these policies (Tömmel 2011b). Taken together, the EU, more than any federal state, constitutes a system of close interrelations between the European and the national levels in both its institutional structure and its decision-making procedures. As such, the Union effectively represents the divergent interests of these levels and mediates between them.

The process of intertwining is not limited to the European and the national levels alone; the regional level is becoming increasingly involved, too. With the Committee of the Regions, the 'third' level of government has gained a direct and independent voice in the EU, while the European level, represented by the Commission, has gained a voice in the regions – in particular, through the monitoring committees in cohesion policy (see Chapter 9). We can see that intertwining increasingly spans multiple arenas of decision-making at different levels of governance.

At this point, let us return to Scharpf's thesis of a 'joint decision trap' in intertwined systems. Obviously, in the Union there are frequent occasions on which a stalemate in deliberations might arise, but this happens less frequently than one might expect. Veto positions, although omnipresent, are not detrimental to decision-making. The dense intertwining among the various levels allows the institutions to mediate between conflicting interests, to decouple divergent arenas of decision-making, to compensate veto players with package deals and side-payments, or to develop convergent views on certain policy issues. These mechanisms seem to have worked quite effectively, so that the 'joint decision trap' closed far less often than Scharpf expected when he first published his seminal article on this issue (Scharpf 1985, 1988; see also Scharpf 1999, 2006, for a reconsideration of the issue).

Overall, we can conclude that the EU is an intertwined system *par excellence*. Close inter-relations among the three levels of government characterize the European polity. The EU's core institutions as well as their substructures represent both the national and the European level in decision-making. In addition, each European institution incorporates the national perspective into its procedures and performance. Yet, the European level as a whole remains relatively independent, although not sovereign. Taken together, it is the multiple inter-relations of the European polity that sustain the EU as a negotiated order and which facilitate decision-making, rather than block it.

## The Union as a multi-level system

If we characterize the Union as a negotiated order and an intertwined system, we implicitly also define it as a multi-level system. Dealing with this dimension of the EU might seem superfluous, but I explicitly focus on it here because this is the systemic dimension most often mentioned in the literature (see, e.g., Hooghe and Marks 2001; Benz 2004; Neyer 2012). Moreover, the term 'multi-level' refers to more than just the inter-relation between levels. Because the nature of the relationship may vary widely, it is of major concern to us here. The crucial question in my analysis therefore centres upon the nature of the systemic nexus that has emerged amongst the levels of the EU, and the mechanisms that produce and reproduce it.

The multi-level structure of the EU results from the fact that, to a large extent, the state level determines outcomes at the European level. Yet, the multi-level structure is also the result of the impacts of European decisions on the member states. It is these impacts that constitute a systemic nexus among the levels (see Chapter 9). Thus, European legislation, whether in the form of directly binding regulations or directives requiring transposition into national legislation, has extensive impact at the 'lower' levels. Besides their direct effects, they may spark regulatory adaptations in a wide range of issue areas in the member states. Furthermore, since EU legislation primarily focuses on closing regulatory gaps, or searching for innovative solutions beyond those practised by the member states, the European and national regulations evolve as complementary in substantive terms. Yet, ultimately, European regulations significantly constrain the autonomy of the member states (Scharpf 1999, 2006) and, at the same time, consolidate the systemic nexus.

Furthermore, the multi-level system of the EU is both constituted and consolidated through the process of policy implementation. Negotiations among the levels of government increasingly limit the ability of the member states to act independently (see Chapter 8). In competition policy, for example, negotiations between the Commission and national governments ensure compliance with European competition rules. Negotiations also serve to build compromises on the design and the implementation of policy in the area of cohesion policy. In both cases, negotiations compensate for the absence of clear hierarchical relationships between the levels. Furthermore, the implementation of European policies in the member states has led to the inclusion of the 'third' level of government in the multi-level structure, although this was not the expressed desire of national governments. As a consequence, subnational units were able to gain a certain degree of autonomy within national political systems (Hooghe and Marks 2001; Keating and Hooghe 2006). Even the coordinative procedures of the OMC, which are becoming progressively more common in European governance, can contribute to building a systemic nexus, by virtue of their ability to induce national and regional authorities to observe European objectives and adapt to transnational competitive mechanisms (see Chapter 8).

In the multi-level system of the EU, the interactions between the government levels are, to a great extent, framed by policy networks. Kohler-Koch (1999) therefore considers the EU to be a system of network governance. However, policy networks, despite being omnipresent in European governance, are neither the defining criterion of EU governance, nor the Union as a political system. They serve primarily as an institutional setting for multi-level interactions, where clearly-defined hierarchical relationships are lacking (Börzel and Heard-Lauréote 2009). Nevertheless, hierarchies play an indirect role in these networks, as the actors – and, lately, the levels involved – command divergent power resources.

In summary, we can see that the European polity clearly constitutes a multi-level system. The multi-level structure not only incorporates the European and the national government levels, but lately encompasses the regional level, too. Remarkably, this development holds true for all regions of the Union, independent of the organization of the state as either federal or unitary. Except in the case of legislation, the systemic nexus among the levels is not based on clear hierarchical relationships. Instead, it reflects indirect mechanisms of political steering: negotiations, voluntary cooperation, competitive arrangements (see Chapter 8). The levels are loosely coupled through policy networks that also display a non-hierarchical structure. The hierarchies that emanate from the diverging power resources of the actors and government levels involved nevertheless play a role, though primarily on a case-by-case basis.

## The structure of the Union as a whole

After having examined three dimensions of the European polity, we are left with the task of characterizing the Union as a whole. In other words, we must identify the structural core that underlies the negotiated order, the intertwined system, and the multi-level system. These three characteristics of the Union are all typical elements of federal states, which might suggest that the Union could also be considered a federal system. Indeed, some scholars conceptualize the EU as a federation (Burgess 2000, 2006; Kelemen 2003; Harbo 2005; Hueglin and Fenna 2006; Nicolaïdis 2006). However, even for these scholars it is evident that the EU lacks certain core characteristics of federal states (Tömmel 2011a). First, the European level is not sovereign; it lacks the ability to decide on the scope of its own powers. Second, the 'lower' levels, represented by the member states, are far more autonomous than the lower levels in federal states. In fact, the member states are sovereign, even though their sovereignty is constrained to a certain extent by European law. Third, the cooperation of the member states in the framework of the EU is less binding than it would normally be in a federal system. That is why the term '*sui generis*' is most appropriate for the EU (Jachtenfuchs 1997). The Union clearly constitutes a new type of political order. And yet, such a classification obfuscates comparisons with other forms of political order, as it blurs the fact that the Union evolved as an amalgam of systemic elements pertaining to well-known political orders (Olsen 2010).

Against this background, I conceptualize the Union as a political system based on a *unique* combination of two principles that arise out of very different political orders: intergovernmentalism and supranationalism. Obviously, this concept is not new, but was used, or implicitly assumed, by many scholars (e.g. Weiler 1981; Bartolini 2005a; Beck and Grande 2007; Neyer 2012).These principles are most clearly expressed in the institutional configuration of the Commission in relation to the Council and the European Council, which together form the core of the dualistic or bicephalous structure of the Union. It is this two-headed structure that constitutes the key characteristic of the EU and clearly distinguishes it from both international organizations and (federal) states. Moreover, it is this same two-headed structure that supports the EU's evolution as a negotiated order, an intertwined system, and a multi-level system. However, since many authors regard either one or the other side of this bicephalous structure as dominant, they interpret the EU as similar to either an international organization, or a (federal) state.

Thus, in essence, the EU is based on two interwoven principles. The interplay between these principles constitutes the dynamism that fosters the evolution of the political system and provides it with stability. The combination of these two principles constitutes a new type of political order. This order can be considered supranational, in that its decisions and laws are, in many cases, binding on the member states. At the same time, this order is directed by the member states and, thus, subject to the principle of intergovernmental cooperation. It is this antagonistic combination of well-known principles of political order that constitutes the dualistic structure of the political system. In the next section, I analyze the dynamics inherent in this system that result in a rapid evolution and differentiation of the EU's institutional structure.

## The dynamics of the EU's evolution

The previous section highlighted the EU as a bicephalous system, marked by the interaction between two contradictory principles: intergovernmentalism, representing the national perspective; and supranationalism, representing the European perspective (see, instead of many others, Beck and Grande 2007). This section explores the significance of this dualistic structure in the evolution of the Union as a political system. I focus mainly on the dynamics that advance the process of European integration and its institutional diversification.

I begin by reiterating some of the conclusions from the earlier analysis:

1.  The EU is characterized by the combination of two contradictory principles, which is institutionally expressed in the dualistic structure of the system. The Commission and the Councils – that is, the Council of Ministers and the European Council – as two interdependent institutions constitute the core of this dualistic structure. Since the Commission and the Councils are the most powerful institutions in the European polity, they form the heads of this structure.

To reflect this power constellation, I use the term 'two-headed' or 'bicephalous' system (see Chapter 1). All the other institutions gravitate towards these two centres of power.

2. The interdependence between these two poles of power creates a specific pattern of interaction between them. The respective institutional actors engage in a permanent struggle for dominance in shaping the process of integration.

3. Since the Commission and the Councils have divergent power resources at their disposal, the struggle for dominance to shape the form that integration takes results in a two-tracked process of building and differentiating the EU's institutional structure. The Commission, using its *procedural powers* in order to expand its influence, pushes institution-building and networking mainly at the informal level. The Council and the European Council, by contrast, having the *powers of decision-making* in legislation and Treaty revisions at their disposal, formally modify existing institutions, or even create new ones in order to enhance their own position of power, and constrain the power and influence of the Commission.

4. The combination of the two interwoven principles in the EU does not indicate a transitory stage in the Union's development; neither is it evidence of an incomplete polity. It is to be viewed as the main characteristic of the Union.

I now go on to discuss the bicephalous structure of the EU in greater detail, and explain the interaction between the core institutions and the processes of system-building that ensues. This will substantiate why the bicephalous structure of the EU is not a transient phenomenon but, rather, a core characteristic of the European polity. In this way, I offer a theoretical approach that attempts to explain the dynamics of the Union's evolution as a highly-differentiated, bicephalous political system.

## The bicephalous nature of the Union

Obviously, a bicephalous systemic structure implies the presence of two more or less equally powerful institutions that act as the 'heads' of the system. In the case of the EU, these institutions complement one another in their powers and functions. As noted previously, the powers of decision-making, both in primary and secondary law-making (i.e. Treaty revisions and legislation), are in the hands of the Council and the European Council, even though the former shares legislative powers with the EP. For its part, the Commission has an almost exclusive right of initiative in legislation and extensive executive powers. These two spheres of power and influence are separate, yet intertwined, so that the corresponding institutions are mutually dependent in their activities. In order to take decisions, the Council and the European Council are dependent on the Commission's proposals; in other words, they rely on the Commission to act as the motor of integration. This is mainly the case where the Council of Ministers seeks to act in the legislative procedure. The European Council is not dependent on Commission proposals, but acts autonomously. However, in practice, it often takes advantage of such proposals and of the Commission's executive and supervisory functions. The internal fragmentation inherent in the Council and the European Council prevents them from taking on the role as motor of integration themselves. For the same reason, they are dependent on the Commission's executive actions, particularly the Commission's ability to monitor and enforce compliance with European decisions and regulations with a neutral authority. Basically, the Council and the European Council face problems of collective action (Tallberg 2006) and have therefore delegated these functions to the Commission (Majone 2009). For its part, the Commission depends on the Council and the European Council to take all major and minor decisions, and to negotiate the necessary compromises. In addition, the Commission needs their backing for the implementation and enforcement of European decisions and regulations in the member states.

In summary, the Commission performs tasks that reflect the collective will of the Council and the European Council. However, these must be endorsed by explicit decisions of the Councils. In this way the complementary division of powers between the two heads of the bicephalous structure ensures that the project of integration will advance, even when there are clear rifts between the member states. The Commission and the Council as well as the European Council are fairly autonomous, yet interdependent institutions. They constitute two centres of power that are opposed but, at the same time, complement each other. All of the other European institutions gravitate towards one or the other of these centres of power.

There are, however, some objections to this characterization of the EU. One objection would maintain that the Union does not have a bicephalous structure but, rather, a hierarchical structure that is headed by the Council and, particularly, the European Council. Such views underlie many conventional textbooks (e.g. Bache *et al.* 2011), as well as theories on integration based primarily on intergovernmentalism (e.g. Moravcsik 1998). According to this position, the Council and the European Council together constitute the decisive centre of power, while the Commission holds only delegated powers and, consequently, is clearly subordinated to it. The Commission, in pursuit of its own institutional self-interest, may assume a more independent stance in some situations but, in spite of that, the Council and the European Council could, according to this position, easily contain such tendencies, or even revoke the Commission's powers.

Indeed, when we consider the EU only in terms of the distribution of formal powers, these views are quite plausible. However, when we take into account the *de facto* power of the Commission, which often manifests behind the scenes, it becomes harder to justify this viewpoint. After all, even though the powers of the Commission were initially delegated by the member states, they have evolved over the years into a fairly independent resource. As many empirical studies and theoretical explanations have shown, the Commission could even use its powers to limit the declared interests of the member states (see Chapter 1). Furthermore, any attempt to revoke the powers of the Commission would surely come with the price of undermining the entire system.

One might also argue that the Commission does, indeed, possess significant powers, but it is the Council and the European Council that delegate these powers to it. In this case, the relationship between the Commission and the Councils can be conceptualized according to principal–agent theory (see Chapter 1 and e.g. Pollack 1996; Majone 2005). The Council and the European Council, as the principals, define the basic objectives; the Commission is then obliged to pursue them. The Commission, as the agent, may pursue these objectives independently from divergent interests among the members of the Council, or the European Council. However, as with all relatively independent agents, the Commission may also pursue its own institutional self-interest and, thus, enhance its independence. It can even deviate from the objectives set by the Council or the European Council – as it may, for example, under pressure from strong interest groups (processes referred to in the literature as 'shirking' and 'capturing'). This understanding of the relationship between the central institutions of the EU, it would seem, reinforces the Councils' strong position of power in relation to the Commission. At the same time, it concedes a certain degree of independence to the Commission. However, it tends to disregard the interplay between the two institutions. European objectives are defined and policy is shaped only through this interplay. Furthermore, this perspective disregards the fact that the Commission is a political institution, even though it exercises politics in a somewhat unconventional manner. Nonetheless, the members of the Commission are not experts but, rather, broadly-qualified and experienced politicians. In contrast, in principal–agent relationships the agents are often explicitly established as apolitical organizations staffed by experts. Such independent agencies are also vested with limited and clearly-defined terms of reference, whereas the Commission, as the motor of integration, acts under an open mandate to take the initiative in all European affairs. Furthermore, the Commission's *raison d'être* is not primarily to increase its own independence, as it already enjoys a fairly autonomous position. Instead, its role is, insofar as it can, to shape the decisions of the Councils in such a way as to advance the cause of European integration. This is the way the Commission enhances its own position of power.

A third argument against the characterization of the Union as a bicephalous structure might claim that the system rests not on two, but on three centres of power, with the Parliament forming the third. Scholars could even claim that it rests on four different institutions, if they also take the Court of Justice into consideration. These arguments take the formal institutional configuration of the EU as the exclusive criterion for defining its structure, and disregard the actions of the institutions and the contradictory forces underlying them. The contradictory forces arise, on the one hand, out of the collective interests of the EU as a whole, and, on the other, out of divergent national interests. In other words, there are two – not three or four – sets of conflicting interests that underpin and dominate integration. We have seen that the Parliament primarily represents the common interests of the European electorate. It does so through its actions and its institutional position. This implies that it primarily acts in a European, or supranational, manner; this, in turn, implies that, in fact, it supports the principles underlying the Commission's activities. That does not dispute the fact that the Parliament, as with all European institutions, also takes national perspectives into account. Furthermore, even though the Parliament actually shares legislative powers with the Council, it lacks powers that the Commission – and, especially, the Council and the European Council – have at their disposal. In particular, the Parliament cannot engage in institution-building and, thus, cannot shape the nature of the European polity. The Parliament does, to a degree, act to balance the Commission and the Council, but it is not a third, independent player that takes a completely different role. A similar argument applies to the role of the Court of Justice in the EU. It is true the Court is an important player in the Union and its judgements have had major impact on European integration. Thus, the Court has often acted to support the supranational principle. In concrete terms, the judgements of the Court may confirm the Commission's position and, as such, we can say that the Court often acts in support of the Commission. However, as an independent institution, dedicated to the review of EU decisions and legislative acts, the Court can only interpret existing law. It does not intentionally take steps to foster integration, and not at all in building and shaping the institutional structure of the EU.

At this point, it is important to emphasize that the concept of the EU as a bicephalous system is based on an understanding of the division of powers between the Commission and the Councils, and, perhaps even more importantly, on the specific interdependent interactions between them. All other institutions function *within* this contradictory relationship. Thus, the Parliament and the Court of Justice often take a position that corresponds to that of the Commission, either deliberately, or, as a matter of fact, even unintentionally. In some cases, parliamentary decisions or judgements of the Court can be more in line with the preferences of the Council or the European Council. European institutions generally do not align themselves with one specific side in the bicephalous structure of the EU; rather, they mainly act in favour of one of the two basic interests and principles that underlie this structure. Nevertheless, every European institution is permeated by both principles of integration; and every institution interacts with the others so as to mediate between these two principles. In the case of the Commission and the Council, as well as the European Council, the mediation between the two principles occurs largely internally, as their institutional substructures embody the opposite principle. This enhances the position of both sides in the struggle for dominance in shaping European integration. In the following section, we take a closer look at the dynamics that result from the interactions between these institutions.

## The interaction between the Commission and the Council

As we have seen, the relationship between the Commission, on the one hand, and the Council and the European Council, on the other, is at once antagonistic and interdependent. Both sides of the bicephalous structure struggle for power and dominance in shaping European integration. This, however, does not mean that the performance of these institutions is defined by concrete struggles. On the contrary, the relationship between the Commission and the Council or European Council is marked by a cooperative and consensual spirit. Furthermore, the Commission's relationship with the European Council is of a more of indirect nature. It is the strategies of both sides of the bicephalous structure that focus on achieving a *de facto* dominant position. Therefore, I characterize their *structural* relationship as marked by struggles.

As I have indicated, the Commission and the Councils have diverse power resources at their disposal. The Councils command the *powers of binding-decision-making*. Thus, the Council of Ministers determines European regulation and legislation. In this way, it directs and oversees the substance of integration. The power of the European Council is even more important, as it can decide on the institutional and constitutional order of the Union as a whole and, as a result, it can advance or hinder integration and system-building. Nonetheless, the powers of both the Council and the European Council are not absolute. They are restricted through the internal fragmentation that derives from the diverse interests of the member states.

The Commission, in contrast, does not appear to hold extensive powers, as it only controls powers that have been delegated to it, such as the right of initiative and some executive functions. In order to make these powers effective, it relies on the decisions and actions of the member states in the Council or European Council. However, the Commission has ensured itself an influential voice in European decision-making and national level implementation by developing and optimizing certain procedures. Hence, the Commission commands *procedural power* to fulfil its role as the motor of integration and the guardian of the Treaties.

Thus, both parts of the bicephalous structure rely on different power resources that do not counter but, rather, complement one another. Through these powers, both parts propel the institutional evolution of the EU. The Commission, by skilfully shaping procedural norms, attempts to influence and constrain the scope of Council or European Council decisions as much as possible. The Councils, in turn, respond to the Commission's pressures by improving their own decision-making procedures. The Commission also reacts by refining its procedural methods – in particular, by drawing in an increased number of external actors to the policy formulation and implementation processes. Even though these actors might have initially been guided by national perspectives, they often adopt more European perspectives. With the support of such actors, the Commission has succeeded in increasing the pressure on the Council or European Council to take decisions that are more in line with European objectives. The Councils, for their part, react to this situation by improving and differentiating the intergovernmental procedures of decision-making and by cementing them in formalized institutional arrangements (Tömmel 2010).

By modifying and improving their own decision-making procedures in relation to one another, the two parts have built and strengthened the institutional structure of the EU and the way it operates. A brief look at the history of European integration confirms this (see Chapter 2 and 3). Over time, the Commission has succeeded in gradually shaping decision-making and interaction among the European institutions, including the Parliament, the Court, and the advisory bodies. In addition, it has successfully recruited a multitude of advisors to assist in the formulation of policy. Commission advisors are comprised of delegates from national and regional governments and administrations, as well as independent experts and representatives of economic and societal interests. This latter group includes business associations, organized along national, sectoral, or European lines, as well as members of individual firms, trade unions and representatives of organized civil society, and other interested individuals. This broad spectrum of stakeholders that participate in the preparation of decisions and the formulation of policies is organized through policy networks. Since these networks also provide vertical links between the various levels of government, the Commission has been able to create a systemic nexus between these levels and thereby advance the evolution of the EU as a multi-level system and a multi-actor system (see Chapters 9 and 10). Taken together, the Commission has sought to achieve European goals by optimizing the decision-making process and strengthening its own power position in relation to the Council and European Council. In so doing, it has pushed forward the process of system-building, albeit primarily through establishing mainly informal or weakly-formalized institutional structures.

In contrast to the Commission, the Council and, particularly, the European Council have deliberately enhanced the intergovernmental procedures and formally established new institutions in order to construct the Union's political system. This development had already begun in the 1960s with the strengthening of unanimous voting through the Luxembourg Compromise and with the establishment of COREPER. In the 1970s and 1980s, national governments created the European Council and, later, granted it official status in the Treaties. The late 1980s were also marked by the formal establishment of the comitology committees, whose functions are to oversee and restrict the executive tasks of the Commission (see Chapter 5). The 1990s saw the creation of the second and third pillars as intergovernmental annexes to the European house. At the same time, a series of agencies was established, independent of both the Commission and the Councils. The overall development of intergovernmental institution-building has culminated with the Lisbon Treaty, which established the European Council as an official and formal institution of the EU, and created permanent presidencies for the European Council, as well as the Foreign Affairs Council. These most recent institutional innovations highlight the member states' explicit political will to take the lead in the EU (Tömmel 2010).

In addition to the efforts to shape the formal institutional structure of the EU, the European Council also re-introduced and broadened the reach of qualified majority voting. At the same time, it expanded the legislative rights of the EP. This development is reflected in the Lisbon Treaty, which introduced a completely new voting system (see Chapters 3 and 4). As a result of these modifications, the threshold for qualified majority in the Council is comparatively low. It will actually be only a little more than an absolute majority. Many scholars view the trend to push back unanimous voting and repeatedly to lower the threshold for qualified majority voting as enhancing supranationalism in the EU. In contrast, I see it mainly as a calculated step towards facilitating decision-making in the Council, as it limits the veto power of individual, and even groups of, member states (Tömmel 2010). This actually strengthens the relative weight of the intergovernmental part of the bicephalous structure. In a similar manner, differentiated integration that acts to exclude Euro-sceptic states from certain steps towards full integration serves to constrain veto players. This also strengthens the intergovernmental side of the system. The four most important projects of differentiated integration – the Schengen agreement, the Social Protocol of the Maastricht Treaty, EMU and the Treaty stipulations on 'enhanced cooperation' – have not led to a 'Europe of different speeds'. Rather, they have increased the number of states participating to a level far greater than initially expected. This is especially evident in the case of EMU.

None of these institutional innovations would have been necessary, if the Councils had been in command of a *de facto* supreme authority in the EU, and if they had been in the position to fully exploit their formal powers, independent of internal differences. Since this has not been the case, these steps must be viewed as attempts to improve the Councils' capacity to act and to exercise leadership in the EU (Tömmel 2010). At the same time, these institutional innovations serve to restrict the creeping expansion of the powers of the Commission, exercised mainly through procedural means (Pollack 1994, 2000). Even though these procedural powers are not obvious, they do have a strong impact on the process of integration.

In summary, we can state that the Commission and the Council and European Council have become entangled in a contentious and contra-dictory relationship, as they attempt to fulfil their respective functions within the system and to pursue their institutional interests. By attempting to dominate their counterpart (the Council and European Council), or at least to maintain the balance of power between the two institutions (the Commission), both sides contribute to the evolution of the institutional structure of the EU. The Commission frames the procedures to formulate and implement policy, and thus creates a multitude of informal or weakly-organized networks for interaction. The Council and particularly the European Council enhance the capacities of intergovernmental deci-sion-making by relying on formal, treaty-based regulations. This takes place in two ways. First, it happens by creating additional institutional structures. In addition, it arises through the amendment of the proce-dures for decision-making to constrain veto players in intergovernmental decisions. Both these strategies are clearly reflected in the most recent constitutional reform of the EU, the Lisbon Treaty.

The Commission and the Councils, through their actions and inter-play, give shape to the EU as a negotiated order, an intertwined system, and a multi-level system. These dimensions of the European polity are solidified by diversifying the procedures of decision-making within and between institutions, by creating extensive substructures for the core institutions, and by including an ever-growing number of external actors in European affairs. Once again, the Commission supports this develop-ment by creating a myriad of informal institutions, whereas the Council and the European Council establish formal institutional structures and rules. These forms of institution-building serve to mediate more effec-tively between European and national perspectives in the process of integration. The Commission fosters the diffusion of the European perspective throughout the member states as well as down to the regional and local level, and to non-state actors at all levels. The Council and the

European Council, for their part, tend to pool national perspectives in an increasing number of institutions and arenas at European level.

In short, we can conclude that the Commission and the Councils, even though their relationship is marked by friction, act in a complementary way to build the European polity. This explains why the relative balance of power between them has always been maintained. Even though national governments have acted through the European Council to enhance their own position of power with Treaty amendments, they have never attempted to alter or to weaken the formal position of the Commission. Instead, they have only ever confronted the Commission with a more diversified intergovernmental structure for formal decision-making. This is proof that, if European integration is to proceed without major obstacles, the Union is in need of two relatively autonomous, yet interdependent, centres of power.

## Theoretical explanations

In order to explain the dynamics of the evolution of the EU in theoretical terms, we can turn our attention to functional arguments. Every member state has basically two different and partly contradictory interests in European integration. First, they hold an interest in the rapid progression of integration and, second, they have an interest in shaping integration so that it is compatible with, or even beneficial to, their own economic, political, and societal system. It is thus necessary to mediate between these interests. The bicephalous institutional structure of the Union provides the framework for this mediation. More precisely, this mediation is rendered effective through the institutional setting that separates those decisions that are directed at furthering the process of integration (i.e. those that define the common good) from those that reflect specific interests and preferences of the member states seeking to maximize utility (i.e. those marked by bargains among the member states) (Scharpf 1992). The functionalist line of reasoning, however, substantiates only the basic bicephalous structure of the Union and not the dynamics of system-building. It does not specify the interaction between the institutions of the EU and its outcomes: that is, the manifold compromises around the shape of integration and the ensuing institutional diversification of the polity. For an explanation of these processes, I refer to the concept of actor-centred institutionalism put forth by Mayntz and Scharpf (1995; see also March and Olsen 1989; Olsen 2010). In this view, actors have a certain degree of freedom to act, even though they are constrained in their activities by institutional conditions and arrangements.

In using this concept, I assume that both sides, the Commission as well as the Council and the European Council, fulfil the functions assigned to them by the Treaties and pursue strategies that will enable them to carry out their functions effectively. They are, however, constrained by the institutional setting in which they operate, as well as by the activities and actions of their counterparts. For this reason, the elaborate proposals that the Commission defines often fail to be adopted because decision-making is stalled in the Council or European Council. The outcome may be non-decision, or a dilution of the proposals put forth by the Commission. On the flipside of the coin, the Councils are regularly presented with extremely complex and far-reaching proposals towards integration, which often exceed by far what they are willing to implement. It may even be hard to assess the consequences of these proposals for the political systems or certain constituencies of the member states. While these situations do not represent constraints in the narrow sense of the word, they put pressure on the Council and the European Council to take decisions. Extensive Commission proposals, however, might exacerbate the divergences among the member states. Consequently, the ability of the Council and the European Council to take binding decisions is further constrained.

In its attempts to overcome the constraints it faces, the Commission adapts its proposals to bring them in line with the views of the delegates of the member states and stakeholders. This has the advantage of allowing the Commission to perfect its own modes of decision-making and, ultimately, to build transnational coalitions that share its interest in advancing the process of integration (Tömmel 2011b; see also Haas 1958). A similar impact may also be felt through the Commission's efforts to perfect policy implementation in the member states by negotiations and cooperation with national and regional administrations and non-state actors. Under the guidance of the Commission, loosely organized networks allow it to transcend, at least to some degree, the institutional constraints inherent in its limited formal powers.

The Council and the European Council function in different ways in order to cope with the constraints arising, on the one hand, from the activities of the Commission and, on the other, from their own internal fragmentation. They do so by diversifying and refining the procedures of decision-making, both horizontally and vertically, so as to enhance their function as a filter. They achieve this goal at the highest political level (i.e. the European Council), as well as at the level of experts. They make use of legislation and Treaty revisions to accomplish this goal. The Council and the European Council establish formalized procedures and corresponding institutions as a counterweight to the Commission's 'creeping competences' (Pollack 1994, 2000) and its informal acquisition of power. In this way, the Councils create highly-differentiated opportunities for the articulation and representation of the interests of the member states and their constituencies. At the same time, however, they constrain veto positions in their own ranks in order to improve their decision-making capacities and their ability to constrain Commission activism. Thus, the outcomes of European decision-making are determined by the interaction between the Commission and the Council, as well as the European Council, and also between the actors and institutions mobilized by both sides. Insofar as European decisions are determined by the balance of power between these interacting forces, so too are the degree, the substance and, above all, the institutional configuration of European integration. The interaction between the core institutions of the EU and their substructures evolves within the framework of the constraints set by the bicephalous configuration of the EU. However, it also evolves as a consequence of deliberate choices and activities of the actors involved.

## Conclusion

In this concluding chapter, we have looked at the EU as an emerging political order that evolves beyond the nation state. We first classified the European polity according to its institutional structure and its practices of decision-making. This led us to identify the European Union as a negotiated order, an intertwined system, and a multi-level system. These three dimensions of the European polity are highly interdependent. Together, they constitute a system that displays similarities with a federation. Yet, we do not consider the EU to be a classical federation, since the 'upper' level lacks sovereignty while the 'lower' level – the member states – continue to be sovereign, even though their sovereignty is, to a certain extent, constrained by European law. We therefore characterize the European polity as a dualistic or bicephalous system.

The bicephalous structure of the EU represents two systemic principles – intergovernmentalism and supranationalism – which underlie the European polity. Although, as we have seen above, both these principles permeate the activities of all European institutions, either one or the other clearly dominates the core institutions. Thus, we can identify the Commission, the Court, and the Parliament with the supranational principle, while the Council and the European Council clearly represent the intergovernmental principle. The essential function of the EU as a political system is to mediate between these principles, which either represents the general interest in promoting European integration, or the particular interests of the member states in adapting this process to their specific needs and preferences. Accordingly, the core institutions and, particularly, the Commission and the Councils are involved in a dynamic interaction that tends to mediate between these principles. Thus, the systemic structure of the EU represents both common or transnational interests that ultimately foster the supranational dimension of the EU, and a wide variety of national interests that tend to shape integration in a way that it is compatible with the existing economic, political, and societal systems of the member states. The interplay between the institutions and actors representing these interests, in turn, supports the evolution of both formal and informal institutional structures and procedural norms in the EU, and results in a two-tracked process of system-building. In other words, it reproduces and increasingly diversifies the dualistic or bicephalous structure of the EU.

## Looking forward: external challenges and internal frictions

This final part of the book provides a brief outlook on the future of the EU, and how the system might cope with the manifold frictions and challenges that confront it. I start with a brief overview of the most recent phase of integration, to give a sense of the direction the process will take in the near future.

At the beginning of the twenty-first century, a heated debate emerged around the *'finalité européenne'*; that is, the final objective of European integration and the final shape of the Union as a political system. The debate was opened by the then German Minister of Foreign Affairs, Joschka Fischer. In a speech to students at the famous Humboldt University in Berlin, he clearly defined the *'finalité'* as the creation of a European federation (Fischer 2000). Unsurprisingly, he avoided the question as to whether the European Council or the Commission should be transformed into a federal government. In any case, he was clear on the issue of democratizing the EU. In his view, the Council of Ministers and the EP should be transformed so as to constitute a genuine two-chamber system.

It was not long before reactions to these proposals could be heard from France. In a speech before the German Bundestag, French President Chirac clearly rejected the federal option (Chirac 2000). His tone was polite but, on the issue, he was definite. Instead of a federation, he proposed a moderate form of De Gaulle's *'Europe des patries'* (Europe of the fatherlands). More critical voices were heard from the UK, even though the government did not express an official opinion. From start to finish, this debate again highlighted the inevitable stalemate that follows the question of the *'finalité européenne'*. After more than 60 years of progress towards integration, the views and visions of the member states on what the EU might be or might become, continue to diverge as widely as ever (Hurrelmann 2005: 202–32). Intergovernmentalism and (federal) supranationalism appear to be irreconcilable options.

This is not surprising since the EU, as we have seen, rests on a unique combination of both of these principles. This combination, first established on the basis of an initial compromise between the member states, was successively reproduced through gradual steps towards reform. At every step, these reforms were backed by a carefully balanced compromise among the member states. However, the basic consensus thus achieved is not sufficient to decide on a 'grand design' that would give shape to the EU, based on the preferences of one side or the other. On the contrary, efforts in this direction would deeply split the Union and endanger the balance of power on which it currently rests. It is therefore not surprising that the debate on the *'finalité européenne'* disappeared as suddenly as it had emerged. Instead, political leaders turned their attention to the resolution of the most pressing problems of the day.

These problems have dominated the European agenda for decades, and have been subsumed under two 'grand' objectives: widening the EU and deepening integration. Most recently, the resolution of the international financial and sovereign debt crisis has emerged and dominates all other issues on the agenda. However, this issue is also clearly linked to the question of widening the EU and deepening integration: whether to further integrate – or disintegrate – the Union, and whether to further enlarge in view of growing economic disparities between the member states.

The goals of widening the EU and deepening integration have accompanied the process of building the Union since its inception. It is generally assumed that these two goals are difficult to reconcile. For this reason, they are usually pursued in succession, with steps towards enlargement followed by steps toward deepening integration and vice versa. During the first decade of the twenty-first century, the EU attempted to pursue both of these objectives simultaneously, as they appeared to be closely interlinked. Hence, the plans for Eastern enlargement, which nearly doubled the number of member states of the EU, were seemingly only possible if the institutional structure and decision-making in the Union were significantly improved. Accordingly, a fundamental revision of the Treaties was launched in anticipation of Eastern enlargement.

If widening the EU was accomplished with surprisingly little controversy, deepening integration has proven to be more contentious, as it required a fundamental revision of the Treaties. This took, as we have seen, nearly 10 years to be accomplished. However, in spite of these achievements, the EU continues to face serious problems that arise out of the most recent steps to enlarge the Union and deepen integration. Furthermore, these problems are exacerbated by new challenges. Paradoxically, in order to cope with them, the Union once again faces two possible options: enlarging its membership and deepening integration.

With regard to *enlargement*, several neighbouring states are knocking quite loudly at the doors of the EU. Turkey could achieve the status of an accession state – accession negotiations were opened in 2005, but they soon stalled because of major dissent on certain political issues. The small states of the former Yugoslavia as well as Ukraine, a large state in the EU's immediate neighbourhood, have also been given reason to strive towards accession. However, at present, they are far from fulfilling the conditions set by the EU. The EU's enlargement policy faces a funda-mental dilemma: if the Union aspires to support democratic consolida-tion in neighbouring states, and thereby improve its own security, it needs to offer these states a credible prospect of accession. However, if it makes this same offer to all aspirants, and particularly to large states, it risks 'imperial overstretch' (Beck and Grande 2007). In addition to these prob-lems, the EU suffers from a tangible lack of support for further enlarge-ment on the part of the citizens of Europe. Obviously, this undermines the policy of widening the Union from within.

The question of *deepening integration* is at present dominated by the economic and financial crisis, which has evolved to a sovereign debt crisis and, consequently, a crisis of the Euro-zone. In a variety of ways, this crisis has highlighted the weaknesses of the EU. It accentuates the eternal problem of economic disparities between the member states and political dissent among national governments. The solution to the crisis lies in forceful common action at the European level and in solidarity with economically weaker states. Unfortunately, the conditions for undertaking such steps are lacking; even worse, they are deteriorating, since national political leaders increasingly blame other states for causing the crisis or preventing swift solutions. Thus, for the first time, a Euro-pean issue clearly dominates national political agendas and politicizes election campaigns. Populist parties, particularly those on the right of the political spectrum, take advantage of the citizens' general mistrust as a means of furthering their own purposes and fuelling public dissent with the policies of the EU.

Not surprisingly, at the European level, deep dissent between the European institutions and among national governments dominates the scene. The Commission has presented extensive proposals for further integration, involving bold steps into the supranational direction. For example, it recently launched plans for tighter economic surveillance of the economic policies of the member states, and it attempted to set up programmes for economic recovery in those states hit most severely by the sovereign debt crisis and the ensuing austerity policies. However, the Council and the European Council dismissed these proposals. Some member states also support taking steps towards enhancing the Union's supranational dimension. Germany, for example, advocates more supra-nationalism through its projects for strict fiscal austerity. However, when France proposed to establish a '*gouvernement economique*', an economic government at European level, Germany suddenly became an advocate of national autonomy. Other member states are outright opposed to any steps in the supranational direction. For example, the UK and the Czech Republic used their veto to prevent the Fiscal Compact from becoming European law. Some political forces and the UK media have even discussed the option of exiting the Union. In the face of such deep dissent, national governments in the Council and European Council continue to act in the usual manner. They continue to raise a variety of objections against any advancement. They hesitate to take decisions, or delay making them, in order to preserve their national interests. Yet, in the very last minute of a summit meeting, they produce *ad hoc* regulations and measures as sticking-plasters for the most pressing problems of the day. Meanwhile the citizens of the member states, more than ever, lose confidence in the problem-solving capacity of the EU. Even worse, many citizens perceive the EU as the source of all the problems and withdraw their support for any further integration. Political debates at national level, the rise of anti-EU parties in nearly all member states, and recent election results all indicate the citizens' distrust in the EU and its political leaders.

The problems do not stop here: the EU faces frictions from within and must deal with a long list of pressing issues. Will it succeed in taking vigorous action to tackle the detrimental impacts of the economic and financial crisis? Will it be able to maintain inter-state cooperation with all member states participating on an equal footing? Will the enlarged Union be able to embark on major steps towards deepening integration, or will it inevitably find itself entangled in forms of differentiated integration? Will the Union be able to speak with one voice in external affairs, or will the member states continue to set the tone, and thus relegate the EU to the role of an insignificant actor on the international stage? And, most importantly, will the EU be able to offer a durable solution to the sovereign debt and Euro crisis? Finally, can the EU further proceed as a project exclusively directed by European elites, while the citizens do not lend support to it?

Whatever course European integration takes in the future, certain core characteristics of the system will persist. In order to consolidate and advance the level and the degree of integration, the EU will have to depend on highly-sophisticated and diversified mechanisms for balancing the interests of, and building consensus among, the member states and the constituencies they represent. This implies that the basic structure of the EU, characterized by the delicate balance of the two systemic principles, will not change in the near future. In other words: the dualistic or bicephalous structure of the EU will continue to constitute its core characteristic. It is this structure that offers the best opportunity to advance the process of integration in incremental steps and stages. It will allow for collective action, and still preserve the autonomy of the member states. However, if progress is to continue, it will be necessary to achieve the close involvement of those who, until now, have been largely excluded from the project of European integration: the citizens of Europe.

# References

Abromeit, H. (1998) *Democracy in Europe. Legitimising Politics in a Non-State Polity* (New York: Berghahn).

Akman, P. and H. Kassim (2010) 'Myths and Myth-making in the European Union: The Institutionalization and Interpretation of EU Competition Policy', *Journal of Common Market Studies*, 48(1): 111–32.

Alfé, M., T. Christiansen and S. Piedrafita (2008) 'Implementing Committees in the Enlarged European Union: Business as Usual for Comitology?', in E. Best, T. Christiansen and P. P. Settembri (eds), *The Institutions of the Enlarged European Union: Continuity and Change* (Cheltenham: Edward Elgar Publishing): 205–21.

Alonso Garcia, R. (2002) 'The General Provisions of the Charter of Fundamental Rights of the European Union', *European Law Journal*, 8(4): 492–514.

Alter, K. J. (2001) *Establishing the Supremacy of European Law: The Making of an International Rule of Law in Europe* (Oxford: Oxford University Press).

Alter, K. J. (2009) *The European Court's Political Power: Selected Essays* (Oxford: Oxford University Press).

Andersen, S. S., and T. Burns (1996) 'The European Union and the Erosion of Parliamentary Democracy: A Study of Post-parliamentary Governance', in S. S. Andersen and K. A. Eliassen (eds), *The European Union: How Democratic Is It?* (London: Sage): 227–51.

Armstrong, K. and C. Kilpatrick (2007) 'Law, Governance or New Governance? The Changing Open Method of Coordination', *Columbia Journal of European Law*, 13: 649–77.

Auel, K. (2007) 'Democratic Accountability and National Parliaments: Redefining the Impact of Parliamentary Scrutiny in EU Affairs', *European Law Journal*, 13(4): 487–504.

Auel, K. and A. Benz (2007) 'Expanding National Parliamentary Control: Does it Enhance European Democracy?', in B. Kohler-Koch and B. Rittberger (eds), *Debating the Democratic Legitimacy of the European Union* (Lanham, ML: Rowman & Littlefield): 57–74.

Avbelj, M. (2013) 'Differentiated Integration – Farewell to the EU-27?', *German Law Journal*, 14(1): 191–211.

Avery, G. (2004) 'The Enlargement Negotiations', in C. Fraser (ed.), *The Future of European Integration and Enlargement* (London: Routledge): 35–62.

Axelrod, R. (1984) *The Evolution of Cooperation* (New York: Basic Books).

Bache, J., S. George and S. Bulmer (2011) *Politics in the European Union* (Oxford: Oxford University Press).

Bachtler, J. and C. Mendez (2007) 'Who Governs EU Cohesion Policy? Deconstructing the Reforms of the Structural Funds', *Journal of Common Market Studies*, 45(3): 535–64.

Balzacq, T. and A. Hadfield (2012) 'Differentiation and Trust: Prüm and the Institutional Design of EU Internal Security', *Cooperation and Conflict*, 47(4): 539–61.

Bartolini, S. (2005a) *Restructuring Europe. Centre Formation, System Building, and Political Structuring between the Nation State and the European Union* (Oxford: Oxford University Press).

Bartolini, S. (2005b) 'Should the Union be Politicised? Prospects and Risks', *Notre Europe Policy Paper*, 19: 39–50.

Bauer, P. (2011) 'The Transition of Egypt in 2011: A New Springtime for the European Neighbourhood Policy?', *Perspectives on European Politics and Society*, 12(4): 420–39.

Beach, D. (2008) 'The Facilitator of Efficient Negotiations in the Council: The Impact of the Council Secretariat', in D. Naurin and H. Wallace (eds), *Unveiling the Council of the European Union. Games Governments Play in Brussels* (Basingstoke: Palgrave Macmillan): 219–37.

Beck, T. (2012) 'Banking Union for Europe – Risks and Challenges', in T. Beck (ed.), *Banking Union for Europe – Risks and Challenges* (London: Centre for Economic Policy Research): 9–16.

Beck, U. and E. Grande (2007) *Cosmopolitan Europe* (Cambridge: Polity Press).

Begg, I. (2010) 'Cohesion or Confusion: A Policy Searching for Objectives', *European Integration*, 22(1): 77–96.

Benz, A. (2004) 'Multilevel Governance – Governance in Mehrebenensystemen', in A. Benz (ed.), *Governance – Regieren in komplexen Regelsystemen. Eine Einführung* (Wiesbaden: VS-Verlag): 125–46.

Benz, A. (2009) 'Combined Modes of Governance in EU Policymaking', in I. Tömmel and A. Verdun (eds), *Innovative Governance in the European Union: The Politics of Multilevel Policymaking* (Boulder, CO: Lynne Rienner): 27–44.

Beyers, J. (2004) 'Voice and Access: Political Practices of European Interest Associations', *European Union Politics*, 5(2): 211–40.

Beyers, J. (2005) 'Multiple Embeddedness and Socialization in Europe: The Case of Council Officials', *International Organization*, 59, Fall: 899–936.

Beyers, J., R. Eising and W. Maloney (2008) 'Researching Interest Group Politics in Europe and Elsewhere: Much we Study, Little We Know?', *West European Politics*, 31(6): 1103–28.

Blauberger, M. (2009) 'Of "Good" and "Bad" Subsidies: European State Aid Control through Soft and Hard Law', *West European Politics*, 32(4): 719–37.

Blavoukos, S., D. Bourantonis and G. Pagulatos (2007) 'A President for the European Union: A New Actor in Town?', *Journal of Common Market Studies*, 48(2): 191–219.

Börzel, T. A. (2010) 'European Governance? Negotiation and Competition in the Dhadow of Hierarchy', *Journal of Common Market Studies*, 45(2): 231–52.

Börzel, T. A. and K. Heard-Lauréote (2009) Networks in EU multi-level governance: Concepts and Contributions', *Journal of Public Policy*, 29(2): 135–52.

Börzel, T. A. and T. Risse (2000) 'When Europe Hits Home: Europeanization and Domestic Change', European Integration Online Papers (EIoP) 4(15). Retrieved from: http://eiop.or.at/eiop/texte/2000-015a.htm

Borchardt, K.-D. (2010) *The ABC of European Union Law* (Luxembourg: Publications Office of the European Union).

Bouwen, P. (2009) 'The European Commission', in D. Coen and J. Richardson (eds), *Lobbying the European Union: Institutions, Actors, and Issues* (Oxford: Oxford University Press): 19–38.

Brack, N. (2012) 'Eurosecepticism at the European level: The Case of the

'Untidy Right' in the European Parliament', *Journal of Common Market Studies*, 51(1): 85–104.

Brandsma, G. J. (2010) 'Accountable Comitology', in M. Bovens, D. Curtin and P. 't Hart (eds), *The Real World of EU Accountability* (Oxford: Oxford University Press): 150–73.

Brandsma, G. J. and J. Blom-Hansen (2012) 'Negotiating the Post-Lisbon Comitology System: Institutional Battles over Delegated Decision-making', *Journal of Common Market Studies*, 50(6): 939–57.

Bretherton, C. and M. Mannin (2013) *The Europeanization of European Politics* (Basingstoke: Palgrave Macmillan).

Bretherton, C. and J. Vogler (2006) *The European Union as a Global Actor* (London: Routledge).

Brown Wells, S. and S. F. Wells (2008) 'Shared Sovereignty in the European Union: Germany's Economic Governance', *Yale Journal of International Affairs*, 30: 30–43.

Brunazzo, M. and E. Domorenok (2008) 'New Members in Old Institutions: The Impact of Enlargement on the Committee of the Regions', *Regional & Federal Studies*, 18(4): 429–48.

Bulmer, S. (1993) 'The Governance of the European Union: A New Institutionalist Approach', *Journal of Public Policy*, 13(4): 351–80.

Bulmer, S. (1998) 'New Institutionalism and the Governance of the Single European Market', *Journal of European Public Policy*, 5(3): 365–86.

Buonanno, L. and N. Nugent (2013) *Policies and Policy Processes of the European Union* (Basingstoke: Palgrave Macmillan).

Burgess, M. (2000) *Federalism and the European Union* (London: Routledge).

Burgess, M. (2004) 'Federalism', in A. Wiener and T. Dietz (eds), *European Integration Theory* (Oxford: Oxford University Press): 25–44.

Burgess, M. (2006) *Comparative Federalism: Theory and Practice* (London: Routledge).

Burley, A.-M. and W. Mattli (1993) 'Europe before the Court: A Political Theory of Legal Integration', *International Organization*, 47(1): 41–76.

Busuioc, M. (2013) 'Rule-making by the European Financial Supervisory Authorities: Walking a Tight Rope', *European Law Journal*, 19(1): 111–25.

Cameron, F. (2011) 'The EU's External Action Service – Golden or Missed Opportunity?', in G. Müller-Brandeck-Bocquet and C. Rüger, *The High Representative for the EU Common Foreign and Security Policy – Review and Prospects* (Baden-Baden: Nomos): 235–58.

Caporaso, J. (1996) 'The European Union and Forms of State: Westphalian, Regulatory, or Post-modern?', *Journal of Common Market Studies*, 34(1): 29–52.

Cecchini, P. (1988) *The European Challenge 1992: The Benefits of the Single Market* (Aldershot: Gower).

Checkel, J. T. (1999) 'Social Construction and Integration', *Journal of European Public Policy*, 6(4): 545–60.

Chirac, J. (2000) 'Rede des französischen Staatspräsidenten Jacques Chirac vor dem Deutschen Bundestag', 27, June. Retrieved from: http://www.bundestag.de/kulturundgeschichte/geschichte/gastredner/chirac/chirac1.html.

Christiansen, T. and M. Dobbels (2013) 'Non-legislative Rule Making after the Lisbon Treaty: Implementing the New System of Comitology and Delegated Acts', *European Law Journal*, 19(1): 42–56.

Christiansen, T. and P. Lintner (2005) 'The Committee of the Regions after 10 Years: Lessons from the Past and Challenges for the Future', *EIPASCOPE* 1.

Christiansen, T. and C. Reh (2009) *Constitutionalizing the European Union* (Basingstoke: Palgrave Macmillan).

Cini, M. (2008) 'Political Leadership in the European Commission: The Santer and Prodi Commissions, 1995–2005', in J. Hayward (ed.), *Leaderless Europe* (Oxford: Oxford University Press):113–30.

Cini, M. and L. McGowan (2008) *Competition Policy in the European Union*, 2nd edn (Basingstoke: Palgrave Macmillan).

Clark, J. and A. Jones (2011) '"Telling Stories about Politics": Europeanization and the EU's Council Working Groups', *Journal of Common Market Studies*, 49(2): 341–66.

Coen, D. (2007) 'Empirical and Theoretical Studies in EU Lobbying', *Journal of European Public Policy*, 14(3): 333–45.

Coen, D. (2009) 'Business Lobbying in the European Union', in D. Coen and J. Richardson (eds), *Lobbying the European Union: Institutions, Actors, and Issues* (Oxford: Oxford University Press): 145–68.

Coen, D. and J. Richardson (eds) (2009) *Lobbying the European Union: Institutions, Actors, and Issues* (Oxford: Oxford University Press).

Cohen, J. and C. Sabel (2003) 'Sovereignty and Solidarity: EU and US', in J. Zeitlin and D. M. Trubek (eds), *Governing Work and Welfare in a New Economy: European and American Experiments* (Oxford: Oxford University Press): 376–406.

Cole, T. (2005) 'The Committee of the Regions and Subnational Representation to the European Union', *Maastricht Journal of European and Comparative Law*, 12(1): 49–73.

Commission of the European Union (2006) 'Green Paper European Transparency Initiative', Brussels, 03.05.2006, COM (2006) 194 final.

Conceição-Heldt, E. (2012) 'EU Agricultural and Fisheries Policies: An Economic and Environmental Disaster!', in H. Zimmermann and A. Dür (eds), *Key Controversies in the European Union* (Basingstoke: Palgrave Macmillan): 161–8.

Cooper, I. (2012) 'A "Virtual Third Chamber" for the European Union? National Parliaments after the Treaty of Lisbon', *West European Politics*, 35(3): 441–65.

Corbett, R. (2007) *The European Parliament*, 7th edn (London: Harper).

Corbey, D. (1995) 'Dialectical Functionalism: Stagnation as a Booster of European Integration', *International Organization*, 49(2): 253–84.

Costa, O. (2011) 'The European Parliament and the Community Method', in R. Dehousse (ed.), *The 'Community Method': Obstinate or Obsolete?* (Basingstoke: Palgrave Macmillan): 60–75.

Council of the European Union (2013a) Council Configurations. Retrieved from: http://www.consilium.europa.eu/council/council-configurations?lang=en.

Council of the European Union (2013b) List of Council preparatory bodies, Annex I, January 2012. Retrieved from: http://register.consilium.europa.eu/pdf/en/13/st05/st05581.en13.pdf.

Council Regulation (EC) No 1083/2006, of 11 July 2006, 'Laying Down General Provisions on the European Regional Development Fund, the European Social Fund and the Cohesion Fund and Repealing Regulation (EC) No. 1260/1999', OJ L 210: 25.78.

Court of Justice (2013a) Statistics: Annual Report 2011. Retrieved from: http://curia.europa.eu/jcms/upload/docs/application/pdf/2012-06/ra2011_statistiques_cour_en.pdf).

Cowles, M. G. (1995) 'Setting the Agenda for a New Europe: The ERT and EC 1992', *Journal of Common Market Studies*, 33(4): 501–26.

Crum, B. (2004) 'Towards Finality? An Assessment of the Achievements of the European Convention', in A. Verdun and O. Croci (eds), *Institutional and Policy-making Challenges to the European Union in the Wake of Eastern Enlargement* (Manchester: Manchester University Press): 200–17.

Crum, B. (2008) 'The EU Constitutional Process: A Failure of Political Representation?', RECON Online Working Paper 2008/08, June.

Curtin, D. and M. Egeberg (2008) 'Tradition and Innovation: Europe's Accumulated Executive Order', *West European Politics*, 31(4): 639–61.

Daugbjerg, C. (2012) 'Globalization and Internal Policy Dynamics in the Reform of the Common Agricultural Policy', in J. Richardson (ed.), *Constructing a Policy-making State? Policy Dynamics in the EU* (Oxford: Oxford University Press): 88–103.

Daugbjerg, C. and A. Swinbank (2007) 'The Politics of CAP Reform: Trade Negotiations, Institutional Settings and Blame Avoidance', *Journal of Common Market Studies*, 45(1): 1–22.

DeBardeleben, J. and A. Hurrelmann (eds) (2011) *Transnational Europe: Promise, Paradox, Limits* (Basingstoke: Palgrave Macmillan).

Decker, F. (2012) 'Electing the Commission President and the Commissioners directly: A proposal', *European View*, 11: 71–8.

Decker, F. and J. Sonnicksen (2009) 'A Direct Election of the Commission President: A Presidential Approach to Democratising the European Union', ZEI Discussion Paper C 192.

Decker, F. and J. Sonnicksen (2011) 'An Alternative Approach to European Union Democratization: Reexamining the Direct Election of the Commission President', *Government and Opposition*, 46(2): 168–91.

De Grauwe, P. (2010) 'Crisis in the Eurozone and How to Deal with it', CEPS Policy Brief 204.

De Grauwe, P. (2013) 'Design Failures in the Eurozone: Can They be Fixed?', *LSE 'Europe in Question' Discussion Paper Series 57*.

Dehousse, R. (1992) 'Integration vs. Regulation? On the Dynamics of Regulation in the European Community', *Journal of Common Market Studies*, 30(4): 383–402.

Dehousse, R. (1998) *The European Court of Justice* (New York: St. Martin's Press).

Dehousse, R. (2011) 'The "Community Method" at Sixty', in R. Dehousse (ed.), *The 'Community Method': Obstinate or Obsolete?* (Basingstoke: Palgrave Macmillan): 6–15.

Della Porta, D. and M. Caiani (2009) *Social Movements and Europeanization* (Oxford: Oxford University Press).

Deloche-Gaudez, F. (2001) 'The Convention on a Charter of Fundamental Rights: A Method for the Future, Notre Europe, *Research and Policy Paper* 15, November.

Del Sarto, R. A. and T. Schumacher (2005) 'From EMP to ENP: What's at Stake with the European Neighbourhood Policy towards the Southern Mediterranean?', *European Foreign Affairs Review*, 10: 17–38.

De Schoutheete, P. (2012) 'The European Council', in J. Peterson and M. Shackleton (eds), *The Institutions of the European Union*, 3rd edn (Oxford: Oxford University Press): 43–67.

Deutsch, K. W., S. A Burrell, and R. A. Kann (1957) *Political Community and the North Atlantic Area: International Organization in the Light of Historical Experience* (Princeton: Princeton University Press).

Dinan, D. (2001) 'Governance and Institutions 2000: Edging towards Enlargement', *Journal of Common Market Studies*, 39, Annual Review: 25–41.

Dinan, D. (2002) 'Institutions and Governance 2001–02: Debating the EU's Future', *Journal of Common Market Studies*, 40, Annual Review: 29–43.

Dinan, D. (2004a) *Europe Recast: A History of European Union* (Boulder, CO: Lynne Rienner).

Dinan, D. (2004b) 'Governance and Institutions. The Convention and the Intergovernmental Conference', *Journal of Common Market Studies*, 42, Annual Review: 27–42.

Dinan, D. (2005) 'Governance and Institutions: A New Constitution and a New Commission', *Journal of Common Market Studies*, 43, Annual Review: 37–54.

Dinan, D. (2006) 'Governance and Institutional Developments: In the Shadow of the Constitutional Treaty', *Journal of Common Market Studies*, 44, Annual Review: 63–80.

Dinan, D. (2007) 'Governance and Institutional Developments: Coping without the Constitutional Treaty', *Journal of Common Market Studies*, 45, Annual Review: 67–87.

Dinan, D. (2008) 'Governance and Institutional Developments: Ending the Constitutional Impasse', *Journal of Common Market Studies*, 46, Annual Review: 71–90.

Dinan, D. (2009) 'Institutions and Governance: Saving the Lisbon Treaty - An Irish solution to a European Problem', *Journal of Common Market Studies*, 47, Annual Review: 113–32.

Dinan, D. (2010a) 'Institutions and Governance: A New Treaty, a Newly Elected Parliament, and a New Commission', *Journal of Common Market Studies*, 48, Annual Review: 95–118.

Dinan, D. (2010b) *Ever Closer Union? An Introduction to the European Community*, 4th edn (Boulder, CO: Lynne Rienner).

Dinan, D. (2011) 'Governance and Institutions: Implementing the Lisbon Treaty in the Shadow of the Euro Crisis', *Journal of Common Market Studies*, 49, Annual Review: 103–21.

Dinan, D. (2012) 'The EU as Efficient Polity', in H. Zimmermann and A. Dür (eds), *Key Controversies in the European Union* (Basingstoke: Palgrave Macmillan): 33–40.

Down, I. and C. J. Wilson (2008) 'From "Permissive Consensus" to "Constraining Dissensus": A polarizing Union?', *Acta Politica*, 43: 26–49.

Duff, A. (2010) *Post-national Democracy and the Reform of the European Parliament* (Paris: Notre Europe).

Duff A. (2013) 'On Dealing with Euroscepticism', *Journal of Common Market Studies*, 51(1): 140–52.

Dyson, K. H. F. and L. Quaglia (2010) *European Economic Governance and Policies: Commentary on Key Historical and Institutional Documents. Volume I* (Oxford: Oxford University Press).

Dyson, K. and A. Sepos (eds) (2010) *Which Europe? The Politics of Differentiated Integration* (Basingstoke: Palgrave Macmillan).

Earnshaw, D. and D. Judge (1997) 'The Life and Times of the European Union's Co-operation Procedure', *Journal of Common Market Studies*, 35(4): 543–64.

Eberlein, B. and D. Kerwer (2004) 'New Governance in the EU: A Theoretical Perspective', *Journal of Common Market Studies*, 42(1): 121–42.

Egan, M. (2001) *Constructing a European Market: Standards, Regulations and Governance* (Oxford: Oxford University Press).

Eisele, G. (2008) 'Towards Visibility and Representativeness? Perspectives of the European Economic and Social Committee', in M. Freise (ed.), *European Civil Society on the Road to Success?* (Baden-Baden: Nomos): 87–107.

Eising, R. and B. Kohler-Koch (2005) 'Interessenpolitik im europäischen Mehrebenensystem', in E. Rainer and B. Kohler-Koch (eds), *Interessenpolitik in Europa* (Baden-Baden: Nomos): 11–78.

Elgie, R. (1998) 'Democratic Accountability and Central Bank Independence: Historical and Contemporary, National and European Perspectives', *West European Politics*, 21(3): 53–76.

Elgström, O. (ed.) (2003a) *European Union Council Presidencies: A Comparative Perspective* (London: Routledge).

Elgström, O. (2003b) '"The Honest Broker"? The Council Presidency as a Mediator', in O. Elgström, O. (ed.), *European Union Council Presidencies: A Comparative Perspective* (London: Routledge): 38–54.

Eriksen, E. O. and J. E. Fossum (2007) 'Europe in Transformation: How to Reconstitute Democracy?', Paper to EUSA Conference 2007, Montreal.

European Commission (1985) 'Completing the Internal Market', White Paper from the Commission to the European Council, COM (85) 310 final.

European Commission (1997) 'Agenda 2000: For a Stronger and Wider Union' (Brussels: European Commission).

European Commission (2010) 'Report from the Commission on the Working of Committees during 2009', Brussels, 2.7.2010, COM(2010)354 final.

European Commission (2012) 'Communication from the Commission to the European Parliament and the Council: A Roadmap towards a Banking Union', Brussels, 12.9.2012, COM (2012) 510 final.

European Commission (2013a) 'Departments'. Retrieved from: http://ec.europa.eu/about/ds_en.htm.

European Commission (2013b) 'Report from the Commission on the Working of Committees during 2012', Brussels, 10.10.2013, COM (2013) 701 final.

European Commission (2014) 'Codecision, Statistics'. Retrieved from: http://ec.europa.eu/codecision/statistics/index_en.htm.

European Parliament (2013a) 'Elections 2013, Share-out of MEP's Seats among 28 EU Countries'. Retrieved from: http://www.europarl.europa.eu/news/en/pressroom/content/20130610IPR11414/html/Elections-2014-share-out-of-MEPs%27-seats-among-28-EU-countries.

European Parliament (2013b) 'Composition of Parliament'. Retrieved from http://www.europarl.europa.eu/aboutparliament/en/004a50d310/Composition-of-Parliament.html.

European Parliament (2014a) 'Conciliations and Codecisions'. Retrieved from: http://www.europarl.europa.eu/code/about/statistics_en.htm.

European Parliament (2014b) 'Committees'. Retrieved from: http://www.europarl.europa.eu/committees/en/full-list.html.

European Parliament (2014c) 'News'. Retrieved from http://www.europarl. europa.eu?en/news-room/content/20130906STO18828/html/Find-out-more-about-the parties.

European Parliament (2014d) 'Results of the 2014 European elections'. Retrieved from http://www.results-elections2014.eu/en/election-results-2014.html.

European Union (2013a) 'Court of Justice of the European Union'. Retrieved from: http://europa.eu/about-eu/institutions-bodies/court-justice/.

Eurozone Portal (2013) 'History of the Eurogroup'. Retrieved from: http://www.eurozone.europa.eu/eurogroup/history/.

Falkner, G., O. Treib, M. Hartlapp and S. Leiber (2005) *Complying with Europe: EU Harmonisation and Soft Law in the Member States* (Cambridge: Cambridge University Press).

Falkner, G. and O. Treib (2008) 'Three Worlds of Compliance or Four? The EU-15 Compared to New Member States', *Journal of Common Market Studies*, 46(2): 293–313.

Farrell, H. and A. Héritier (2004) 'Interorganizational Negotiation and Intra-organizational Power in Shared Decision Making: Early Agreements under Codecision and their Impact on the European Parliament and Council', *Comparative Political Studies*, 37: 1184–212.

Featherstone, K. (2011) 'The Greek Sovereign Debt Crisis and EMU: A Failing State in a Skewed Regime', *Journal of Common Market Studies*, 49(2): 193–217.

Featherstone, K. and G. A. Kazamias (eds) (2001) *Europeanization and the Southern Periphery* (London: Frank Cass).

Featherstone, K. and C. Radaelli (eds) (2003) *The Politics of Europeanization* (Oxford: Oxford University Press).

Fischer, J. (2000) 'From Confederacy to Federation – Thoughts on the Finality of European Integration', Speech at the Humboldt University in Berlin, 12 May 2000, in C. Joerges, Y. Meny and J. H. H. Weiler (eds), *What Kind of Constitution for What Kind of Polity. Responses to Joschka Fischer* (Firenze: Robert Schuman Centre for Advanced Studies, European University Institute): 19–30.

Follesdal, A. and S. Hix (2006) 'Why There is a Democratic Deficit in the EU: A Response to Majone and Moravcsik', *Journal of Common Market Studies*, 44(3): 533–62.

Freise, M. (2008) 'European Civil Society on the Road to Success?', in M. Freise (ed.), *European Civil Society on the Road to Success?* (Baden-Baden: Nomos): 9–19.

Friedrich, D. (2008) 'Actual and Potential Contributions of Civil Society Organizations to Democratic EU Governance', in M. Freise (ed.), *European Civil Society on the Road to Success?* (Baden-Baden: Nomos): 67–86.

Garrett, G. (1995) 'From the Luxembourg Compromise to Codecision: Decision Making in the European Union', *Electoral Studies*, 14(3): 289–308.

Garrett, G. and G. Tsebelis (1996) 'An Institutional Critique of Intergovernmentalism', *International Organization*, 50(2): 269–99.

Geary, M. J. (2012) 'The Process of European Integration from The Hague to Maastricht, 1969-92: An Irreversible Advance?', Debater a Europa, *Periodico do CEIDA e do CEIS20*: 6–23.

General Secretariat of the Council (2013) 'Guide to the Ordinary Legislative Procedure', October 2010. Retrieved from: http://www.consilium.europa.eu/uedocs/cmsUpload/QC3109179ENC.pdf.

Genschel, P. (2007) 'Why No Mutual Recognition of VAT? Regulation, Taxation and the Integration of the EU's Internal Market for Goods', *Journal of European Public Policy*, 14(5): 743–61.

Gehring, T. (2005) 'Gesellschaftliche Rationalität durch die Differenzierung von Entscheidungsverfahren', in T. Gehring, S. Krapohl, M. Kerler, and S. Stefanova (eds), *Rationalität durch Verfahren in der Europäischen Union: Europäische Arzneimittelzulassung und Normung technischer Güter* (Baden-Baden: Nomos): 27–61.

Gehring, T. and M. Kerler (2008) 'Institutional Stimulation of Deliberative Decision-making: Division of Labour, Deliberative Legitimacy and Technical Regulation in the European Single Market', *Journal of Common Market Studies*, 46(5): 1001–23.

Giegerich, B. and W. Wallace (2010) 'Foreign and Security Policy: Civilian Power Europe and American Leadership', in H. Wallace, M. A. Pollack, and A. Young (eds), *Policy-Making in the European Community*, 6th edn (Oxford: Oxford University Press): 431–77.

Gilbert, M. (2003) *Surpassing Realism: The Politics of European Integration since 1945* (Lanham, ML: Rowman & Littlefield).

Gillingham, J. (2003) *European Integration, 1950–2003: Superstate or New Market Economy?* (Cambridge: Cambridge University Press).

Ginsberg, R. H. (2007) *Demystifying the European Union. The Enduring Logic of Regional Integration* (Lanham, ML: Rowman & Littlefield).

Gocaj, L. and S. Meunier (2013) Time will Tell: The EFSF, the ESM, and the Euro Crisis, *European Integration*, 35(3): 239–52.

Gostynska, A. (2012) 'President of the European Council Ahead of his Second Term: An Assessment and Perspectives', Polish Institute of International Affairs, *Bulletin*, 45(378): 720–21.

Gray, M. and A. Stubb (2001) 'The Treaty of Nice – Negotiating a poisoned chalice?', *Journal of Common Market Studies*, 39, Annual Review: 5–23.

Greenwood, J. (1997) *Representing Interests in the European Union* (New York: St Martin's Press).

Greenwood, J. (2007) 'Review Article: Organized Civil Society and Democratic Legitimacy in the European Union', *British Journal of Political Science*, 37: 333–57.

Greenwood, J. (2011) *Interest Representation in the European Union*, 3rd edn (Basingstoke: Palgrave Macmillan).

Greven, M. (2000) 'Can the European Union Finally Become a Democracy?', in M. Th. Greven and L. W. Pauly (eds), *Democracy beyond the State? The European Dilemma and the Emerging Global Order* (Lanham, ML: Rowman & Littlefield): 35–62.

Groenleer, M. (2009) *The Autonomy of European Union Agencies: A Comparative Study of Institutional Development* (Delft: Eburon).

Grossmann, E. (2004) 'Bringing Politics Back in Rethinking the Role of Economic Interest Groups in European Integration', *Journal of European Public Policy*, 11(4): 637–54.

Guéguen, D. (2011) *Comitology: Hijacking European Power*, 3rd edn (Brussels: European Training Institute).

Haas, E. B. (1958) *The Uniting of Europe: Political, Social and Economic Forces 1950–1957* (London: Stevens & Sons).

Haas, P. (1992) 'Introduction: Epistemic Communities and International Policy Co-ordination', *International Organization*, 46(1): 1–35.

Habermas, J. (2001) *The Postnational Constellation: Political Essays* (Cambridge: Polity Press).

Häge, F. M. (2012) *Bureaucrats as Law-Makers: Committee Decision-Making in the EU Council of Ministers* (London: Routledge).

Hall, P. A. and R. C.R. Taylor (1996) 'Political Science and the Three New Institutionalisms', *Political Studies*, XLIV: 936–57.

Harbo, F. (2005) *Towards a European Federation? The EU in the Light of Comparative Federalism* (Baden-Baden: Nomos).

Hartlapp, M. (2009) 'Extended Governance: Implementation of EU Social Policy in the Member States', in I. Tömmel and A. Verdun (eds), *Innovative Governance in the European Union: The Politics of Multilevel Policymaking* (Boulder, CO: Lynne Rienner): 221–36.

Hartlapp, M., J. Metz and C. Rauh (2013) 'Linking Agenda Setting to Coordination Structures: Bureaucratic Politics Inside the European Commission', *Journal of European Integration*, 35(4): 425–41.

Hayes-Renshaw, F. (2007) 'From Procedural Chore to Political Prestige: Historic Development and Recent Reforms of the Presidency of the Council', *Österreichische Zeitschrift für Politikwissenschaft* (ÖZP), 36(2): 107–23.

Hayes-Renshaw, F. (2009) 'Least Accessible but not Inaccessible: Lobbying the Council and the European Council', in D. Coen and J. Richardson (eds), *Lobbying the European Union: Institutions, Actors, and Issues* (Oxford: Oxford University Press): 70–88.

Hayes-Renshaw, F., W. van Aken, and H. Wallace (2006) 'When and Why the EU Council of Ministers Votes Explicitly', *Journal of Common Market Studies*, 44(1): 161–94.

Hayes-Renshaw, F. and H. Wallace (2006) *The Council of Ministers*, 2nd edn (Basingstoke: Palgrave Macmillan).

Heidbreder, E. G. (2011) *The Impact of Expansion on European Union Institutions: The Eastern Touch on Brussels* (New York: Palgrave Macmillan).

Heidenreich, M. and G. Bischoff (2008) 'The Open Method of Co-ordination: A Way to the Europeanization of Social and Employment Policies?', *Journal of Common Market Studies*, 46(3): 497–532.

Heisenberg, D. (2005) 'The Institution of 'Consensus' in the European Union: Formal versus Informal Decision Making in the Council', *European Journal of Political Research*, 44: 65–90.

Héritier, A. and C. Reh (2012) Codecision and its Discontents: Intra-organisational Politics and Institutional Reform in the European Parliament', *West European Politics*, 35(5): 1134–57.

Héritier, A. and M. Rhodes (eds) (2011) *New Modes of Governance in Europe: Governing in the Shadow of Hierarchy* (Basingstoke: Palgrave Macmillan).

Hix, S. (2005a) *The Political System of the European Union,* 2nd edn (New York: Palgrave Macmillan).

Hix, S. (2005b) 'Why the EU needs (Left–Right) Politics? Policy Reform and Accountability are Impossible without It', *Notre Europe Policy Paper* 19: 1–28.

Hix, S. (2008) *What's Wrong with the European Union and How to Fix It* (Cambridge: Polity Press).

Hix, S. and B. Høyland (2010) *The Political System of the European Union*, 3rd edn (Basingstoke: Palgrave Macmillan).

Hix, S. and C. Lord (1997) *Political Parties in the European Union* (Basingstoke: Macmillan).

Hix, S., A. G. Noury and G. Roland (2005) 'Power to the Parties: Cohesion and Competition in the European Parliament 1979–2001', *British Journal of Political Science*, 35(2): 209–234.

Hix, S., A. G. Noury and G. Roland (2007) *Democratic Politics in the European Parliament* (Cambridge: Cambridge University Press).

Hodson, D. (2012a) 'The Eurozone in 2011', *Journal of Common Market Studies*, 50, Annual Review: 178–94.

Hodson, D. (2012b) 'Managing the Euro: The European Central Bank', in J. Peterson and M. Shackleton (eds), *The Institutions of the European Union*, 3rd edn (Oxford: Oxford University Press): 199–218.

Hodson, D. and I. Maher (2001) 'The Open Method as a New Mode of Governance: The Case of Soft Economic Policy Coordination', *Journal of Common Market Studies*, 39(4): 719–46.

Hönnige, C. and A. Kaiser (2003) 'Opening the Black Box: Decision-making in the Committee of the Regions', *Regional and Federal Studies*, 13(2): 1–30.

Hoffmann, S. (1966) 'Obstinate or Obsolete? The Fate of the Nation State and the Case of Western Europe', *Daedalus*, summer issue: 862–915.

Hoffmann, S. (1982) 'Reflections on the Nation-state in Western Europe Today', *Journal of Common Market Studies*, 21(1–2): 21–37.

Holzinger, K., C. Knill and A. Lenschow (2009) 'Governance in EU Environmental Policy', in I. Tömmel and A. Verdun (eds), *Innovative Governance in the European Union: The Politics of Multilevel Policymaking* (Boulder, CO: Lynne Rienner): 45–61.

Hooghe, L. (1996) 'Building a Europe with the Regions: The Changing Role of the European Commission', in L. Hooghe (ed.), *Cohesion Policy and European Integration: Building Multi-Level Governance* (Oxford: Oxford University Press): 89–126.

Hooghe, L. and G. Marks (2001) *Multi-Level Governance and European Integration* (Lanham, ML: Rowman & Littlefield).

Howorth, J. (2007) *Security and Defence Policy in the European Union* (Basingstoke: Palgrave Macmillan).

Howorth, J. (2011) 'The "New Faces" of Lisbon: Assessing the Performance of Catherine Ashton and Herman van Rompuy on the Global Stage', *European Foreign Affairs Review*, 16(3): 303–23.

Howorth, J. (2012) 'Decision-making in Security and Defense Policy: Towards Supranational Inter-governmentalism?', *Cooperation and Conflict*, 47: 433–53.

Howse, R. and K. Nicolaïdis (eds) (2003) *The Federal Vision: Legitimacy and Levels of Governance in the United States and the European Union* (Oxford: Oxford University Press).

Hrbek, R. (2004) 'Europawahl 2004: neue Rahmenbedingungen – alte Probleme', *integration*, 27(3): 211–22.

Hueglin, T. O. and A. Fenna (2006) *Comparative Federalism: A Systematic Inquiry* (Peterborough, Ontario: Broadview Press).

Huget, H. (2007) *Demokratisierung der EU. Normative Demokratietheorie und Governance-Praxis im europäischen Mehrebenensystem* (Wiesbaden: VS-Verlag).

Hurrelmann, A. (2005) *Verfassung und Integration in Europa: Wege zu einer supranationalen Demokratie* (Frankfurt am Main: Campus)

Jachtenfuchs, M. (1997) 'Die Europäische Union – ein Gebilde sui generis?', in K.-D. Wolf (ed.), *Projekt Europa im Übergang? Probleme, Modelle und Strategien des Regierens in der Europäischen Union* (Baden-Baden: Nomos): 15–36.

Jachtenfuchs, M. (2001) 'The Governance Approach to European Integration', *Journal of Common Market Studies*, 39(2): 245–64.

Jachtenfuchs, M., T. Dietz and S. Jung (1998) 'Which Europe? Conflicting Models of a Legitimate European Political Order', *European Journal of International Relations*, 4(4): 409–45.

Jeffery, C. (2000) 'Sub-national Mobilization and European Integration: Does it Make Any Difference?', *Journal of Common Market Studies*, 38(1): 1–23.

Jeffery, C. and C. Rowe (2012) 'Social and Regional Interests: The Economic and Social Committee and the Committee of the Regions', in J. Peterson and M. Shackleton (eds), *The Institutions of the European Union*, 3rd edn (Oxford: Oxford University Press): 359–81.

Jessop, R. (2003) *The Future of the Capitalist State* (Cambridge: Polity Press).

Joerges, C. (2012) 'Europe's Economic Constitution in Crisis', *Zentra Working Papers in Transnational Studies*, 6: 1–28.

Jordan, A., D. Benson, R. Wurzel and A. Zito (2012) 'Environmental Policy: Governing by Multiple Policy Instruments?', in J. Richardson (ed.), *Constructing a Policy-making State? Policy Dynamics in the EU* (Oxford: Oxford University Press): 104–24.

Judge, D. and D. Earnshaw (2003) *The European Parliament* (Basingstoke: Palgrave Macmillan).

Kantola, J. (2010) *Gender and the European Union* (Basingstoke: Palgrave Macmillan).

Karakatsanis, G. and B. Laffan (2012) 'Financial Control: The Court of Auditors and OLAF', in J. Peterson and M. Shackleton (eds), *The Institutions of the European Union*, 3rd edn (Oxford: Oxford University Press): 241–61.

Kassim, H. and D. G. Dimitrakopoulos (2007) 'The European Commission and the future of Europe', *Journal of European Public Policy*, 14(8): 1249–70.

Kassim, H. and J. Peterson (2013) 'Leadership in the European Commission', in H. Kassim, J. Peterson, M. W. Bauer, S. Connolly, R. Dehousse, L. Hooghe and A. Thompson (eds), *The European Commission of the Twenty-First Century* (Oxford: Oxford University Press).

Katz, R. S. (1997) 'Representational Roles', *European Journal of Political Research*, 32: 211–26.

Kaunert, C. (2010) 'The Area of Freedom, Security and Justice in the Lisbon Treaty: Commission Policy Entrepreneurship?', *European Security*, 19(2): 169–89.

Keating, M. and L. Hooghe (2006) 'Bypassing the Nation-state? Regions and the EU Policy Process', in J. Richardson (ed.), *European Union: Power and Policy-making*, 3rd edn (Milton Park, Abingdon: Routledge): 269–86.

Kelemen, R. D. and G. Majone (2012) 'Managing Europeanization: The European Agencies', in J. Peterson and M. Shackleton (eds), *The Institutions of the European Union*, 3rd edn (Oxford: Oxford University Press): 219–40.

Kelley, J. (2006) 'New Wine in Old Wineskins: Promoting Political Reforms through the New European Neighbourhood Policy', *Journal of Common Market Studies*, 44(1): 29–55.

Keohane, R. O. (1984) *After Hegemony – Cooperation and Discord in the World Political Economy* (Princeton, NJ: Princeton University Press).

Keohane, R. O. and S. Hoffmann (eds) (1991) *The New European Community: Decision-making and Institutional Change* (Boulder, CO: Westview Press).

Kirchner, E. J. (1992) *Decision-making in the European Community: The Council Presidency and European Integration* (New York: St Martin's Press).

Kleine, M. (2007) 'Leadership in the European Convention', *Journal of European Public Policy*, 14(8): 1227–48.

Knill, C. (2003) *Europäische Umweltpolitik: Steuerungsprobleme und Regulierungsmuster im Mehrebenensystem* (Opladen: Leske+Budrich).

Knill, C. (2006) 'Implementation', in J. Richardson (ed.), *European Union: Power and Policy-making*, 3rd edn (Milton Park, Abingdon: Routledge): 351–75.

Knill, C. and J. Tosun (2012) 'Governance Institutions and Policy Implementation in the European Union', in J. Richardson (ed.), *Constructing a Policy-making State? Policy Dynamics in the EU* (Oxford: Oxford University Press): 309–33.

Knipping, F. (2004) *Rom, 25. März 1957: Die Einigung Europas. 20 Tage im 20. Jahrhundert* (München: dtv).

Kölliker, A. (2006) *Flexibility and European Integration: The Logic of Differentiated Integration* (Lanham, ML: Rowman & Littlefield).

König, T. (2007) 'Divergence or Convergence? From Ever-growing to Ever-slowing European Legislative Decision Making', *European Journal of Political Research*, 46: 417–44.

König, T. and L. Mäder (2013) 'Non-conformable, Partial and Conformable Transposition: A Competing Risk Analysis of the Transposition Process of Directives in the EU 15', *European Union Politics*, 14(1): 46–69.

Kohler-Koch, B. (1999) 'The Evolution and Transformation of European Governance', in B. Kohler-Koch and R. Eising (eds), *The Transformation of Governance in the European Union* (London: Routledge): 14–35.

Kohler-Koch, B. (2007) 'The Organization of Interests and Democracy in the European Union', in B. Kohler-Koch and B. Rittberger (eds), *Debating the Democratic Legitimacy of the European Union* (Lanham, ML: Rowman & Littlefield): 255–71.

Kohler-Koch, B. (2011) 'Zivilgesellschaftliche Partizipation: Zugewinn an Demokratie oder Pluralisierung der europäischen Lobby?', in B. Kohler-Koch and C. Quittkat (eds), *Die Entzauberung partizipativer Demokratie. Zur Rolle der Zivilgesellschaft bei der Demokratisierung von EU-Governance* (Frankfurt am Main: Campus): 241–71.

Kohler-Koch, B. and R. Eising (eds) (1999) The Transformation of Governance in the European Union (London: Routledge)

Kohler-Koch, B. and C. Quittkat (eds) (2011a) *Die Entzauberung partizipativer Demokratie. Zur Rolle der Zivilgesellschaft bei der Demokratisierung von EU-Governance* (Frankfurt am Main: Campus).

Kohler-Koch, B. and C. Quittkat (2011b) 'What is "Civil Society" and Who Represents it in the European Union?', in U. Liebert and H.-J. Trenz (eds), *The New Politics of European Civil Society* (London: Routledge): 19–39.

Kohler-Koch, B. and B. Rittberger (eds) (2007) *Debating the Democratic Legitimacy of the European Union* (Lanham, ML: Rowman & Littlefield).

Kurpas, S., C. Grøn and P. M. Kaczyński (2008) 'The European Commission after Enlargement: Does More Add Up to Less?', *CEPS Special Report*, February.

Ladrech, R. (2010) *Europeanization and National Politics* (Basingstoke: Palgrave Macmillan).

Larsson, T. and J. Murk (2007) 'The Commission's Relations with Expert Advisory Groups', in T. Christiansen and T. Larsson (eds), *The Role of Committees in the Policy-Process of the European Union: Legislation, Implementation and Deliberation* (Cheltenham and Northampton: Edward Elgar): 64–95.

Laursen, F. (2010) 'The EU as an International Political and Security Actor after the Treaty of Lisbon: An Academic Perspective', *Dalhousie EUCE Occasional Paper* 9: 1–23.

Laursen, F. (ed.) (2011) *The EU and Federalism: Polities and Policies Compared* (Surrey: Ashgate).

Lavenex, S. (2009) 'Transgovernmentalism in the Area of Freedom, Security, and Justice', in I. Tömmel and A. Verdun (eds), *Innovative Governance in the European Union: The Politics of Multilevel Policymaking* (Boulder, CO: Lynne Rienner): 255–71.

Lavenex, S. (2010) 'Justice and Home Affairs: Communitarization with Hesitation', in H. Wallace, M. A. Pollack, and A. Young (eds), *Policy-Making in the European Community*, 6th edn (Oxford: Oxford University Press): 457–77.

Leconte, C. (2012) 'Eurosceptics in the Rotating Presidency's Chair: Too Much Ado about Nothing?', *European Integration*, 34(2): 133–49.

Lehmann, W. (2009) 'The European Parliament', in D. Coen and J. Richardson (eds), *Lobbying the European Union: Institutions, Actors, and Issues* (Oxford: Oxford University Press): 39–69.

Lehmkuhl, D. (2009) 'Cooperation and Hierarchy in EU Competition Policy', in I. Tömmel and A. Verdun (eds), *Innovative Governance in the European Union: The Politics of Multilevel Policymaking* (Boulder, CO: Lynne Rienner): 103–19.

Leibfried, S. (2010) 'Social Policy', in H. Wallace, M. A. Pollack, and A. Young (eds), *Policy-Making in the European Community*, 6th edn (Oxford: Oxford University Press): 243–78.

Lenschow, A. (2010) 'Environmental Policy: Contending Dynamics and Policy Change', in H. Wallace, M. A. Pollack, and A. Young (eds), *Policy-making in the European Community*, 6th edn (Oxford: Oxford University Press): 307–30.

Lenz, T. (2012) 'Spurred Emulation: The EU and Regional Integration in Mercosur and SADC', *West European Politics*, 35(1): 155–173.

Leuffen, D., B. Rittberger and F. Schimmelfennig (2012) *Integration and Differentiation in the European Union* (Basingstoke: Palgrave Macmillan).

Lewis, J. (2005) 'The Janus Face of Brussels: Socialization and Everyday Decision Making in the European Union', *International Organization*, 59, Fall: 937–71.

Lewis, J. (2012) 'National Interests: the Committee of Permanent Representatives', in J. Peterson and M. Shackleton (eds), *The Institutions of the European Union*, 3rd edn (Oxford: Oxford University Press): 315–37.

Lieb, J. and A. Maurer (2009) 'Der Vertrag von Lissabon. Kurzkommentar', *Diskussionspapier der FG 1 und FG 2*, SWP Berlin.

Liebert, U. and H.-J. Trenz (eds) (2011) *The New Politics of European Civil Society* (London: Routledge).

Lindberg, L. and S. A. Scheingold (1970) *Europe's Would-Be Polity: Patterns of Change in the European Community* (Englewood Cliffs, NJ: Prentice Hall).

Lipgens, W. (ed.) (1986) '45 Jahre Ringen um die europäische Verfassung: Dokumente 1939–1984 – Von den Schriften der Widerstandsbewegung bis zum Vertragsentwurf des Europäischen Parlaments' (Bonn: Europa-Union-Verlag).

Long, T. and L. Lörinczi (2009) 'NGOs as Gatekeepers: A Green Vision', in D. Coen and J. Richardson (eds), *Lobbying the European Union: Institutions, Actors, and Issues* (Oxford: Oxford University Press): 169–85.

Lord, C. (2004) *A Democratic Audit of the European Union* (Basingstoke: Palgrave Macmillan).

Lord, C. (2007) 'Democratic control of the Council of Ministers', *Österreichische Zeitschrift für Politikwissenschaft (ÖZP)*, 36(2): 125–38.

Lord, C. (2008) 'Still in Democratic Deficit', *Intereconomics*, 43(6): 316–20.

Lord, C. and E. Harris (2006) *Democracy in the New Europe* (Basingstoke: Palgrave Macmillan).

Lowi, T. J. (1964) 'American Business, Public Policy, Case Studies, and Political Theory', *World Politics*, 16(4): 677–715.

Ludlow, N. P. (2009) 'The European Commission and the Rise of Coreper: A Controlled Experiment', in W. Kaiser, B. Leucht and M. Rasmussen (eds), *The History of European Union: Origins of a Trans- and Supranational Polity 1950–72* (New York and London: Routledge): 189–205.

Magnette, P. (2005a) 'In the Name of Simplification: Coping with Constitutional Conflicts in the Convention on the Future of Europe', *European Law Journal*, 11(4): 432–51.

Magnette, P. (2005b) 'The Politics of Regulation in the European Union', in D. Geradin, R. Munoz and N. Petit (eds), *Regulation through Agencies in the EU: A New Paradigm of European Governance* (Cheltenham: Edward Elgar): 3–22.

Magnette, P. and K. Nicolaïdis (2004) 'The European Convention: Bargaining in the shadow of rhetoric', *West European Politics*, 27(3): 381–404.

Mailand, M. (2008) 'The Uneven Impact of the European Employment Strategy on Member States' Employment Policies: A Comparative Analysis', *Journal of European Social Policy*, 18(4): 353–65.

Majone, G. (ed.) (1996) *Regulating Europe* (London and New York: Routledge).

Majone, G. (2002) 'Functional Interests: European Agencies', in J. Peterson and M. Shackleton (eds), *The Institutions of the European Union* (Oxford: Oxford University Press): 299–325.

Majone, G. (2005) *Dilemmas of European Integration: The Ambiguities and Pitfalls of Integration by Stealth* (Oxford: Oxford University Press).

Majone, G. (2009) *Europe as the Would-be World Power: The EU at Fifty* (Cambridge: Cambridge University Press).

March, J. G. and J. P. Olsen (1984) 'The New Institutionalism: Organizational factors in political life', *American Political Science Review*, 78(3): 734–49.

March, J. G. and J. P. Olsen (1989) *Rediscovering Institutions: The Organizational Basis of Politics* (London: Macmillan; New York: Free Press).

Marks, G., L. Hooghe, and K. Blank (1996) 'European Integration from the

1980s: State-centric versus Multi-level Governance', *Journal of Common Market Studies*, 34(3): 341–78.

Marsh, M. and S. Mikhailov (2010) 'European Parliament Elections and EU Governance', *Living Reviews in European Governance*, 5(4): 1–30.

Maurer, A. (2008) 'The German Council Presidency: Managing Conflicting Expectations', *Journal of Common Market Studies*, 46, Annual Review: 51–9.

Maurer, A. (2012) *Parlamente in der EU* (Vienna: Fakultas).

Mayntz, R. and F. W. Scharpf (1995) 'Der Ansatz des akteurzentrierten Institutionalismus', in R. Mayntz and F. W. Scharpf (eds), *Gesellschaftliche Selbstregelung und politische Steuerung* (Frankfurt a Main: Campus): 39–72.

Mazey, S. (2012) 'Policy Entrepreneurship, Group Mobilisation and the Creation of a New Policy Domain: Women's Rights and the European Union', in J. Richardson (ed.), *Constructing a Policy-making State? Policy Dynamics in the EU* (Oxford: Oxford University Press): 125–42.

Mazey, S. and J. Richardson (eds) (1993) *Lobbying in the European Community* (Oxford: Oxford University Press).

Mazey, S. and J. Richardson (2006) 'The Commission and the Lobby', in D. Spence (ed.) with G. Edwards, *The European Commission*, 3rd edn (London: Harper): 279–92.

MacRae, H. (2010) 'The EU as a Gender Equal Polity: Myths and Realities, *Journal of Common Market Studies*, 48(1): 155–74.

McElroy, G. and K. Benoit (2010) 'Party Policy and Group Affiliation in the European Parliament', *British Journal of Political Science*, 40: 377–91.

McGowan, L. (2005) 'Europeanization Unleashed and Rebounding. Assessing the Modernization of EU Cartel Policy', *Journal of European Public Policy*, 12(6): 986–1004.

McNamara, K. R. (2002) 'Managing the Euro: The European Central Bank', in J. Peterson and M. Shackleton (eds), *The Institutions of the European Union* (Oxford: Oxford University Press): 164–85.

Menendez, A. J. (2013) 'The Existential Crisis of the European Union', *German Law Journal*, 14(5): 453–526.

Milward, A. S. (1984) *The Reconstruction of Western Europe, 1945–51* (London: Methuen).

Milward, A. S. (2000) *The European Rescue of the Nation-state* (London: Routledge).

Mitrany, D. (1966) *A Working Peace System* (Chicago: Quadrangle Books) (first publication: 1943).

Monar, J. (2002) 'Institutionalizing Freedom, Security, and Justice', in J. Peterson and M. Shackleton (eds), *The Institutions of the European Union* (Oxford: Oxford University Press): 186–209.

Monar, J. (2007) 'Justice and Home Affairs', *Journal of Common Market Studies*, 45, Annual Review: 107–24.

Monar, J. (2010a) 'The Rejection of the EU–US SWIFT Interim Agreement by the European Parliament: A Historic Vote and its Implications', *European Foreign Affairs Review*, 15(2): 143–51.

Monar, J. (2010b) 'The "Area of Freedom, Security and Justice": "Schengen" Europe, Opt-outs, Opt-ins and Associates', in K. Dyson and A. Sepos (eds), *Which Europe? The Politics of Differentiated Integration* (Basingstoke: Palgrave Macmillan): 279–92.

Moore, C. (2008) 'A Europe of the Regions vs. the Regions in Europe: Reflections on Regional Engagement in Brussels', *Regional & Federal Studies*, 18(5): 517–35.

Moravcsik, A. (1991) 'Negotiating the Single European Act: National interests and conventional statecraft in the European Community', *International Organization*, 45(1): 19–56.

Moravcsik, A. (1993) 'Preferences and Power in the European Community: A Liberal Intergovernmentalist Approach', *Journal of Common Market Studies*, 31(4): 473–524.

Moravcsik, A. (1998) *The Choice for Europe: Social Purpose and State Power from Messina to Maastricht* (Ithaca, NY: Cornell University Press).

Moravcsik, A. (2002) 'In Defence of the "Democratic Deficit": Reassessing Legitimacy in the European Union', *Journal of Common Market Studies*, 40(4): 603–24.

Moravcsik, A. (2004) 'Is There a "Democratic Deficit" in World Politics? A Framework for Analysis', *Government and Opposition*, 39(2): 336–63.

Moravcsik, A. (2008) 'The Myth of Europe's "Democratic Deficit"', *Intereconomics*, 43(6): 331–40.

Moravcsik, A. and K. Nicolaïdis (1999) 'Explaining the Treaty of Amsterdam: Interests, Influence, Institutions', *Journal of Common Market Studies*, 37(1): 59–85.

Mosher, J. S. and D. M. Trubek (2003) 'Alternative Approaches to Governance in the EU: EU Social Policy and the European Employment Strategy', *Journal of Common Market Studies*, 41(1): 63–88.

Müller-Brandeck-Bocquet, G. and C. Rüger (eds) (2011) *The High Representative for the EU Foreign and Security Policy – Review and Prospects* (Baden-Baden: Nomos).

Neuhold, C. and P. Settembri (2007) 'The Role of European Parliament Committees in the EU Policy-making Process', in T. Christiansen and T. Larsson (eds), *The Role of Committees in the Policy-Process of the European Union: Legislation, Implementation and Deliberation* (Cheltenham and Northampton: Edward Elgar): 152–81.

Neunreither, K. and A. Wiener (eds) (2000) *European Integration after Amsterdam: Institutional Dynamics and Prospects for Democracy* (Oxford: Oxford University Press).

Neyer, J. (2006) 'The Deliberative Turn in Integration Theory', *Journal of European Public Policy*, 13(5): 779–91.

Neyer, J. (2010) 'Justice, not Democracy: Legitimacy in the European Union', *Journal of Common Market Studies*, 48(4): 903–21.

Neyer, J. (2012) *The Justification of Europe: A Political Theory of Supranational Integration* (Oxford: Oxford University Press).

Neyer, J. and A. Wiener (eds) (2011) *Political Theory of the European Union* (Oxford: Oxford University Press).

Nicolaïdis, K. (2006) 'Constitutionalizing the Federal Vision?' in A. Menon and M. Schain (eds), *Comparative Federalism: The European Union and the United States in Comparative Perspective* (Oxford: Oxford University Press): 59–91.

Nicoll, W. (1994) 'Representing the States', in A. Duff, J. Pinder, and R. Pryce (eds), *Maastricht and Beyond: Building the European Union* (London: Routledge): 190–206.

Niemann A., S. A. L. Schröder and M. C. Tunick (eds) (2008) 'Recovering from the Constitutional Failure: An Analysis of the EU Reflection Period', *ZEI Discussion Paper*, C 182.

Nugent, N. (1991) *The Government and Politics of the European Communities*, 2nd edn (London: Macmillan).

Nugent, N. (1994) *The Government and Politics of the European Communities*, 3rd edn (London: Macmillan).

Nugent, N. (2001) *The European Commission* (Basingstoke: Palgrave Macmillan).

Nugent, N. (2010) *The Government and Politics of the European Union*, 7th edn (Basingstoke: Palgrave Macmillan).

Obradovic D. (2009) 'Regulating Lobbying in the European Union', in D. Coen and J. Richardson (eds), *Lobbying the European Union: Institutions, Actors, and Issues* (Oxford: Oxford University Press): 298–334.

*Official Journal of the European Union* (2013), L 66, Volume 56, 8 March 2013, : 121.

Olsen, J. P. (2010) *Governing Through Institution Building: Institutional Theory and Recent European Experiments in Democratic Organization* (Oxford: Oxford University Press).

Ovey, J. D. (2002) *Between Nation and Europe. The SPD and Labour in the European Parliament, 1994–1999* (Opladen: Leske & Budrich).

Padoa-Schioppa, T. (ed.) (1987) *Efficiency, Stability and Equity: A Strategy for the Evolution of the Economic System of the European Community: A Report* (Oxford: Oxford University Press)

Parsons, C. (2003) *A Certain Idea of Europe* (Ithaca, NY: Cornell University Press).

Paterson, William E. (2011) 'The Reluctant Hegemon: Germany Moves Centre Stage in the European Union', *Journal of Common Market Studies*, 49, Annual Review: 57–75.

Pedler, R. H., and K. S. C. Bradley (2006) 'The Commission: Policy Management and Comitology', in D. Spence (ed.), *The European Commission* (London: Harper): 235–62.

Peterson, J. (2004) 'Policy Networks', in A. Wiener and T. Dietz (eds), *European Integration Theory* (Oxford: Oxford University Press): 117–35.

Pierson, P. (1996) 'The Path to European Integration: A Historical Institutionalist Analysis', *Comparative Political Studies*, 29 (2): 123–63.

Pinder, J. (1991) *European Community: The Building of a Union* (Oxford: Oxford University Press).

Pollack, M. A. (1994) 'Creeping Competence: The Expanding Agenda of the European Community', *Journal of Public Policy*, 14: 95–145.

Pollack, M. A. (1996) 'The New Institutionalism and EC Governance: The Promise and limits of Institutional Analysis', *Governance*, 9 (4): 429–58.

Pollack, M. A. (1998) 'The Engines of Integration? Supranational Autonomy and Influence in the European Union', in W. Sandholtz and A. Stone Sweet (eds), *European Integration and Supranational Governance* (Oxford: Oxford University Press): 217–49.

Pollack, M. A. (2000) 'The End of Creeping Competence? EU Policy-making since Maastricht', *Journal of Common Market Studies*, 38 (3): 519–38.

Pollack, M. A. (2003) *The Engines of European Integration: Delegation, Agency and Agenda Setting in the EU* (Oxford: Oxford University Press).

Pollack, M. A. (2004) 'New Institutionalism', in A. Wiener and T. Dietz (eds), European *Integration Theory* (Oxford: Oxford University Press): 136–58.

Princen, S., and B. Kerremans (2010) 'Opportunity Structures in the EU Multi-

Level System', in J. Beyers, R. Eising and W. A. Malony (eds), *Interest Group Politics in Europe: Lessons from EU Studies and Comparative Politics* (London: Routledge): 27–44.

Puetter, U. (2012) 'Europe's Deliberative Intergovernmentalism: The Role of the Council and European Council in EU Economic Governance', *Journal of European Public Policy*, 19(2): 161–78.

Quaglia, L. and E. Moxon-Browne (2006) 'What Makes a Good EU Presidency? Italy and Ireland Compared', *Journal of Common Market Studies*, 44 (2): 349–68.

Quittkat, C. (2011) 'The European Commission's Online Consultations: A Success Story?', *Journal of Common Market Studies*, 49 (3): 653–74.

Quittkat, C. and B. Kohler-Koch (2011) 'Die Öffnung der europäischen Politik für die Zivilgesellschaft – das Konsultationsregime der Europäischen Kommission', in B. Kohler-Koch and C. Quittkat (eds), *Die Entzauberung partizipativer Demokratie. Zur Rolle der Zivilgesellschaft bei der Demokratisierung von EU-Governance* (Frankfurt am Main: Campus): 74–97.

Rasmussen, Anne (2011) 'Early Conclusion in Bicameral Bargaining: Evidence from the Co-decision Legislative Procedure of the European Union', *European Union Politics*, 12(1): 41–64.

Raunio, T. (2012) 'Political Interests: The European Parliament's Party Groups', in J. Peterson and M. Shackleton (eds), *The Institutions of the European Union*, 3rd edn (Oxford: Oxford University Press): 338–58.

Raveaud, G. (2007) 'The European Employment Strategy: Towards More and Better Jobs?', *Journal of Common Market Studies*, 45(2): 411–34.

Regalia, I. (2002) 'Decentralizing Employment Protection in Europe: Territorial Pacts and Beyond', Centro Interdipartimentale WTW – Work, Training and Welfare, Working Paper 4.

Regelsberger, E. (ed.) (1997) *Foreign Policy of the European Union: From EPC to CFSP and Beyond* (Boulder, CO: Lynne Rienner).

Regulation (EU) No 1303/2013, of the European Parliament and the Council of 17 December 2013, 'Laying down common provisions on the ERDF, the ESF, the CF, the EAFRD and the EMFF and laying down general provisions on the ERDF, the ESF, the CF, and the EMFF and repealing Council Regulation (EC) No 1083/2006', OJ L 347: 320–469.

Reh, C. (2008) 'The Convention on the Future of Europe and the Development of Integration Theory: A lasting imprint?', *Journal of European Public Policy*, 15(5): 781–94.

Reh, C., A. Héritier, E. Bressanelli and C. Koop (2010) 'The Informal Politics of Legislation: Explaining Secluded Decision-Making in the European Union', Paper prepared for the APSA Annual Convention, Washington, 2–5 September 2010.

Reif, K. and H. Schmitt (1980) 'Nine Second-order National Elections: A Conceptual Framework for the Analysis of European Election Results', *European Journal of Political Research*, 6(1): 3–45.

Reiter, R. (2010) *Politiktransfer der EU. Die Europäisierung der Stadtentwicklungspolitik in Deutschland und Frankreich* (Wiesbaden: VS-Verlag).

Rhodes, M. (2010) 'Employment Policy: Between Efficacy and Experimentation', in H. Wallace, M. A. Pollack and A. Young (eds), *Policy-Making in the European Community*, 6th edn (Oxford: Oxford University Press): 283–306.

Rieger, E. (2005) 'Agricultural Policy: Constrained Reforms', in H. Wallace, W.

Wallace and M. A. Pollack (eds), *Policy-Making in the European Union*, 5th edn (Oxford: Oxford University Press): 161–90.

Risse, T. (2004) 'Social Constructivism and European Integration', in A. Wiener and T. Dietz (eds), *European Integration Theory* (Oxford: Oxford University Press): 159–76.

Risse, T. and M. Kleine (2007) 'Assessing the Legitimacy of the EU's Treaty Revision Methods', *Journal of Common Market Studies*, 45 (1): 69–80.

Rittberger, B. (2005) *Building Europe's Parliament: Democratic Representation beyond the Nation State* (Oxford: Oxford University Press).

Rittberger, B. (2010) 'Democracy and European Union Governance', in M. Egan, N. Nugent and W. E. Paterson (eds), *Research Agendas in EU Studies: Stalking the Elephant* (Basingstoke: Palgrave Macmillan).

Roberts-Thomson, P. (2001) 'EU Treaty Referendums and the European Union', *Journal of European Integration*, 23(2): 105–37.

Roederer-Rynning, C. (2010) 'The Common Agricultural Policy: The Fortress Challenged', in H. Wallace, M. A. Pollack and A. Young (eds), *Policy-Making in the European Community*, 6th edn (Oxford: Oxford University Press): 181–205.

Rosamond, B. (2000) *Theories of European Integration* (Basingstoke: Palgrave Macmillan).

Rosamond, B. (2008) 'Review Article: Open Political Science, Methodological Nationalism and European Union Studies', *Government and Opposition*, 43(4): 599–612.

Rose, R. and G. Borz (2013) 'Aggregation and Representation in European Parliament Party Groups', *West European Politics*, 36(3): 474–97.

Ross, G. (1995) *Jacques Delors and European Integration* (Cambridge: Polity Press).

Rowe, C. (2011) *Regional Representation in the EU: Between Diplomacy and Interest Representation* (Basingstoke: Palgrave Macmillan).

Rüger, C. (2011) 'A Position under Construction: Future Prospects of the High Representative after the Treaty of Lisbon', in G. Müller-Brandeck-Bocquet and C. Rüger (eds), *The High Representative for the EU Foreign and Security Policy – Review and Prospects* (Baden-Baden: Nomos): 201–33.

Ruzza, C. (2004) *Europe and Civil Society: Movement Coalitions and European Governance* (Manchester: Manchester University Press).

Sabel, C. and J. Zeitlin (2008) 'Learning from Difference: The New Architecture of Experimental Governance in the EU', *European Law Journal*, 14(3): 271–327.

Sabel, C. and J. Zeitlin (eds) (2010) *Experimentalist Governance in the European Union: Towards a New Architecture* (Oxford: Oxford University Press).

Sandholtz, W. and A. Stone Sweet (eds) (1998) *European Integration and Supranational Governance* (Oxford: Oxford University Press).

Sandholtz, W. and J. Zysman (1989) '1992: Recasting the European bargain', *World Politics*, 41(1): 95–128.

Sbragia, A. M. (1993) 'The European Community: A Balancing Act', *Publius: Journal of Federalism*, 23: 23–38.

Sbragia, A. M. (2002) 'The Treaty of Nice, Institutional Balance, and Uncertainty', Conclusion to Special Issue on the institutional balance and the future of EU governance, *Governance*, 15(3): 393–412.

Schäfer, A. (2006) 'A New Form of Governance? Comparing the Open Method of Coordination to Multilateral Surveillance by the IMF and the OECD', *Journal of European Public Policy*, 13(1): 70–88.

Schäfer, G F. and A Türk (2007) 'The Role of Implementing Committees', in T. Christiansen and T. Larsson (eds), *The Role of Committees in the Policy-Process of the European Union: Legislation, Implementation and Deliberation* (Cheltenham and Northampton: Edward Elgar): 182–200.

Scharpf, F. W. (1985) 'Die Politikverflechtungs-Falle: Europäische Integration und deutscher Föderalismus im Vergleich', *Politische Vierteljahresschrift*, 26(4): 323–56.

Scharpf, F. W. (1988) 'The Joint Decision Trap: Lessons from German Federalism and European Integration', *Public Administration*, 66, Autumn: 239–78.

Scharpf, F. W. (1992) 'Einführung: Zur Theorie von Verhandlungssystemen', in A. Benz, F. W. Scharpf and R. Zintl (eds), *Horizontale Politikverflechtung: Zur Theorie von Verhandlungssystemen* (Frankfurt am Main: Campus): 11–27.

Scharpf, F. W (1999) *Governing in Europe: Effective and Democratic?* (Oxford: Oxford University Press).

Scharpf, F. W. (2001) 'Notes toward a Theory of Multilevel Governing in Europe', *Scandinavian Political Studies*, 24(1): 1–26.

Scharpf, F. W. (2006) 'The Joint Decision Trap Revisited', *Journal of Common Market Studies*, 44(4): 845–64.

Schelkle, W. (2013) 'Monetary Integration in Crisis: How Well do Existing Theories Explain the Predicament of EMU?', *Transfer*, 19(1): 37–48.

Schimmelfennig, F. (2003) *The EU, NATO, and the Integration of Europe: Rules and Rhetoric* (Cambridge: Cambridge University Press).

Schimmelfennig, F. and U. Sedelmeier (eds) (2005) *The Europeanization of Central and Eastern Europe* (Ithaca, NY: Cornell University Press).

Schmalz-Bruns, R. (2007) 'The Euro-Polity in Perspective: Some Normative Lessons from Deliberative Democracy', in B. Kohler-Koch and B. Rittberger (eds), *Debating the Democratic Legitimacy of the European Union* (Lanham, ML: Rowman & Littlefield): 281–303.

Schmidt, S. K. (2004) 'The European Commission's Powers in Shaping European Policies', in D. G. Dimitrakopoulos (ed.), *The Changing European Commission* (Manchester: Manchester University Press): 105–20.

Schmidt, S. K. (2009) 'Single Market Policies: From Mutual Recognition to Institution Building', in I. Tömmel and A. Verdun (eds), *Innovative Governance in the European Union: The Politics of Multilevel Policymaking* (Boulder, CO: Lynne Rienner): 121–37.

Schmidt, S. K. (2011) 'Law-Making in the Shadow of Judicial Politics', in R. Dehousse (ed.), *The 'Community Method': Obstinate or Obsolete?* (Basingstoke: Palgrave Macmillan): 43–59.

Schmidt, V. (2006) *Democracy in Europe: The EU and National Polities* (Oxford: Oxford University Press).

Schmitter, P. C. (1971) 'A Revised Theory of Regional Integration', in L. Lindberg and S. A. Scheingold, (eds), *Regional Integration: Theory and Research* (Cambridge, MA: Harvard University Press): 232–64.

Schön-Quinlivan, E. (2011) *Reforming the European Commission* (Basingstoke: Palgrave Macmillan).

Schout, A. and S. Vanhoonacker (2006) 'Evaluating Presidencies of the Council of the EU: Revisiting Nice', *Journal of Common Market Studies*, 44(5): 1051–77.

Scully, R. (2005) Becoming Europeans? *Attitudes, Behaviour, and Socialization in the European Parliament* (Oxford: Oxford University Press).

Smismans, S. (2003) 'European Civil Society: Shaped by Discourses and Institutional Interests', *European Law Journal*, 9(4): 473–95.

Smith, M. E. (2001) 'Diplomacy by Decree: The Legalization of EU Foreign Policy, *Journal of Common Market Studies*, 39(1): 79–104.

Smith, M. E. (2004) *Europe's Foreign and Security Policy: The Institutionalization of Cooperation* (Cambridge: Cambridge University Press).

Spence, D. (2006a) 'The President, the College and the Cabinets', in D. Spence (ed.) with G. Edwards, *The European Commission*, 3rd edn (London: Harper): 24–74.

Spence, D. (2006b) 'The Directorates General and the Services: Structures, Functions and Procedures', in D. Spence (ed.) with G. Edwards, *The European Commission*, 3rd edn (London: Harper): 128–55.

Startin, N. and A. Krouwel (2013) 'Euroscepticism Re-galvanized: The Consequences of the 2005 French and Dutch Rejections of the EU Constitution', *Journal of Common Market Studies*, 51(1): 65–84.

Steffek, J., C. Kissling and P. Nanz (2008) *Civil Society Participation in European and Global Governance: A Cure for the Democratic Deficit?* (Basingstoke: Palgrave Macmillan).

Stephenson, P. (2012) 'Sixty Years of Auditing Europe', Paper presented at the Conference: *Sixty Years of European Governance*, York University, Toronto, 13–14 September 2012.

Stone Sweet, A. (2004) *The Judicial Construction of Europe* (Oxford: Oxford University Press).

Streeck, W. (2013) *Gekaufte Zeit: Die vertagte Krise des demokratischen Kapitalismus* (Berlin: Suhrkamp).

Streeck, W. and P. C. Schmitter (1991) 'From National Corporatism to Transnational Pluralism: Organized Interests in the Single European Market', *Politics and Society*, 19(2): 109–32.

Studinger, P. (2012) *Wettrennen der Regionen nach Brüssel: die Entwicklung der Regionalvertretungen* (Wiebaden: Springer).

Taggart, P. (2006) 'Questions of Europe: The Domestic Politics of the 2005 French and Dutch Referendums and their Challenge for the Study of European Integration', *Journal of Common Market Studies*, 44, Annual Review: 7–25.

Tallberg, J. (2003) 'The Agenda-Shaping Powers of the Council Presidency', in O. Elgström (ed.), *European Union Council Presidencies: A Comparative Perspective* (London: Routledge): 18–37.

Tallberg, J. (2006): *Leadership and Negotiation in the European Union* (Cambridge: Cambridge University Press).

Tallberg, J. (2007) 'Bargaining Power in the European Council', *Journal of Common Market Studies*, 46(3): 685–708.

Tallberg, J. (2008) 'The Power of the Chair: Formal Leadership by the Council Presidency', in D. Naurin and H. Wallace (eds), *Unveiling the Council of the European Union. Games Governments Play in Brussels* (Basingstoke: Palgrave Macmillan): 187–202.

Taylor, P. (1983) *The Limits of European Integration* (London: Croom Helm).

Teasdale, A. L. (1996) 'The Politics of Majority Voting in Europe', *Political Quarterly Publishing*, 67: 101–15.

Tömmel, I. (2009) 'Modes of Governance and the Institutional Structure of the European Union', in I. Tömmel and A. Verdun (eds), *Innovative Governance in the European Union: The Politics of Multilevel Policymaking* (Boulder, CO: Lynne Rienner): 9–23.

Tömmel, I. (2010) 'The Treaty of Lisbon: A Step toward Enhancing Leadership in the EU?', *Transatlantic Research Papers in European Studies* (TraPES), 2010 (1). http://www.jmce.uni-osnabrueck.de/fileadmin/Download/EPS/TraPES._Toemmel.pdf.

Tömmel, I. (2011a) 'The European Union: A Federation Sui Generis?' in F. Laursen (ed.), *The EU and Federalism: Polities and Policies Compared* (Farnham: Ashgate): 41–56.

Tömmel, I. (2011b) 'Transnationalism in European Governance and Policy-Making', in J. DeBardeleben and A. Hurrelmann (eds), *Transnational Europe: Promise, Paradox, Limits* (Basingstoke: Palgrave Macmillan): 57–76.

Tömmel, I. (2013a) 'The Presidents of the European Commission: Transactional or Transforming Leaders?', *Journal of Common Market Studies*, 51(4): 789–805.

Tömmel, I. (2013b) 'The New Neighborhood Policy of the EU: An Appropriate Response to the Arab Spring?', *Democracy and Security*, 9 (1–2): 19–39.

Tömmel, I. and A. Verdun (eds) (2009) *Innovative Governance in the European Union: The Politics of Multilevel Policymaking* (Boulder, CO: Lynne Rienner).

Tömmel, I. and A. Verdun (2013) 'Innovative Governance in EU Regional and Monetary Policy-making', *German Law Journal*, 14(2): 380–404.

Treib, O., H. Bähr and G. Falkner (2007) 'Modes of Governance: Towards Conceptual Clarification', *Journal of European Public Policy*, 14(1): 1–20.

Tsebelis, G. (1994) 'The Power of the European Parliament as a Conditional Agenda Setter, *American Political Science Review*, 88, March: 88–142.

Tsebelis, G. and G. Garrett (2001) 'The Institutional Foundations of Intergovernmentalism and Supranationalism in the European Union', *International Organization*, 55(2): 391–438.

Tsebelis, G. and S.-O. Proksch (2007) 'The Art of Political Manipulation in the European Convention', *Journal of Common Market Studies*, 45(1): 157–86.

Tsebelis G. and X. Yataganas (2002) 'Veto-players and Decision-making in the EU after Nice', *Journal of Common Market Studies*, 40(2): 283–307.

Tsoukalis, L. (2011) 'The JMCS Annual Review Lecture: The Shattering of Illusions – and What Next?', *Journal of Common Market Studies*, 49, Annual Review: 19–44.

Turner, S. (2008) 'Expertise and the Process of Policy-Making: The EU's New Model of Legitimacy', in S. Eliasson (ed.), *Building Civil Society and Democracy in New Europe* (Newcastle: Cambridge Scholars Publishing): 160–75.

Urwin, D. W. (1993) *The Community of Europe: A History of European Integration since 1945*, 8th edn (London: Longman).

Van Miert, K. (2000) *Markt, Macht, Wettbewerb: Meine Erfahrungen als Kommissar in Brüssel* (Stuttgart and München: Deutsche Verlagsanstalt)

Verdun, A. (2009) 'Regulation and Cooperation in Economic and Monetary Policy', in I. Tömmel and A. Verdun (eds), *Innovative Governance in the European Union: The Politics of Multilevel Policymaking* (Boulder, CO: Lynne Rienner): 75–86.

Wallace, H. (2010) 'An Institutional Anatomy of Five Policy Modes', in H.

Wallace, M. A. Pollack and A. Young (eds), *Policy-Making in the European Community*, 6th edn (Oxford: Oxford University Press): 69–104.

Wallace, H., J. A Caporaso, F. W. Scharpf and A. Moravcsik (1999) 'Review Section Symposium: The Choice for Europe - Social Purpose and State Power from Messina to Maastricht', *Journal of European Public Policy*, 6(1): 155–79.

Wallace, W. (1983) 'Less than a Federation, more than a Regime: The Community as a Political System', in H. Wallace, W. Wallace and C. Webb (eds), *Policy-Making in the European Community*, 2nd edn (Chichester, NY: John Wiley & Sons): 403–36.

Warntjen, A. (2008) 'Steering but not Dominating: The Impact of the Council Presidency on EU Legislation', in D. Naurin and H. Wallace (eds), *Unveiling the Council of the European Union. Games Governments Play in Brussels* (Basingstoke: Palgrave Macmillan): 203–18.

Weiler, J. H. H. (1981) 'The Community System: The Dual Character of Supranationalism', *Yearbook of European Law*, 1: 267–306.

Weiler, J. H. H. (1994) 'Journey to an Unknown Destination: A Retrospective and Prospective of the European Court of Justice in the Arena of Integration', in S. Bulmer and A. Scott (eds), *Economic and Political Integration in Europe: Internal Dynamics and Global Context* (Oxford: Blackwell): 131–68.

Weishaupt, J. T. and K. Lack (2011) 'The European Employment Strategy: Assessing the Status Quo', *German Policy Studies*, 7(1): 9–44.

Werts, J. (2008) *The European Council* (London: Harper).

Wessels, W. (2008) *Das politische System der EU* (Wiesbaden: VS-Verlag).

Westlake, M. (2006) 'The European Commission and the European Parliament', in D. Spence (ed.) with G. Edwards, *The European Commission*, 3rd edn (London: Harper): 263–78.

Westlake, M. (2007) 'Why Presidencies Still Matter', Österreichische Zeitschrift für Politikwissenschaft (ÖZP), 36(2): 157–65.

Westlake, M. (2009) 'The European Economic and Social Committee', in D. Coen and J. Richardson (eds), *Lobbying the European Union: Institutions, Actors, and Issues* (Oxford: Oxford University Press): 128–42.

Westlake, M. and D. Galloway (eds) (2006) *The Council of the European Union*, 3rd edn (London: Harper).

Whitaker, R. (2011) *The European Parliament's Committees: National Party influence and Legislative Empowerment* (London: Routledge).

Wiener, A. and T. Dietz (eds) (2004) *European Integration Theory* (Oxford: Oxford University Press).

Wilks, S. (2010) 'Competition Policy: Towards an Economic Constitution?' in H. Wallace, M. A. Pollack and A. Young (eds), *Policy-Making in the European Community*, 6th edn (Oxford: Oxford University Press): 133–55.

Willke, H. (2007) *Smart Governance: Governing the Global Knowledge Society* (Frankfurt am Main/New York: Campus).

Wonka, A., F. R. Baumgartner, C. Mahoney and J. Berkhout (2010) 'Measuring the Size and Scope of the EU Interest Group Population', *European Union Politics*, 11(3): 463–76.

Wozniak Boyle, J.R. (2006) *Conditional Leadership: The European Commission and European Regional Policy* (Lanham, ML: Roman & Littlefield).

Yataganas, X. (2001) 'The Treaty of Nice: The Sharing of Power and the Institutional Balance in the European Union – A Continental Perspective', *European Law Journal*, 7(3): 242–91.

Young, A. (2010) 'The Single Market: Deregulation, Reregulation, and Integration', in H. Wallace, M. A. Pollack and A. Young (eds), *Policy-Making in the European Community*, 6th edn (Oxford: Oxford University Press): 107–131.

Zito, A. R. (2010) 'European Agencies as Agents of Governance and EU Learning', in A. R. Zito (ed.), *Learning and Governance in the EU Policy Making Process* (London: Routledge): 122–41.

Zürn, M. (1998) *Regieren jenseits des Nationalstaates. Globalisierung und Denationalisierung als Chance* (Frankfurt am Main: Suhrkamp).

Zürn, M. (2000) 'Democratic Governance beyond the Nation-state: The EU and Other International Institutions', *European Journal of International Relations*, 6: 183–221.

# Index